D1575251

NEW BOOK

SETTLING
THE
SCORE

NED ROREM

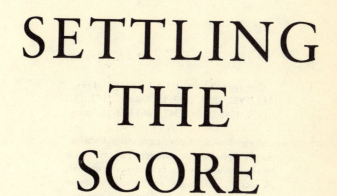

SETTLING THE SCORE

Essays on Music

HARCOURT BRACE JOVANOVICH, PUBLISHERS

San Diego   New York   London

to James Holmes always

HBJ

Copyright © 1988, 1987, 1986, 1985, 1984,
1983, 1982, 1978, 1977, 1975, 1974, 1972, 1971,
1970, 1969, 1968, 1967, 1963 by Ned Rorem

Library of Congress Cataloging-in-Publication Data
Rorem, Ned, 1923–
Settling the score : essays on music / Ned Rorem.
p. cm.
Includes index.
ISBN 0-15-180895-3
1. Music—History and criticism. I. Title.
ML60.R7845 1988
780—dc19   87-28080

Printed in the United States of America
Design by Beth Tondreau Design
First edition

A B C D E

PERMISSION ACKNOWLEDGMENTS

"Living with Gershwin." Copyright © 1985 by Ned Rorem. Reprinted from *Opera News*, March 16, 1985.

"Copland's Birthday (at 70)." Copyright © 1974 by Ned Rorem. Reprinted from *Pure Contraption* by Ned Rorem, published by Holt, Rinehart and Winston, Inc.

"Copland at Eighty-five." Copyright © 1985 by The New York Times Company. Reprinted by permission from *The New York Sunday Times*, November 10, 1985.

"A Medal for Lenny." Copyright © 1987 by Ned Rorem. Address delivered upon the presentation of the MacDowell Medal to Leonard Bernstein, Peterborough, N.H., on August 9, 1987.

"William Flanagan: In Memoriam." Copyright © 1970 by Ned Rorem. An address delivered at a memorial concert for William Flanagan at New York's Whitney Museum, April 14, 1970. Reprinted from *Critical Affairs* by Ned Rorem, published by George Braziller, Inc. under the title "Bill Flanagan (1923–1969)."

"Flanagan's Music." Copyright © 1967 by Ned Rorem. Written for *The American Composer's Alliance Bulletin*, No. 4, 1961. Reprinted from *Music and People* by Ned Rorem, published by George Braziller, Inc. under the title "Flanagan."

"Looking for Sam." Copyright © 1983 by Ned Rorem. Reprinted from *Carnegie Hall Stagebill*, February 1983.

"A Note on Barber's *Antony and Cleopatra*." Copyright © 1978 by Ned Rorem. Excerpted from the chapter "A Cultured Winter" in *An Absolute Gift* by Ned Rorem, published by Simon & Schuster.

"Lord Byron in Kansas City." Copyright © 1982 by Ned Rorem. Written for *The New Republic*, May 6, 1982. Reprinted from *Pure Contraption* by Ned Rorem, published by Holt, Rinehart and Winston, Inc.

"Smoke Without Fire." Copyright © 1972 by Ned Rorem. Written for *The New Republic*, April 8, 1972. Reprinted from *Pure Contraption* by Ned Rorem, published by Holt, Rinehart and Winston, Inc.

"Foss Improvises." Copyright © 1968 by Ned Rorem. Reprinted from *Music and People* by Ned Rorem, published by George Braziller, Inc.

"Cage's HPSCHD." Copyright © 1978 by Ned Rorem. Excerpted from the chapter "A Cultured Winter" in *An Absolute Gift* by Ned Rorem, published by Simon & Schuster.

"A Paragraph on Crumb." Copyright © 1978 by Ned Rorem. Excerpted from the chapter "A Cultured Winter" in *An Absolute Gift* by Ned Rorem, published by Simon & Schuster.

"Elliot Carter: A Book Review." Copyright © 1972 by Ned Rorem. Written for *The New Republic*, February 26, 1972. Reprinted from *Pure Contraption* by Ned Rorem, published by Holt, Rinehart and Winston, Inc.

"Richard Cumming's Songs." Copyright © 1983 by Ned Rorem. Reprinted from the liner notes for Cambridge Record CR S2778: *Richard Cumming: Cycles and Songs*.

"Ezra Pound as Musician." Copyright © 1968 by Ned Rorem. Reprinted from *Music and People* by Ned Rorem, published by George Braziller, Inc.

"Notes on Debussy." Copyright © 1971 by Ned Rorem. Written for *The American Record Guide*,

March 1971. Reprinted from *Pure Contraption* by Ned Rorem, published by Holt, Rinehart and Winston, Inc.

"Pelléas and Pierre." Copyright © 1971 by Ned Rorem. Written for *The American Record Guide*, March 1971. Reprinted from *Pure Contraption* by Ned Rorem, published by Holt, Rinehart and Winston, Inc.

"Notes for Debussy's *En blanc et noir*." Copyright © 1987 by Elektra/Asylum/Nonesuch Records. Liner note for Nonesuch Record 9-79161-2: *Claude Debussy: Etudes for Piano and En blanc et noir*. Reprinted by permission.

"Ravel." Copyright © 1975 by Ned Rorem. First published by *Commentary Magazine*, May 1975, under the title "Notes on Ravel." Reprinted from *An Absolute Gift* by Ned Rorem, published by Simon & Schuster.

"Ravel and Song." Copyright © 1984 by Columbia Records Inc. Liner note for CBS Record M39023: *Ravel's Songs*. Reprinted by permission.

"Dancing to Ravel." Copyright © 1978 by Ned Rorem. Excerpted and adapted from the chapter "A Cultured Winter" in *An Absolute Gift* by Ned Rorem, published by Simon & Schuster.

"Ravel's House." Copyright © 1986 by Architectural Digest Publishing Corp. Reprinted from *Architectural Digest*, September 1986, under the title "Historic Houses: Maurice Ravel at Le Belvedere; A Serene Setting for the French Composer."

"Francis Poulenc: A Souvenir." Copyright © 1963 by Ned Rorem. First published simultaneously in the USA by *The Village Voice*, February 21, 1963, under the title "Francis Poulenc (1899–1963)"; and in Great Britain by *Tempo Magazine*, Spring 1963, under the title "Francis Poulenc: A Memoir." Reprinted from *Music and People* by Ned Rorem, published by George Braziller, Inc.

"Afterthoughts on Francis." Copyright © 1968 by Ned Rorem. Written for *The American Record Guide*, September 1968. Reprinted from *Music and People* by Ned Rorem, published by George Braziller, Inc.

"Poulenc's *Dialogues*." Copyright © 1977 by Ned Rorem. Written for *Opera News*, February 5, 1977. Reprinted from *An Absolute Gift* by Ned Rorem, published by Simon & Schuster.

"Poulenc's Chamber Music for Winds." Copyright © 1984 by Ned Rorem. Liner note for Erato Record STU 71539: *Francis Poulenc: Musique de Chambre pour instruments à vent*.

"Bernac and Poulenc." Copyright © 1967 by Ned Rorem. Written for *High Fidelity Magazine*, November 1967. Reprinted from *Music and People* by Ned Rorem, published by George Braziller, Inc.

"The Rosenkavalier Diary." Copyright © 1983 by Ned Rorem. First published by *Opera News*, March 12, 1983, under the title "A Rose Journal: Personal Impressions of *Der Rosenkavalier*."

"A Strauss Biography." Copyright © 1967 by Ned Rorem. First published by *The New York Times Book Review*, April 23, 1967. Reprinted from *Music and People* by Ned Rorem, published by George Braziller, Inc.

"Notes on Weill." Copyright © 1984 by Ned Rorem. Reprinted from *Opera News*, January 21, 1984.

"Nabokov's Bagázh." Copyright © 1975 by Ned Rorem. First published by *The New York Times Book Review*, December 14, 1975. Reprinted from *An Absolute Gift* by Ned Rorem, published by Simon & Schuster.

"Stravinsky via Craft." Copyright © 1972 by Ned Rorem. First excerpted from an article in two parts, "Stravinsky and Whitman," written for *The New Republic*, June 3, 1972. Reprinted from *Pure Contraption* by Ned Rorem, published by Holt, Rinehart and Winston, Inc.

"Variations on Mussorgsky." Copyright © 1986 by Ned Rorem. Reprinted from *Opera News*, February 1, 1986.

"Rubinstein at the Movies." Copyright © 1978 by Ned Rorem. Excerpted from the chapter "A Cultured Winter" in *An Absolute Gift* by Ned Rorem, published by Simon & Schuster.

"About Toscanini." Copyright © 1968 by Ned Rorem. Written for *The American Record Guide*,

CONTENTS

THREE
GERMANS, RUSSIANS, AND OTHER EUROPEANS

FOUR
POPULAR MUSIC

FIVE
THREE LANDSCAPES WITH FIGURES

SIX
OF SONGS AND WORDS

SEVEN
ODDS AND ENDINGS

INTRODUCTION

Two considerations guided the assembling of these essays: homogeneity of tone and non-duplication of material still in print. I have been writing about music since 1959, when obliged to do so as composer-lecturer at Buffalo University. After the publication of two Diaries in the mid-1960s I began writing on other matters—geography, fiction, decoration, clothes, sex, indeed anything requested by such diverse organs as *Commentary* and *Christopher Street*—albeit always from the vantage of a musician. Since 1966 I've published six collections, each a very mixed bag with no central focus and each, except for *Setting the Tone*, long out of print.

Settling the Score is therefore my first anthology that, whatever its failings, can boast purity of subject: everything is on music. Now with the complementary volume *Setting the Tone*, almost all my non-diary prose is available—some 120 articles (minus scattered pieces on non-musical matters that will turn up in some future book). The non-duplication premise makes for minor inconveniences. For instance, my most re-printed essay, "The Music of the Beatles," composed in 1967 for the *New York Review of Books* and now in *Setting the Tone*, would have been useful between the present covers, since it was the springboard for ensuing pieces on the Beatles and on other pop considerations appearing here. Similarly articles on Poulenc and Debussy and Ravel, featured in *Setting the Tone*, might have lent a sense of completion had they been included here.

Chronology has been ignored; rather the entries in *Settling the Score* have been organized by category. Thus the earliest writing, "Flanagan's Music" (1959), follows the most recent, "A Medal for Lenny" (1987). It seems fitting that this span of twenty-eight years should be flanked by portraits of two dear composer friends.

It also seems fitting (I'd not noticed it until I began writing this paragraph) that of the sixty-two essays only one, "Variations on Mussorgsky," concerns pre–twentieth-century music; only one, "Homage to

Julius Katchen," concerns an interpretive artist (I am, after all, a live composer preoccupied with my fragile species in the fragile present, while many another writes about the past); and only one, "Robert Jacobson Gone," concerns a musical nonpractitioner.

Robert Jacobson's venerable magazine *Opera News* is where most of my writings on contemporary opera first were read, always in conjunction with productions at the Metropolitan Opera: Gershwin's *Porgy and Bess*, Mussorgsky's *Khovanshchina*, Poulenc's *Dialogues des Carmélites*, Strauss's *Der Rosenkavalier*, and Weill's *Mahagonny*. The color, the emphasis, the shape, even the grammar of an article depends not only on the year it was penned, but also on the occasion. So the sometimes-academic stance of these opera essays is dropped for the more buoyant moments of public speech. "Why I Write as I Do," for example, was designed to be read aloud at a meeting of the American Music Center in January 1974. ("What shall I talk about?" I had asked Hugo Weisgall, chairman of the meeting that would feature three other composers. "Oh, just talk about why you write as you do, and keep it down to fifteen minutes.") "A Medal for Lenny" was likewise tailored for microphone, the occasion being the bestowal by the MacDowell Colony of an honor to Leonard Bernstein. "William Flanagan: In Memoriam" was delivered at a memorial concert at the Whitney Museum in April 1970. (The aforementioned "Flanagan's Music" first came out in the *American Composer's Alliance Bulletin*.)

Other entries, originally spoken, are more informal still, having been improvised for television (on a Critics Roundtable shared with Alexander Cockburn, Harold Hayes, and Jack Richardson on New York's PBS Channel 13 in 1974 to 1975), then written down after the fact. These include "Dancing to Ravel," "Rubinstein at the Movies," "Anita Ellis and Barbra Streisand," "A Paragraph on Crumb," "Cage's *HPSCHD*," and "A Note on Barber's *Antony and Cleopatra*."

Between 1972 and 1974 I wrote a dozen pieces for *The New Republic*. These include "Stravinsky via Craft," "Britten's *Death in Venice*," "Our Music Now (1974)," and "Smoke without Fire"; also reviews of a book about Elliott Carter and of a new opera by Virgil Thomson. A word on these last two: since adolescence, although my cultural vocabulary has broadened, my taste has remained the same. Other than once disdaining and now enjoying the sound of Brahms, I've experienced no esthetic about-face. But I *have* altered attitudes about colleagues. The words on Elliott Carter, written nearly sixteen years ago and reproduced here, strike me on rereading as careful, a touch remote, certainly respectful. A few years later I would write of Carter dithyrambically as deserving of all praise. More recently I've became sharply critical of him. The violent shift does not reflect a change of heart about Carter's music, which has never really meant much to me; rather it's a lashing out at having been, for the first time ever, duped by a highly paid public relations machinery that marketed the notion of Carter as Great Man. The words on Thomson's opera, and by extension on Thomson's work in general, reflect another kind of lashing out, this time at a person who during my formative years was as crucial as a parent from whom I needed to be weaned. Like Carter's, Thomson's music never "spoke" to me, but it wasn't until reviewing *Lord Byron* that I confessed this to the world. Virgil, not thrilled, dropped me for some time. I justified my action by claiming that if as a critic Virgil had dished it out for decades, he should be able to take some of the same medicine. In fact, Virgil felt the student had betrayed the master. When our friendship shakily began to repair itself, I vowed never again to counter him. Years later, at a revival of *Lord Byron*, I had reason to revise my opinion, now finding both the score and Jack Larson's libretto witty, touching, exquisite, and honest. Meanwhile I've elsewhere written about Virgil's music in phrases that I believe have pleased him. Then why reprint this review, and in a book that under other circumstances I might have dedicated to him? Because it's history, because it's me at a certain period, and because it does contain some novel truth.

"Where Is Our Music Going?" and "About Toscanini" first appeared in the *American Record Guide*. So did the first two paragraphs of "Copland's Birthday (at Seventy)," presented, along with a score of other homages by friends, to the composer at an Essex House banquet in November 1970. The additional paragraphs were added when the article appeared in my book *Pure Contraption*. "Copland at Eighty-five" was commissioned by the Sunday *New York Times* fifteen years later to the day.

The Sunday *Times* was also the first home of "Song Singing in America," "On Nearing Sixty," "The American Composer Speaks," " A Strauss Biography," "Peter Yates on Twentieth-Century Music," "Great Songs of the Sixties: A Book Review," and "Nabokov's *Bagázh*" (the last five in the *New York Times Book Review*).

And the Sunday *Times* was responsible for "Against Rock," which it printed on October 26, 1969, as an attack on rock critic Richard Goldstein, fostering it into a cause célèbre, which editor Sy Peck relished in those days. Goldstein (whom I've never met but have since come to respect for his pages in the *Village Voice*) answered me disparagingly the following Sunday, and for two Sundays after that the "Letters" column teemed with pros and cons. "Against Rock" was concocted as an antidote to my infatuation with the Beatles. As they decayed pop music became, and has remained, a strictly commercial blight, even as the proselytizing around it became increasingly solemn and silly. Today I reject it utterly, and fear it.

"Afterthoughts on the Beatles" was first published in my book *Music and People* (1968), while "Last Thoughts on the Beatles" came out in the *Village Voice* in the autumn of 1967. The *Voice* also hosted "Francis Poulenc: A Souvenir" on the occasion of that composer's death in 1963.

Other articles were conceived as liner notes for records: "Notes on Debussy," "Pelléas and Pierre," "Notes for Debussy's *En blanc et noir*," "Ravel and Song," "Poulenc's Chamber Music for Winds," "Richard Cumming's Songs," and "*Last Poems of Wallace Stevens*: An Album Note."

"Foss Improvises" was first in *Musical America*, "Looking for Sam" in the Carnegie Hall program booklet, "Bernac and Poulenc" in *High Fidelity*, and "Afterthoughts on Francis" in *Music and People*. *Commentary* published "Ravel" in remembrance of that musician's hundredth birthday in 1975, and *Architectural Digest* commissioned "Ravel's House'" in 1986. I based the latter study on instinct and common sense, using what I love about my favorite composer's works and superimposing that onto my reaction to the fabulous color reproductions, supplied by the magazine, of the villa at Monfort-l'Amaury. I've never set foot in Ravel's house.

"Ezra Pound as Musician" first served as a preface to the reprint (by Plenum Press in the early 1960s) of a small volume called *Antheil and the Treatise on Harmony* written by Pound in the 1920s.

The remaining essays first saw light as follows:

"Charles Rosen's *The Classical Style*" was originally a letter to Philip Rahv about why I couldn't review Rosen's book for Rahv's new magazine *Modern Occasions*. He deleted "Dear Mr. Rahv" and "Sincerely yours" and published the letter as a critique in 1971.

"Ladies' Music" came out in *Vogue* in 1968, with the title hideously changed to "Woman: Artist or Artist-esse?" (Ten years later I wrote a complementary essay called "Women in Music," which appears in *Setting the Tone*.)

"Notes on Sacred Music" dates from the January 1973 issue of *Music: The Magazine of the American Guild of Organists*.

"The Well-Dressed Composer," under its original title "Makers of Manners," was confected at the wish of my old friend Patrick O'Higgins, who gave it to *Harper's Bazaar*, which refused it as being too chichi, so *Vogue* published it in 1968.

The piece on Julius Katchen was written as an epitaph and published by *High Fidelity* in 1969. If Bill Flanagan had been my best friend among composers, Julius was certainly my best among pianists. I thought of him as "my" pianist, even as the late Nell Tangeman and the late Donald Gramm were "my" singers. I owe them everything.

"Our Music Now (1984)" was one of a dozen contributions to *ASCAP In Action*, all of them, except mine, optimistic.

"*Jesus Christ Superstar*" was in *Harper's Magazine*, June 1971.

"The More Things Change: Notes on French Popular Song" was written in the summer of 1968 for Leo Lerman's *Mademoiselle*.

"Poetry of Music" was originally presented as a lecture titled "Words without Song," delivered in April 1969 at New York University, commemorating the one hundred-fiftieth anniversary of Walt Whitman's birth. (The "Postscript on Whitman" was at that time part of this lecture.) It was first published in *London Magazine*.

"Anatomy of Two Songs," as explained in the context, comes from a long-ago diary and was printed in my first collection, *Music from Inside Out*, in 1967.

As always I am deeply indebted to Jim Holmes. He provided the book's continuity, edited every page, and came up with the title *Settling the Score*.

To Marie Arana-Ward, my editor at Harcourt Brace Jovanovich, I extend a bouquet for her belief in such a noncommercial project and for her mannerly patience about matters of which she is aware.

Ned Rorem,
August 10, 1987

ONE

AMERICAN
COMPOSERS
Tributes and Reviews

LIVING WITH

GERSHWIN

Although I was only thirteen when he died in July of 1937, George Gershwin had already grown so crucial to the collective unconscious that half the world seemed to stop. Five months later when Maurice Ravel died (I was fourteen now), the other half stopped. The realities of love and death were suddenly as real as they would ever become.

I've just listened nonstop to fifty-three songs by George and Ira Gershwin, and the effect is no less exhilarating than if the songs had been by Robert Schumann or Charles Ives or indeed by Ravel. George's tunes are as memorable, Ira's texts as apt as those of the truest songmakers of yore. Ella Fitzgerald, the wistful baritone (she's as content cooing below the staff as sopranos are fifteen steps higher) proves as ideal a match for this team as Lotte Lehmann and Donald Gramm and Maggie Teyte were for the others. How she tints the tones (never an irrelevant ornament, only an occasional tilde) one by one, like those gray roses blushing toward pink in early Technicolor movies, then blends them into a bouquet of melody that evokes, over and over and over, your own first love. For the songs are virtually always about love—lost, found, longed for, disposed of—never about death. Death will come only with *Porgy and Bess.*

Hearing the songs in one fell swoop, most of them familiar as family, I realized I'd been living with Gershwin since the age of reason. Actually each of us lives daily with this most famous of modern composers, whose art surges forth from Musak all over the globe. Weaned on him, like most kids of the swing era, I never differentiated between Gershwin's basic worth and Ravel's but took him for granted (as I did Ravel) without analyzing wherein lay his charm and craft. At ten, thrilled by Paul Whiteman's theme song, I bought *Rhapsody in Blue* at the store next to the Frolic moviehouse on Chicago's Fifty-fifth Street (sheet-music shops,

3

now all but extinct, grew all over town then), and it still reposes on the piano, with my name childishly scrawled upon that friendly blue-and-gray Harms edition. Two years later my parents, ever alert to the Urban League and other racial betterment groups, came home late one night, flushed and dazzled and forever changed by the local premiere of the Negro spectacle *Porgy and Bess*. I envied them. "Summertime" took its place on the piano next to *Rhapsody in Blue*. Over the next decade, while learning by schooling the concert repertory from Couperin to Copland, I was learning by osmosis the words and airs of every Gershwin song. In the mid-1940s, as pianist for Eva Gauthier, I was often regaled by tales about another pianist she once hired, the young George Gershwin, who, on a program that began with piano-vocal excerpts from Schoenberg's *Gurreleider*, accompanied Madame Gauthier in "Stairway to Paradise," "Innocent Ingenue Baby," "Swanee," and "Do It Again." They brought down the house—with nobody questioning the legitimacy of such odd bedfellows. In 1948 I won the George Gershwin Memorial Award for my *Overture in C* (the piece did not deserve the prize, but I did), the premiere of which, under Mishel Piastro and the New York Philharmonic, was my first brush with the big time. On the program were Alec Templeton playing *Concerto in F*, Avon Long scatting "It Ain't Necessarily So," and Oscar Hammerstein, who in front of the audience handed me the award money, which was spent on a ticket to France where I stayed ten years. By the early 1950s, now myself an American in Paris, I was catching on to the Gershwin songs by their local plumage ("Quelqu'un m'adore" for "Somebody Loves Me," "Journée brumeuse" for "A Foggy Day," which seemed as smooth in French as in Ira's spirited English.

Ira's spirited English concerns me here. If as the stuff of good songs his words (called lyrics in Tin Pan Alley) don't quite vie with Goethe's, they are less bathetic and a good deal tighter than some of the poetasting used by, say, Schubert and Fauré. Witty, too, and ingeniously contrived. In the whole catalog I find but one trite line ("Oh if we ever part/Then that might break my heart"), and but one strained inversion ("And so all else above/I'm waiting for the man I love"). It's fun to play games of comparison ("You've got what gets me/What gets me you've got," writes Ira Gershwin in *Girl Crazy*; "I adore what you burn; you burn what I adore," writes Henry James in *The Tragic Muse*), or ponder the implications of lines like "I want to bite my initials on a sailor's neck" or "All the sexes from Maine to Texas," which seem every bit as equivocal as the *Erlkönig*. Ira likes to drop names such as Schopenhauer as something de trop when Eros is near (who disagrees?), or to suggest that "any Russian play" will guarantee fewer clouds of gray than when Eros has gone. The antiliterary Ira scores literary points about love, even as the learned Prioress in Poulenc's *Dialogues des Carmélites* loses meditational points about death when she realizes in her agony that a lifetime of prayer comes to naught in the end.

Ira's points are set to music by George according to the conventions of his day. He doesn't stretch the vocal line beyond a major tenth; is not melismatic—that is, doesn't use more than one note to a syllable (neither does Poulenc, his exact contemporary); and the shapes of each song are pretty much the same: a casual prelude succeeded by the requisite thirty-two-bar refrain of *a-a-b-a*. Yet there is as much variety—rhythmic, chordal, speedwise—as in the vocal output of Ravel. If a mannerism appears common from song to song, it's the tendency toward pentatonicism—arches confected from black-key rambling. Take at random "The Lorelei," "They All Laughed," "Maybe," "The Half of It," "Looking for the Boy," and see how each is built from the same rising sequence. Also the so-called blue note, a lowered third or seventh that *was* jazz in the 1920s (Darius Milhaud, striving toward timeliness, used more blue notes in his *Création du monde* of 1923 than did Gershwin in his *Rhapsody* of the same year), might seem overused were it not that each impulse takes on its own identity, then soars with a virile energy evoking a world as vulnerable and vast as the current world seems cool and stunted. For one belonging to both worlds, I find that every song still sends shivers of excruciating nostalgia up my spine, something no other music, past or present, seems to do anymore.

I've gone on at some length to show that George Gershwin's songs are no different in quality from those of the other named composers. But they are profoundly different in kind. His are popular, theirs are classical—the two halves of the world that seemed to stop for awhile, at least for me, back in 1937. These two genres have forever traveled parallel paths, but so distant as to be not even rivals.

Popular and classical, of course, have come to be meaningless categories, the one referring to being well liked, the other to a specific period in musical history. Some classical music is in fact popular, some pop songs have turned into classics. Still, I shall continue to use these terms here, since most readers know perfectly well what I'm talking about, but will redefine the terms as variable and invariable. Popular music is variable in that notes are improvised according to the player's mood. Classical music is invariable in that the same notes are played on all occasions. If in fact the two forms of music do sometimes trade devices (slick arrangements on the one hand, aleatoric cadenzas on the other), they nonetheless remain psychologically separate in the public ear.

True, the thirty-two-measure layout with its restricting lyrics does constrain the standard show tune's sense of structural adventure, keeping that aspect of it . . . well, invariable. (The term lyrics applies, I suppose, not to a species of verse but to words written simultaneously with, or sometimes after, the music. In the domain of so-called art song, music is built on pre-existing words, words sometimes hundreds, thousands of years old. Except for Messiaen, is there a living art song composer who writes his own "lyrics" as so many of the jazzmen do?) True again, the more fluid texts generally chosen by classical composers permit them, from one song to another, to vary the shape and length ad infinitum. Beyond these exceptions any pop song can, genuinely and persuasively, be played fast, slow, high, low, soft, loud, and be sung by any sex in any language with any accompaniment from guitar solo through chamber septet to a 1,000-piece orchestra. But can you imagine, say, Debussy's piano-vocal setting of Mallarmé's *Soupir* being sung by Sarah Vaughan with her irritating oversell, in English translation, transposed down a fifth, speeded up to allegro, and backed by the Boston Pops?

Given these distinctions, where does George Gershwin fit in? Gershwin's songs, his show tunes, are pure pop, or—as he would have said, ignoring our myriad current subdivisions—jazz. They withstand all manipulation, from the fuzzy-tragic wail of the late Billie Holiday (who was not even a fact when Gershwin died), with her vague groups of jam sessioneers, to Ella Fitzgerald's cool-as-sherbet diction backed by Nelson Riddle's great big band dolling up the tunes to within an inch of their lives. His concert music, notably *An American in Paris* and *Concerto in F*, is classical in that it is not adapted by "stylists" but performed intact. (Alone, *Rhapsody in Blue* inhabits a halfway house, being ostensibly a konzertstück but reshuffled, like Chabrier's *España*, for every profit-making combination imaginable.)

Porgy and Bess? *Porgy and Bess* is grand opera in the highest sense and belongs in the world's great theaters. As a show-tune composer Gershwin is pop, as author of *Porgy* he is classical, but he is never both at the same time. The only other musician to straddle this schizophrenic fence successfully is Leonard Bernstein. Can it be more than coincidence that both men are American Jews and that both have been obsessed with musical realizations of the dybbuk? The dybbuk is a split-personality-inducing soul that, according to *Webster's*, "enters the body of a man and controls his actions until exorcised . . ."

Gershwin's ever-thwarted wish to study privately with the Great led to the oft-quoted reactions of Ravel—"You would stop writing good Gershwin and start writing bad Ravel"—and of Stravinsky—"With your royalties it's I who should take lessons from you." Interestingly, although Gershwin did write a lot of *good* Ravel, his opera shows no influence whatsoever of Stravinsky, not even in the balletic picnic scene marked *Molto barbaro* where he could have nicely appropriated the eccentric "aboriginal" cross rhythms of *The Rite of Spring*. But jazz, finally a more magnetic lure for him than any classical composer could have been, derives not from an eccentric but a steady beat; indeed almost nowhere in the hotly danceable oeuvre of Gershwin does one find meters other than in a normal four. The brief 5/4 dance in that picnic scene, or the *trouvaille* of offbeat accents in early tunes like "Fascinatin' Rhythm," would seem as child's play to even a Tchaikovsky or a Brahms. In the long run Stravinsky, with his early *Tango* and later *Ebony Concerto*, took more from Gershwin than Gershwin ever took from him.

The texture of *Porgy and Bess*, like that of all jazz, derives (via its original Creole ambiance?) from French impressionism, rather than from German romanticism. Scarcely a chord is built on other than major or minor sevenths (or ninths or elevenths), *à la française*, rather than on the dominant or diminished triads and sevenths in use across the Rhine. Not that Gershwin's nest, like the magpie's, wasn't laced with a bit of everything around. *Porgy and Bess*, which was launched in Boston on September 30, 1935, owes a trick or two to *Wozzeck*, which had been performed seventeen seasons earlier in Philadelphia, not to mention to *Tosca* of 1900, as well as to (Gershwin had foresight) *Peter Grimes*, *West Side Story* and *Dialogues des Carmélites*. It was as influential as it was influenced.

For example, in my well-thumbed score I've noted that the opening scene alone, within the first four minutes, features the Honey Man's arietta which wavers, as Britten loved to waver, twixt the Dorian and Lydian modes; the invocation of the men's chorus ("Roll dem bones!", which melts from a C-sharp dominant into an F-sharp minor seventh even as Poulenc's women's chorus melts, in the same key, from "Dominus tecum" into "Benedictus tecum"; and Serena's admonition ("See that hussy drinkin' like any man!"), instantly preceded by Puccini's chimes in parallel fifths and succeeded (as Bess guzzles) by gurgling clarinets out of Berg's "water music," then followed head-on by a Bernsteinian sequence of blue harmony in a minor-on-major stack-up. And does that onstage out-of-tune piano come from *Wozzeck*, from Weill's *Mahagonny*, or is the device as old as theater itself?

In themselves the ingredients of *Porgy and Bess*—harmony, counterpoint, rhythm, melody, orchestral color, vocal concept for both solos and chorus, and the integrity of overall construction—are each first-rate in quality, professional in execution, and, despite the stolen threads common to most creators, utterly personal in impact. Like Mussorgsky, Gershwin was an elegant primitive; his own ways were ultimately more telling than those of his slick adapters. As to from where he learned, other than from Schillinger and from trial and error, not only the craft of instrumentation but the art of imbuing his music—first in single songs, later in whole garlands of song called musical comedies, finally in a three-hour drama—with the salubrious sap that makes it blossom and cohere from top to bottom, I wouldn't know. Does an artist *learn* such things?

Gershwin's meter, then, is mostly square, albeit with contagious syncopations within and over the bar, while his harmony is mostly built on secondary major and minor sevenths or on triads with added sixths (and those streams of parallel seconds, so rife in the *Rhapsody*, flow years later onto the set of *Porgy*). What of the other ingredients in his opera?

Melody, being the most personal, is the most memorable component of any composer's dialect. Melody is what makes a composer a composer. The vocal solos in *Porgy and Bess* are arias rather than songs because they are nonextractable; because the tunes follow—though sometimes deviously—where the words lead rather than being stuffed into a thirty-two-bar cage; and because they float upon an expanded operatic range. Unlike show tunes they do not have introductions, though they might have recitative preludes, even very "constructed" ones (Bess's preparation for the second-act duet—"It's like this, Crown . . ."—rises in a brief space from a relaxed low E to a wrenching high B). Nor are they as uniquely syllabic as show tunes. Each character has his theme, including the comprehensive quotidian "character" of Catfish Row, whose lilting 12/8 berceuse is never intoned. But alone Porgy has a leitmotiv, that is, a strictly instrumental shadow that precedes or follows him. The "sultry" nature of this leitmotiv—a sequence of ascending parallel fifths supporting a design made from a descending fifth swooping to a blue note attacked by a lewd acciaccatura—has come to be identified with fallen women more than with crippled men. Thus Porgy's tune, for those who don't know the context, sounds like Bess's.

Excepting the ubiquitous "Summertime," the closest thing to a straight song is the Strawberry Woman's air, nine sweet measures, concise and poignant as a Chanler Epitaph or an Auvergnois ditty (like Poulenc, Gershwin had a gift for inventing his own folk music). But have you ever heard this air sung as written, without those cute "selling" interpolations of squealed ritards? Why do performers mistrust simplicity?

Gershwin's prosody was as good as it needed to be. He probably didn't think much about it. Like most "natural" songwriters he was just that, natural, letting the impulse trail the curve of speech, colloquial and even Jewish though that speech might be. If a syllable seems falsely stressed, it is the false stress of folk song wherein a verse is nudged to fit the tune, not vice versa. In Serena's plaint "Ole *Man* Sor-*row*," the dislocated emphases on the second and fourth beats are there to match the correctly emphasized "My *man's* gone *now*." Here incidentally is a song about death if ever there was one (in 3/4 time, unlike nearly every other aria in *Porgy*), concluding with a cadenza right out of a Jewish funeral.

Counterpoint, in the schoolbook sense of the noun—five species, Palestrina, canon, undifferentiated simultaneous voices (is a fugue a family in perfect accord, or a madman talking to himself?)—plays no stronger a role in Gershwin's than in any other twentieth-century composer's works for the "lyric stage," with the possible exception of Hindemith's. But in the sense of the verb *counterpoint*, Gershwin's opera is filled with it. Small woodwind motives sneak between big vocal phrases and garnish, or *counterpoint*, the main surge, as in "Summertime." All around the choral lament for Clara, threads from other fabrics (mainly the Bess-Crown duet) are rhythmically and melodically counterpointed. In the final spiritual cum rumba "I'm on My Way," Porgy's solo is counterpointed with, in the orchestra, both "You Is My Woman" and the bass's own leitmotiv. In the hurricane scene a six-part chorus screams out for several minutes, a *tour* of storm force in an unmetered simultaneity no less ingenious than *Lucia*'s sextet, whose six exponents deliver six independent notions at the same time. However, in the 600-page vocal score there is but one short moment, a 2-page bridge of strings (at the start of the second act, leading from "It Takes a Long Pull" to "I Got Plenty O' Nuttin' "), that could properly be termed counterpoint, a sort of aborted *fugato* to no purpose.

"Do you do your own orchestration?" the layman often asks classical composers, having been struck with the contradictory idea, fostered by old movies about pop composers, that orchestration, being arcane, needs to be farmed out to hacks. In fact orchestration, that most tangible aspect of a composer's craft and hence the easiest to talk about, is not an art but a physical science dealing in checks and balances that can be mastered by anyone. The answer to the layman's question is: "If I don't, who does?"

Is orchestration part of composition? Yes, insofar as a piece is "composed" of—made up of—various ingredients, including instrumentation. But no, insofar as a piece of music, unlike a painting, must exist before it is colored. True, few Broadway and no Hollywood composers orchestrate their own music (union regulations); still, their music is there to be orchestrated. They may have the colors in mind while composing, but the coloring and the composing remain separate processes.

After 1923, which saw the advent of *Rhapsody in Blue*, his first so-called classical concert piece, Gershwin orchestrated all of his own music. And although we know more about Monteverdi's operas than we do about Gershwin's so far as *procedure* of orchestration is concerned (the lead sheets, abbreviations, makeshift rehearsal scores for *Porgy* having all vanished), the net result is crystalline, never overladen or intrusive. Aware of the basics—that strings are the body of any orchestra, woodwinds the soul, brass the clothing, and percussion the jewelry (the less you wear, the more effective)—Gershwin did occasionally go against typecasting. By and large, though, he didn't take more chances than, say, Respighi, whose sonorities he emulated a bit too closely for comfort (on page 508 of the *Porgy* score you will not hear, as marked, "a Sleeping Negro" but "The Pines of Rome"). Yet somehow, indefinably, his scoring is identifiably his. Who but Gershwin would have chosen, as background for Serena's impassioned recitative "Oh, Doctor Jesus," a soft trill, not on a drum or a cello but on a *piano*!

Just as the neighborhood Catfish Row plays its musical part in *Porgy and Bess*, so does the Chorus announce its own intense identity in a role longer, timewise and pagewise, than that of both principals combined. As cast member the Chorus is more indispensable even than *Carmen*'s chorus, being composed of personalities. Yet so familiar are the seventeen arias that we forget they are almost incidental—some a mere ten measures long—as against the grand set numbers of the group that account for three-quarters of the opera. The opera, thanks in large part to the choruses that support it like marble pillars placed between moments of slapstick and joy and horror and death, is in any case adeptly structured, with slows and fasts and highs and lows and mobs and solos and sads and sillies, all satisfyingly intermixed, each exquisite in itself. George's innate sense of unity owes much to the dozen earlier collaborations with Ira. (The book for *Of Thee I Sing*, sans music, won the Pulitzer prize in 1933.) Yes, the third act flags, especially when Crown's meaningless "A Redheaded Woman" comes out of left field, and later when a resetting of the normal tone seems to drag on forever before the ghastly truth is sprung on the hero. But beyond this there's scarcely an uninspired or superfluous minute in all of *Porgy and Bess*. In effect the framework would seek to disavow (not with entire success) the set-piece format of Gluck or Weill, or indeed of Gershwin's own show-biz past, in favor of the unbroken line of Debussy and Wagner. *Porgy*, no more than *Pelléas* and *Parsifal*, needs applause.

Another lay observation: "You write such good songs, you're meant to write great operas." The two expressions, if not mutually exclusive, don't often overlap. Schubertian gift is of tune and poetry, of short breath, of shaping form while the iron is hot, of starting and ending a work in a frantic inspirational space—in sometimes the mere time it takes to notate it. Verdian gift is of theatricality and prose, of the long line, of reworking matter even when cold, of spending perhaps years in getting it down. The opera composer's talent is dramatic first, lyrical second—and sometimes never. The song composer's talent is the reverse. A few—Mozart, Poulenc, Britten—play both the Elysian fields, and George Gershwin is one of these blessed.

Is there a Negro voice? Maybe—though Ella Fitzgerald doesn't much have it. We are *not* all the same; opposites attract. It's no fiction, contends

Margaret Mead, that black folks all got rhythm, though it's not heredity either. Since the poor can't afford nursemaids, they carry infants on their bosoms or backs; the papoose thus continually interacts with his parents' daily doings and has only to knock if he wants something. He is reared in purposeful metrical throbbing, which well-off nontactile Wasps are not. Similarly group singing, with its extrovert interpolations by Baptist soloists, makes for the gleeful croon, the silky tear, which have come to be associated with the black sound. Leontyne Price retains it throughout her repertory (except in spirituals!). Younger black singers raised in the North can fake it, which is more than Helen Jepson could do in the old Red Seal recording of "Summertime."

If *Porgy and Bess* belongs in the world's great theaters, does that mean it could be played convincingly by an all-white cast? Yet if you claim that Puccini and Wagner are credible with blacks so why not *Porgy* with whites, doesn't the claim deny *Porgy*'s identity as a demonstration of the black condition? *Tosca* and *Tannhauser* are not demonstrations of the white condition. *Is* there a white condition—and by extension a white voice?

These notions nagged me when in the early 1960s I received a grant to write a work for the New York City Opera. What finally emerged as *Miss Julie* was only the last of several projects, some half completed, then dropped. Among these was *Mamba's Daughters,* a darkly violent play adapted (for Ethel Waters) from the novel by DuBose and Dorothy Heyward, which I was making into a libretto. The story unfolds in the same milieu, known as Gullah, as Catfish Row. Working first with James Baldwin, I had regularly to audition my arias (Betty Allen learning them on spec) for the motherly Mrs. Heyward, who always found them "not Gershwiny enough." She was betting on another *Porgy*, which, being one of a kind, was a losing proposition. Yet she put me in touch with Eva Jessye, choirmistress of *Porgy*'s first production, who actually rehearsed my choruses. Feeling compromised, I dropped the project. By the time Jenifer Heyward, after her mother's death, came up with the rights, I was otherwise engaged. My true reason for the "engagement," as I see it now, was that I had no right to those rights. How could a white artist, however compassionate, presume to depict a black nightmare from the inside out? I could identify with femaleness perhaps, since half my ancestors were women. But none of my ancestors was black. Artists contain all sexes but not all races. Still, shouldn't a true artist be able to enter any psyche? And weren't the Heywards and Gershwins white? Yes, but maybe theirs was a white man's image of the black man. I sensed that the difference between black and white corresponded to the difference between jazz and classical, and I didn't want to seem like Grace Moore, missing the point by rolling her *r*'s in "Minnie the Moocher."

Philadelphia, September 21, 1984. Is there a black person still around who had once known Gershwin? Although we've both taught at the Curtis Institute for years, our paths (because our "days" are different) have never crossed. So this afternoon by prearrangement I stop by the Barclay Hotel for an hour's chat with Todd Duncan. Manly and gorgeous at eighty-two, effusive yet proper, radiating culture and enunciating with the resonant voice that created the role of Porgy in 1935 and repeated it 1,200 times, Mr. Duncan asks after my parents whom he'd met years ago, and seems touched to learn that my first true piano teacher had been his friend Margaret Bonds. I tell him a bit about my adventure with Dorothy Heyward. He proffers keen appraisals of today's singers. We decide against having tea. Then he talks about *Porgy and Bess*.

There was, he tells me, a sort of switch from typecasting at his first meeting in 1934 with George Gershwin. Duncan, a sedate and formally trained thirty-two-year-old bass, had been summoned from his studies in the South to audition for this brash and brilliant white boy in a 72nd Street penthouse where only brother Ira was present. Duncan was the hundredth candidate for the role. Yet after his rendering of a three-minute canzonetta, George asked, "Will you be my Porgy?" (The very young Jean-Pierre Aumont, after a three-minute audition in Paris that same year, heard Cocteau declare, *"Vous serez mon Œdipe."* Those were the days when creators loomed larger than their interpreters.) Duncan's answer: "Well, I'd like to hear your music first, Mr. Gershwin." With Ira as kibitzer, George sang what existed of the opera "in his awful—awful but wonderful—voice, which was pure Charleston Negro. I was disconcerted," says Duncan, "even appalled, by the crassness of the piece. Until 'Summertime.' Then I literally wept for what this Jew was able to express for the Negro."

Did he ever feel that Gershwin was outside looking in? That Gershwin condescended? No, Duncan never once questioned the book's integrity, nor the music's, despite being publicly chastised by certain of his people for playing a crippled criminal. Indeed the whole production was denounced by black groups for its Uncle Tomism and phony dialect (which in fact was a pastiche of Gullah filtered through Ira's Manhattanite imagination and realized helter-skelter by the singing actors, most of whom had never been to Charleston).

Yet working with Gershwin remains the high point of Duncan's public life. "Mr. Gershwin loved his own music, believed in it, was always anxious to hear it sung. At the final rehearsals he realized he had put down on paper accurately something from the depth of the soul of the South Carolina Negro." As for Todd Duncan's own interpretation of, for example, "I Got Plenty O' Nuttin' "—which during the early performances gradually took on his mannerisms, adapted by ensuing Porgys, specifically the half-shouted phrase "No use complainin' "—Duncan confesses he was merely aping the way the composer first sang it to him! His many performances at parties and benefits, with Gershwin at the piano, Duncan found to be transcendentally supportive occasions.

Eva Gauthier, drawing on memories individually accurate but collectively confused, years ago told me that the composer died from a malady passed on from Simone Simon. We know today, of course, that the cause was an inoperable brain tumor. Is Mr. Duncan aware of Gershwin's romantic life?

"Well, he was quite fond of Kitty, you know. Kitty Carlisle."

New York, November 2, 1984. If Kitty Carlisle was half as alluring fifty years ago as she is this afternoon, it's easy to see why Gershwin was fond of her. She will give a dinner party for twenty-four guests later tonight, so she warns me that the phone may often ring. It does. During the first protracted hiatus while Kitty—sitting marvelously erect, tailored skirt slit up to the thigh, phone crooked twixt chin and shoulder, a writing pad on her lap—attends lucidly to affairs of state (she heads the New York State Council of the Arts), I discreetly inspect pictures and books (Chagall and Dufy prints, photos of Arlene Francis and Nancy Reagan as well as of Cecil Beaton and of Kitty's late husband, Moss Hart, whose autobiography—several copies—is in evidence); the view from the window (Manhattan Bank, Madison Avenue branch); music on the Steinway ("The Man I Love," other Gershwiniana); and a vast sheaf of extraordinary roses, a pale pumpkin color.

"I'm going to write my own book, so don't expect me to talk too much," she announces on hanging up. "But yes, we went out regularly, both here and in Hollywood. George was my first entrée to the grand life. It's no secret that he was a wonderful pianist, and not just of his own pieces. But he never practiced. He didn't have time to practice, he was always performing. Like everyone else those days we'd go to Harlem—in ermine and pearls!—where George listened very, *very* assiduously to the great players of the time. In each nightclub we'd make a bet as to which tune the band would strike up first, his 'Lady be Good' or my 'Love in Bloom' "—the second being the theme song of the 1934 movie *She Loves Me Not* in which Kitty starred with Bing Crosby. The phone rings again.

If, as I like to believe, even the nonvocal music of a country stems from the language spoken in that country (Beethoven's sonatas take on the stresses of the German tongue, Arab flutes sound scratchy like Arab speech, etc.), then don't the dialects within a language affect the music, too? Sure, there is a Negro voice; but do blacks have a different laryngeal structure from whites, the way Swedes are fairer than Chileans? Does the nation make the song, or the song the nation? Are Russian bassos bred to intone those deep lines, or are those deep lines conceived to assuage Russian bassos? There's a Jewish voice, too, rising from the cantor's free cry and sometimes, as in George Gershwin's case, joining the cry of special streets. Did the *Porgy* cast turn his music black? Was it in itself black? Or has it come, with the intervening generations, to mean black now to us—if it does? Dialects do alter with the generations. Gershwin's slang was of a time. Who can say what he, who died in 1937, would have made of Billie Holiday (that archblack mezzo with her all-white repertory, whose career began that year) and her loose way with "I Wants to Stay Here" versus Leontyne Price's strict way or Anita Ellis's frantic way or Nina Simone's hostile way? How would he have felt about his arias, as opposed to his show tunes, being revamped? What, for that matter, did he think of Kitty's voice?

"No, he didn't drink," she allows in reply to a question about the Harlem clubs. "Jews don't drink. At least they didn't then. . . . Yes, he wanted to marry me, it would have suited him." By this she means that Gershwin wanted an old-fashioned wife, one his Orthodox family could approve of and at the same time one who could help him with his music by testing each new song as it came out.

Is she Jewish, too? Not in any religious way. But she emphasizes Gershwin's own Jewishness, as Todd Duncan had emphasized his subliminal negritude, as the stabilizing force that lent verisimilitude to the music. These are the romantic viewpoints of performers. Composers themselves have no such viewpoints about why they compose, or at least about why they compose the *way* they compose.

Asked what it means to be a Jew, she has no ready answer, at least not for herself. Then carefully she says, "I suppose, since the Holocaust, it means solidarity." Long pause. "Of course, George didn't know the Holocaust."

Her last two phrases hang in the air like a Zen koan. Does it make sense to suggest that *Porgy and Bess* could not have been written by a Gentile? Or that it could not have been written by a black?

The cook comes in to confirm the menu. The phone rings again as I slip away.

The old question of Opera in the Vernacular, Yes or No? is of course endlessly arguable. But in *The Muses Are Heard*, Truman Capote's quaint account of the *Porgy and Bess* Russian tour of 1955, a new slant is proffered. Because the denizens of Catfish Row are God-fearing, extremely erotic, cocaine addictive, uncritically superstitious, and sing out loud that people can be happy with plenty of nuttin', the production risked being taken, from the Communist viewpoint, as a picture of racial exploitation by southern whites. Thus the director planned to deliver a precurtain speech stating that *Porgy and Bess* is set in the past and no more reflects the present than if it were about life under the czars. But opening night was not the resounding success that international hype was seeking. The translated libretto was unavailable in time, and the uncomprehending audience sat on their hands. During the funeral scene, Capote wrote, "While the murdered man's widow sings a lament, the mourning inhabitants of Catfish Row sway in a tribal circle around the corpse. At this point, an important Soviet dignitary turned to a correspondent and said in Russian, 'Ah, now I see! They are going to *eat* him.' "

What is the answer? To have an all-black American cast learn Russian? I have always thought that music, especially non-vocal music, is the least universal of languages. What can we (or the Russians) make of the vital intent of Eskimo or Korean or Hindu music, or indeed, now so long after the inception, of Gershwin's brand new language?

My father—who as I write resides with Mother in New Jersey and continues active as America's most innovative consultant on medical economics—my father was born eight years before Debussy's *Pelléas*, six years before the death of Oscar Wilde, and four years before George Gershwin saw the light of day. These dates seem removed, historical, mysterious. Yet I still speak with Father nearly every day (I've just given him Todd Duncan's regards), asking advice on how to deal with the modern world.

If because he died young Gershwin now seems remote, so does the fact of *Porgy*. Mysteries remain within the text. When is the action? The published score, composed in 1934 (and, incidentally, dedicated simply "To My Parents"), bears the indication *Charleston, the recent past*. The novel, published in 1926, draws upon a news item of the teens (about a cripple, "Goat Sammy," who assaulted a woman) and supposedly draws also upon DuBose Heyward's own recollection of the 1911 hurricane. The "kindly" white man in the second act, Mr. Archdale, posts bail for Peter because "his folks used to belong to my family." But Gershwinophile Robert Kimball situates the action "in the 1930s," and no one then could have matter-of-factly had folks who were slaves. Also, what happens to Clara? If Crown survived, couldn't she and Jake have survived, or at least shouldn't their fates be explained?

Is *Porgy and Bess* a tragedy? Who is the hero? If Crown is the nominal villain, while Sportin' Life's merely a son of a bitch, virtually all the characters in the first act, except Porgy, turn their backs on Bess when she needs a friend. ("The God-fearing women and the God-damning men!") Meanwhile Porgy-as-murderer goes unpunished—is indeed condoned by his peers, although he played the coward at the police station—whereas Crown (also a murderer) is the sole character to display courage as he ventures out to save Clara in the eye of the storm.

"No other American composer had such a funeral service as that held last Thursday for Gershwin," wrote Olin Downes in 1937. "Not a MacDowell, nor a Chadwick, not a Stephen Foster or John Philip Sousa received such parting honors." A few months later George Antheil wrote: "He has been recognized by everybody except those whose . . . understanding he most craved—the American Composer . . . [Even Virgil Thomson's words on Gershwin] were often as condescending as the others . . . America's 'recognized abroad' serious symphonic composers have remained strangely silent."

Serious. That was the aim of high art, an aim that in itself now seems less serious than solemn in our ever more agile age of Akhenatons and Alices. Arnold Schoenberg, a fellow portrait painter and tennis opponent during the mid-1930s, wrote this when his friend Gershwin died: "Many people do not consider [him] a serious composer. But they should understand that, serious or not, he is a composer—that is, a man who lives in music and expresses everything, serious or not, sound or superficial, by means of music, because it is his native language." Schoenberg does not add that *he* finds Gershwin's music, or even his own, serious, nor is the word defined.

Two years earlier Gershwin himself had said, "I chose the form I have used for *Porgy and Bess* because I believe that music lives only when it is in serious form. When I wrote the *Rhapsody in Blue* I took 'blues' and put them in a larger and more serious form. That was twelve years ago and the *Rhapsody in Blue* is still very much alive, whereas if I had taken the same themes and put them in songs they would have been gone long ago."

Virgil Thomson's *Four Saints in Three Acts*, produced one year before *Porgy and Bess* in 1933, was (although not on a Negro subject) the first opera ever to utilize an all-black cast. Thomson, two years Gershwin's senior, had this to say in 1935 about the all-black *Porgy*: "The music . . . is not very different from his previous output of serious intent, except insofar as staging helps cover up the lack of musical construction. Hence it is no longer possible to take very seriously any alibi for his earlier works. . . . Gershwin has not and never did have the power of sustained musical development. . . . It is clear by now that Gershwin hasn't learned . . . the business of being a serious composer, which one has long gathered to be the business he wanted to learn. . . . His efforts at recitativo are as ineffective as anything I've heard. . . . I do not like fake folklore, nor fidgety accompaniments, nor bittersweet harmony, nor six-part choruses, nor gefiltefish orchestration." Not for thirty years did Thomson render further judgment on *Porgy and Bess*. In 1965 in the *New York Review of Books* he wrote simply that "although the theme is . . . a white man's view of Negro life (hence phony throughout), its translation into melody is a lovely one because Gershwin was a pure heart." That is all our greatest music critic ever wrote about George Gershwin.

Postcript. There is but one instance of filching from a pop peer. The tune "I Can't Sit Down" owes itself to Cole Porter's "I Get a Kick out of You." To atone for this melodic plagiarism, Gershwin adorns it with an ingenious ostinato stolen from Poulenc's first *Mouvement perpétuel*. The two thefts conjoined (like simultaneously patting your head and rubbing your stomach) melt into a single utterance that sounds like pure George.

Yes, Britten and Gershwin each loved to float between the Dorian and Lydian modes. Isn't Scriabin's "mystic chord" a harmonic version of the same penchant? A six-part chord in root position, with fourth raised and seventh lowered, is Lydian lain upon Dorian.

All musical aspects of Lorin Maazel's *Porgy* disc are apt except the rhythmic. He is square by being unsquare. Rather than rely on the page, Maazel coddles, plays with, *interprets* the beat (hear the first-act piano), thinking thus to lend a free and jazzy mood. But jazz isn't free. Jazz depends on metronomic regularity, like a Chopin nocturne: the rubato "meaning" of the right hand relies on the impersonal strictness of the left.

As in the only other extant recording, recitatives here are reinstated in the name of authenticity, while references to "niggers" are conscientiously deleted. Reversal of freedom-of-speech trend. Is this bowdlerization kosher? Maybe, but it ain't Gullah.

What Debussy's tone poems are for nature travelogues, Gershwin's tone poems are for Manhattan skylines. Defiled and devalued, the art of these men became the lingua franca for 1940s movie musicians. But defilement is not in question when I hint that *Rhapsody in Blue* would have been substantially different without the model of Debussy's *Ballade des femmes de Paris*. Nor is devaluation in question when you hear Earl Wild's dazzlingly honest piano improvisations on *Porgy and Bess*, in the hot tradition of Liszt's opera transcriptions, on the record called *Wild About Gershwin*.

I skipped gym to see *Queen Christina* at the Frolic. The next year Rouben Mamoulian directed *Porgy and Bess*. He worked with both Garbo and Gershwin, the sphinx and the extrovert. This means no more than it means, except that a child makes links where he finds them. Besides *Porgy*, *Peter Grimes*, and *Four Saints*, how many operas can you name wherein the curtain rises on fishermen repairing nets? And doesn't the "Buzzard Song" with its flailing clarinets remind you of Bartók's "Lake of Tears"?

———

What the pop composer puts on paper (or whistles into a Dictaphone, as with Noël Coward and Irving Berlin and others who can't read or write music) is less a composition than something to be recomposed, while what the classical composer puts on paper is final. Performers of these two kinds of music, by virtue of their specialized training, do not overlap, although their careers, like church and state, have always run parallel. The only creators, as I wrote earlier, who've spanned the bridge are Gershwin and Bernstein. *Porgy* belongs more utterly to Gershwin than, say, *Sweeney Todd* belongs to Stephen Sondheim, because Gershwin is responsible for the sonority and placement of every note in the score. Of course, he was wrong about his songs—that since they weren't "serious" they wouldn't last. Were you forced to name the second greatest (anyone can name the first) melodist in our century, could you possibly place Puccini or Poulenc or Jerome Kern, Mahler or Ives or Harold Arlen, Messiaen or Chanler or Richard Rodgers ahead of the wondrous George?

(*1984*)

COPLAND'S BIRTHDAY
(AT SEVENTY)

Dear Aaron: It has been twenty-seven years since we first met. That was at the suggestion of Lenny Bernstein, who said you liked knowing what young composers were up to. Although as a student from Curtis I was intimidated by the thought of contact with the Dean of American Music, you received me warmly in that now-vanished studio on 63rd Street. On the piano was your *Short Symphony*, which Stokowski was to perform the next week. On your shelves were *Quiet City* and *El Salón México*, which at the time comprised the only "serious" American music (besides Leo Sowerby and John Alden Carpenter) I'd ever heard. In a wee voice I sang you songs of mine; you asked if "tunes came easily" to me. And you asked about mutual friends in my hometown of Chicago. That was that for a while.

Today I am four years older than you were then. Much has occurred meanwhile to you and me in that musical field we both plow, our furrows crisscrossing occasionally, yet I feel scarcely any alteration in our roles. I'm still intimidated by your reputation, and perhaps you still wonder if my tunes come easily. Yes, the tunes flow. And let us hope that twenty-seven years hence your reputation will be based on the continuing variations of your vast output.

Such was the substance of my festschrift contribution offered the septuagenarian last night after a colossal meal at Essex House. The past—any past—is golden by definition, and surely a certain warmth surrounds all memory of Aaron. Yet the letter reads more sentimentally than my actual sentiments. In *Music and People* I drew as ample a portrait of the man as my needs demanded. What follows is a postscript.

In the early postwar years Aaron Copland and Virgil Thomson were the Rome and Avignon of American music. Young composers joined one faction or the other; there was no third. Both were from France through Nadia Boulanger, but Aaron's camp was Stravinsky-French and contained a now-vanished breed of neoclassicist like Alexie Haieff and Harold Shapero and Arthur Berger, while Virgil's branch was Satie-French and contained a still-vital breed of neocatholic like Lou Harrison and John Cage and Henry Brant. (The Germanisms of Wolpe-via-Schoenberg were as yet quiescent.) The few lone wolves such as myself were still socially partial to one or the other. I saw a good deal less of Aaron than of Virgil—if only because the latter was my employer for a while (I was his part-time copyist during 1944 and 1945).

Beyond an occasional letter of reference or a pat on the back, neither musician, during three decades of fraternizing, has ever lifted a finger toward my music, be it by performance, verbal recommendation, or through their copious writings. Automatically they were more important to me than I to them—they were older; to this day I recall every word that each ever said, and can realize how their professional behavior has indelibly stamped mine. Yet this comes of tenacity: instruction is taken, not given, and they set an example just by being themselves. Beyond those elements of themselves that were at the disposal of anyone, I owe nothing to either man.

Looking through old diaries, I recover this "artistic entry" from Hyères dated August 9, 1953, which I still like but no longer comprehend:

> To say his music's empty does not imply vacuous or arid. It means empty. Emptiness is a state, a state can be changed, something empty could be something full (or half full, or half empty). Aaron's music *contains* emptiness, which is a benefit, not a derogation. There lies its force. The music is transparent, *dépouillée*, like a fish net that can be used only as a fish net, giving you the opportunity to *see* the emptiness which of course cannot be seen. A colorless fish net containing nothing. Copland flings it, further filtering, over our ears, and the music that gathers in memory is often full of many things including beauty. Music full of fullness is dangerous.

Five film scores by Aaron Copland in the 1940s represented the most distinguished Hollywood had yet heard. His music was no more illustrative than his predecessors', it was more illustrious. Aware of sound's pliability when conjoined with sights (any sound "works" with any sight, but the sound dictates the final meaning of the sight, i.e., certain music could make a comic scene tragic—truly tragic), he didn't resort to clichés but gave new tonal measurements to old situations. Though these scores have been turned into concert suites and live on their own merits, the effectiveness of the films without the music is open to question.

Does that paragraph hold true? Did Hollywood actually need distinction? Did Copland really eliminate clichés or merely introduce new ones? Do his concert suites live on? Are the movies so ineffective without the music?

Can you name one film score, other than for a documentary, that deserves to enter, even in altered form, the concert repertory as many a ballet has? Are the Copland movie suites, with all their fame, really weakened versions of his ballet suites? Documentaries aren't interfered with by too much text and plot. Prokofiev's *Alexander Nevsky* is really a documentary. So is Georges Auric's *Le Sang d'un poète*. Ironic that Thomson's movie music, being documentary, will probably survive Copland's!

The great Steiner and Waxman scores just can't cut it out of context. (Those of Rod McKuen or John Barry can't cut it even *in* context.) At best they remind us of their source, not of themselves. The most thrilling movie scores are not improvisatory solderings, like those by pit pianists in silent days and brought to their apex by Copland. They are precomposed set pieces like the slow waltz of George Delerue that haunted *The Conformist*, or like the concerto Johann Sebastian Bach composed for *Les Enfants terribles*.

(Movies of presumably abstract images accompanied by music are unfeasible. Two abstractions cancel each other—though visions soon assume logical shape, as they must, like clouds. Formal sound is helpful for underlining compact story lines; distillations of life are granted unity through the additional artifice of music.)

The feast at Essex House was followed by *louanges* and presentations from the Great, and terminated with *Danzón Cubano* performed at two pianos by Copland and Bernstein with the *élan* of a pair of drunken sailors—all harmless fun. And warmer certainly than our memorial for Bill Flanagan some months ago, when Aaron's contribution was a speech, the burden of which lay in how much Bill had always admired his (Aaron's) music.

(While weights within our frontiers shift with the years, outside impressions remain fixed. Paul Jacobs relates this backstage bonbon: Stockhausen, in New York and onstage for a series of sold-out performances, spots Aaron Copland in the hall during a rehearsal. So Stockhausen introduces his girlfriend. "I'd like you to meet the great American composer Virgil Thomson.")

(*1970*)

COPLAND AT
EIGHTY-FIVE

As a teenager at Philadelphia's very proper Curtis Institute in 1943, I would occasionally head for New York to get into mischief. One weekend before boarding the train (I was off to see Virgil Thomson, whom I'd never met, about becoming his copyist), Shirley Gabis said, "Why not drop in on my old friend Lenny while you're up there." I did. Accordingly Bernstein put me onto Copland—"Aaron likes knowing what young composers are up to"—and I spent an afternoon bleating my tunes for the famous musician. Well, I took the job with Virgil, became an instant fan of Aaron's and of Lenny's, and for the next forty-two years with many an up and a down I've remained staunch friends with all three men. Some weekend!

Meanwhile there has built up around Copland bits of conventional wisdom that bear inspection. On a recent television homage I found myself stating, as by rote, that Copland had invented out of whole cloth what it means to be American. Now, wasn't it Thomson who first legitimized the use of homegrown fodder for sophisticated palates, a use Copland borrowed intact for his second period—the period of open prairies and Appalachian springs? What's more, hadn't Virgil, like Poulenc, invented his own folk music (you won't find his church-tune pastiches and cowboy ditties in hymnals and songbags), while Aaron, like Stravinsky, incorporated preexisting lore into his scores? Certainly Aaron was out to find the American way, but whether the Brooklynite would have chosen just this way without the Missourian Thomson's pioneering is speculative. As to the periods, they can now be viewed as mere textbook labels after the fact. Copland's oeuvre is history: each work—from the once "problematic" *Variations* through the "lean" *Rodeo* to the "thorny" *Inscape*—can now be heard as flowing from the same economical pen. His music, all of it, is accessible to the big public, with (and this is his crucial inheritance from Boulanger) never a note too many.

On the same TV program we learned, again through the iteration of received ideas, that Aaron Copland is a saint. The broad acceptance of his sanctity stems less, I think, from his sturdy need for self-promotion (which all artists possess) than from his fanatic sense of the value of other people's work (which few artists possess). Even in private Aaron is a public person, enjoying gossip but not uttering it, witty and generous, yes, but also stoic and immutable. Yet to be a saint one must have been a sinner, and it lessens the man to assume he is above temperament. I have observed Aaron livid with impatience at the longueurs in a French peer's sonata, heard him sigh from betrayed affection, submitted to his ire at what I'd written about a friend of his, known him to be more than tempted by the flesh. Bland sins, I admit. But then, Aaron is more artist than saint. Saints are a dime a dozen but true art is scarce, and one could argue that Aaron Copland has changed the world for the better, while Joan of Arc never changed it at all.

Last week I told the composer George Perle that Copland has branded us all in America, even those who repudiate him, since the very act of repudiation is acknowledgment of Copland's force. I've said this so often it's dogma, so I was disconcerted when George replied, "He never influenced me. In fact, I've influenced him. After all, he finally came over to the serial technique, while I never went over to his side." Indeed Aaron did "come over" to the twelve-tone system during his so-called third period. Retrospectively this seems an act of hysteria, of not wanting to be left behind. In the 1960s Aaron had the world at his feet, except for that small portion older composers most crave: young composers. The young at that moment were immersed in Bouleziana, a mode quite foreign to Copland's very nature (as to the nature of Stravinsky, who also sold out to the system).

The more things change, the more they stay the same. Today I teach at Curtis. Lenny's everywhere. Virgil thrives. Shirley has married George Perle. And Aaron Copland is again loved by the young, though less as model than as a fact of sonic geology, like a throbbing song-filled Rock of Gibraltar.

(*1985*)

A MEDAL FOR LENNY

We have no sacred monsters anymore, no larger-than-life Stravinskys whose every gesture fires the collective imagination. Even our performing artists are now sold as regular guys, while American saints are fundamentalist hacks snatching expensive halos from each other.

We have no general practitioners anymore. If in Europe the breed once flourished, from Leonardo da Vinci to Jean Cocteau, over here jacks-of-all-trades have always been suspect. We are specialists. A doctor who treats your foot isn't likely to treat your ear, much less write a play, lest he in turn be treated as superficial. Those blessed with more than one gift are punished for spreading themselves thin.

As sole exception to these assertions we have Leonard Bernstein, the epitome of glamour combined with quality, and thank heaven for him— the heaven of the golden gods of yore.

His triumphs are known to all. No need to reiterate that Bernstein's books and lectures have shaped the way America listens. No need to recall that his mastery of keyboard and podium has defined the notion of American performance. No need to stress that while the scope of his programs spans centuries, it italicizes his homeland, bringing into relief our sense of American craft. Nor is there need to add that as champion of liberal causes he is as scrupulous as to the causes of art.

Now if he were all this but had never composed a note, it would, as he has said of others on Passover, have been sufficient. But the notes he has composed are what concern us here today, for the MacDowell Colony, to its very name, symbolizes musical creation even as Bernstein embodies it. And so for this quarter hour I would like to talk first about Bernstein the writer of music, then about Bernstein as he figures in musical society.

He is a composer whose influence on other composers is at once vast and vague. Vast, because in giving Broadway opera a good name— eclectic though he be—he spawned a genre that changed the very skel-

27

eton of our musical theater. Vague, because the effect of eclectics on others is by nature as ambiguous as the effect of others on them. Take my case. Such reputation as I may enjoy seems to lie in songs; and I've always felt that Lenny and I were as different as night and day. Yet last month when I played again his *Jeremiah Symphony,* the first piece of his I ever heard in public, I realized what I may never have wanted to admit—how for decades this heady draft had been infusing my own music. My very first song, on a Chaucer lyric, was modeled on the Hebrew plaint in his final movement, and by extension almost every song I've penned has had a taste of his recipe.

What is his recipe?

Start with the rhythm. Bernstein's meters are generally eccentric, even when depicting casualness. Yet despite the off-center basic beat, the assemblage of beats retains a steadiness that inspires listeners to action that involves regular motion—like dancing, picking apples, making love. His tempos meanwhile are convincing at any speed, with that potential for infinite variety that distinguishes major from minor artists. His fast music is inherently fast, not slow music played fast, just as his slow music is inherently slow.

His counterpoint is second to none when he chooses, but he doesn't often choose, except sometimes in choral writing. Then he plays different colors against each other, as a great theater man like Verdi does, rather than the same colors at different pitches like Bach does.

Bernstein's harmony is at once rich and lean. Not only the rainbows conjured from a pure triad, but wildly complex chords are often expressed in but three voices. His harmony derives from his melody, not the other way around.

Melody, of course, is the sovereign ingredient of music, the one that makes a composer a composer. Without it, nothing else counts. Bernstein's sense of tune is all-embracing, infectious, strange. All-embracing, because it informs every bar of his instrumental catalog, not just the sung airs. Infectious, because once heard it is never forgotten; yet even at the hundredth hearing I, for one, never quite know where it's leading me—which is why it's strange. I do know that Bernstein is the most recent, maybe the last, in the line of great vocal writers that began with Monteverdi, as distinct from the line of more formal writers like Beethoven.

His orchestration, since he's not much given to tricks, stumps the analytic ear with its ingenuousness. As with his tunes, I never know quite how he confects this or that sonority, and the *not knowing* is, from one composer to another, a high compliment. When on referring to the score I discover that his solution for some mystical effect is utterly plain, I wonder why *I* never thought of it. Still, what truly matters in music is that which can't be imparted except through itself; even the composer isn't always clear about how he makes things tick. Anyone can learn to write a perfect piece, but not how to make that piece breathe and bleed. Bernstein's pieces bleed and breathe. Expressivity is their goal, simplicity their device.

So much for his grammar. What about his language?

People usually speak of derivation as though it were naughty, and not the very soul of composition. All art is clever theft. The act of covering your traces is the act of creation, for that act is *you*. If you have something to say, that something will gleam through, even though you bend over backward to be *un*original. If traces of his beloved Haydn or Mahler exist in Bernstein's scores, they exist only in intent—in the crispness or angst—not in sound. Indeed, I find in him no sound of any musician east of the Rhine. Bernstein's precursors are rather Debussy and Copland. Yet the eclectic student's work is instantly recognizable as his own, and those very precursors can be shown to have robbed *their* pasts. I have a theory that one can also rob the future. The Debussy theme that Bernstein used for his *Facsimile* was in fact a facsimile of Bernstein's, simply because the American's use of the theme is more poignant.

As for the Copland connection, the younger man was clearly drawn to the open-air thrift of the older, the unapologetic use of jazz and folk tune, the Parisian transparence of both style and content. Yet Copland somehow seeks to secularize his speech, while Bernstein seeks the reverse. Maybe their very resemblance underlines their basic difference. What, therefore, is the final effect of Bernstein's ingredients when mixed together—the tunes, lines, pulses, chords, hues, and influences?

All of his music has the theatricality of religious ritual. Not just the Roman Catholicism of his huge *Mass*—which reflects the original multimedia spectacle that for millennia has been sung, acted, danced, tasted, and sniffed—but the High Anglican Waspery of the *Chichester Psalms* and the Audenesque *Age of Anxiety,* the Low Baptist gospel impelling many of his show-biz songs and even some of the concert ones, the pristine Hellenism of his Platonic *Serenade,* the medieval cabalism of *Dybbuk,* and the Old Testament tragedy of *Jeremiah Symphony* and

Kaddish. Even the nonvocal chamber works, like the little *Clarinet Sonata,* seem to have their own scenarios, their exits and entrances and built-in altars at which one prays for a better world.

To define him is, finally, to define any artist. An artist is like everyone else only more so, so Bernstein is like every other artist. Only no other artist is like him.

We first met in early 1943 at his West 52nd Street walk-up. He was already famous, although it would be another eight months before he'd make headlines with his Philharmonic debut. Fame is to some extent a frame of mind, and the young Lenny was every bit as charismatic and self-aware as the star who sits here now.

On his piano, next to Copland's *Piano Sonata,* was a just-finished song called "You've Got to Be Bad to Be Good." I'd have liked using that title for these notes. In fact, yes, experience, including "badness," does aid toward understanding of art, but toward lucid dispersal of art no one knows better than Lenny that you've got to be *good* to be good. Certainly you've got to be good to be *bad*—to *get away with* being bad. It's said he's sometimes overbearing, but is that not balanced by his judgment, sense of related values, indeed by his goodness? Not moral goodness, of course, for art has nothing of morality. He does aim high, but is his aim higher than that of, say, Anton Bruckner, notorious for his modesty? Is Bernstein's unleashed ego really bigger than yours or mine? It's not that he seeks to be the center—he *is* the center that others seek, for he has that rare knack, which can't be faked or bought, of listening to you alone as though *you* were the center despite your stammering, or of wanting to convince you alone no less than an audience of thousands.

Still, he soars above the fray, does not appear on talk shows, does not—unlike Stravinsky—lash out at his critics or respond publicly to would-be biographers. He does work hard, and plays hard, but as befits the sacred monster he leaves to others the machine of his glory. The more famous some artists grow, the more others proclaim: "If only he wouldn't waste himself so!" But waste is not misuse of one's talent; it's lack of use of one's talent—the contrary of Lenny's splendiferous generosity. Still, successful people, if they have brains, don't think of themselves as successful. They know what the public does not know—they know what they've not yet done. Bernstein too wears the crucial badge of all true artists: perpetual self-doubt.

In the intervening smoke-filled insomniac years since 1943, self-doubt notwithstanding, Lenny has brought to life a mountain of first-rate works of his own, and of a hundred colleagues. His premieres of my works have shown that, if as a composer I sometimes become Lenny, as a conductor he turns into me. When performing my music, his metabolism is so in tune with my own that he might as well have written the music himself. Other composers here will attest to this—his bloodstream is theirs during the length of their piece.

We live in an unhealthy age where non-pop composers are not even a despised minority. To despise something, that something must exist, whereas our composers are mostly invisible even to the cultured American public who otherwise digs Jackson Pollock or Merce Cunningham or Saul Bellow. Our age is equally unhealthy in that musical taste is determined by nonessential citizens—critics and managers—parasites who decree that solely music of the past is what counts, for it pays.

Lenny is the only major musical figure in our world who demonstrates that the living creator is the center of his art. Of Bernstein the pacifist, the Socratic rabbi, the unchic radical, the family man who laughs and reads and loves and dies, it is Bernstein, the composer's interpreter, who is most urgent, for he knows that the composer *is* his music, just as music *is* the composer. He alone grasps the ontology of the art. Whatever Bernstein does musically is right, even when it's wrong; the composer is always right, because he is the originator.

And the performer? you may well ask at this point. After all, music reviewing has become almost exclusive commentary on the performance of music rather than on the music itself. The performer is that oxymoron: an essential irrelevance. Essential because he displays the music, irrelevant because another performer might do it just as well.

What then of Bernstein, always a composer but sometimes a performer? If he were not a composer, he would not be the world's best conductor. Alone among conductors he knows that the essence of music is not what it sounds like, but what the sounds are intended to communicate. Since he too is a composer, he knows that the magic lies not in the communication of sound, but in the sound of communication. He is no more faithful to the score than any performer, but he is faithful always to the composer's intent. A score is but an approximation, while intent is immutable.

Bernstein, on his "Omnibus" series, was once lauded for taking the magic out of music through his gift of explaining music. But Bernstein does not explain—he reveals. Like the Celebrant in his own *Mass,* at the moment of Elevation he discloses the sacred elements to all; and we understand that no explanation is possible.

However little I have just said in analysis of both the music and the man, it is still too much. Such analysis cannot be done in words. To think it can is the critic's error. Just as critics of words use words, so critics of music use . . . words. The only valid criticism of a piece of music is another piece of music. If you want to know how much I love Lenny, listen to my songs. In discussing any great artist, the parts of speech are inadequate. Or as the poet Wallace Stevens says, "Not Ideas about the Thing but the Thing Itself."

And so, precious Lenny, the day is yours, and so is the century. You are what we all would be, the Thing Itself.

(*1987*)

WILLIAM FLANAGAN:
IN MEMORIAM

Nagged by that awful question "Do you consider yourself foremost a writer or a musician?" he of course answered, "A musician." For, like myself, Bill Flanagan became an author by virtue of whatever reputation he had earned as a composer, not the other way around.

We were the same age and of similar convictions—namely, that there was still blood in tonality, breath in the simple line, and that the flesh of music could be grafted onto the skeleton of poetry and given life by the singing voice, with a feeling of heightened naturalness for the listener. We remained close if competitive allies for twenty-three years. During some of those years we presented a very popular series, the Rorem-Flanagan concerts, of vocal music by Americans.

A decade ago, for the Bulletin of the American Composer's Alliance, at Flanagan's invitation and with his blessing, I wrote a survey examining virtually all of his compositions, relating them to his working habits and those habits to his life pattern. His output up to then had been small by any standard: less than three hours of music produced over fourteen fairly active years. During the nine years that remained of his life, Bill composed proportionately even less: about a half-hour's worth of completed score. Since this remainder does little to alter the survey, I have no more to add by way of analysis about Flanagan the creator. His catalog, for better or worse, is closed.

About Flanagan the man we all will speculate indefinitely. He was much more complicated than his music. Like his songs he was sad, but he was more intelligent than they—if one can speak of songs as in themselves containing intelligence. His perceptions were diamond hard; his logical, original, Jesuit-trained mind was such that very little escaped it. Very little except, of course, himself. His real body, which drank at West Village bars, could not keep pace with his fantasy of that body, which drank at the Fountain of Youth. He literally danced himself to death. As the action, or rather nonaction, of the hero in his opera *Bartleby* set the tone for much of Flanagan's own life-style, so the contagious tune in his *Illic Jacet* foresang his death: ". . . in love with the grave./And far from his friends and his lovers/He lies with the sweetheart he chose."

I used to be embarrassed by discussions about the waste of an artist's life cut short. (Remarks like "If only Schubert had lived, think of the beauty he would have bequeathed!" sound presumptuous.) I used to think artists died when their work was over; since obviously their work was over when they died, that settled the discussion. (I never rationalized Sibelius's long final period of nonproduction; he alone could have done that.) I used to feel fatalistic about man being granted an allotted time to say his piece. (Proof was Poulenc's collapse the morning after he had inscribed the double bar on his last work in progress, answered all letters, and was wondering what to do.)

Today I firmly believe Bill Flanagan died too soon. He left so much undone! True, his last completed work (and by general consensus his best), *Another August*, was finished more than two years before his death. But of the many pieces still under way, not one will be realized— a pity for a man whose production was already frugal. From that production there is not even a "signature" work identifying him, as Copland's *Appalachian Spring* or Barber's *Adagio for Strings* identify those composers. Nor did he leave one unflawed song, which could seem ironic given the chiseled, albeit purple, intent of his musical speech, a speech that wanted to say only what needed saying.

But need and speech are separate, especially within an insecure syntax; Bill's conservatory background had not been rigorous enough to allow him the discipline of simplicity. The proper balance that generates a surplus from which an artist draws and learns was for Bill gained through the labor pains of trial and error. I used to kid him about being too smart for prolificity, but he didn't find that funny. He could not practice Forster's motto for creation—speak before you think—but continued to censor, restrain, throttle his muse. The result was a paradoxical fusion of extreme conservatism with extreme unusualness, in effect if not in flavor like Satie.

His critical prose was something else. Though we may never see his presumably near-finished two volumes, on American music and on American theater, there exists an uncollected mass of published reviews and articles sufficient to fill a sizable book with his special personality: astute, tailored, funny, touching, correct, and wise. He was America's most literate spokesman for music's New Right, or the post-avant-garde, a music no longer embarrassed by classical molds or by expressivity as points of departure. These he defended from the inside out through his dual-natured but enviably modest authority as composer-critic. It is not too much to say he fought a losing battle for his life.

Not even the French can convincingly generalize about the creative process: how artists do, or should, work. For schizoid composers who are also writers, it seems nonetheless obvious that these two vocations satisfy rival drives. Bill's prose was elegant and clear, while his music was turgid and painfully delivered. Half of what he left as completed compositions were, in my opinion, sketches for completed compositions. Still, the other half, along with his prose, comprises tender and truthful treasures, all the more precious for their rarity.

(1969)

FLANAGAN'S MUSIC

Every true artist has two faces: one we see in the flesh, the other we see through his work. Although sometimes the marriage of these natures appears compatible, it is more often filled with the sound of broken dishes. William Flanagan is not an exception—he is a true artist, and positively schizoid.

There is, for example, no composer of my acquaintance more articulate than he in musical discourse, as both his conversation and perceptive journalism of a decade have proved. His comments generally contain a wholesome objectivity toward the musical manners of his time and, in particular, an awareness of the mechanisms that produce such trends. His critical face is pitilessly cultured, first telescoping musical values, then microscoping their cause and structure in focus.

Yet Flanagan's creative face is almost wholly sensual. He forsakes the intellectual and performs with the remotest consciousness, which is not to say that he minimizes technique; simply that he cannot for the life of him see it as an end in itself. He has always composed through desire, never through duty, always written what he wanted, never what he "should," according to current academies. If Flanagan the critic is a man of the mind, Flanagan the composer is a man of the heart. In an age when young and old alike push toward greater musical complexity, Flanagan continues to shed the extraneous. When serial music is as common as breakfast cereal and electronic objectivity all but official, Flanagan allows a subjective tonal style to persuade him. In refusing to conform to the nonconformists, he presents himself as the most *avant* of the avant-garde.

It is, of course, his business to be *au courant du dernier cri*—that is how he earns a living. Yet his own music embodies nothing of the fashionable, and (like Ravel, who, with Copland, is the twentieth-century musician closest to his heart) he has never been absorbed into ever-shifting stylistic quicksand. In the *Herald Tribune* he wrote:

Last evening was as nostalgic as it could be. For it was a program of American music composed during the forties and as such is unsullied by the turn to ostentatious complexity that was to characterize much of our music during the fifties. The agonizing reappraisal of central-European dodecaphonic technique—soon to become a howling influence among American composers—was at this time only a dubious murmur; the mass defection to the musical *récherché*—12-tone or otherwise, for better or for worse, was yet to come. . . .

Flanagan yearns here, as ever, for the more easy communicative style that ripened in America nearly twenty years ago during our cultural isolation from Europe and that today we can reevaluate with the blessing of hindsight. His musical "birth" is of that time, and in growing he has remained faithful to its premise if not to the specific mannerisms of the period.

A sensual faith is doubtless what first attracted him to the intimacy of the small vocal forms, an area in which he has always felt most at home, yet to which Americans are but seldom drawn. I believe that it was in defiance of his own intellect that Flanagan favored this expression. Let him explain that predisposition:

In Tanglewood, in 1947, I had written a batch of songs that I took very seriously. I don't recall that I had thought this bias so unusual because young composers that not-so-distant day ago were comparatively undogmatic. The concept of *laissez-faire* where musical practice and style were concerned was, with normal and healthy exception, the order of the day. The struggle for a properly contemporary musical language had been, most of us felt, the business and achievement of our immediate predecessors; that had supplied the "how" and, in so doing, had left us with the musico-syntactical wherewithal to concentrate on the "what." If my "what" was a poem, the fun of searching for and perhaps finding the special musical thing that would make it a song, none of my teachers or student colleagues thought it at all strange—or, rather, if they did they didn't say so.

Today, with a volume of symphonic and chamber works to his credit, Flanagan still thinks of music as sung. Arrest even his orchestral music at any given turn of phrase (no matter how outlandish), and the phrase will somehow echo the singer within him. The characteristic of the phrasal turn will be brevity; its origin the blues. His songs (no, all of his pieces) are replete, thank heaven, with melody. But he resorts rarely to the *grande ligne*, those immediately memorable long-spun tunes that we associate with the Romantics. His melodic concept resembles rather Debussy's: the contagion is less instant but more pervasive, a serum that, once injected, lingers longer than the tone of old love. Billie Holiday (her way with a tune, not the tunes she sang) was the source and soul of Flanagan's early songs and, more subtly and indirectly, of even his nonvocal music. By truncating the acceptable, Miss Holiday rendered banality classic. One could choose a worse teacher.

But this was hardly formal instruction so much as it was free pollen involuntarily fertilizing a young man whose sonorous tongue was French, whose first exposure to symphonic music had been by way of Hollywood and its background composers, and whose orientation had been the best popular culture of the day. How did he blend these influences?

By taking the sounds of his time by instinct, he attempted little disguise in the beginning. His harmonic speech was therefore that of the men to whose work he had, as a fledgling composer, first been attracted: principally Aaron Copland and David Diamond, under whose alternate tutelage he produced, among other things, a sheaf of songs that were far more than typically student affairs. Whereas their accompaniments now seem overrefined, their vocal lines remain among the most infectious of Flanagan's catalog. Today he realizes that his "bias" of the 1940s *was* unusual: "As the American public begins to accept the European concept of the small, elegantly designed automobile," he wrote in the *Herald Tribune*, "our musical style-setters—the composers—have yet to come to terms with another, far older European concept: that of the 'little master.' Our writers bend ever toward the musical grand slam." Or, in the same article: "Song composers are face to face with basics. 'Form' will be dictated by the text rather than by a pre-described mold. And the song composer who denies having made subtle and personal harmonic discoveries in searching out the musical framework for a poem is probably not the genuine article—not a real song composer."

The texts for these early songs are nearly all by Americans, and their choice reveals a face of yet-different complexion from either the lucid critic or the sensuous lyricist. With the exception of a handful of songs—like the delicious "A Valentine to Sherwood Anderson" (1948), text by Gertrude Stein—Flanagan was lured by despondent verse: poems on mistrust, abandonment, death, with the solitude of male solidarity providing dubious textual relief. "The Dugout" (1946) and "Send Home

My Long Strayed Eyes" (1949), texts by Siegfried Sassoon and John Donne, respectively, are all but unbearably somber, yet their lyric content is such that one can hear them daily without pall, while the heart bleeds for the man who once felt urged to compose them. Though the language of their composition derives much from his teachers, the syntax of Flanagan's expression *within* this language is highly personal.

He might very well have been divulging the secret that lies behind the success of these early songs when he wrote:

> The vocal line is a song's most elusive property. Its curves, its metrical pulse should be one with the rhythmic flow of the language; it should also come to the tricky terms of consonant-vowel properties. Practically anyone can be taught to write a just, accurately prosodized declamation, but the expenditure of these same considerations for a *bona fide* lyric utterance—this, in the end, is what distinguishes a song from a mere musical "setting."

Those early songs most surely are not "mere musical settings," but to this day Flanagan is not quite sure what made them tick. They were, if you wish, inspired: the beginner's luck of the relatively untrained. If his syntax was already personal, by the early 1950s his musical speech was fast shedding its derivative overtones. A choral version of *Billy in the Darbies*, composed in the days immediately preceding 1950, represents a bridge between the gifted novice and the independent creator. It is the first of Flanagan's three large pieces on the words of Herman Melville, whose sentiments in themselves seemed to embrace every nuance of hopelessness and poignant affection that so appealed to the young composer. But if their shared theme is a blank wall (it will become even blanker in the opera *Bartleby*), the loneliness is controlled by an intensity that by now owes little to anyone but the composer himself.

The cycle *Time's Long Ago* (1951), six songs to poems by Melville, is the first wholly successful extended work by the maturing composer. Pain again is the keynote. With *Time's Long Ago*, we come upon a musical texture far more sophisticated than any hitherto encountered in Flanagan's work. The favored secondary seventh and ninth chords are still in evidence, but their distributions have been altered by expanding intervals into new meanings—like Picasso's distortions through elimination of the unnecessary. The intensified tonal chromaticism again is new for Flanagan, as indeed is the fresh use of the same diminished and augmented sounds that are so studiously avoided in the composer's

previous works. The essentially diatonic vocal line is jagged and ever leaping out of the home octave. The cycle is hard of texture and, with that,
more dissonant than any work in Flanagan's catalog before or since.

These devices are furthered in the disturbing opera *Bartleby*, an hour-
long work composed over a five-year period in the past decade. Again
the text is Melville's, and again the choice generates a heat of desperate
humiliation. In brief, the story concerns a deranged subaltern whose
sole response to all requests is "I would prefer not to." He voluntarily
sequesters himself and dies of starvation. The pathetic atmosphere is
solidified by Flanagan's near-flawless drama of sound. The composer
has never—before or since—delivered himself of so elegant an agony
in such ambitious terms. Even so, a traumatically bad instrumental performance rendered its unique hearing (two scenes in concert presentation, 1954) a fiasco both in performance and in the press. When witness
to the initial collapse of a major creative gesture, one tends toward
discouragement. More than that, for reasons best known to himself,
Flanagan withdrew from the competitive scene, and for three years, like
Bartleby, he "preferred not to." This purely musical seclusion engendered no new works, allowed no publicity of the old ones. With the
spooky expiration of Bartleby, a part of its creator died.

But two years ago Flanagan emerged from this fallow silence, to all
intents and purposes a changed man. Perhaps his engagement as a reviewer for the *Tribune*, which almost automatically reinstated him in
the public swim, helped instrument the metamorphosis. At any rate, he
began to regain his lost time by composing copiously on somewhat more
optimistic texts, by writing articles, by organizing concerts of American
vocal music, and by submitting his larger orchestral compositions to
major orchestra conductors who have since been playing them thick and
fast.

These orchestral compositions take us back as far as a dozen years.
There are only three of them, and each received its premiere last season
within two months. Yet so extraordinary is their instrumental competence that the composer declared, on finally hearing them, that he would
not alter a note of the scoring—this in homage to the intricate and
thorough orchestral training at the hand of Copland. The first two, *A
Concert Overture* (1948) and *Divertimento* (1949), are mostly gifted
assimilations of what was in the air those days: the Stravinsky of *Scènes
de Ballet*, perhaps a touch of Richard Strauss and Mahler and, of course,
the manners of his two teachers who remained among his prime sources

of supply, Copland and Diamond, both of whose catalogs he had analyzed to the bone by 1950. Still, when one recalls that even in 1949 Flanagan had only four years of compositional experience behind him, the innately adventuresome sense of the orchestra, along with the germs of the individual style that was to result in two years in *A Concert Ode* (1951), looms large.

The *Concert Ode* is a ten-minute jewel of high pathos and likely to enter the standard orchestral repertory. I know of few other pieces (Honegger's *Pastorale d'été* is one) that can so constantly sustain the *Ode*'s sensitivity of fingertips on a broken heart. A year before the appearance of the *Ode*, Flanagan was to complete one of the lesser items in his catalog, a *Sonata for Piano* (1950). Some of the Sonata's stronger elements were salvaged and transplanted directly into the *Ode*, but the piece, like similar work on the part of many good songwriters, runs to facile accompaniment figuration.

Flanagan's preoccupation with song has left him little time for non-vocal chamber music. Apart from the *Piano Sonata*, he is represented by only one other published work in this medium, a *Chaconne* for violin and piano (1948). This work predates the Sonata by two years and yet is much finer, no doubt because the violin is treated as human utterance. Composed during Flanagan's study with Diamond, the work reflects more than any other Diamond's influence on the young composer.

Still, such stylistic influences all but vanish in the cycle on A. E. Housman's *The Weeping Pleiades* (1953), set for baritone, flute, clarinet, violin, cello, and piano. This is no garland of gentle ditties but a series of virile thrusts. The cello line, which serves as a frame at the start and finish (thus implying true cyclic design), acts like some strange water engulfing an island whose sole inhabitant is ultimately forced to cry out. And cry out he does through a now-mastered way with solo colors whose independent tensions melt into a common dynamo. The force of this cycle is not surpassed by its composer's "comeback" gesture, a huge number called *The Lady of Tearful Regret* (1959) on careless verse by his close friend, the future playwright Edward Albee. A rambling cantata for two singers and seven instruments, it resembles an oriental garden path leading through a maze of vocal virtuosity into Flanagan's newest "period."

Typical of this period is a calm sureness, a patient conviction that he knows who and what he is within the present domain of musical and extramusical chaos. This conviction is, perhaps, not removed from tragedy, but at least the symptoms of the antisocial storm have subsided. This resignation can be ascertained in the three new songs to poems by Howard Moss—the best of his career, taken altogether.

William Flanagan, the creative musician, has always remained loyal to the values that initially attracted him to the art of musical composition. And he has been able to accomplish genuine growth without need for translation into modish dialects. "I am concerned with the *sound* of music," he says. More preoccupied with sound than with lost causes, he is in quest of attractive results rather than in manipulation of theory. He once told me he is quite as much gratified by the *sound* of Ethel Merman's blatant hysteria at the end of *Gypsy* as he is by the *sound* of a novelly spaced instrumentation in Stravinsky.

On the negative side, Flanagan's preoccupation with sound has occasionally led him in a sound-for-its-own-sake direction that has perhaps limited certain works to too much of a single kind of beauty. Acidity and dramatic contrast are sometimes lacking. Sense of theater develops solely through the hearing of one's music. If Flanagan's larger works remained unplayed until quite recently, he now has more performances per square foot than the majority of his contemporaries, and this practical lesson astounds his new textures.

For example, he had not previously been a "practical" composer (save his accompaniment to a pair of film documentaries in the 1940s); but today his palette has increasing contrasts as he writes with concrete ends in view. His backgrounds for solo clarinet composed for *The Sandbox* represent, for all their scantness, a venture into rich variety employing highly chromatic techniques. His recent and regular collaboration with the best singers of the country has produced a new song collection, which, while retaining the enigmatic musical "rightness" of his earlier works, is more satisfyingly vocal for listener and singer alike. As for the accompaniments, their refinement is less serene.

Along with the new theatrical sense, which was instinctively manifest in *Bartleby*, Flanagan now nourishes a necessary appetite for extroversion. Much as he demonstrates a penetrating wit in society, his art has hitherto been shy of humor. A work in progress, *Notations for Large Orchestra*, promises to bring forward and integrate his native penchants, and to underline the breathing vitality latent in all artists and indispensable to all art.

(1959)

LOOKING
FOR SAM

Even as you read these words, somewhere in the world Samuel Barber's *Adagio for Strings* is being played. As the most performed "serious" piece by an American, the *Adagio* dispels two notions of conventional wisdom: that what is popular is necessarily junk and that the late improves upon the early. If Barber, twenty-five years old when his piece was completed, later aimed higher, he never reached deeper into the heart, and he is still held most dearly for works composed before his fortieth birthday.

Forever weaving and reweaving their web around our globe, what do the *Adagio*'s strings sing to us if not a sad, brief perfection? The perfection is not that of, say, a sapphire, for the sound has no glitter, is not "expensive." Rather it is like some forgotten love letter retrieved intact from a cedar chest, penned with vast and tender elegance, yet vaguely irrelevant. If the irrelevance is itself irrelevant now (for what dates more than timeliness?), it nonetheless seems to be, along with the elegance, Samuel Barber's defining property.

I write "seems to be" advisedly, wondering if the defining property might not also be conventional wisdom—a trick of memory. During his life Barber was probably the only musician in a land of iconoclast cowboys for whom elegance was a virtue; when he left us two years ago at seventy he took with him, for better or worse, a concept of craft stemming from that virtue.

Now insofar as it means control and taste, is *elegance* quite the noun for the art of Barber? Does one confound the product with the person, well wrought in shape but overwrought in content, coolly French on top yet Brahmsian beneath? And insofar as it means aloof and unruffled, is elegance indeed the term for the person, and is his product inevitably suave? Listen again to the *First Symphony*, frantic and—if you will—

43

ill-bred throughout its nineteen minutes, or to the trivial and vulgar *Excursions* for piano. Then think back to the man himself, as Apollonian a creature who ever stopped chatter on entering a room, as canny and cultured a friend as one could desire on his good days, yet with on occasion the cutting manners that only those born rich can get away with (or think they can) and with the *terre à terre* opportunism that every composer, rich or poor, has harbored since before Haydn.

Does a composer resemble his music? Assuming we can define what music "means," what humans are made of, or even the four humors as they pertain to art, then certainly a composer resembles his music, since by definition one cannot exist without the other. Still, biographers often disengage the two, as though the animal source were a necessary evil to be shunned or purified. Art is not True Life, to be sure, but it *is* a distilled life, and who else's but the artist's?

In July 1946 the Tanglewood Festival school reopened after the war. Twelve student composers graced the campus, six (including me) with the resident teacher Aaron Copland, and the others with Bohuslav Martinu, the guest teacher. After the first day Martinu was injured in a fall and was replaced by Nikolai Lopatnikoff. Twice weekly the two composers' classes joined, and at one of these meetings I presented an analysis of Barber's *Essay for Orchestra* to the frosty curiosity of my colleagues. (Barber's unabashed lyricism, known as Post Romantic, was not too terribly in vogue back then; what's more, as the only live composer favored by Toscanini, Barber was no less a figure of awe than of envious derision.)

In 1947 I was again in Copland's group, and again the guest teacher, this time Arthur Honegger, suffered a fall and had to be replaced. Barber happened to be on the premises—he was touring the Cape and had stopped by for the weekend to hear Koussevitzky conduct his Overture to *The School for Scandal*—so he was drafted. Again that summer were the composers' meetings, and at one of these I first met Sam. But I had heard him earlier, behind closed doors, coaching Eleanor Steber in what seemed a most magical song—yet was it a song?—all the more exquisite in that it was in that strangest of tongues: English! I too wrote songs, but except for a handful of these my output till then had been stillborn; and those songs had come so easily I felt something must be wrong with them. Wasn't art supposed to be hard? And wasn't Song then (as now) a superfluous medium? Those Tanglewood bull sessions were knotty, long-winded, theoretic, "meaningful." Meanwhile Sam Barber was our sole songwriter, one who seemed always to have access to "real" singers. Avoiding the nonvoiced American specialists with lunatic reputations, he understandably favored divas with big, gorgeous sound boxes. True, he had written "Monks and Raisins" for the bizarre Povla Frijsh (who could deny her?), and soon after we met he would sculpt his *Mélodies passagères* for the one-of-a-kind Pierre Bernac (whose link with Poulenc had grand cachet), but they were Europeans. Mainly, however, one then thought of Barber as the composer of *Nuvoletta* and *Knoxville* for the established Steber, even as he would later compose the *Hermit Songs* and *Prayers of Kierkegaard* for the up-and-coming Leontyne Price. Sadly it was not to songs but to stars that the public was and is drawn, and without arias even stars aren't certain magnets. If foreign composer-singer tandems like Poulenc and Bernac or Britten and Pears once had box office in the United States, the famous home boy, without an orchestra behind his soloist, did not. When Barber and Price, as pianist and soprano, were offered as a package during the early 1950s, they had too few bids to continue.

But back to the bull sessions. When in deference to the songwriting Sam the question of Song was broached, how tantalizing to hear him say, "Yes, all composition is difficult, but why song more than 'straight' music? Why the fuss about prosody and diphthongs and declamation and word quantities? Why not write as you speak?" Which is the reason vocalists enjoy him, and why my dim guilt was assuaged. When I showed him my analysis of his *Essay* from the previous year, he found it absolutely faultless and (like most analyses) absolutely beside the point.

One hears Sam in his songs as unmistakably as one sees Julia Child in her recipes, and not least because he was himself a singer. Inside all composers lurks a prima donna longing to get out, yet they are famed for their vile voices. Sometimes, as with Marc Blitzstein, a composer's wheezy larynx works to his advantage, particularly when his songs are talky show tunes with "personality." (Indeed, during the long run of *Threepenny Opera*, all of the regularly changing cast of performers seemed to be hired according to how much they sounded like Blitzstein.) Mostly, though, singing composers sabotage themselves. Two exceptions: Reynaldo Hahn, whose Dictaphone rendition of *Chansons grises* shows a clean, affecting tenor enough removed from his original inspiration not to fall prey to self-indulgence; and Barber, whose still-available disc of his own *Dover Beach*, made forty-eight years ago, reveals a true, gentle baritone of professional class, albeit with the rolled *r*'s of upper-crust Philadelphia. Barber in fact minored in voice at Curtis in the 1920s and, being Louise Homer's nephew, frequented a milieu where the human instrument was a practical, not a theoretic, matter.

And yet is firsthand knowledge a prerequisite of first-rate work? I used to see Sam at parties where, if coaxed, he would accompany himself—though never in his own music—in some dear goody of yore, "Pale Hands" being a favorite. What he mocked was precisely what he once most "felt," for his own early efforts were close to the bone of Carrie Jacob Bonds. Which explains their continuing popularity on safe recital programs. Despite his very classy choice of authors (Prokosch, Hopkins, Horan, Lorca, Rilke), his most famous songs lacked profile. Consider the setting, dating from 1939, of the rather nondescript verses of James Agee (whose prose six years later would serve as text for the masterly *Knoxville*). It is neither the simple tune nor the primary harmonies of *Sure on this Shining Night* that render it bland (songs by Chanler and Bowles and Citkowitz sound far spicier, while being no more "advanced"), but that the ear searches vainly for a signature. The accompaniment may echo snatches of Canteloube's Auvergne orchestrations, all the rage in those days, but the air could have been concocted by anyone. Anyone, that is, with a big technique.

From whence the technique?

Sam was a mere fourteen years old when he began at the Curtis Institute with the only composition professor he would ever have: Rosario Scalero, already elderly, Latin by birth but Teuton by nature (he had known and worshiped Brahms), a wizardly contrapuntist but an intrepid reactionary feeding on the residue of his failure as a creative artist. Indeed, when I myself "took" from the maestro during a weird season two decades later, I found his attitude toward Sam to be no less grudging than prideful, crediting himself not just for the younger man's fame but for the very melodies he penned. Well, those melodies were pretty solid, and so were all other accoutrements of Sam's musical structure—harmony, polyphony, rhythm, and orchestration—as they obtained to various forms, small and large. His sheer scope was vaster than any American's of the time, including Copland's, and his know-how with opera as with song, ballet as with symphony, concerto as with sonata, stemmed from the whip hand of Scalero that cast him finally as a national glory.

But if his modes of expression were varied, his language was not. Often highly chromatic but always deeply tonal, Sam spoke one dialect all his life. He did not evolve, as Beethoven or Stravinsky are said to have evolved, but, like Chopin or Ravel, sprang full blown from the head of his muse and spoke his conservative piece as persuasively at twenty as at seventy. It might even be argued that some of his later works (the *Piano Concerto*, the *Toccata Festiva* for organ) can now, like Prokofiev's, be heard as bombast and *remplissage*.

In the competitive rat race Sam was a loner, a not-quite-magnanimous aristocratic who never lectured or visited schools. Nor could he inure himself to the angry young. Sam was categorically intolerant of many a peer and of all the electronic and aleatoric children who, in their turn, found him anachronistic. Was he deluded in his tastes? Art is not about taste, nor need an artist be "right" about his contemporaries (that's a critic's job) so long as he is right about himself. Sam was pretty much right about himself from the start; he knew how to do what he wanted to do.

His audience?

There is no one audience. There are as many audiences as there are artists who presume to display the fact of themselves, and these don't often overlap. Beethoven's public is not Mozart's, but insofar as they may coincide the Mozart-Beethoven public is not Vivaldi's, and Vivaldi's is not Monteverdi's, which is not Messiaen's, which is not Steve Reich's. But if Reich's audience consists largely of nonmusicians—indeed of people who may never have been to a concert—while, say, Elliott Carter's is largely of practitioners, Sam Barber's audience, while smaller than Reich's and bigger than Carter's, contains members of both. No professional composer, although he might disdain Barber for frothiness as another despises Carter for obtuseness, would summarily dismiss either man as they might dismiss Reich. Barber's fan club does contain listeners who feel unthreatened by such "modern music," but it also contains real musicians. If his influence has been less than Copland's for the plain reason that he lacks an identifiable style, he has through some paradox identifiably influenced such high-tone creators as Lee Hoiby and John Corigliano.

Now let it be stated that although I in a sense am among Sam's audience, I never quite cared for the person, nor do I quite need the music: both are too rarefied, unpredictable, neurotic, and, well, too elegant for me to deal with.

No sooner is that last sentence written than I'm assailed by contradictions. If I do not need Sam's sounds, how account for his ever-haunting "Anthony O'Daly" smiling through my most-sung song, "The Silver Swan," a parentage no one has pointed out in the thirty-four years since that swan was hatched? For what reason have I kept over the years those dozen letters I now reread, finding in each a generosity somehow mislaid? Why am I covered by gooseflesh when the live voice of this dead acquaintance fills the room, as now it does, with *Dover Beach* lending a patina of precious antiquity to the very furniture? And where is the speaking voice that phoned a month before he died to confer about a mutual friend in need?

If frequent contact plus sharing of victory and woe are what make for friendship and qualify the valid memoirist, then I'm not the one to recall Sam Barber in any formal fashion. We moved in different circles. Also, we were almost the only ones whose catalogs were colored by Song, and that fact in turn was colored—at least for me—by a certain rivalry. One may question the propriety of one composer publicly discussing another, especially when that other lies underground. Yet as I seek to retrieve Sam, these lines serve as sketches for a portrait that someday I hope to flesh out in full. Obviously I would never have begun sketching were it not for that *Adagio* in the first paragraph, an *Adagio* whose strings, thank God, are still and always twining about our world.

(*1982*)

A NOTE ON BARBER'S
ANTONY AND CLEOPATRA

Music, by its so-called abstraction (its absence of literary meaning, which thus paradoxically gifts it with infinite meaning), becomes a flexible power, and very tough. If in movies and plays where it is used secondarily—that is, as background—music can't actually make or break a scene, it can certainly set a mood and even change an author's intent from sad to glad. By the reverse token, in opera, where music is primary, the composer's intent is hard to sabotage by even the most willful mind. Still, in their infinite wisdom directors often do their worst to "illustrate" music. Béjart managed to make both Berlioz and Stravinsky sound measly in the garish shade of his misrepresentations.

More recently Zeffirelli, hired in 1966 by the Metropolitan Opera to open the new house, nearly killed not only composer Samuel Barber but Shakespeare by infecting them with elephantiasis. At the premiere the stage's giant turntable was broken beneath tons of tulle, Roman armies, live goats, and camels. The blame fell unjustly on the composer, who, disgraced in fortune and men's eyes, produced little thereafter.

A second chance for a new work that fails the first time is risky and rare, at least within the same generation. It occurs sometimes for a play, but never for an opera. This precedent has now been broken for Barber's *Antony and Cleopatra*. Nine years after its flop at the Met, it has been revised and reheard successfully at the Juilliard School.

Stripped of its "camelflage," the new version is improved through minor additions, major subtractions, a straightforward set, Menotti's tentative mise-en-scène, and a cast who as actors are no worse than most singers. We can now judge this opera for what it is.

What it is is no closer to Shakespeare than the Shakespearian excursions of Verdi, Berlioz, Tchaikovsky, Prokofiev, Britten, Debussy, and Diamond; but it is close to Barber at his most deliciously skilled. The overall sound is hyperromantic out of Glière via Elgar and a Hollywood sound track, while the thematic substance is never less than serviceable and sometimes rises high, especially when the texture is leanest, as during Antony's long suicide scored just for kettledrum and flute. The dramatic sludge is the fault of a play that is more political than amatory. Love-making verses had to be borrowed from elsewhere (the duet "Take, O take those lips away") and sound inappropriate to this pair of middle-aged politicians.

The total, almost nose-thumbing, eschewing of novelty seems itself novel—an experiment in the bland. But Barber's vehicle also is touching and large. It deserves to stay in our part-time repertory as much as, for example, the various Janáček revivals, because it is the last American opera in the grand tradition.

(1975)

LORD BYRON
IN KANSAS CITY

Virgil Thomson's opera *Lord Byron* is not a masterpiece, but it is indubitably a piece by a past master. The composer's claim to mastery dates back to 1928 when he completed his first opera, *Four Saints in Three Acts*, on a text of Gertrude Stein's. When the work was produced six years later it became, as everyone knows, an overnight cause célèbre and has remained one ever since. Though never a repertory piece—only safe soap operas are that—it is among the four or five or maybe fewer staples in our bare American cupboard. *Four Saints in Three Acts* nourishes through its vitality; even a wretched performance is somehow viable.

Like all art it is rather mad and so beyond definition, yet like all madness it has a canny logic all its own. The music is neither particularly beautiful nor even interesting. Its chief originality lies in its willful diatonicism at a time when dissonance was the rage. Nor is the libretto especially gripping when taken alone. Worse, it is poetry, a dangerous ingredient in theater. The magic of *Four Saints* issues from a marriage made in heaven. Never have two artists so realized their individuality precisely by sacrificing it to a common cause. Stein and Thomson took not only talent but their very presence from each other. Alone, neither has fashioned a work of comparable strength.

A generation later, soon after Gertrude Stein's death, Virgil Thomson composed a second opera to a scenario of hers, *The Mother of Us All*, on the life of Susan B. Anthony. From the opening drum roll the sound is like *Four Saints:* always the plain phrases with their modernistic touches (triads used polytonally) soldering the Baptist-sounding hymns of the composer's Kansas City childhood. And always the point-blank verse of Stein's, so ideal to Thomson's setting. The same happy chemistry is at work, though less "abstract" than before, and American as baseball.

Now, after still another generation, we have a third opera from Virgil Thomson in this year of his diamond jubilee. And he has a new co-author. During the 1950s Thomson contemplated a posthumous script of Gertrude Stein's, talked about subjects with Robert Lowell and Robert Penn Warren, and got past the talking stage with one poet, Kenneth Koch, whose marvelous *Angelica* was in fact born and weaned under the musician's guidance, and then rejected. Finally in 1962 he met the person who was to realize a project he had long coveted.

Jack Larson lived then as now in Los Angeles, an occasional actor and writer of theater pieces and poems that contained a calculated innocence resembling Gertrude Stein's. Undoubtedly the Steinian element first attracted Thomson to Larson's work. The composer proposed a collaboration on the subject of Byron's life, was accepted, and together they worked on the opera for seven years.

Attended by the most distinguished audience in America and covered by the international press, *Lord Byron* received its world premiere on April 20 at the Juilliard School of Music. Jack Larson's three-act libretto turned out to be hearty and touching, if a bit heavy on exposition and light on variety. His scenario begins and ends in Poets' Corner at Westminster Abbey where Byron has been denied burial, and where he is mourned not only by living friends but by the shades of his immortal peers. The interim action occurs in flashbacks treating of Byron's appeal to women (and men) despite a clubfoot, of his lifelong liaison with his sister Augusta whose pregnancy gives rise to gossip that occasions the poet's marriage to Annabella Milbank, of his seven years on the Continent (depicted through an extended ballet sequence), and of Byron's death in Greece. Finally, again in Westminster Abbey, the poet's intimate journal with all its compromising contents is burned before the eyes of his friends and lovers, who then retreat sadly to the outer world. Byron's ghost appears and is welcomed by the statues into their poetic midst.

Larson has quoted Byron's own words when the poet himself sings. He uses familiar passages ("You walk in beauty"), but more ingeniously he has drawn from the poet's letters to concoct such quatrains as:

> Give your baby kisses, kisses from his Mrs.
> Kisses from his sis's, kisses kisses
> Ramble scramble jumble cum tumble cum all 'a hug
> Duck! kisses, kisses. Goose! kisses, kisses.

Larson's overall style is mock-heroic, and not unexpectedly a bit too Steinian for comfort. If our first impression is of children making up an opera as they go along, with fuzzy logic but flawless declamation, we quickly accept their terms and are intrigued at how snugly words and music fit together. But the fit is mechanical. In writing to Thomson's specifications Larson has provided a blueprint, not the real thing. Since there are no submerged reefs on which the music might founder, neither are there risks. Despite the subject there is no sense of tension, much less of tragedy.

The music is pure Thomson. Carefully planned, with appropriate airs and witty ensembles, the vocal conceptions are at all times what singers call "gracious." The sound is lean, harmonic opulence and rhythmic complication being as foreign to Thomson's vocal scoring as to bel canto. The piece is made mostly out of unpretentious tunes flowing from a source rich in old favorites ("Auld Lang Syne," "Saviour Breathe an Evening Blessing," "Ach du Lieber Augustin," and "Believe Me, If All Those Endearing Young Charms" are quoted in full). If the composer seems preoccupied with natural prosody at the cost of a soaring line, with reviving the long-dead whole-tone scale, with literalism or mickey-mousing (as in the parallel seconds depicting an incestuous tickle), those devices—derivations, really—have come to form Thomson's language, which he speaks with his unique accent.

The accent now sounds outmoded. The faux-naïf notion of transporting Kansas City nostalgia to George III's London seems surrealistically amusing, but is quite unconvincing. What functions brilliantly for Susan B. Anthony cannot begin to sustain the passionate sweep of Lord Byron's character. Ironically, much of the music's appeal as seen on the page is lost in the hall. By fleshing out the melodies, the orchestra relieves them of their personality, which is essentially skeletal; the music becomes less "dumb" than it is, and loses thereby. As for the vocal lines, since everyone sings the same *kind* of music, there is a lack of differentiation that turns to monotony. The monotony was not bothersome in *Four Saints*, which followed no story, nor are saints expected to present contrasts, to "do" anything. But that was in another time and place, and what worked with Gertrude cannot work without her.

Thomson supervised the entire production, which John Houseman, who staged the original *Four Saints* nearly forty years ago, directed. Alvin Ailey choreographed the ballet sequence. Costumes and sets were by Patricia Zipprodt and David Mitchell, respectively, and Joe Pacitti provided lighting. Except for the Juilliard chorus, which was below acceptable standard, and the Juilliard orchestra, which was above mere student excellence as conducted by Gerhard Samuel, none of these contributors was more than just professional. Most of the solo singers were not even that. This was unfortunate, because *Lord Byron* would not appear to possess the spontaneous combustion of Thomson's previous operas. It will need to be ignited by the fire of others.

Virgil Thomson's composing gift has never relied on interesting ideas, but on the uses to which dull ideas can be put. Displacing the ordinary, he renders it extraordinary—that is his stock-in-trade.

His music has little to do with romance or the grand statement, for it is as removed from the scene of action as cherubim are removed from the scenes they decorate. His music does have to do with joy, never carnal joy but the pure joy of merely being—again like cherubim (or saints). Thomson's lifelong effort would seem to have been to cleanse his art of *meaning*, in the Beethovenian sense, of sensuality or suffering or what we call self-expression, seeking instead, like pre-romantics such as Mozart, to delight. To this day his method of delight is through the constant lightheartedness of primary triads, avoiding like the plague the lush "subjectivity" of secondary sevenths or ninths. One cannot know whether Thomson intends his music as satiric, yet most of it for fifty years does sound that way. And for fifty years it has not changed much. Whatever the secret of Thomson's message, the message remains the same, the composer believes continually in it.

Like the status of Elliott Carter's music which nobody seems to challenge (probably on the grounds that it's so complex it must be deep), for half a century nobody has ever publicly contested the status of Thomson's music (probably on the grounds that it's so simplistic there must be more to it than meets the ear). A composer's impulse is usually apparent in even his worst works. With Thomson it is often difficult to hear the raison d'être—why he let certain pieces "pass," why he even bothered to write them down. The difficulty arises from the fact that he is not only a composer but the most stylish music critic of the twentieth century; how then can he not exercise the same perception toward his own work as toward that of others?

It is true that Thomson has been a pathfinder, that he wrote our first prestigious operas and film scores, that the prestige lay in the use of indigenous material, and that this material in turn was adopted by more "sophisticated" composers who gave it the slick American Sound. It is also true that Thomson's music, for all its originality, does not have very much to say. And is it so original? Outside his operas, has he accomplished anything not accomplished through the folkloric phantasmagorias of Charles Ives, or through the tongue-in-cheekeries of his idol Erik Satie? Ives aimed emotionally higher than Thomson and hit the mark. Satie composed in *Socrate* one of the most serious pieces of all time. Emotion and seriousness are not what we identify with Thomson's music, though finally they are the yardsticks by which all meaning is measured.

(*1972*)

SMOKE WITHOUT FIRE

The New York City Opera last month presented the local premiere of Lee Hoiby's *Summer and Smoke*, based on Tennessee Williams's play, and all factors of the production conspired toward what should have been a successful experience. The libretto, by off-Broadway prodigy Lanford Wilson, was the very model of how to strip a script to the bone without killing it. Lloyd Evans designed expensively lush yet subtle costumes and an ingenious unit set, through which the lighting of Hans Sondheimer filtered with just the right level of nostalgia. The house orchestra sounded lavish and inspired as always under Julius Rudel's baton, while the clean direction of Frank Corsaro appeared carefully rehearsed.

The music at any given moment was perfectly lovely, sometimes beautiful, occasionally masterful. No one today composes more graciously than Hoiby for the human voice, and John Reardon and Mary Beth Peil sang their lead roles with eloquence, the grandly arching melodies emerging from an audible and clearly set text. The composer's instrumentation was foolproof, always full yet never overwhelming. His theatrico-musical layout, planned with contrasts of fast and slow and dark and light, flowed logically through two extended acts. Indeed everything about the thing worked except the thing itself.

What made it all fall flat? Some of the above virtues were partly responsible, for by the end of the evening they had soured into vices. Consistently "lovely" writing turns quickly bland. Arching melodies are but one of many means for italicizing thought or action, and are effective in inverse proportion to their frequency of use. Instrumentation, no matter how expert, is finally uninteresting when always full; rarely did Hoiby indulge in chamber music or venture into other than safe sonorities; special effects (offstage bands, an unseen guitar) were banal effects. One agreeable moment did feature a singing lesson that ostensibly parodies salon music, but since Hoiby is in fact a salon musician, the moment succeeded not as parody but as the hit tune of the show.

One might suppose that merging the talents of our most experienced young opera composer with those of our most lyrical playwright would produce fireworks instead of a fizzle. The failure lies not so much in Hoiby's language as in his pronunciation of that language and timing of the delivery. His musical contrasts, by themselves logical, had little dramatic logic as organic development of the text; the highs and lows seemed therefore inconsequential and ultimately undifferentiated.

The problems not faced by Hoiby were those of linking the theatrical and musical structures—problems of knowing when silence is louder than busyness, of where opposition produces more tension than illustration.

It is not unfair to ask that an opera score reveal drama and add dimension by fleshing out meanings of the necessarily skeletal libretto. Lee Hoiby's devices resolutely failed to alter the emphasis of any character's motion or word. If the libretto is the shadow of the original play, then Hoiby's music is not the body but the accompaniment of a shadow, and thus superfluous to our understanding of Tennessee Williams's touching tale of frustration—a tale that nonetheless shines through the camouflage of sonorous smoke.

The pallor of *Summer and Smoke* reflects the general sickness of American opera. There are indeed only three real operas by Americans that may be considered valuable: Thomson's *Four Saints in Three Acts*, Gershwin's *Porgy and Bess*, and Moore's *Ballad of Baby Doe*. Except for the last named, even these are scarcely performed. While it is tempting to credit this situation to the current managements—the most reactionary of all performing-arts representation—it is really the composers who are to blame. Regardless of their musical language, twentieth-century American composers tend to be conservative in appearance, and in social and private affairs. They do not issue manifestos; they ultimately dismiss "bad boys" such as John Cage or even Lukas Foss (who, like George Antheil of yore, are known only for being bad boys); seldom does one of them try to give the public a serious jolt, much less disabuse the public of its own notion of what opera is.

What opera is, is restriction. It is Art, therefore serious. It is Expensive, therefore cautious. It is Story, therefore narrative bound. Above all, opera is European Heritage, therefore unmanufacturable from American blueprints. Of the three valuable operas mentioned above, only *Baby Doe* operates with the restrictions. As noted, only *Baby Doe* is scheduled regularly by our national managements. To ignore restrictions is to suffer performance droughts, as do Thomson and Gershwin, whose names are nonetheless world famous; to observe restrictions is to choke to death, as do *Vanessa, Regina, Lizzie Borden, Miss Julie*, the list is endless.

It does not seem possible even to re-define opera in its original terms of spectacle and entertainment now that ballet has quit the opera stage to mature so effectively as an independent form. Those few works that exemplify opera as it was in the beginning—a pageant-like mixture of acting, singing, and dance—are now called by their creators "theater pieces." No doubt Leonard Bernstein's latest such piece, his *Mass*, is, strictly speaking, the only modern true opera presently in the public consciousness. If so, how ironic that the most avidly received musical work in recent American history is an opera that dares not speak its name.

(*1972*)

FOSS IMPROVISES

The intense and diverse gifts of Lukas Foss are no secret. For years he has been a famous composer, lecturer, conductor, world traveler and goodwill champion, most skillful of pianists, and finally professor. Such indefatigability has now overstepped mere self-expression and (like Foss's orderly-minded countryman Schoenberg) sought to found a school. He has fused his talents in a practical theory whereby composer, performer, and audience presumably share the simultaneous joys of creation.

Foss explains it as "system and chance music," based on new premises with a symbolic notation of his own contrivance. That notation is translated into sound by the performer who "holds the reins," correcting rather than surrendering to chance. The rigid planning makes spontaneity feasible when an ensemble rather than a soloist is involved. And the listener is pleased. To this end, Foss and his Improvisation Chamber Ensemble now give us an R. C. A. Victor recording with the title *Studies in Improvisation*.

The composer and his excellent colleagues (particularly clarinetist Richard Dufallo) maintain that one welcomes an expression that need not presuppose immortality to claim validity—the "validity" being the fascination of ever-changing contours, risk, unrepeatability, and absorption in a process wherein anything may happen anytime and never again.

If the prime function and appeal of these *Studies* lie in unpredictability and lucky accidents that should be heard live, a recording becomes as contradictory to the raison d'être as a series of filmed kaleidoscope images. The Victor release by definition offers nothing unpredictable after one hearing, and must be considered solely as a static document. Nor does the composer pretend to perpetuity, wishing only to distribute his still-rough experiments, that others may develop them with more sophistication.

To judge the disc, then, is not to judge the intent. As heard here, the elements of chance and control become oil and water, neither very pure.

To cite Morton Feldman (who should know) the music of chance necessarily avoids stylistic rhetoric. Rather than chancing a choice, its practitioners "choice a chance," as Lou Harrison used to say. On Foss's improvised tightrope, the risks are run over a wide net of standard compositional formulas. They emerge like unrealized doodlings from the composer's notebook, for each piece bears his stamp (or that of his past influences) and not that of a mass personality.

The ultimate effect of the album's larger pieces is of a long-hair jam session lacking the urgency of jazz—and jazz has never needed self-justifications like those on the record's jacket. The shorter pieces have a certain initial poise: their predetermined sections all sound "right," but they too collapse when the haphazard effect disjoins the formal causes. The listener is addressed by Babel, not by an artist with well-wrought communicable ideas.

The law of averages presupposes low points for anyone as prolific as Foss (or Milhaud or Hindemith). Perhaps his experiments are more telling when incorporated into bigger "set" pieces such as the recent *Time Cycle*. In themselves they are smaller than the sum of their parts.

(1966)

CAGE'S *HPSCHD*

Lukas Foss is a triple threat: composer, conductor, pianist—and more than just first-rate as each of these. He's also an organizer. Five years ago he took over the venerable Brooklyn Philharmonia and concocted a series of marathons: six hours of one composer or of one period performed to satiety—sometimes several programs occurring simultaneously in separate halls. Occasionally the marathon is of strictly contemporary music, a subseries called "Meet the Moderns." It was to the most recent of these that I hied me last week.

The Brooklyn Academy is harder to find than an elephant graveyard, which it's about as cheerful as. It contains a suite of gloomy rooms and stairways around which have been constructed three vast ugly concert halls with sharp acoustics. In these halls four separate full-length concerts were presented. Three of these featured an international cast of every persuasion. For Lukas is nothing if not catholic. Five years ago various "schools" of composers warred with each other; today they often share the same bed without complaint.

While three concerts were being presented consecutively downstairs, a fourth was presented simultaneously upstairs. This consisted of one work, John Cage's four-hour *HPSCHD* (pronounced "harpsichord") for six harpsichords and mixed media.

If not the best, Cage's was certainly the most famous piece of the evening because it lasts so long and costs so much. I'm not quite sure what *HPSCHD* is for—what we're supposed to *do* while experiencing it—but it's embarrassing by its déjà vu, a quality not found in even the most conservative of the other pieces. I gave it as much as my eardrums could afford (about eleven minutes).

Of the other pieces I most enjoyed Gregg Smith's settings of William Blake, smooth French vocal writing unblushingly lush and very charming; Jacob Druckman's *Valentine for Solo Contrabass*, a short, witty piece played not with a bow but with a drumstick by Donald Palma all in black, looking suave against the dark red of the huge instrument and very charming; Englishman Peter Maxwell Davies's *Missa super L'homme armé*, with its amusingly unhip British jazz and theatrical whoops, all very charming (although his practice of having the singer declaim rather than intone the Latin verses is not a musical solution to the problem of presenting text); and Charles Wuorinen's *Speculum speculi* for six disparate instruments, which despite a certain spikiness was also kind of charming. Charm indeed was the keynote, even of Cage's piece. And although the crime of charm ten years ago was punishable with exile (and even today the word makes these living composers turn in their unquiet graves), surely charm—by which I mean color for its own sake—is what attracts the young to these works.

Though there weren't many young, or many anyone. Those who were, were devoted and stayed to the bitter end.

I did not. It grew late, so I skipped the panel of composers, which was the postlude. However, I've heard most of what composers have to say, and learn less from what they say than from what their music says—except for John Cage, whose arguments *are* his music.

Cage, like most household utensils, gets rusty and needs resharpening from time to time. His arguments grow lax: he justifies poetry with poetry, thereby stopping conversation. When we say it's just noise, he quotes E. E. Cummings: "In just spring . . ." and asks, "Is spring just?" But assuming Cummings had a meaning, "just" can mean mere, only, deserved (just rewards), fair (he's fair and just), exact, specific.

A throw of the dice if a piece is to be long or short. If it's long, we the public must accept this, though when the piece is over we're closer to death than we would be if the piece had been short. We have made a gift of time to the whim of dice.

People always used to ask, "What do you think of Cage?" or "What do you think of Menotti?" Today they're facts of life.

If Cage proceeds on false presumptions (namely, that noise is music if you know how to listen), his explications are always winning, which is why the question-and-answer period is the best part, and may indeed be the most musical part, of his evenings.

(1974)

A PARAGRAPH
ON CRUMB

Went last night to hear George Crumb's *Songs, Drones, and Refrains of Death*. The vogue for Crumb is dumbfounding. That his six effects in search of a mind should appeal to the vulgar is comprehensible: disembodied colors shine bright. That the effects should pass unquestioned by executants is also understandable: anyone can produce them and they get a big hand. But that critics should fall for it—should indeed have created the vogue—is as depressing as the toadying by the cream of PEN to Yevtushenko a few years back (though Russia's Rod McKuen, as an alien guest with political principles, extrapoetical though they may have been, did bring extenuating terms). There is something subversive—worse, hickish—about Crumb's persistent setting of García Lorca's Spanish, mooning on each big-scope syllable of *muerte* or *luna* with a meaningless meaningfulness that must sound silly to native ears. If his music had some Yankee viewpoint! But it exudes mere memories of Falla. Many a great work remains great for my mind, though my body rejects it (the *Missa Solemnis*, for instance, or the *Goldberg Variations*). Even my mind concedes no greatness for others (Schubert's piano sonatas, the Berlioz machines). Crumb's language depends on what was a speech defect chez Varèse. The language is neither interior nor exterior, but derivative gimmick. Assembling the tassels of fifty years ago, he's made his main dress, adding associative titles and literal quotations. But who is *he*? The Vonnegut of music. Admittedly Crumb has "reintroduced" expressivity to avant-garde concerts, which comes as a quaintness to blasé ears, but his music is nothing *more* than expressivity—hanging unqualified in air.

(1975)

63

ELLIOTT CARTER:
A BOOK REVIEW

The art of Elliott Carter understandably provokes contrasting attitudes. Some who know and care contend wistfully that he is the last great master; others, mostly from among the young, feel that if the species is dying, it's no loss to them. Harold Schonberg, usually outspokenly contemptuous of all categories of new music, remains deferential in his dislike of Carter, while Virgil Thomson says "Carter's chamber music is the most interesting being composed today by anyone anywhere," and John Simon bizarrely suggests that Carter (whose experience with and interest in the sung word is avowedly edgy) could be the savior of American musical comedy. Meanwhile his detractors find in this composer a subtle parvenu.

If a master is one who writes masterpieces, who aims high and hits the mark, using as weapon the "big statement" (a piece inherently long and with profound intent, like the post-Beethoven sonata forms, as opposed to inherently short pieces like Webern's), then Elliott Carter fills the bill. But it is true that the big statement, descending as it does from nineteenth-century preoccupations, has indeed grown extinct, the victim of giganticism, at least in purely instrumental repertories. (Most of the important gestures of the so-called serious music world—and all of them from the pop world—have, since *Le Sacre du printemps* in 1912, involved the human voice.) Carter is the only composer after Bartók who can make a convincing big statement in nonvocal mediums, particularly in the otherwise atrophied string quartet. He stands isolated in his mastery, as much through uniqueness of viewpoint as through genius.

This singular position was gained neither easily nor early. Born in 1908, Carter did not settle into himself until his mid-forties. Before that his music sounded rather commonplace—not in the sense of vulgar, which can be thrilling (like Gershwin as contrasted with Cole Porter, or Weill as contrasted with Reynaldo Hahn), but in the sense of second-rate, which can be dull (like all those neo-classical composers as contrasted with Stravinsky). Carter's composition of the 1930s and early 1940s was of the "accessible" Coplandesque brand; he felt "a social responsibility to write interesting, direct, easily understood music." Had this music in fact been "interesting" or, more important, successful in its day, one wonders where Carter might be now. Around 1950 he made the intellectual decision to focus, as he puts it, "on 'advanced' music, and to follow out with a minimal concern for their reception, [his] own musical thoughts along these lines. . . . If a composer has been well taught and has had experience," Carter adds about himself, "then his private judgment of comprehensibility and quality is what he must rely on if he is to communicate importantly."

He was communicating importantly enough by 1955 to have replaced Aaron Copland as national father figure, and to be the only American taken seriously on their terms by the elite of European composers. And though he jumps through no hoops, his position remains secure in 1972 when half of being an artist lies in self-promotion. Like Roger Sessions he has never pushed his persona along with his product, a stance nearly as anachronistic as his choice of musical terrain. If for no other virtue than integrity, Elliott Carter at sixty-four finally deserves a book-length study. *Flawed Words and Stubborn Sounds* is not, however, it.

Although more than three-fourths of the volume consists of an edited transcript of Carter's replies to queries posed by one Allen Edwards, the result seems somehow unauthentic. Edwards has chosen not only the format but (pathetically) the tone of the famous Stravinsky-Craft *Conversations*. He has proceeded on the assumption that his subject is "a composer I know I am not alone in regarding as the most important to have appeared in America," and then exempts himself from literary responsibility ("The defects that remain in the final text are ones for which I am motivated to ask the reader's indulgence because of my conviction of the overriding value of the perspective here gained"). From the painful ejection of the very first question the book sags, for the protagonists lack the Craft-Stravinsky gift of gab; their scholarly exchange does not of itself result in the literature that should be the one excuse for this kind of publication. Mr. Edwards depicts the two of them in an ivory tower of Babel, satirizing a situation that Carter in reality deplores.

Not even by comparison can Elliott Carter come to life, except in a few instances of anecdotage (for example, a description marked by admiring tenderness for Nadia Boulanger), or of working method. This is to be pitied, because Carter's answers often contain ideas, explanations, and recollections that in their present raw form could be transformed into an excellent *written* (not transcribed) book. His comments on American education provide a most attractive indictment of a system that at every turn stifles the imagination, preaches a materialistic concept of success, and advocates allegiance to an often-narrow vision of the American way. But his youthful friendships with Ives, Alfred North Whitehead, Ralph Kirkpatrick, and other fabulous greats are alluded to only teasingly, as though "personal" discussion would soil the higher purposes in question. His pessimistic appraisal of what a composer can expect by way of public acclaim and respect might make some impress on the public conscience were it tightened into a formal essay. And surely he has more to say about the problems of vocal composition than the meager half page allotted to it.

Elliott Carter's ideas about his own music, reduced to lowest terms, are neither complicated nor especially original (his notions about orchestration, for instance, or the celebrated "invention" called metric modulation), but they are necessarily valuable as statements by a vital artist "in process." Perhaps one day he'll authorize a less pompous biography or, better still, collect his own thoughts in essay form. Contrary to what Edwards declares in his foreword, Elliott Carter surely has time for this. Any artist does.

The title from Wallace Stevens seems inappropriate. Despite Carter's modesty (in one footnote he refers to this complex theoretical exchange as "bits of useful information [which] may help a few readers to understand something about what it is for one person, at least, to write music in the United States"), his own words are not really flawed, except inasmuch as any discussion of art, however complete and learned, becomes de trop before the fact. Nor are his musical sounds at all stubborn, although his endless compositional patience might be so termed. But even the best books on music can only demonstrate points, while music itself proves points. On closing this book we ache from structure-talk and long for living notes.

(*1972*)

RICHARD CUMMING'S
SONGS

Richard Cumming is a survivor, being of that handful of Americans who were writing first-rate tonal songs thirty-five years ago and who, in their madness, persisted in writing such songs to this day. If the fall of song and the rise of serial music coincided with the end of the late war, the two phenomena are probably unrelated. As vocal recitals began fading from the scene, that portion that was always deemed expendable anyway—the light "modern" group, occasionally featuring a subgroup in English—was the first to go. Conservatories taught singers an antique repertory in all languages but their own. Not a single American vocalist, even today, earns a living primarily as a recitalist, and as such, what concerts a vocalist gives rarely contain songs in his native tongue. Composers younger than Cumming (he was born fifty-five years ago in Shanghai, but looks like a Yankee quiz kid), when they used the voice at all, used it in instrumental layouts, treating it more for sonority than as purveyor of text.

Thus Richard Cumming could seem an anachronism: a survivor not only in an uncalled-for medium, but speaking a dialect that in itself sounds dated. Yet aren't there now intimations that firm tonality—even the simplest diatonicism—is no longer a pariah to trendsetters and that song as an expressive medium is making a comeback? Alas, unlike so many prodigal sons returning to the fold on the C-major bandwagon, Richard is not given a party; all these years he stayed home being good, so who noticed when his work came back into style?

Well, Cambridge Records noticed. The present disc, in the guise of retrospective homage, is not only a beacon on the precious past (of Cumming's seventy songs to date, nineteen are here represented, most of them at least two decades old), but, let us hope, a pioneer toward things to come again. As for the interpreters, were I forced to name but three American singers of importance to the agonizing art song, two would be Donald Gramm and Carole Bogard. But Cumming is no more lucky with their services than they are with his delectably singable goodies to wrap their gorgeous and experienced tongues around.

Now to particulars. Such criticism as may emerge in the next paragraphs are medals of faith, the composer being among the few I esteem.

The songs of Richard Cumming—or Deedee ("little brother" in Chinese), as he is called by friends—are without exception doggedly tonal and easily parsed. They offer little of contrapuntal or rhythmic fascination: such line-against-line forays as do occur are of the most primary, and the meters are generally in a simple two or three. Indeed, like the truest songs since the dawn of time, those of Cumming are all chords and tune. The chords, complex in their secondary eleventh and thirteenth pileups, sound nonetheless innocent in their evocations of the suaver 1940s nightclubs. The tunes are prosodically natural, following the lilt and dip of the verse, and seldom gliding other than at the tempo of speech. The accompaniments are mostly just that—repeated grounds that support the vocal thread, like Schubert's, not independent strands that weave their own web, like Debussy's. As rendered by their maker (and here again Cumming is an anachronistic survivor in that, like most composers before 1900, he is his own best performer), the piano parts take on a definitive cast, seemingly unduplicatable, brittle, dark, velvety, amber, strangled, whatever is needed. I realize that these adjectives are descriptive of music only after the fact, but they must do.

His hue and texture, about half the time, skirt what once were the risky borders of cheapness (but is that still a real risk?). Cumming is never trite or bland, and his vulgarity is of the highest, I mean, the lowest: of the earth, the "people." He was raised, like all of us, humming pop tunes. The net effect of Cumming's songs (as opposed to, say, Diamond's or Britten's or Milhaud's or anyone's in Germany) is one of optimism; even the grimmest are friendly as fudge, and I have a sweet tooth.

Within his entire oeuvre there lurks not a shadow of his three mentors—Sessions and Bloch and Schoenberg, with whom he studied in the late 1940s—as though to deny them utterly were his sole salvation. Yet he is the most derivative composer since Francis Poulenc, and like Poulenc, whom he also resembles shamelessly, he is not ashamed of being shameless as he slides along his sometimes-treacly path. For like the cuckoo laying eggs only in the nests of other species, yet hatching thoroughbred cuckoos, Cumming takes what he needs and makes it his own. What he needs is the safer side of the recent past.

What is a song cycle? A century ago a cycle was the musical version of many interrelated lyrics, usually in narrative sequence, by a single author. Later composers of cycles held them together by using only one poet, but whose poems were unrelated. Today a cycle's definition is looser still, being whatever a composer chooses to call by that name. The poems are often by widely different writers, the binding ingredient being solely the composer's personality.

We Happy Few is the only cycle in Richard Cumming's long list of piano-vocal works. It is a true cycle despite being subtitled, almost casually, *Ten Songs for Voice and Piano*. The texts are culled from a period spanning 5,000 years, but it is hard to imagine any one of them sung without the others, so tightly melded are they by contrasts of soft and loud, sad and silly, fast and slow. (Let me immediately stress that, to his theatrical credit, the fasts of Cumming are inherently fast, not like, say, Fauré's, which are slows played fast; and his slows are kinetically slow, not like, say, Honegger's, which are fasts played slow.) Melded they are too by theme, which, though a bit too approvingly military for my Quaker heart, is deadly serious. Tailored in 1963 to the specific credentials of Donald Gramm and premiered by him and the composer on a Ford-sponsored program in New York the following year, this collection as a whole is the best piece by Richard Cumming.

Opening like a Britten fanfare in the grand improvisatory manner, with Henry V's Crispian harangue, the music soon flows from the Avon to the Mississippi, so heavily does Cumming rely on lowered thirds and sevenths. Is it an illicit pleasure to hear the Bard's verbs fall on hot blue notes? Is Cumming's lush view of Shakespeare less congruous than Prokofiev's lean or Foss's quaint or Diamond's angular one?

The grave Egyptian chaconne "To Whom Can I Speak Today?"—built on an eight-note motto—in text may predate the Shakespeare by forty-five centuries, but the sentiment of a land smote by war seems to emerge logically from the previous song.

"Fife Tune" on three stanzas of John Manifold is a filler. A merry note was needed so a merry note is sounded as ironic set-up for the brief, haunting "Here Dead We Lie." In this realization of Houseman's tragic quatrain, Cumming's various vices conspire to blend into a perfect virtue. And hear how Gramm scales down his force to a sad, sad whisper throughout this—this nineteenth-century torch song.

Lawrence Durrell's "Ballad of the Good Lord Nelson" is the cycle's showstopper (a long, wry polka for the piano, a tongue-twisting patter song for the baritone), while Richard Lovelace's famous "I could not love thee dear so much" is as touchingly turned as to befit a Mabel Mercer.

"A Sight in Camp," built from one of Walt Whitman's proselike reactions to the Civil War, becomes a truly important song, certainly the most important on this record. The piano provides a sober, melancholy canvas of hollow octaves upon which the voice traces three poignant portraits of stricken soldiers. The least scrumptious song that Cumming ever penned, in its very restraint lies its superior strength.

How could I not be pleased—or should I say placated—by the setting of Archibald MacLeish's wittily frightening "End of the World," since it is dedicated to me? But did Deedee realize that the chunk he borrowed from my ditty, "My Papa's Waltz" was in turn stolen from an earlier song of mine, "Whiskey Drink, Divine," which came from Satie's "Je te veux," which was filched from the waltz factories of Vienna? Nothing's new. And in fairness to Ives, let it be noted that the song's second half would not be quite thus were it not for the Connecticut master's "William Booth," which nonetheless, through some alchemy, seems pure Cumming.

Less happy in its derivations is the next, "Grave Hour," on a Rilke poem, which draws too close for comfort to Barber's "A Desire for Hermitage" blurred with Ravel's "Le gibet."

The closing number, too, in all of its rollicking Biblicality, owes much to Bernstein, yet keeps up its fiery splendor till the curtain falls.

Well, if the fourth, fifth, and seventh songs are at once masterful and moving, the others are no less than appropriate, and all are expert for the voice. Ask any singer.

Carole Bogard stars on the disc's flip side in a medley of nine gems, some rare, some common, hewn between 1958 and 1981. Her crystalline timbre, pristine diction, and controlled sense of sonic curve serve as a sensible leash—or as a kind of necessary contradiction—to the sometimes-dangerous opulence of Cumming's martini harmonies.

"Fordham University Summer," a hail-and-farewell duet for Bogard and Gramm in the shape of a Latinized mazurka, ripples irresistibly through the words of one Hugo Leckly. This leads directly to a second duet, this one for soprano and oboe—a plaintive modal folk song on an Old English text.

Now follow four settings of William Blake (two of them conceived for and first sung by the incomparable Jennie Tourel in 1958). That "The Sick Rose" has been musicalized by just about every composer born since Blake does not render Cumming's setting the less singular, with its low, driven, candid, hurting simplicity. "Memory, Come Hither," a delectable allegretto, has such an infectious tune that one asks why the composer never brings back the so-charming eighth-note device used only in the fourth measure. "London" has the piano sweating evocatively like the very fog filling this hapless urban painting. "The Little Black Boy" is doubtless useful for program builders who are always at a loss for first-rate catchy numbers; but the poetry, with its old-fashioned conceit ("I am black, but O! my soul is white"), is not from among the great Blake's prouder moments, and Cumming's samba makes a Sambo of the singer.

The most recent song (1981), on Emily Dickinson's "Heart, we will forget him," was concocted for Bogard and all she does best—sustained cantilena, sudden softs on highs, poignant enunciation. She intones it here against a cello tune reminiscent of Stephen Foster.

The last songs, collectively named *Other Loves*, on three poems of Philip Minor, date from 1974 and seem as inseparable as those in *We Happy Few*. The Minor poems are just that: excellent in the style of Edna St. Vincent Millay, but falling short in their denouements. (Interestingly, like the songs of the flawless and thrilling and neglected songwriter Theodore Chanler, with his poetaster Father Feeney, Cumming's better songs are made from lesser poetry.) "Summer Song," twining its languorous five-beat figurations around a melody of noble wistfulness, recalls those faraway summers when Bill Flanagan (not a survivor) was writing songs almost as persuasive as this. "Night Song" is pure pop, constructed like many of the others ("Here Dead We Lie," "Going to the Wars," "The Sick Rose," "London," "As Dew") as a straightforward air over a nonindependent chordal sequence. "Love Song" is stylishly cute.

Rereading these assessments, I do not find the required liner notes so much as critical reviews. Have I too-often fallen back on the facile "this reminds me of"? Comparisons can be odious (Brahms, when his *First*

Symphony was likened to Beethoven's *Ninth*: "Any fool can see that!"), but they can be fragrant, too.

We went to different schools together, Deedee Cumming and I. Americans, we were both writing songs at opposite ends of the globe during our early twenties. When we finally met in New York in 1956, we discovered that we and only a few others (Flanagan, Daniel Pinkham, who else?) were playing the game. Naturally our influences stemmed from our immediate predecessors (Thomson, Barber, Copland, Citkowitz, Bowles, Diamond), and naturally we compared ourselves with each other. My thumbnail reactions here are thus not castigation but location.

Though Richard Cumming is like many others, no one is quite like him; that is all that counts in an artist. And a true artist he has surely become—one of the only song composers in the world.

(*1983*)

EZRA POUND
AS MUSICIAN

Nothing is more bemusing than to discover in reappraisal that certain opinions once voiced by the truly great now appear quite naive. The discovery is bemusing (rather than exasperating) because it invariably occurs in areas outside the Great Man's "specialty." (Had he been naive *within* that specialty, he would not by definition have been great.)

Specialists are what artists (also scientists and candlestick makers) of our century mostly become; if they develop an affection for one of the sister arts, they fall prey to the same failings as any amateur: the confounding of acquaintance with knowledge, of conviction with greatness, effort with ability. One thinks of Paul Claudel's or Henry James's verbalizations on painting—or this very remark on James and Claudel! When the concern is music, which it is here, a practicing musician merely smiles patiently as, say, André Gide tells him what Chopin is all about or as E. M. Forster—even Shaw—explains the art through poetic rather than analytic description. Composers, of course, class performers as laymen and consider men like Rubinstein or Casadesus as more "sensical" when playing than when writing, or writing about, music. Perhaps in a pinch a philosopher such as Susanne Langer can be attended precisely because she exorcises the phony inspirational Hollywoodiana from musical art.

Some poets are original and instructive when they discuss peripheral (i.e., theatrical) usages of music, sometimes even when they make librettos for their composer friends. But when venturing suggestions as to how their verse should be musicalized, or how the music itself should be built, they tread risky water—the very water in which Ezra Pound nearly drowned.

Nearly, but not quite. Between the two is continuing life. And life, with all that implies of curiosity and scholarly enthusiasm, is what in the 1920s the poet had in abundance.

Music reportage is more appropriate for performance than for composition, for how the execution occurred than for what was executed, for what McLuhan calls (I think) the "hot medium" than for what stays put. Berenson wrote real literature about paintings of the past because those paintings are stationary (hence, paradoxically, continual): they can be *referred to*. But Shaw's criticism of nineteenth-century musical execution becomes (since the performance is gone forever) less literature than history. There exists today a whole new style of recording criticism, and records, like pictures, stay put. But since, as the saying goes, God didn't intend music to be heard on discs, such art is makeshift. (Occasional music *is* designed to be heard only on recording, although nothing could be more self-contradictory than, for example, a record of "chance" music—and several exist.)

As to the instructive virtue of musical criticism, it tells the public who wasn't there what happened last night, or the public who *was* there what to *think* about what happened last night. To composers it will teach nothing about the quality or construction of pieces (score reading teaches that), but will maybe teach them something about how pieces can be played—including their own.

The music commentator, then, falls roughly into either of two classifications: (1) that of reporter on what just happened (press reviewer of concerts) or on what is happening (tastemaker); and (2) that of reporter on what once happened (historian, biographer) or on what was happening (authors on the evolution of harmony out of plainchant and counterpoint).

Pound, by self-ordainment, becomes classified under each of these categories, though by what authority it is hard to say, for no one seems to know much about his formal musical training. He has, I'm told, passed much of his adult life in near contact with the once-successful violinist Olga Rudge; and during the 1920s in France he hobnobbed (as did all literati) with various creative musicians, mostly American. One still suspects that his auditory education was come by less through discussion with these persons than through rigorous study of the prosodic values of Provençal, a language—like all others before the fifteenth century—quite intertwined with music. Certainly Pound's intellectual knowledge about music far surpassed his practical knowledge; his main concern (at least before meeting George Antheil) seemed to have been the relationship between words, word rhythms, and music. "Poetry atrophies when it gets too far from music, music when it gets too far from the dance" (*ABC of Learning*). And certainly also, emotional references to music are everywhere apparent in his verse, from *A Lume Spento* of 1908 to his 1956 translation of Sophocles' *Women of Trachis*. And names of musicians are scattered throughout the *Cantos*.

On this *propos* let me cite the very talented young triple-threat musician, my friend Robert Hughes, who in 1958 visited Pound at St. Elizabeth's and wrote me later as follows:

I went down from Buffalo as part of a recorder quartet led by Forrest Read, a Pound scholar who has published on the *Cantos* (Columbia University Press, if I remember correctly). We played Gabrieli *Canzone* out on the lawn for Pound and his wife, and Pound said it was only the second time he had heard live music during his incarceration there—the first time having been a pianist brought by Stokowski. In addition to the soprano recorder I had my bassoon along, and having read that Pound at one time had played the instrument I offered it to him. He declined saying that he gave it up in the 20s in order to take up boxing with Hemingway. I asked him about *Le Testament* and he said that as a consequence of the war he had no idea where the manuscript or a copy could be found. He did, however, say that he had a page or two of his unfinished opera *Cavalcanti* and promptly fetched it from his room. It looked like a Ruggles manuscript—very large notes scribbled on broad wrapping paper. We played it for him: a simple troubadour-type tune, not terribly distinguished as a melody, but with a certain grace and ease for the voice.

Le Testament? A lost manuscript? An unfinished opera? Indeed yes! From his special knowledge Pound had, in the 1920s, composed an opera. Whatever that opera's ultimate worth, is there another poet of the past two centuries who can claim as much?

The text was drawn from François Villon's *Grand Testament* (1461), a number of funereal bequests in whimsically "argotic" yet highly poignant medieval forms of versification. The resulting libretto (or should it be termed rather a "chant-fable"?) amounts to an intoned "autobiography" of Villon in one act of around forty minutes. The musical score itself is certainly the work of a nonprofessional; for example, it is much more finicky for the eye than it need be for translation by the ear. Although Antheil helped both in the exegesis and in the actual notation, the result remains that of an amateur: measures shifting from an unreasonably complex 5/8 to 13/16 to etcetera could easily be simplified and still provide the smooth modal vocality intended by the poet. Nevertheless a self-justifying foreword to the manuscript deserves a quotation:

> This opera is made out of an entirely new musical technic, a technic, for certain, made of sheer music which upholds its line through inevitable rhythmic locks and new grips . . . a technic heretofore unknown, owing to the stupidity of the formal musical architects still busy with organizing square bricks in wornout . . . patterns . . . a powerful technic that grips musical phrases like the mouths of great poets grip words.
>
> There is really nothing more to say. Those *who want to understand*, will understand Villon.
>
> As the opera is written in such a manner so that nothing at all is left to the singer, the editor would be obliged if the singer would not let the least bit of temperament affect in the least the correct singing of this opera, which is written as it sounds! Please do not embarrass us by suddenly developing intelligence.

Paris thus heard it in 1926, and Virgil Thomson, who was there, declared "the music was not quite a musician's music, though it may well be the finest poet's music since Thomas Campion . . . and its sound has remained in my memory." The foreword's insecure insolence notwithstanding, the opera is of genuine and hauntingly unclassifiable beauty.

The beauty, though, was of such impractical difficulty that it was not until 1962 that the opera received a second hearing in a version made for the BBC by the Canadian composer Murray Schafer. Such is the material of the music that, like Mussorgsky, who is submitted to much rearrangement (or more properly, like the *Art of the Fugue*), *Testament* "speaks" as well in various instrumentations. The Paris version was apparently for only two human voices, solo violin (Olga Rudge), and a *corne*, which is a twelve-foot instrument from medieval France. Schafer's bilingual rendition is a good deal more sophisticated, using full chorus, several soloists, and a complex of instruments, including saxophone, mandolin, and rattled bones.

A few summers ago Gian-Carlo Menotti induced the poet from his Rapallo seclusion to attend another performance (only the third, and the first one ever staged) of *Testament* at the Spoleto Festival. In preparation for this event Menotti engaged two protégés, the bright composers Lee Hoiby and Stanley Hollingsworth, to revamp the work, shortening it and standardizing the notation. The result was then choreographed by John Butler and offered to an elite international public whose reception was apparently one of high respect, puzzled indignation, and a standing ovation. The ovation was as much for Pound the poet as for Pound the composer. As for Pound the man, his presence at the spectacle is said to have been noncommittal, even dazed, and his brief spoken preamble was preceded by an untheatrically long silence.

Silence has come to be the tone of Ezra Pound today. I, for one, as a composer thinking of a poet, find the fact unutterably touching and telling—the silence in music, and in poetry, of one who once spoke perhaps not wisely but too well.

Robert Hughes said Pound thought little now about his music of the past, that it was remote, like all our pasts, like dreams, and that he is, silently, completing his life of Cantos.

This then—a career as composer of a single opera performed but thrice over a forty-year interval—represents Pound's qualification as music commentator. A qualification *after the fact*—for his book, which is the object of this discussion, was begun as early as 1918 and published a year before the first presentation of the opera.

The title is *Antheil and the Treatise on Harmony with Supplementary Notes by Ezra Pound*. It is divided into four sections of unequal length: "The Treatise on Harmony," "Antheil," "William Atheling," and "Varia."

The style, unlike the author's music, is pontifical, tries for wit, sometimes achieves rapidity and wisdom, more often ponderousness. A cultured lay genius like Pound can insist on learning the hard way (i.e., on his own) what a professional is simply taught at school and takes for granted. The lay genius will present the professional with his "unique" discoveries, while the professional, dull though he be, heaves a sigh for the genius, for the genius could have saved so much time by merely opening a book.

Pound gives us emotional talk on practical subjects, practical talk on esthetics. One quickly senses that he, at least below the surface, may feel less on home ground here as he speaks (so to speak) from outside in, than in, for instance, *ABC of Reading*, his other scholarly treatise, where he really speaks from inside out. Though "treatise" this present work is not—which is precisely what saves it—it contains none of the documentary orderliness of the usual doctorate. The effect is rather one of obsessions fragmented into a manner both folksy and grand, occasionally incomprehensible, not unlike the utterances of Ives or even, curiously, John Cage's *Diary*.

Antheil, who provides the impetus for the major portion of the volume, appears (despite Pound's obstinate veneration of him) to provide an excuse onto which the writer latches his theories—or rather his conclusions. By far the chief reason, in the cold of our time, to allow the hot air of these conclusions to flow interestingly over us, is because of the man, now almost historical and certainly silent, who once so feverishly committed them to paper.

Part One, "The Treatise on Harmony," starts right off with an unfair question (though who expects poets to be fair?): "What, *mon élève*, is the element grossly omitted from all treatises on Harmony . . . ?"

Does the *élève* now stare blankly because he must assume there's just one reply to this arbitrary query (a reply, what's more, unavailably cached within the questioner's smugness)?

Supposing, however, the pupil answered: "The element of space," meaning that the psychic sense of a stationary (vertical) harmony, or any sequence of harmonies, shifts according to place, as when sounded in a deserted cathedral rather than a crowded chamber.

He would be wrong. For teacher's answer is: "The element of Time. The question of the time-interval that must elapse between one sound and another if the two sounds are to produce a pleasing consonance or an *interesting* relation, has been avoided."

"Pleasing" and "interesting" aside, this concept may be less unique than Pound realized, although in 1923 it was stimulating. To his credit he develops (or rather, randomly restates) this notion, not with conclusions of eyes, which are only means in music, but always of ears, which are ends. His reactions were dictates of blood circulation, though not the blood of corpses. "Pure theory" (he cites Ernst Friederich Richter) "can not . . . concern itself with practice." And more deliciously (quoting one Sauzay): "Il faut se borner à penser que J.-S. Bach écrivait la musique par certains procédés dont la loi générale nous échappe."

His concern with acoustics was as deeply special as that of, say, Lou Harrison today, yet always (and this is not so frequent as you'd think) as applied to *sound*, the audible glowing of nature as opposed to the "academicism [which] is not excess of knowledge [but] the possession of *idées fixes* as to how one should make use of one's data." Yet in his joy at debunking pedantry he could become pedantic himself ("There is nothing sacred about the duration of the second," etc.), but his ultimate and whimsical wish was to render the physics of sound so complex that composers would grow discouraged, would "give up trying to compose by half-remembered rules, and really listen to sound." How even more welcome today, in the dreary ice of our "serious" musical fray, would be that warm wish come true!

One wonders how the impact of this opening chapter might have resounded were its spontaneous information better coordinated. Then again, coordination might have detracted from the rugged urgency that finally reaches us more as poetry than as knowledge—poetry, as everyone knows, dealing more with word sequence than with idea.

George Antheil. His name to our young is not even a name, and his performances number zero. But yesterday he was not only the self-proclaimed *Bad Boy of Music*—such was titled his autobiography—but the official bad boy (or "leftist," as the avant-garde was then named) of most expatriate 1920s intellectuals, the literary ones rather more than the musical. Gertrude Stein received him although she knew nothing of music; Virgil Thomson promoted him both in journalism and in the organization of far-out concerts; James Joyce, a great Purcell fancier, discussed him as the prime mover of the now-common machinery-in-art movement and even considered collaborating with him on an opera; while Hemingway owed to his influential relations the publication of *In Our Time*.

Mr. Pound it was, though, who eventually, for better or worse, immortalized him in the present book. The aging poet's apotheosizing of this very young composer amounts in fact to a conglomeration of bons mots on art, bons mots so occasionally cogent yet wild they become impossible to summarize other than by illustration.

Stravinsky is quickly put down in favor of (or at best equated to) Antheil:

> Stravinsky arrived as a comfort, but one could not say definitely that his composition was new music; he was a relief from Debussy; but this might have been merely the heritage of Polish folk music manifest in the work of an instinctive genius. . . . Stravinsky's merit lies very largely in taking hard bits of rhythm, and noting them with care. Antheil continues this; and these two composers mark a definite

break with the "atmospheric" school; they both write horizontal
music. . . .

Why was Stravinsky a comfort? And how—though it makes little
difference—was his composition not "new"? Certainly he was less a
"relief" than (and doubtless he himself would admit it) a *continuation*
or outgrowth of Debussy. It is unclear how Polish music was reflected
in this oh-so-Russian; as for his being horizontal, if one must equate
music to the linear, Stravinsky, at least in the 1920s, was most certainly
vertical—that is, harmonic.

Later remarks on Stravinsky provide their own commentary:

> The "Sacre" stands, but its cubes, solid as they are, are in proportion
> to [Antheil's] Ballet mécanique as the proportions of architecture are
> to those of town planning. . . . "Noces" falls to pieces. After the Ballet
> it sounds like a few scraps of Wagner, a Russian chorale (quite good),
> a few scraps of Chopin, a few high notes "pianolistic."

Good God! But then Pound is elsewhere correct in maintaining that
the "authentic genius will be as touchy . . . about the differences between
his own particular art and all others, as, or than, he will about any
possible analogies with the arts."

> Antheil has . . . noted his rhythms with an exactitude, which we may
> as well call genius . . . has purged the piano, has made it into a re-
> spectable musical instrument. . . . Antheil is probably the first artist to
> use machines, I mean actual modern machines, without bathos. [There
> is nowhere mention of Varèse.] I think that music is the art most fit
> to express the fine quality of machines. Machines are now a part of
> life. . . . A painting of a machine is like a painting of a painting. The
> lesson of machines is precision, valuable to the plastic artist, and to
> the literati. . . .

Then he approvingly quotes Antheil: " 'the failure of Stravinsky [!] . . . In
accepting Satie as a master, we see that he [Stravinsky] was nothing but
a jolly Rossini.' "

This chapter elsewhere offers such tantalizing propositions as: "Prose
is perhaps only half an art . . . you can not get a word back into the
non-human." Then it moralizes in a manner so démodé that the eyebrows
of a Larry Rivers today, or even of a Boulez, would scarcely be raised;

while a Frank O'Hara could only agree about longevity as it pertains to artists rather than to their work, artists seldom anymore seeming to care about posterity, or even about the word *art*: "The thorough artist is constantly trying to form an ideograph of 'the good' in his art; I mean the ideograph of admirable compound-of-qualities that make any art permanent."

Pound goes on to quote appraisals by Antheil himself, Antheil who notes a "constant tirade against improvisation": "Debussy, soul of ardent virgin, clear and sentimental implanted in great artistic nature." (Ironically, Debussy's own assessment of Grieg, of all people, had not been too unlike this and—if you will—was equally "false": he compared the Norwegian's music with the sounds heard in old folks' homes, to the taste of bonbons stuffed with snow!)

Antheil is finally defined by Pound as "possibly the first American or American-born musician to be taken seriously . . . [who] has made a beginning; that is, in writing music that couldn't have been written before."

Since any composer worthy of the name, be he conservative or experimental, writes music that by definition couldn't have been written before, Antheil's fellow musicians of this period were mostly a good deal more resistant to him than were the authors. He himself a few years later—whether by abandon or ousting or nostalgia—quit the French musical scene for California where he continued to turn out vast amounts of not-too-often-played scores (influenced no less by machines than by Hedy Lamarr, to whom his *Heroes of Today* is dedicated), and to write journalism on subjects quite unrelated to his field. In 1959 he died in comparative obscurity, and to date his music has not been revived by either Right or Left.

What did Antheil himself think of Pound's overly personal, often disordered and irrelevant, yet sycophantic précis of his oeuvre? In the postwar retrospect of 1945 he tells us:

> It seems terribly unfair of me, at this time, to proceed to criticize Ezra Pound, now that the poet has fallen into disgrace. But, I emphasize, I would write these pages exactly this way if Ezra had become an international hero instead. For from the first day I met him Ezra was never to have the slightest idea of what I was really after in music. I honestly don't think he wanted to have. I think he merely wanted to use me as a whip with which to lash out at all those who disagreed

with him, particularly Anglo-Saxons; I would be all the more effective
in this regard because I was an "unrecognized American."

And he beautifully adds: "The main clues of a composer's life are in his
music; but it is not always so easy to read them."

And how do Antheil's surviving peers esteem him? Well, listen, for
instance, to the 1967 assessment by Peter Yates, who, in my opinion,
is now America's leading spokesman for twentieth-century music:

> . . . the young American George Antheil [took] what then seemed the
> obvious course of using noise without exploring it. Antheil's expla-
> nations after the event tried to rationalize a successful headline-seeking
> stunt into a considered esthetic achievement. In fact, it was most
> successful in its headlines. The sound lacks variety; the typewriters
> used for instruments do not compete effectively with the several pi-
> anos; the pianos are borrowed from Stravinsky's far more successful
> use of them in *The Wedding*; the airplane propeller is no more than
> Strauss's wind-machine in *Don Quixote*; and the rattling and banging
> of the percussive elements do not combine to produce musical sub-
> stance. Similar faults are evident in much of the noise-music which
> has been composed since that time. Antheil's superficiality became
> more evident in later compositions, imitating the surfaces of more
> competent composers.

Or listen to the Britisher Wilfrid Mellers, who (partly from the objectivity that springs from physical distance, partly from the subjectivity
of a truly devoted love for us) in 1965 published *Music in a New Found
Land*, the most definitive book to date on American music:

> . . . Antheil claims that [*Ballet mécanique*] is built mathematically on
> the Time-Space concept, like musical engineering, or modern archi-
> tecture in sound. He admits that Varèse preceded him in this concept.
> In any case, compared with the works of Stravinsky and Varèse, *Ballet
> mécanique* has only historical, not musical interest. . . . [He] used ar-
> ithmetical durations of silence as early as 1924, partly as a result of
> studying Oriental music. . . . [However] the work's motor rhythms
> relate it to Western music, and it does not get far with the space-time
> concept.

Or to the 1966 avowal of a personal sponsor from their mutual heyday,
Virgil Thomson, who presumably needs no introduction:

My estimate (in 1926) of him as "the first composer of our generation" might have been justified had it not turned out eventually that for all his facility and ambition there was in him no power of growth. The "bad boy of music" . . . merely grew up to be a good boy. And the *Ballet mécanique*, written before he was twenty-five, remains his most original piece.

Like the pseudonymous Monsieur Croche behind whom Debussy hid, like Bernard Shaw's Corno di Bassetto, indeed like many a nineteenth-century critic who, for one or another reason (usually to protect professional status) adopted a false cognomen, Ezra Pound from 1917 to 1920 wrote fortnightly in the *New Age* under the pen name of William Atheling. In 1923 these admittedly badly written musical "shiftings" were submitted to Antheil, who bestrewed them with marginalia. This conjointed enterprise constitutes the third, and probably most personal, portion of Pound's treatise. Most personal—partly because Antheil's italicized interpolations are fairly incidental agreements and none too witty (examples: "A bad musician will only admit a name so well-known that there can be no question about it. He is a bad musician because he has no 'guts' anyway"; or, commenting on a remark that the British concert performer is chosen from the exclusively eviscerated strata of the community: "How funny it must be in England"; or: "I bow gracefully"; or simply: "Bravo!!"), and partly because here Pound expounds on what instinctively a great poetical layman can most "know" about: performance (as opposed to composition) and what he terms the "musicking" of verse, namely, prosody.

A telling wisdom careens in the wake of platitude: "Hundreds of musical careers have been muddled because performers have not understood how entirely music must lead its own life; must have its own separate existence apart from the audience. . . ." Then: "An era of bad taste probably gathers to itself inferior matter from preceding periods. An indiscriminate rummaging in the past does not help to form a tradition."

Still, when talking of words and music, he deserves quotation in any (but there *aren't* any!—except my own, and I didn't know Pound then) manual on how to make a song:

There are different techniques in poetry; men write to be read, or spoken, or declaimed, or rhapsodized; and quite differently to be sung. Words written in the first manners are spoiled by added music; it is superfluous; it swells out their unity into confusion. When skilled men write for music then music can both render their movement . . . tone by tone, and quantity by quantity; or the musician may apparently change the word-movement with a change that it were better to call a realization. Music is not speech. Arts attract us because they are different from reality. Emotions shown in actual speech poured out in emotion will not all go into verse. The printed page does not transmit them, nor will musical notation record them phonographically.

Thematic invention in music has coincided with periods when musicians were intent on poetry, intent on the form and movement of words. Thematic invention is the weakest spot in contemporary music *everywhere*. The rhythms of French are less marked, but only in France do we find a careful study of the verbal qualities. I do not think I have shown any delirious or unbalanced appreciation of the modern French, but among their song-setters are practically the only contemporary song-setters whom one can respect.

The best poets have been nature poets only incidentally. Nature appears here and there in their work, but is not singled out for their subject-matter. Whatever "religion and Christianity" may still mean to the populace and to the modern heath-dweller, religion as exploited by artists of the last century has been mostly exploited as convenient furniture and not from any inner necessity.

One might take exception to other of his songwriting generalities:

The perfect song occurs when the poetic rhythm is in itself interesting, and when the musician augments, illumines it, without breaking away from, or at least without going too far from the dominant cadences and accents of the words; when ligatures illustrate the verbal qualities, and the little descants and prolongations fall in with the main movements of the poem.

Still, we will all agree that:

In the finest lyrics the music comes from the words and so enriches, reinforces, illuminates them. We will recapture this art of illuminating only when we have musicians capable of literary discrimination, capable of selecting *cantabile* words, and of feeling the fine shades of their timbre, of their minor hurries and delays.

Other jewels can also be detached from their setting and thrown out loose here:

Our decadence may be due to the fact that the educated are now too stupid to participate in the arts. . . .

You cannot compare Music since Beethoven with the early thin music which is like delicate patterns on glass. Since Beethoven people have thought of music as of something with a new bulk and volume. . . .

One must, perhaps, find one's ideal artists in fragments, never whole and united. . . .

Tchaikowsky: a certain cheapness is imminent in this composer. He is not cheap all the time, or even, perhaps, most of the time but he keeps one in a state of anxiety. . . .

Occasionally there is a gaffe like "We noticed how *stupid* Liszt was, and how little he knew about chords" (if Liszt didn't know about chords, nobody did), followed by facile banality like "Opera is a diffuse form . . . made to cover light after-dinner conversation," followed by pedantic advice like "It is a good thing for singers to get off the beaten track and hunt up music that is lying in desuetude." (Most music lying in desuetude lies there because God—meaning Lack of Talent—willed it so.)

Special divisions in a similarly inconsistent genre are devoted to the piano (called "pye-ano"), to the fiddle, the lieder school ("which is wrong"), to ballet, to Chopin and Scriabin and Mozart; and deep in the morass shines a gemlike essay on Oriental music as compared to Provençal poetry.

The whole comes off as a succinct cluster of aphoristic Gallic *pensées* translated into the grouchiest Americanese.

"Varia" gives us more of the same, though it is chiefly directed toward composers. The bulk originally appeared in the *New Masses* and in the *New Criterion*.

Composers are all too aware of being at "the mercy of the executant, and the executant is at the mercy of his endocrines," but they may be amused to see their craft reduced to "knowing what note you want; how long you want it held; and how long one is to wait for the next note, and in making the correct signs for these durations." Pound smartly adds that "it is for lack of just such simple statements . . . that the misunderstandings arise between the musician and the well wisher"; then, for the first time in the whole book, qualifies his authority: " . . . apart from accommodating notes to words, I am an incompetent amateur."

This very amateurism led this very professional Idaho poet, while he was overwhelming world scholarship, to wish to do as much for musical art. That wish was therefore to prove that George Antheil had taken, "or at any rate [had] found a means that can take, music out of the concert hall." This removal presumably would disseminate formal sound throughout an even vaster world than his own literary one and bestow it upon the people, as tribal ceremonies had been bestowed in the past, or sea chanteys or labor songs. Such has ultimately occurred, moreover, for better or worse, through our John Cage, who would be pleased to read that the "aesthete goes to a factory . . . and hears *noise*, and goes away horrified; . . . the composer hears noise, but he tries to (?) 'see' (no, no), he tries to *hear* what kind of noise it is." Indeed Antheil *had* talked vaguely of "tuning up" whole cities, of "silences twenty minutes long *in the form*," et cetera, though he never put these functions to the test.

Antheil, by our witness today and by his admission yesterday, served as sacrificial goat for a genius whose *gauche prévoyance* had in itself little influence, but was in fact an image of what distortedly would come to pass. If for no other reason then, Pound's treatise is worth a reperusal. For strange as it may seem, few scholars know of this book though they've hazily heard of Pound's opera, while few musicians know of the opera though they've hazily heard of this book.

Any jottings of the Great (Pound was and is great)—even a billet-doux or laundry list (and this volume is much more than that)—become by definition important, deserving the concentration of cultured laymen and all other fellow artists.

(*1963*)

THE AMERICAN
COMPOSER SPEAKS

Everyone knows that American composers today are verbally articulate, but it may come as a surprise to learn that they were already articulate—that they even existed—two centuries ago. Gilbert Chase illustrates the point in his compilation of thirty essays by as many composers, from William Billings in 1770 to Earle Brown in 1963 (*The American Composer Speaks*). The intervening styles are as diverse as the contributing personalities, and a chronological perusal is nearly as entertaining as a survey of the short story. Nearly. The concerns, being all in the same key, become a bit tedious. Artists' personal obsessions seem invariable despite social advancement or cultural upheaval, and those obsessions (expressed with charm or rancor) center on the need to define American music, to put down the rival camp, to bridge the artist-public gulf, and to bemoan the lack of just rewards for their labor. Chase's role is not that of referee but of host. Carefully he introduces each participant and situates the circumstances of all the selections. Many of the latter are necessarily superficial, being extracts from more comprehensive works; others toward the end were specifically requested for this volume, and present thorough views on aspects of the current musical scene.

Now the current musical scene is almost as fluctuating as that of painting, whose generation's time span has shrunk to about four days. Which is one reason why those articles written since the last war seem more old-fashioned than those of the eighteenth century. Also, with few exceptions, twentieth-century musicians have a less memorable literary tone than their predecessors, though most are clear and unsentimental in their opinions.

With a style that is sheer joy to read, William Billings speaks of compositional rules: "Nature is the best Dictator. . . . Art is subservient to Genius, for Fancy goes first. . . . I think it is best for every Composer to be his own Carver." His prose is suave yet artless, while his music was rough-hewn as an old church door. The same holds for Francis Hopkinson, whose beguiling and opportunistic "Dedication to His Excellency George Washington" is included. One wonders if that president's reaction was closer to that of Queen Bess or Lyndon Johnson. But one no longer need speculate when, a few years later, John Hewett details an agonizing visit to the White House of President Tyler.

Stephen Foster was the hit-songster of his time, yet then as now the money went to interpreters, leaving the composer without even the benefit of a performing-rights fee. Such pre-ASCAP troubles are shown poignantly in Foster's letters: "I find I cannot write at all unless I write for public approbation and get credit for what I write." He lamented that his "style of music [was] so cried down by opera mongers," yet naively asserted—"this song is certain to become popular as I have taken great pains with it." Louis Gottschalk, Foster's contemporary, resolved the financial problem by becoming his own performer, and as such was something of an international Liberace. He complained that his homeland was the last to recognize his talents, for as he modestly states: "I was the *first* American pianist." But his writings are never glib, usually elegant, sometimes penetrating precursors of Susanne Langer: "Music is a psycho-physical phenomenon (which begins where words leave off). . . . We discover in its general character an agreement with our physical state . . ."—and he goes on to explode the fallacy that music may possess specific literary connotations.

MacDowell, once hailed as *the* Great American Composer, was also something of a psychologist: ". . . to recognize the existence of decidedly unpleasant music . . . would be the first step toward a proper appreciation. . . ." His esthetic stressed form above what he termed sensuousness, although in practice his composition was by definition sensuous, since it was intensely German—though he thought of it as American. Yet like his forebears he was unable satisfactorily to define the term, not realizing that Americanism is an attitude and not a formula. (The best definition probably comes from Virgil Thomson some fifty years later: "The way to write American music is simple. All you have to do is to be an American and then write any kind of music you wish.")

In opposition to MacDowell, Arthur Farwell (who wrote in 1903 but died as recently as 1951) sympathized with the French and suggested we submit more to their influence. Which of course we finally did. He nonetheless felt we already had a distinguishing signature, and all that

American composition needed was publicity. Which of course we finally got. His colleague Henry Gilbert was less optimistic. In an article dated 1915 he gives an aperçu of the artist's economy; though stylistically clumsy and redundant, it could have been written in our days.

Our days, psychologically speaking, actually predated Gilbert and began with Ives. The latter's Epilogue from *Essays Before a Sonata* (1920) is a model of spirited English, depicting the creative procedure once and for all.

From there we are led, by way of the reactionary Daniel Mason (the Jewish influence in American music is a "menace to artistic integrity"), through the progressive Henry Cowell ("Contemporary music makes almost universal use of materials formerly considered unusable"), the likably innocent Gershwin ("If music ever became machine-made . . . it would cease to be art"), the knowledgeably pompous Roy Harris ("Our sense of rhythm is less symmetrical than the European. . . . America waits calmly between the Pacific and the Atlantic while the tide of the Mississippi rises and falls with the seasons"), and even the rustic Jelly Roll Morton ("You got to be able to come down in order to go up")—to the recent crop of not-so-young iconoclasts.

Of these last, I find John Cage's habitual intelligence about all things sonorous and Harry Partch's witty concern for human speech values particularly farseeing and literate. By contrast, Arthur Berger's words on the Stravinsky school seem no longer cogent, and Gunther Schuller's on jazz (1956) appear by their very "timeliness" out of date. As for Milton Babbitt, he not surprisingly gives the impression that whoever doesn't think as he does doesn't exist. But quite surprisingly, he illogically equates music with mathematics by suggesting that a concert audience should be as formally equipped as an audience at a lecture about advanced mathematics, as if science weren't a means to an end and art an end in itself. They all speak of progress, of evolution, as though these terms were more inevitably applicable to a healthy musical growth than to a cancer.

"One of the present problems among musicians is that of keeping abreast of the time," declared Elliott Carter in 1958, and the point was proved when William Flanagan the same year maintained that opera was all the rage among younger composers. It isn't now.

To Roger Sessions perhaps one must allow the last word, since his thesis is the least ax-grinding, the most inclusive. He offers a rundown on every current trend in this country's music, and while praising the vitality, he points out the dangers of the *embarras de richesses* now available to the young. Best of all, he dispels the misconception that "a period in which musicians think and talk so much about art must necessarily be a sterile one." Composers, good and bad, have always done a lot of talking, good and bad. The present volume is a perfect example.

(*1967*)

TWO

DEBUSSY, RAVEL, AND POULENC

NOTES ON
DEBUSSY

Claude Debussy has become history. He is already open to reinterpretation as opposed to mere misinterpretation. Nearly eighty years have passed since *L'après-midi d'un faune* struck Parisian academia as rather bland, while today its composer is paired by the young with Scriabin as someone positively psychedelic. Yet some still live who knew and worked with Debussy; and it seems like only yesterday that he overhauled at least one childhood.

He was my key to France. His music very early unlocked and exposed my innate Francophilia.

Born five years after his death, I did not know Debussy's name during my first decade. At ten I knew only the keyboard literature of middle-class beginners, especially something called "Mealtime at the Zoo." But when I became eleven, one afternoon like any other, my new piano teacher, Mrs. Rothschild, in her sunny apartment on Chicago's Kenwood Avenue, played for my unsuspecting ears *L'Isle joyeuse*. That was my undoing. The sounds did not reveal Watteau's rarefied past so much as open a door to modern Paris, which, years later, would become my residence.

Now, looking back, people ask if that stay in France influenced my life and music. But I went to France because I was already French, not the other way around. And Debussy lit the way home.

By twelve, in 1936, I knew his whole output from *Lindaraja* to *Khamma*, had mulled the still-puzzling notation of *Des pas sur la neige*, choreographed the saxophone *Rapsodie*, and sighed at the misprints strewn throughout the Durand editions that to this day remain unrectified. That spring Edward Lockspeiser's biography appeared with news about Debussy's cool professionalism and stormy domesticity. And that summer my parents took my sister Rosemary and me to Europe. Which is when

I learned that nature imitates art—if nature may include the ambience of cities. My dream life has always occurred, so to speak, *in advance*: not, as Freud had it, sorting out yesterday, but previewing tomorrow. Like dreams, like art. Just as today New Orleans evokes the reality of Blanche DuBois more than of itself, so the land of Paris seemed already familiar through Debussy, and the Mediterranean reflected his private vision more than literal clouds.

How should he be played?

When I still went to concerts, Debussy was given in all possible manners, from the icy precision of Toscanini's *La Mer* to Bernstein's steaming carnality, from the Lisztian elegance of Gieseking's *Images* to Browning's "objective" intelligence, and from the "authentic" liberties of Maggie Teyte's *Green* to Jenny Tourel's tougher ruby-hued wisdoms. What with these sacred monsters around, the French themselves—Ansermet, Cortot, Bernac—did not strike one as definitive. (When in 1940 the Bartóks at Northwestern University performed the two-piano *En blanc et noir*, Bob Trotter and I were allowed to be page turners. There was no room for objective appraisal, the occasion being legendary, and Béla being inferior to his wife as keyboard artist. Still, devotion flowed. For had not Bartók, on a visit to Paris in the early 1900s, longed to meet Debussy? He was told: "Let us introduce you to d'Indy. Debussy will just insult you. Do you want to be insulted by Debussy?" "Yes.")

Even if composers had the last word on how they should be heard, Debussy's own surviving interpretations are too blurred for much use. Recording in 1902 with Mary Garden, he sounds merely remote, and *D'un cahier d'esquisses* is most memorable for wrong notes. Nevertheless Debussy clearly played his own pieces straighter than Ravel played his. Misty music, to sound misty, must be played without mist, while pristine music, to make its point, should be played pristinely. Ravel's scores were hammered like Cellini goblets into inevitable shapes with not one inlaid jewel misplaced, so his own carefree recorded renditions come as a surprise with that Chopinesque left hand always anticipating the right.

Is it safe to suggest that, just as composers are not final authorities on their own music, so the French are not the ultimate interpreters of theirs? French music should probably not be "interpreted" at all.

France has produced many a great musician (though not, like Germany, a great musical audience: the French public's discipline is centered around the sense of sight, which in traditions of art requires less group work than the sense of sound); but the proprietary attitude held by French performers for their composers ignores the *distance* that I, for one, find helpful for Debussy, urgent for Ravel. French performers seem either too indulgently romantic, like Jacques Thibaud, or too lovingly crisp, like Casadesus.

When, as with much French composition, intimations of mood, speed, and color are economically built into the note lengths and into the chordal spacing (which, especially in the orchestration, gives that "transparent" effect), rather than indicated by "expression marks" and instrumental doublings, then, as the saying goes, to let the music speak for itself would be the logical solution for performance, a solution inappropriate for German composition.

(No sooner are the foregoing generalities proposed, than Georges Prêtre's image rises to refute each word.)

Once I wrote: "Because we enjoy Ravel more than Debussy we assume he's less good than; another generation will acknowledge Ravel as better precisely because he's more enjoyable." Taken literally, that statement needs a grain of salt. Yet if it implies that pleasure, being suspect, no longer serves as criterion for judgment (except in rock), it also implies we need new twists if we persist in playing off these Frenchmen against each other. To disdain the likening of them, as one did thirty years ago (how could great individuals be likened!), now feels frustrating.

The game's a basis for evaluation: Try to view simultaneously two rivals of the same national and musical language, and through their similarity rather than difference define their "school," to the disadvantage of neither. You will see the composers as two sides of one coin. Ravel and Debussy become the body and soul—the mother and father—of modern France. Pair off Strauss and Mahler, Bartók and Kodály, Ives and Ruggles. Or take Boulez and Stockhausen (yes, they speak the same national and musical language, the Frenchman being by inclination and residence a German, and their mutual artistry being the original of the current Esperanto).

Do not forget that resemblance and influence are not synonyms. His influences are what, when disguised by his personality, make an artist an artist. Of course, to disguise the things he has taken from others, he must first be conscious of those things; only second-raters proclaim their originality, blind to the origins bursting their seams. Nothing springs from nothing. The so-called creative act lies in reconditioning borrowed objects, in making them yours, in speaking Esperanto in your own translation.

Debussy appears less the unique innovator when we examine his early works—before he learned the art of camouflage. Those fudge-colored ninths shifting like lava through the *Sarabande* to *Pelléas* sound uncomfortably close to the ninths of Satie and Rebikov (both, incidentally, Debussy's juniors). *Nuages* paraphrases Mussorgsky's *Sans Soleil*, as does, more than coincidentally, Stravinsky's prelude to *Le Rossignol*. But by the turn of the century Debussy had become himself: himself in a position to be stolen from.

Now the chances are that Stravinsky's Nightingale emerged directly from the Clouds rather than from the mere Sunlessness of a fellow Russian. In any case, since no one, not even Oscar Wilde, was ever born fully clothed, Stravinsky seems as inevitable a parturition of the paternal Claude de France (Debussy's name for himself) as, say, Poulenc does of the maternal Ravel.

En bateau, Brouillards, La Cathédrale engloutie, L'Îsle joyeuse, Voiles, Jardins sous la pluie, Poissons d'or, Ondine, Reflets dans l'eau. So much of his piano music concerns water! Much of that, in turn, is formally his most experimental.

There's orchestral water too. *La Mer* is often called his masterpiece and balanced against Ravel's *Daphnis et Chloé* by those same people who agree that Ravel in formal matters was the classicist, while Debussy played the role of free versifier. These two works demonstrate the reverse: *La Mer* is a symphony, *Daphnis* a rhapsody. They may well be their composers' principal orchestral pieces, though if masterpieces must be cited, look (as with most composers, except Beethoven) to the vocal works: *Pelléas et Mélisande* and *L'Enfant et les sortilèges*.

As everyone knows, water means mother, and *mer* sounds like *mère*. Now psychoanalysts can prove points everywhere except in art. *Maman* being the dominant figure of Ravel's little opera, is it idle to ponder Ravel's fixation on the descending fourth whenever he sets that word to music? By extension shall we ponder the descending fifth, which is the dominant figure of his non-vocal *Daphnis*? Result: A fifth, being a fourth upside down, suggests that water by any other name smells of inversion. Or: How ridiculous the mind over musical matter!

Much has been made of his new forms, or rather of his desire to dispense with old forms by creating a continuous middle without beginning or end. As far as I can see, this desire remained just that. Indeed, despite revolution in all other areas of composition, not until John Cage did the twentieth century see deviations from standard musical shapes (none, for example, from Schoenberg, Stravinsky, or Boulez), and the musical as opposed to theatrical intent of these deviations is open to question.

Except for an isolated later song such as *Placet futile*, where the structure is dictated by the poet, Debussy's forms were pretty accessible. Certain *Préludes* like *Canope* or *Voiles* have an eccentric organization, but no more so than piano pieces by Satie that predate these by twenty years—pieces novel because they contain no development, simply the addition of blocks, or endless repetitions, which, *faute de mieux*, do vaguely suggest an eternal middle.

Consider Debussy's *Études*, which many call his crowning achievement and treat either with affection (Stravinsky: "[My] favorite piano opus in the music of this century"); with deference (Lockspeiser: "A summary of the composer's entire pianistic creation"); or with veneration (Charles Rosen: "A statement of what he had done, and could do, to the art of music . . . a concentration of such severity that it is difficult to follow the musical thought at first hearing"). The *Études* do deserve great praise; and some of them are formally curious, for instance, *Pour les agréments*, or *Pour les sonorités opposées*. Others, like those in thirds or in sixths, are no more "advanced" than the *Mazurka* of twenty-five years earlier: the sole continuity device comes from the statement of a foursquare figure, followed by its literal restatement. In the *Mazurka* the device sounds youthful, in the *Études* simplistic.

Like Scriabin, Debussy had his mystical moments (which Messiaen inherited), but also, like Robert Schumann, his boyish moments (which Messiaen did not inherit). His coy use of grace notes, like a lifted eyebrow, on the word *nu* in *Placet futile* seems if not cheap at least highschoolish, and taints an otherwise sophisticated experience.

What made him special? Formally he was not "new." Melodically he was short of breath, given to evolving fragments rather than spinning threads. Harmonically he derived consecutively from Satie and Massenet (in *L'Enfant prodigue*), and from Russia, Cambodia (*Pagodes*, etc.),

Spain (*Ibéria*, etc.), even America (*Golliwog's Cakewalk*, etc.), and finally from the very Stravinsky he himself had so influenced. Rhythmically, too, he was rather predictable.

He was special because he was better than others playing the same game. The game can be called "sound," sound taking precedence over shape, over language. Surely, if the key word for, say, Palestrina is line, for Puccini is tune, for Bach is structure, for Prokofiev rhythm, for Berlioz energy, then for Debussy the word is sound. Surely, too, that explains his popularity as a sensualist among today's young. For although ironically sound figures less than style or content in pedagogical discussions of music, it is the one ingredient to identify and distinguish this art from all others.

Never let him be defined as an Impressionist, that being a term for painters who seek to avoid literal representation. When a musician tries for impressionism, he seeks to *become* literal.

Richard Strauss was younger than Debussy, though one might correctly say that he closed the nineteenth century while Debussy opened the twentieth, because we now realize Strauss's frenzy to have been not essentially innovative but agonized. No younger composer of value came from Strauss as Strauss came from Wagner. He was the last Romantic, Debussy the first Modern.

(*1970*)

PELLÉAS AND PIERRE

One can detest opera yet love *Pelléas et Mélisande*. One can love opera yet detest *Pelléas*. And one can love both, so long as one doesn't seek in *Pelléas* those extrovert arias or mob scenes characteristic of bel canto or Sturm und Drang genres. The piece is unique in France's lyric-theater history (being free of set numbers) and in its composer's catalog (being his sole completed essay in the form). Even *Parsifal*, *Pelléas*'s German cousin, resembles him only physiologically, the temperament of Claude Debussy's masterpiece being thoroughly French.

The Frenchness comes from an understated sensuality. Instrumental choirs are seldom doubled, even in loud passages, while the vocal parts are without melisma. A noncathartic tastefulness pervades the score, providing innuendo rather than, say, the open hysteria of a *Salome*.

The leanness of the work's each component would seem to preclude a performable translation, the French tongue (especially Debussy's use of it), like French music, being more immutable than Italian or German. Yet I first heard *Pelléas* in Philadelphia in English, without frustration, while various productions in Paris led me rashly to wonder if the French always misjudge their perspective toward this opera as toward so much of their other music. The most glorious Mélisande, after all, remains the first, Scotland's Mary Garden; nor has a tradition grown around the role as around Norma or Lucia, Isolde or Elektra. I reasoned that a sensible case could someday be made, if not for an Englished *Pelléas*, at least for an authoritative version by non-French artists. A recent New York City Opera production reinforced the reasoning.

But a hearing of the present recording (Boulez conducting a Covent Garden ensemble, Columbia M3-30119) makes clear that even if a singer's origins are irrelevant, he must at least preserve a Debussyan viewpoint. The weakness of this particular ensemble does not lie in its internationality per se (none of the cast is French)—a foreign accent being more acceptable than a foreign attitude—but the score's first twenty minutes expose the personalities and vocal attributes of all five protagonists, and these singers are just not at home. They polish the surface, but do not themselves shine from within the verbal and musical speech. In the Covent Garden performance that preceded this recording, all except Elisabeth Soederstroem were singing their roles for the first time; this may explain why all (again except for Soederstroem), in dramatic concept, tone of voice, and projection of language, resemble students.

For example, though the part of Golaud evolves more richly than the others, Donald McIntyre's portrayal is bland and nondeveloping, his sound unclean if not unpleasant, his diction careful but still stumbling.

The adolescent Pelléas, willfully self-involved and passive, is also exuberant and generous, as text and music make clear. Thus a presumably youthful-sounding tenor was chosen for this production rather than the usual baryton martin. Yet George Shirley's top is strident and inaccurate, and his lower registers are conscientious but unlovely. If the pronunciation of his l's and r's sometimes intrudes on the mood, his main vice lies in being too cautious. Pelléas may be sentimental, but he is also carnal and playful: wrapped in Mélisande's tresses, he's having fun. George Shirley's young Pelléas sounds old.

David Ward's old patriarch sounds young. Like Polonius, Arkel may be sage or senile or both; whatever characterization Debussy may have pictured, the notes allotted by the composer to the king do invite a resonance not here apparent. Ward's interpretation lacks life, timbre, focus, contrast.

As Geneviève, the Australian mezzo Yvonne Minton does the only singing that might be called gorgeous, but only on the staff. Below middle-C she rasps.

Elisabeth Soederstroem, however, is always satisfactory, sometimes heartwarming. Her theatrical viewpoint comes over a bit démodé, but at least she has a viewpoint and her démodé is in the overwrought Opéra-Comique tradition which just possibly was how Debussy coached Mary Garden. Surely Garden, like Soederstroem, had a tinge of accent, some foreigners' very lack of accent being itself an accent, achieved as it is by a technique never wholly invisible. An accent does befit Mélisande more than the others, since she comes from afar.

Alone of the principals, Soederstroem knows that Debussy's vocality is not a series of soldered fragments but a concentrated melody (the "spun out line" reduced to lowest terms, as opposed, say, to Puccini's expansion of it to highest terms or to Webern's ultimate dismissal of such terms), and that it often fills a harmony role by replacing a "missing" instrument.

My aversion to boy sopranos, in chorus or solo, puts me in the class with those "philistines" who hooted the child Yniold off the stage at the dress rehearsal in 1902. Sung by a woman the part seems silly and the music nasty. Sung by a boy, as in the present recording (for the "credibility and almost unbearable terror which it implies," explains the program note), insult is added to the injury of certain ears. Ironically, Anthony Wicks, the English child performing here, sings better French than his five featured colleagues.

Maeterlinck's play is sophisticated, taken at face value rather than for symbolism. Mélisande becomes an Antonioni heroine, wealthy (as are they all) without explanation, who doesn't answer questions and is herself not always given replies. Meanwhile the demented echoes, non sequiturs, and shifting repetitions of speech sound as timeless as nursery rhymes or lovers' quarrels. Debussy responds to the text literally, even occasionally mickey-mousing (despite Satie's warning against letting the scenery "make faces") when there is talk of fountains, sheep, death, creaking gates. Such effects are of course all orchestral.

Indeed, if Debussy demands the same requisites for finished performances as other opera composers—good singers, good orchestra, good blend of the two—he also demands more balanced proportions than, for instance, Donizetti, whose accompaniments can be so-so if the singers are sensational. Therefore, if the vocalists for this recording of *Pelléas et Mélisande* scarcely approach the magic point where expressions merge and catch fire, the loss is partly redeemed by the orchestra, which is sheer perfection.

Pierre Boulez, who knows and could supply good French singing if he wished, has chosen instead, not without a certain wisdom, to star himself in this enterprise. We hear it as a symphonic piece with human voices superimposed. Covent Garden's orchestra is passionate, clean, theatrical, mellow, and tough, while Boulez's tempos are supple as a vast canvas on which his singers are allowed to draw their little lines of tune. But as the actors do not give the impression of being able to "think French" and thus do not sing from inside their roles, they fail to exploit the daft as well as the plaintive features of the libretto. This defect is heightened when conductor Boulez veils, even swallows, the singers with his orchestra. So, despite what he and others these days maintain about the work's not being a dream but a drama of cruelty, the fact remains it *is* a dream, and Boulez makes it sound even more like one by re-evaluating, for better or worse, certain vital dimensions.

(*1970*)

NOTES FOR DEBUSSY'S
EN BLANC ET NOIR

Published comment on *En blanc et noir* is scant and contradictory. Lockspeiser's *Debussy*, for half a century the standard biography, contains but two feeble references: "The pieces for two pianos entitled *En blanc et noir* [were] inspired by the greys of Velasquez . . ."; and "Debussy was becoming a prey to his own 'formulas.' This was his final and most ironic tragedy. . . . At least one of the three pieces for piano duet [*sic*] entitled *En blanc et noir* were [*sic*] topical war pieces. Few of these are played nowadays: they are too dull. And dull music is the last thing one can accept from a composer who sets out merely to delight." From Groves Dictionary: "Among the many miracles of this masterpiece are the textures, some of rich clarity, others hard-edged . . . and a freedom of harmonic movement." Debussy himself, making no reference to Velasquez, said that the movements of his suite "derive their color and feeling solely from the sonority of the pianos."

The suite dates from the composer's last years when the cancer that would kill him in 1918 was already active. "I humbly regret my state of latent death," he wrote to a friend, "and have been writing like a madman." It is tempting to attach a program to these three untitled pieces, originally named *Caprices*. Each is headed by an epigraph suggesting a mood or even a scene. (The white and black, so far as I'm concerned, refer only to the piano keys.)

The first carries this quatrain from the libretto of Gounod's *Roméo et Juliette*:

> Qui reste à sa place
> Et ne danse pas
> De quelque disgrâce
> Fait l'aveu tout bas.

The historian Léon Vallas interprets this as an allusion to those who shunned the "macabre dance" of the battlefield, thereby admitting to some physical defect. Debussy, patriotic to a fault, even to appending *musicien français* to his signature after 1914, was alternately despairing and riled at the very mention of German armies. But the music itself, marked *Avec emportement*, surges with a witty, sensuous enthusiasm broken only fitfully by the odd sonority of a unison *risoluto* fanfare. The movement is dedicated to "A. Kussewitsky"—who turns out to be conductor Serge Alexandrovich Koussevitzky, then a publisher in Europe.

The second movement, inscribed "au Lieutenant Jacques Charlot tué à l'ennemi en 1915, le 3 Mars," is unmistakably imbued with the scent of war. The epigraph is from Villon's *Ballade contre les ennemis de la France*, and the depictions are of a haze of rumbling cannons, skewered bugle blasts, soft drumrolls beneath marching feet, and a Lutheran chorale blended with "La Marseillaise." "I apologize for this anachronism," Debussy wrote his publisher, "but I think it is permissible at a time when the very pavements and the trees of the forests are vibrating to this ubiquitous anthem." The composer had also quoted the ubiquitous anthem three years earlier in *Feux d'artifice*.

Similarly the inscription for the frisky third movement, "Yver, vous n'este qu'un vilain . . . ," is borrowed from *Trois Chansons* on verses of Charles d'Orléans that Debussy had set to music for unaccompanied chorus in 1908. Indeed the entire suite, which lasts a mere thirteen minutes, would seem—literarily, sentimentally, musically—to be a gathering up of the past into a bulwark against the hideous present and an uncertain future. Dedicated "à mon ami Igor Strawinski" (who, though neither could have known it then, would become the logical extension of the older musician until his own death in 1971), this movement, like the others, reassembles every mannerism of Debussy's rather brief career. Like *La Mer*, like *Pelléas*, like all the piano music hitherto, this suite is not formed from broad strokes but from dozens of sparkling mosaics, here glued together by an expert sense of keyboard writing.

En blanc et noir is the last of Debussy's works for two pianos. *Lindaraja*, a Hispanic bonbon from 1901, is generally granted short shrift, but though I've heard it only once (performed in 1940 by the Bartóks), I've never forgotten its gracefully contagious lilt. The other works are arrangements of Wagner, of Tchaikovsky, of Saint-Saëns, and most notably, of Schumann's *Six Studies in Canon Form*. He also arranged

L'après-midi d'un faune for two pianos, along with various other of his own orchestral pieces for one-piano four-hands—a practice of most composers before the advent of the phonograph. *En blanc et noir* itself has something of the look and sound of an arrangement, as though it were the reduction of something more elaborate or the blueprint for a forthcoming orchestral piece. Not that the two-piano writing isn't characteristic; the spacings are well planned, and they "sound." It's that the two pianos seem more like twins than like differentiated and conversational personalities. If contrast does seethe through the suite as it unfolds horizontally, vertically there is no contrast at all: the two pianos continually say the same thing. What they are saying is at all times accessible. Stravinsky must have been wearing earmuffs the day pianist Paul Jacobs overheard him remark that the third piece was entirely atonal and that the final D-major chord was merely a signature, *"me voilà, Claude Debussy, musicien français."* The movement is so unarguably diatonic that any child could whistle it.

Fourteen months before Paul Jacobs was swallowed up by the as-yet-unnamed plague that has since claimed thousands, he gave a public performance in California, with his colleague Gilbert Kalish, of *En blanc et noir.* That performance is what we are given on this recording. (It must have been out of doors; the formal tones are embellished by random crickets, birds, crying babies.) Jacobs was the first notable musician in the world to die of AIDS. He was fifty-three—almost the age of Debussy at the end. And Debussy was the one composer for whom Paul Jacobs had his keenest affinity, and whose music—at least to one taste—he performed more aptly than anyone else. Paul was aware of his own "latent death," and the awareness is doubtless what explains the passionate sympathy of this urgent performance.

(*1986*)

RAVEL

Of those composers I most love, Maurice Ravel is the single one through whose sound I feel the man himself. The feeling can rise straight from a harmony hit in passing, evoking within a split second the vastly non-abstract realm of Paris before I was born: my heart beats in a *salon faubourien* during conversation with an artist I never met in a time that is not, and real tears well up for the unknown that is hyperfamiliar. Time and again this happens as I'm seated at the piano playing Ravel, or hearing him in a concert hall. No other composer pulls quite the same trick.

A century ago (on the hundredth anniversary of Jane Austen's birth) Ravel was born of solvent and understanding parents in the village of Ciboure near the Spanish frontier. These few facts color all that he became. His art straddled the border as it straddled centuries, being in texture as opulent as a tourist's notion of Iberia, in shape as pristine as Rameau, in intent no less modern than ragas or group therapy, and in subject matter mostly antiromantic. Listen again to *Boléro*. ("It's my masterpiece," said the composer. "Unfortunately it contains no music.") French logic drenched in Basque mystery.

Mysterious for its lack of mystery was his worldly life: he didn't read much, didn't carouse, had avuncular crushes and a juvenile taste for enamel toys, heavy spices, mother figures, Siamese cats and pink shirts with mauve suspenders at a time when men donned only dull colors. Beneath garish shirts lay bland discretion.

But the unknown is good press. The two most frequent questions on Ravel: Was he Jewish? Was he homosexual? (One assumes he couldn't be both.) Even his dearest friends could do no more than quote the musician as to his love life: "Basically the only love affair I ever had was with my music." Nobody knows, so everyone cares. Beyond this—and beyond the details of his long, sad agony—the man was less absorbing than the artist. But the artist's method has been finely documented. What to add? This musician, who over the years brought me more than any other, now leaves me at a loss. What we love we long to share but need to hoard.

What we learn as children we question without question. That Ravel's music was standoffish, elegant, well made, and casual I took as fact, like the Oedipus complex or T. S. Eliot's genius, wondering uneasily why that special sound entered me like a heady draft of carnality throttling my Quaker frame to dwell on love and the pursuit of happiness.

It was in the summer of 1936 that I first heard him, on the antimacassared upright in Oberlin, Ohio. While kohlrabi fumes floated from the pantry, my cousin Kathleen performed the *Sonatine*, which awakened me forever. Thinking the composer's name was Reville, I could locate no more of his music.

By 1937 I knew the spelling plus every work on record. I'd even begun composing a bit of Ravel myself. On December 28 of that year, a Tuesday brimming with sunshine, Father (I still picture him there on the sofa) read aloud from the Chicago *Tribune*: FRENCH COMPOSER DIES. (His name didn't yet merit a headline.) Gershwin had gone that summer. Now this. Moved, I sat down and played the *Pavane*. "How obvious," snorted a fourteen-year-old pal when I told him later.

Like Minerva he emerged full blown. Like Chopin he did not "advance," have periods, grow more complex. He entered the world with the true artist's faculty for self-appraisal, and all his life wrote the same kind of music, consistently good. Goodness accounts, as with Chopin, for a proportionately short catalog. Virginity accounts, as with Minerva, for concern about fertility through craft.

Unlike Chopin he was no contrapuntalist. His canonic forays are abortive: those thousand examples of balanced, clean lines are not counterpoints but harmonic shorthand. That fugue in *Le Tombeau de Couperin* is idiosyncratic.

A nation's music resembles its language in all respects, and since French is the only European tongue with no rhythmic tonic accent, any metricalization of a French phrase in music can be construed as correct. Lacking natural pulse, all French music becomes impressionist. French composers when they opt for rhythm exploit it squarely, like children. The spell of *Boléro* resides in its nonvariety, its contrast to Gallic speech which inherently rejects hypnosis, as opposed to American speech which like jazz is pure monotony. (Not for nothing was hypnosis first documented by a Frenchman, Charcot. Where rhythm is a stranger, rhythm is a prophet.)

Boléro has nothing to do with French music, yet only a Frenchman could have composed it.

Ravel's signatures are harmony and tune. His melodies are based on and emerge from chords. His identity (like Puccini's) lies in long line.

Melody is horizontal. No matter how brief or fragmental, melody necessarily unfolds, and so is experienced in time. Like sex and food, melody can be enjoyed in the "now." We react to a tune as it happens, although (unlike sex and food) we cannot judge the tune until it is over, whether the tune is three notes of Webern or three pages of liturgical chant.

Harmony is vertical. Harmony, too, may exist in time (a single chord may be indefinitely sustained), although that is not its defining signal. (A shifting series or progression of chords is just that: chords, not *chord*—harmonies, not *harmony*.) Of course, a progression of simultaneous tunes—counterpoint, as it's named—produces at all moments harmony, that is, vertical noises that result from (but aren't specifically the purpose of) the juxtaposition of moving lines; but these moments are actually points in space rather than in time: no sooner sounded than they perish or are retained like antimatter only in memory, in the past, while melody is experienced solely in the present, like a movie.

Debussy never, not once, even for violins, composed extended melody. His vocal writing, though tuneful, is glorified recitative, while the occasional *grande ligne* hints in his orchestral work are either cut short in mid-orgasm or exhaust themselves too soon for logic. (That brief outburst in *Ibéria*'s middle movement brings no "expected" relief but merely dribbles off.) Such Debussyan tunes as are lengthy, like the vast ending of *La Mer* or in the soaring *Études*, are additive: literal repetitions piled up like pancakes.

Not that he couldn't melodize, but he had other fish to fry. The music of Debussy, that famed roué, leads somewhere, but not to sex. The music of Ravel, that presumed abstainer, usually emulates bodily fulfillment.

We know of Debussy's love-hate of Wagner. But how did a nonlinear type like him react to such limitless ropes of silk as Ravel wove for his dragonfly fiddles in *L'Enfant et les sortilèges*, or to the endless opening theme of *Daphnis et Chloé*, or to that unbroken languor of the solo flute? Do we admire in others what we too can do, or what we cannot?

Ravel and Debussy each had a strong personality and so were inimitable; but they were contemporaries, after all, bearing the same age relationship as Liszt to Franck, or as Copland to Barber. (Satie, whom we think of as Papa, actually lay between them like Lucky Pierre.) Once we agree it's unfair to compare them, it's fun to compare them.

Their color is abundant and varied, but always pure. The difference between French and German orchestration is that the former uses no doubling. Reinforcement, yes; but where in Strauss a string tune is thickened with winds or brass, in Ravel the fat is skimmed off and held in abeyance. This makes for what is known as *transparent* instrumentation—a sound paradoxically opulent and lean. By extension the sound applies to his piano solo and vocal works. Sumptuous bones.

Another unchallenged donnée: Ravel's taste, the good taste—*son goût exquis*—which we accept at face value along with his "sophisticated" wit.

What *is* taste (or wit, for that matter) in music? For programmatic pieces it can be defined, but can the definition be extended (like the orchestral transparency of his piano works) to abstract pieces?

If taste means decorum, boundary, *mesure*, then Ravel's jeweled box holds jewels, Debussy's jeweled box a heart. But to a Mahler that heart is candy, to a Puccini it's gall.

Yes, he had taste. Like all Frenchmen Ravel was blinded by Poe, whose essay "The Philosophy of Composition" influenced him (he claimed) more than any music; yet he never actually envisaged setting Poe's fiction, as Debussy had planned with "The Fall of the House of Usher." Like all Frenchmen Ravel was approached by the gaudy Ida Rubinstein, whose spoken voice (that least musical of instruments, in contrast with the singing voice) was the requisite solo for the works she commissioned; yet he never succumbed to using that voice, as Debussy did in his *Martyre*.

Alone, subject matter determines taste in music. (Music without subject matter cannot be argued as tasteful or tasteless; there are no criteria.) Murder, war, and amorous passion being the texts for nine-tenths of lyric theater, and such texts being beyond taste, most opera is tasteless. Again, Ravel was tasteful there: his sonorous stories never grazed grown-up matters except in parody (licentious doings in *L'Heure espagnole*) or from a safe distance (slave revolt in *Chansons madécasses*). Otherwise he stayed close to home, which is to say, close to the nonsexual side of Colette. Nor did he ever, save for a brief minute in the early song *Sainte* on a poem by Mallarmé, musicalize even a quasi-religious verse: the gods forbid such breach of taste.

Yet who does not forget himself at *L'Enfant et les sortilèges*? Colette's very stage directions are high poetry, and contribute to making this my single most preferred work of the century. Why? Because despite its length, the quality of inspiration remains appropriately fevered while exploiting (no less adroitly than Bach's passions and Wagner's dramas do) each aspect of sonorous speech: instrumental opulence, both solo and orchestral, and vocal expertise, both solo and choral.

(Ravel and Colette, as inevitable a pair as Gilbert and Sullivan, scarcely knew each other.)

How unfair to accuse him of taste! To hear *Daphnis et Chloé* is to hear great art (despite the hideous heavenly choirs, so copied by sound tracks that we hear the original now as a copy), but to see the score is to blush. Each "telling" tune illustrates a mawkish stage direction: the violas pose a question to which the shepherd opens his arms, the harp sweeps upward as the lovers reunite, etc.—what we call mickey-mousing.

Apropos, after Ravel's death his brother, witnessing his first animated cartoon, declared, "That's how *L'Enfant et les sortilèges* should be mounted," a declaration echoed by many another tasteful Frenchman. (Disney is second to Poe on France's short list of esteemed Americans.) *L'Enfant* should never be mounted in any form; like *Saint Matthew Passion* the work's tightness is too elaborately delicate to support visuals.

Influences we avow are, of course, the conscious ones—those we're sure don't show. Once assimilated, the property becomes ours. Magnanimously we admit the theft, safely knowing that no one detects the original beneath our paint. (Unconscious influence alone is damning.) Thus Ravel announces Saint-Saëns, Schubert, Mozart as his progenitors. Who would guess it?

His influence on others? On Poulenc it is obvious, though no one ever points out the harmonic progression of three chords in Ravel's *L'Indifférent* (1905) pilfered intact fifty years later to form the motto of Poulenc's *Dialogues des Carmélites*. More interestingly no one ever points out the cadenza for two clarinets in Ravel's *Rapsodie espagnole* (1908), pilfered intact three years later to form the motto for Stravinsky's *Petrouchka* ballet. That bitonal *Petrouchka* sound outlined Stravinsky's harmony for the next decade, and by extension most Western music for the next half century, yet the sound demonstrably stems from a few casual bars in the French musician's pseudo-Spanish idiom.

He evolutionized keyboard virtuosity more than anyone since Liszt, yet his complete solo piano works fit comfortably into one evening's program.

In his sixty-two years Ravel, who worked constantly, didn't turn out more than eight hours' worth of music, as contrasted with Debussy's sixteen, Beethoven's thirty, Wagner's fifty, Bach's seventy, Ives's two thousand, or Webern's two. Of those eight hours none is slipshod or routine. Not that he was a miniaturist; he was a perfectionist. So was Bach a perfectionist—different times, different mores—but a page of Ravel's orchestration is twenty times busier than a page of Bach's. (Still, since Stravinsky was twice as busy as Ravel, yet twice as prolific, we draw no conclusions.)

He was a classicist, yes, sometimes, in those square-structured suites, concertos, and pastiches with their recapitulations and so-called symmetrical melodies. (Symmetrical is a poor word, since time cannot have symmetry.) But so many other pieces are truly impressionist—all of *Gaspard de la nuit*, most of *Miroirs*, many of the straight orchestra numbers (though none of the thirty-three songs, curiously, since songs, being based on words, are by definition musically free). Such pieces are not so much heard as overheard, come upon, already transpiring before they start, evanescent. Made solely of middles, without beginnings or ends, they emerge from nowhere, from a mist, trouble us for a dazzling while, then without notice vanish like Scarbo, fade like Ondine. Any of these sparklers could be convincing shorter or convincing longer, for they have been spinning always and will always continue, though within human earshot only for those fugitive minutes.

How to perform such pieces! Not, certainly, like the composer himself, with nineteenth-century mushiness, sabotaging the perfect interplay of his puzzles. Vague sounds, to make their point, need precise rendition, just as white on a canvas needs additional pigments to have meaning as white. Play what you see, the notes will take care of themselves. Add no nuances, they are embedded in the score—not, to be sure, as verbal indications but as notated musical calculations. (Yet my heart sinks regularly when baritones, reaching the closing bars of the air to Dulcinée, slow down the meter along with the rhythm: Ravel scored a ritard by elongating note values, not by writing the word *ritard*.)

He needs no interpretation; he should be played like Bach, the way Gieseking played him. Bach takes interpretation; he should be played like Ravel, the way Landowska played him.

I have wanted to disqualify what is often claimed and to add what is seldom said. So I have not bothered to mention that Ravel was barely more than five feet tall or that he never married. I used to know people whom Ravel knew well (soprano Madeleine Grey, violinist Hélène Jourdan-Morhange, composer Roland-Manuel), but none ever revealed much about the man or about his musical attitudes. Today they are dead, Ravel is a hundred, and facts about him grow as unreachable as facts about Shakespeare.

Having touched on all variables of music as they pertain to Ravel, let me recall them quickly:

His rhythmic sense, characteristically French, is vague, except where consciously italicized.

He made no pretense at being a contrapuntalist, and his few stabs at canon (with the exception of the ecstatic false fugue at the close of L'Enfant) are banal.

He was a harmonist born. His harmonies, both in their vertical selves and in sequence, contain the inevitability of greatness, are almost embarrassingly tactile, and are always recognizable as his, despite their providing the unique base for all chordal progressions in pop music internationally for fifty years.

His tunes, spun out for mile upon silver mile, locate him in a camp far from Beethoven or even Debussy, both of whom glued together (always ingeniously) their truncated fragments.

His instrumental hues (again characteristically French) are unadulterated. But if the French have always been noted for economical means, which in turn are the roots of taste, no one has ever focused on taste in, say, Franck or Fauré.

What is called Ravel's wit is his removal, when choosing texts to set, from sober adult romance. (But is the anguished Trio witty? And who finally dares call it or any music anguished?)

The effects of his music, assumed to be restrained and upper class (so as to distinguish them easily from Debussy's), are really nonintellectual and replete with voluptuous yearning. These effects were as fully realized in his earliest works as in his last, in his impressionist pieces as in his formal ones—the latter being, ironically, more "physical" than the former if only because (unlike Debussy) they relied on sonata form, which is the standard musical emulation of sexual intercourse.

The more we know someone's music, the more we know how it should *not* go. Distance is not imitated by softness. If, for example, the more impressionistic of Ravel's piano pieces sound as though they were being eavesdropped upon—like something we become aware of as being whispered downstairs—then they must project. Projection comes through precision, the articulation of musical syntax, which is always crystal clear on Ravel's printed page.

Even without his music, the thought of him makes me feel good.

(1975)

RAVEL AND SONG

It will soon be fifty years since he died, and Maurice Ravel's most every work will enter public domain to be rearranged with impunity and played freely across the globe. Yet even during his life his art was dolled up by others (*Pavane*, as "The Lamp Is Low," was on our Hit Parade), and at his centenary in 1975 Ravel was observed to be "the most played modern composer," his copious posthumous royalties—from *Boléro* mainly—reverting to the widow of his brother's widow's second husband. So much has since been said about the French musician by everyone including myself, that there seems scarcely room for a parsing of some fugitive measure or for a conjecture on some social intimacy, only for occasional private musings about this person whom I adore above all.

Compared with Germany, France has never been a land of song. If song is defined as a brief lyric poem set to music for single voice with piano, Schubert composed more than 600 to Berlioz's 35, Brahms 200 to Chabrier's 16, Wolf 250 to Debussy's 90, and Pfitzner 100 to Duparc's 13. Fauré, Paris's most esteemed *mélodiste*, did write some 100-plus, but Ravel, his most esteemed pupil, wrote a mere 30. Still, if tune is the sovereign ingredient of true music, insofar as true music is always a vocal expression (be it a piano toccata, a tuba trio, or a timpani etude—for inside every composer lurks a singer longing to get out), then Maurice Ravel was among the greatest songsmiths who ever breathed. Metaphorically all of his music was as "sung" as Schubert's, while literally he did use the solo voice newly, in contexts not touched by any of the foregoing—that is, with instrumental groups: not just with orchestra but with small and odd chamber combinations. These combinations were precursors, by format if not by language, of what vocal composers were to write during the 1960s, the single-voice-with-piano medium having by then all but expired. (The sad question of why straight songs are never considered nobly as chamber works, but like organ and choral music are relegated to second-class citizenship in critical columns, is more than can be answered here.)

As one becomes more acquainted with the oeuvre, it appears to have sprung full blown from the master's head, to have remained excellent throughout his lifetime, and to have hardly changed manner or "evolved" in the sense that, say, Stravinsky's music evolved, or Copland's. But remember that Ravel's lifetime, professionally speaking, covered little more than three decades and that his catalog is short. By conservatory standards he was a mediocre student and had no public recognition until age twenty-six—in 1901 with *Jeux d'eau*—and the four years before his death from a brain operation in 1937 were haunted by aphasia and were sterile artistically. The five vocal works mentioned as follows neatly span the thirty golden years.

Shéhérazade (1903). These settings of three opulent lyrics by Tristan Klingsor (the Wagnerian pseudonym of one Arthur Leclère), a likable poetaster who, though two years older than the musician, outlived him by thirty, represent Ravel's first significant orchestral venture. I first heard *Shéhérazade* as an adolescent in Chicago, conducted by Rudolf Ganz, and was bowled over by—what shall I call it?—the contradictions rising from all that unusual shimmer: the sincere elegance, the tailored lust, the sheer sound linked to the sheer sense. Although premiered in 1904 by a certain Jane Hatto, Cortot conducting, and inevitably sung ever since by women, I was told by Ravel's colleague, the fairly reliable Eva Gauthier—for whose classes I played during the 1940s—that both poet and musician had a man in mind as narrator. This notion jibes nicely with the pederastical lilt of especially the final poem *L'Indifférent*; and for those who enjoy Freudian analogies (I myself do not), consider how Poulenc throughout his *Dialogues des Carmélites* uses harmonic progressions stolen from *L'Indifferérent* to support the melodic role of the Father. While enjoying the gorgeous transparence and seductive bitterness of these three songs (yes, each separate note is "visible" through the tremulous jungle of instruments, and every versical nuance seems underlined as by a crimson wire), ponder this dictum of the composer that so contradicts my first impression: "I refuse to confound the conscious of an artist with his sincerity. Sincerity is of no value unless one's conscious helps make it apparent. My conscious compels me toward technical perfection, which I am sure of never attaining, but the important thing is to get nearer all the time." But is there a more perfect work—unless it be another by Ravel—than *Shéhérazade*? Paradoxically, since perfection is in my opinion a minor virtue (beauty limps, and great beauty like the tragic hero is flawed almost by definition), Ravel is the only "big" creator I know whose perfection is never grating and always grand.

Cinq Mélodies populaires grecques (1905). Ravel was a painstaking craftsman, taking months, sometimes years, to "realize" even his shortest works. (Though if those works did not come easily, who can know how protracted may not have been the gestation of the garlands of sound, before their final unchecked flowering, that we owe to the "facile" pens of the Schuberts and Chopins and Poulencs and Hindemiths?) So it is surprising to learn that this little cycle was done in thirty-six hours. True, the songs are "arranged": Ravel had been asked to supply on short notice piano accompaniments for preexisting folk tunes, and his expert métier saw him through. Yet the result, in its so-simple glory, is pure Ravel, for nature imitates art: who will ever hear these tunes in their original pure state without being reinfected by Ravel's delicious contagion? Not, surely, Joseph Canteloube, a composer from the "rival" school of d'Indy, whose lush adaptations of Auvergne folk songs—later made famous in Madeleine Grey's recording—were seeing the light around this time. Do they sound too close for comfort to Ravel's five Greek songs? Or might it be the other way around? (Incidentally, a sixth song, *Tripatos*, was bequeathed by its author to Eva Gauthier, and the manuscript is among her documents, bequeathed in turn to New York's Library of Performing Arts.)

Trois poèmes de Stéphane Mallarmé (1913). Around 1890 Degas said to Mallarmé, "I'd have been a good poet, I have such poetic ideas." "Poetry," answered Mallarmé, "is not about ideas but words." In 1898 Jules Renard wrote in his diary: "Mallarmé writes intelligently like a madman," and "Mallarmé is untranslatable, even into French." Fifteen years after that Ravel, who meanwhile in 1906 had made a musical version of Renard's prosy *Histoires naturelles* (at the premiere of which Renard fell asleep), set three sonnets of Mallarmé, claiming, "I wished to transcribe Mallarmé's poems into music, especially that *préciosité* so full of meaning and so characteristic of him." Here now are my translations of those poems:

SIGH

My soul rises toward your brow where, O peaceful sister,
a dappled autumn dreams,
and toward the roving sky of your angelic eye,
as in a melancholy garden, faithful,
a white plume of water sighs toward heaven's blue!
Toward the compassionate blue of pale and pure October
that onto vast pools mirrors infinite indolence
and over a swamp where the dark death of leaves
floats in the wind and digs a cold furrow
letting the yellow sun draw out into a long ray.

FUTILE PETITION

Princess! envious of the youthful Hebe
rising up on this cup at the touch of your lips,
I spend my ardor, but have only the low rank of abbot
and shall never appear even naked on the Sèvres.

Since I'm not your whiskered lapdog,
nor candy, nor rouge, nor sentimental pose,
and since I know your glance on me is blind,
O blonde, whose divine hairdressers are goldsmiths!

appoint us—you in whose laughter so many berries
join a flock of tame lambs
nibbling every vow and bleating with joy,
appoint us, so that Eros winged with a fan
will paint me upon it, a flute in my fingers to lull those sheep,
Princess, appoint us shepherd of your smiles.

RISEN FROM HAUNCH AND SPURT

Risen from haunch and spurt
of ephemeral glassware
without causing the bitter eve to bloom,
the ignored neck is stopped.

I, sylph of this cold ceiling,
do not believe that two mouths—
neither my mother's nor her lover's—
ever drank from the same mad fancy.

The pure vase empty of fluid
which tireless widowhood
slowly kills but does not consent to,
innocent but funereal kiss!

To expend anything announcing
a rose in the dark.

If it's horse sense or even comprehensibility you're after, you cannot approach Mallarmé as you do Robert Frost. Our John Ashbery, this afternoon at his most ironically abstruse seems sheer clarity beside the Mallarmé of ninety years earlier at his most humorlessly direct. Yet precisely because "poetry is about words," composers love Mallarmé; and since great minds run in the same channels, it's less weird than Debussy himself thought ("a phenomenon of autosuggestion worthy of communication to the Academy of Medicine") when he learned that not only was he simultaneously involved in three settings of Mallarmé, but that two of his choices, *Soupir* and *Placet futile*, coincided with Ravel's. Ravel's are scored for the silvery-velvet mixture of two flutes, two clarinets, string quartet, and piano, instruments chosen to jibe with those of Stravinsky's *Poèmes japonaises* and of Schoenberg's *Pierrot lunaire* for a program that never took place. Debussy's versions, made for voice and piano, are comparable to the younger composer's mainly because many musicologists find—wrongly, to my ears—that each man strained the limits of tonality when confronted by the powerful symbolist. In fact, all six songs, which were to be the last but one in Debussy's catalog (he died in 1918) but which fall squarely in mid-career for Ravel, pivot, albeit chromatically, on a firm pedal point. The only other similarity lies in melodic coincidence: both men start their vocal line *mon âme* on a rising major second, and both, on the word *princesse*, skip a minor sixth—down for Debussy and up for Ravel.

Those same musicologists often refer to Ravel as "tasteful," doubtless meaning "within the bounds." But since no great works are tasteful, and since Ravel wrote many great works, the term echoes a typical Germanism for French music in general. Now could it not be construed that by today's standards Ravel *lacked* taste (those augmented seconds that start *Shéhérazade*, for example, come straight from a De Mille sound track) or would that be saying he abused what, unbeknownst to him, was to become a worldwide cliché? To me his music is tasteful literally: you can taste it. *Placet futile* is plangent as homemade marmalade, poignant as zest of lime, tender as . . . but listen yourself to the magic at *Nommez-nous*—"Appoint us, so that Eros winged with a fan"—when the flute like a sad and sumptuous aftertaste weaves a path from the singer's tongue to yours. Or hear how the violin tremors that open the third song resemble a hummingbird diving into the honey of a Monet rose. Ah, derailed by Ravel's all-glamorous "taste," I stagger into the trap for those who depict by blurred analogy rather than by clean description!

Chansons madécasses (1925–1926). "I am quite conscious of the fact that my *Chansons madécasses* are in no way Schoenbergian, but I do not know whether I should have been able to write them had Schoenberg never written." A curious statement from the most quintessentially French composer of our century about the most quintessentially German. Yet if French means thrift and unsentimental clarity—a skimming the surface "impressionistically"—and if German means single-minded profundity in the sense of belaboring a point, then Ravel did have his Teutonic moments, as witness *Boléro* or that hyper-Viennese *La Valse*, while Schoenberg had his Gallic ones, not only because of the verses but in the fragile instrumental spacings of *Pierrot lunaire*. Still, it's hard to hear their rapport in these three songs by Ravel; nor did he—God rest his soul—foresee his country's music as ever pursuing the trail of his colleagues across the Rhine.

This trio of savage cries for voice, cello, piano, and flute was commissioned by Washington's Elizabeth Sprague Coolidge. The texts, drawn from the eighteenth-century Creole poet Evariste-Désiré de Parny, are in their leanly insidious anticolonialism as timely as tomorrow. It is amusing, however, to discover that although Parny found Madagascans "happy by nature," he declares their music to be "always melancholy." It was Ravel, who believed this cycle to be one of his crucial works, who nevertheless gave thrust to the poems, and not just through his music. The famous shrieks that open the second song were the composer's interpolations to the poem, which originally began simply with "*Méfiez-vous des blancs*." What does music mean? It means whatever a composer wishes. These outcries of "*Aoua! Aoua!*" on descending minor thirds fortified by dissonant piano crunches are identical in prosody, harmony, and rhythm to the peacock screaming his descending minor thirds on "*Léon! Léon!*" in *Histoires naturelles* a quarter century earlier. But *Aoua!* is scary, while *Léon!* is silly. As for scholars who still find suspensions of tonality here, you have only to scan the songs with your harmony teacher: they are as analyzable as Bach. For others who label Ravel classical and objective, listen now to these declarations so wistful, so languorous and lewd.

Don Quichotte à Dulcinée (1932–1933). This set of three songs on words by novelist Paul Morand was designed to be sung in a movie starring Chaliapin. Because of Ravel's illness, the music was delayed (Ibert quickly furnished a score for the film) and not heard until a year later when Paray conducted the premiere with baritone Martial Singher, who is presently thriving in California. The set was Ravel's last completed work. He still heard masterpieces in his brain and felt that his best music was yet to come, but he was incapable of coherent notation. Ravel all his life adored the mystique of Spain and composed fabulous pastiches in homage to that wild country, pastiches that nonetheless retained the French sense of *mesure*. Perhaps it is fitting that the swan song of this sober stylist, who believed he forever fell short of his dream, should be intoned by Don Quixote, a drunk Spanish dreamer in love with a creature of fantasy.

French reticence notwithstanding, Maurice Ravel maintained that man's most elevating pleasure derives from contemplation of the Beautiful or the excitement of the Soul, as distinct from Truth, which is satisfaction of Reason, or from Passion, which is excitement of the Heart. His successful demonstration that "music must be always beautiful" is surely what for so long made him our "most played modern composer." Most played though he was, one must yet ask today, when we are continually besieged by thumping rock bands on beaches and in elevators and from windows and cars all over town, "Why is it never Ravel?" The only answer is: Our world is not made that way.

(1983)

DANCING TO RAVEL

Gide's quip that France's greatest poet was "*Victor Hugo, hélas!*" came constantly to mind as one after another the new ballets trotted themselves out during the New York City Ballet's current "Homage à Ravel."

Choreographically Balanchine's company is the world's best, but it's not that good. True, there is no best anything; and Balanchine for a quarter century has supplied enough invention to satisfy the most jaded minds and hearts. But the core has begun to soften, as happens with all absolute monarchies, and the softening is particularly evident in this festival. None of the seventeen new ballets will outlive the season. I declare this not with relish but with sadness.

Not that the creators were exhausted, but their choice of music was a mistake. Maybe Ravel cannot be danced to, not with any serious artistic result, not even *Daphnis et Chloé*, his only score composed *for* dance. The music seems at once too fragile and too complex for dance, too gorgeous, too self-contained. It doesn't impel movement as Stravinsky's muscularity does, nor do the movers urgently illuminate sounds. On the contrary, both music and dance seem diminished by their union.

This slant's biased. Knowing every note of every piece since prepubescence, I have built-in associations. Dangerous. If you love something deeply, the instinct is both to share and to covet. Suddenly here's all this sound, once "mine," being manipulated in a manner that drains rather than swells.

Stronger the music, weaker the dance. *Daphnis et Chloé* and *L'Enfant et les sortilèges* have always defied choreography. They are the two most beautiful works of our century. The additions by John Taras and by Balanchine were lilies gilded.

Weaker the music, stronger the dance. Of the new Robbins ballets I liked best the first twenty seconds of the six-minute *Une barque sur l'océan*, based on the composer's most amorphous number (and were those five males evoking waves, or people among waves?), and least *Chansons madécasses*, based on the composer's most purposeful—indeed his only "political"—music. Robbins avoided literary content and pasted pale decals onto bright substance. *Ma Mère L'Oye*, willfully rather than naturally childlike, patronized Ravel's most faultless diamonds. (Can one patronize diamonds?) As for *Introduction et Allegro*, if the program didn't state it was by Robbins, I'd have thought the dancers were in self-expression therapy making up the steps as they went along.

Indeed, this arbitrary yet literal translation of music—this letting the notes carry the dancer along (mickey-mousing rather than going against)—was a blight over all. *Pavane*, with chiffon scarf and mourning nymphet, evoked Isadora, who, like the cygnets designed by Jacques D'Amboise, went in one eye and out the other.

Few scores composed expressly to be danced have been first-rate; those that have have mostly outlived their choreography. Of the scores of scores commissioned by Martha Graham only Copland's *Appalachian Spring* has survived on its own. The three greatest pieces commissioned by Diaghilev have *never* had great choreography (can they ever?): *Jeux, Le Sacre*, and *Daphnis*—music that ridicules any dance master who approaches. On the other hand, some of the greatest ballets (and also works by modern dance giants) have been based on already existing music, or on made-to-order music by weaker composers. Really good music and really good choreography, when composed simultaneously by collaborators, seem to cancel each other out. The most famous exceptions are by Balanchine and Stravinsky (except for *Sacre*), and by Copland and Graham. (Naturally I'm concerned strictly with the twentieth century, not with ballets of, say, Rameau, Lully, Tchaikovsky.)

A final irony: The music of Ravel, which is so filled with dance, be it *Boléro, La Valse*, the several Iberian confections, even *Pavane*, does yet defeat any who would literally dance to it.

(1975)

RAVEL'S HOUSE

Maurice Ravel is a composer universally adored even by those who, as the saying goes, don't know anything about music. Like Mozart's, Ravel's appeal lies in a childlike vision yoked by a virtuosic technique to a cool sensuality. Neither prodigy evolved, "got better," went through periods like Beethoven, say, or Stravinsky; both were born full fledged and remained first-rate within a more or less undifferentiated language throughout their famous lives. But there the resemblance ends (although Ravel always claimed Mozart as his chief model). Mozart was an employee of the church and court, composing on commission, crucial to his epoch, yet ultimately dispensable (he went to a pauper's grave); while the Frenchman five generations later was of private means, worked without schedules, was an ornament to his epoch (music is no longer a vital—i.e., paid for—appendage of the state), yet at the time of his death at sixty-two in 1937 he was a national monument and buried with honors.

Following the Great War, his music—particularly the youthful *Pavane* and the ballet for Nijinsky, *Daphnis et Chloé*—had made the composer a household word such as no classical composer is today. But with the joys of success came the horrors of success; Paris, Ravel's home for most of his life, had become a maze of demands in which he found it impossible to work. In 1920, answering to a long-felt need, the composer bought a rather unprepossessing villa in the elegant, somnolent, medieval faubourg of Montfort-l'Amaury, fifty kilometers west of the capital a bit beyond Versailles, not far from Debussy's birthplace at Saint-Germain-en-Laye. The next year, after total renovation (Ravel supervised every remodeling detail, installing a real bathroom with painted tin tub and shower, and even decorated most of the walls himself with stenciled designs à la grecque in black, white, and beige), he took occupancy of the house, which he christened Le Belvédère, and dwelled there for the sixteen remaining years of his life.

Le Belvédère stands at the edge of town on a mounting cobblestone lane (now located at 4 rue Maurice Ravel), and nothing distinguishes it at first from scores of other bourgeois country villas ornamented in Baroque style with trimmings of white woodwork. But on opening the street door that leads into a diminutive entry facing a diminutive den, a visitor is struck by three reactions: It's a doll's house. It's dark. It's surely not the abode of one of the greatest artists France ever produced.

Unlike many small men who are attracted to the large, Ravel, who was five foot two, was always intrigued by the miniature. He was child-like not only in his enthusiasms for a wonderland of toys, but in the very scope of his environment. His domestic decor was no more suited to average-size humans than are the dwarfs' apartments in the Gonzaga Palace of Mantua. His taste for black was a contrast or a concession, it might be argued, to the dazzle of the inner light that many artists feel is sufficient to their work. ("I like a view," wrote Gertrude Stein, "but I like to sit with my back to it.") Not only was Paris, where he frequently visited, the *ville de lumière* with the bistros and nightclubs and glittering conversation that Ravel relished, but the nearby Rambouillet forest, and even his own pocket-size garden, were shot with a continual and gorgeous light; thus the composer felt the need to withdraw from these distractions into the inner realm of his fancy. As for the house not being the messy atelier outsiders picture as the emblem of genius, to Ravel, as to most true artists, the work process was intimate and personal. No one ever saw him at work or found evidence of that work on his desk or piano. His sole pupil, Manuel Rosenthal, said it was "as if the keys of the piano operated directly on the printing press." The only sheet of music now visible in the entire establishment is the *Menuet* from *Le Tombeau de Couperin* on the Erard piano in the little study, and that is doubtless propped up daily by the caretaker. Similarly the violin exposed in the same room is an unlikely sight, since no violinist ever leaves his instrument dangerously vulnerable on a chair. The setting nonetheless evokes the master's closest female friend, violinist Hélène Jourdan-Morhange, for whom he wrote his Violin Sonata and the theatrical *Tzigane*, and the study itself is where he wrote his last great works: *L'Enfant et les sortilèges*, *Boléro*, the two Piano Concertos, *Chansons madécasses*, a dozen songs.

The piano nearly fills the quarters, with a small desk and chair and an étagère of bibelots. Each flat space is covered with objects, some of high value, most of them fakes that Ravel liked to tease his friends with— porcelain sofas and doll furniture, a blown-glass ship on painted waves (which could be manipulated to rock the boat), crystal paperweights with orchid centers, a smoked glass ball on a pedestal that on examination turns out to be a burned-out electric bulb, small vases, brass boxes, a fluffy yellow doll and such bric-a-brac, but absolutely no musical memorabilia. Indeed, the lone sonic reference would seem to lie in the striped or checkered black-and-white motif which, like piano ivories, echoes through the residence in the floor tiles (the pride of the village), towels, cushions, and wallpaper.

The tiny salon next to the wee dining room is a mixture of Empire and Japanese. The *canapé* is flanked by cupboards filled with china—or apparently. Actually they are trompe l'oeil closets where music is stored. The bedroom contains a Directoire bed, copied from Napoleon's *lit de camp*, with a gold canopy, and a fireplace and a sheer wall both decorated in Greek columns by the master's hand. This chamber opens directly onto the garden laid out in Japanese style by the owner, with a graveled terrace bordered by myriad sky-blue pansies that look like elfin plates each holding a poached hummingbird egg.

The only rapport between the rather campy artifice of this cramped and sometimes-ugly property and the sumptuous originality of the *propriétaire*'s never-vulgar music is the sense of utter precision—everything just so.

From the second-story balcony is a view of the wild Rambouillet forest where Ravel loved to stroll for hours alone or with friends like the ineffable Misia, the sculptor Leyritz, or his neighbor Colette for whose libretto of *L'Enfant et les sortilèges* Ravel evoked, in a triumph of vocal and instrumental onomatopoeia, the cries and whispers of this forest, the purrs and squeaks and coos and buzzing of the squirrels and bats and doves and dragonflies.

The house of Maurice Ravel is today a museum, bequeathed to the French government by his younger brother Edouard. The village is now a refuge of well-off visitors seen relaxing at the sensational restaurant Les Préjugés, in the shadow of one of the loveliest Romanesque churches in the Île-de-France and whose stained glass rivals that of the cathedral in Chartres. These visitors are often unaware that up on the hill—inviolate, motionless—stands the home of Maurice Ravel, whose music elsewhere in the world forever throbs with life.

(*1986*)

FRANCIS POULENC

A SOUVENIR

Like his name he was both dapper and ungainly. His clothes came from Lanvin but were unpressed. His hands were scrubbed, but the fingernails were bitten to bone. His physiognomy showed a cross between weasel and trumpet, and featured a large nose through which he wittily spoke. His sun-swept apartment on the Luxembourg Gardens was grandly toned in orange plush, but the floors squeaked annoyingly. His social predilections were for duchesses and policemen, though he was born and lived as a wealthy bourgeois. His villa at Noizay was austere and immaculate, but surrounded by densely careless arbors. There he wrote the greatest vocal music of our century, all of it technically impeccable, and truly vulgar. He was deeply devout and uncontrollably sensual.

In short, his aspect and personality, taste and music each contained contrasts that were not alternating but simultaneous. In a single spoken paragraph he would express terror about a work in progress, hence his need for a pilgrimage to the Black Virgin's Shrine at Rocamadour; his next breath extolled the joys of cruising the Deauville boardwalk. This was no non sequitur but the statement of a whole man always interlocking soul and flesh, sacred and profane; the double awareness of artists and of their emulators, the saints.

And, like artists, he was also a child; his self-absorption was stupefying. I recall once in Cannes his monologue to a baffled bartender about a series of triumphant modulations he had penned that afternoon. I remember also a river of tears as he listened to a record of his own *Stabat Mater*. "Robert Shaw," he wept, "is the greatest performer of our time: his tempi correspond to the very motion of my blood." And I remember a pair of elderly female instructors from the Tours lycée, each sporting a shirt and tie, who came for tea to his country home. While his big, liver-spotted hands popped tiny raspberry tarts into his mouth—washed down with *tilleul* (he seldom touched liquor)—he held forth on private Paris gossip, then talked for an hour about orchestration, all this to uncomprehending listeners, including the chauffeur, who was also at the party.

Yet he was not intellectual. Indeed, as a composer, he was never concerned with poetry's meaning beyond its musical possibilities. Which is why his songs surpass those of, say, Auric, who *knows* too much to release instinct. Songs are nonetheless a collaboration of both poet and musician. And though Poulenc is sung the world over, his chief bard, Paul Eluard, once told me that those songs obliterated the tunes he himself had heard while writing the verses. Which did not keep him from printing:

> *Francis, je ne m'écoutais pas*
> *Francis, je te dois de m'entendre.*

Because Francis was a friend, indiscriminately, generously! (He taught me more than anyone long before I dreamed of knowing him.) Both man and music were delicious—an adjective now suspect to the brain-washed public alerted to disrespect what it might understand or like. The very nature of Poulenc's art is to be liked and understood, which is therefore its momentary defeat.

So, although joyful by inclination, he nursed that special melancholy of the successful ones who are no longer admired by the young. Yet he did not attempt (as others may, if their powers wane) to seduce youth by adopting its mannerisms; his language remained constant. Self-centered though he was, he still remained one of the few composers I know who wasn't bored by the music of others. He regularly studied old scores while keeping his heart open to new trends.

Now that heart has killed him. Curiously, it was not his heart but his liver that plagued him during his later life (as it plagues all Frenchmen), in this case largely psychosomatic. When he was half finished with his *Dialogues* opera, there was a question of being denied the rights by the Bernanos estate. His organs grew paralyzed, he retired to a Swiss hospital where his circulation all but stopped and stigmata appeared on his wrists. He wrote farewell letters to everyone, exclaiming: "In the Middle Ages I'd have been burned alive for less than this!" When the rights were finally granted, he recovered overnight and completed the work, which has since glorified our international stages. There again was the contradictory child.

That child said: "We put words to music; but we must also put to music what is found in the white margin." In translating that marginal whiteness Poulenc, like Ravel, became not different but better than anyone else. Nobody in Paris can do it now. Not since Ravel's death in 1937 (I was fourteen) can I recall being so disturbed as by the news of Poulenc last week. For Poulenc had inherited Ravel's mantle, and today in leaving us he has taken with him the best of what remained in musical France.

(*1963*)

AFTERTHOUGHTS
ON FRANCIS

We were visiting him, Henri Hell and I, for our sumptuous semiannual *goûter*, 5, rue de Médicis, on an already darkening autumn afternoon in 1953. The usual meeting with Francis Poulenc was like uncorking a champagne bottle, but that day he had little sparkle and no appetite for the lusty spread of homemade pear tarts and chamomile tea. Rubbing the large forehead above his closed eyes, he muttered with a grin of nasal irony, "Le groupe des Six vieillit!" (Read: Which one of us will be the first to go?) A few months later Honegger died. But nearly a decade passed before the disappearance of the second of the Six—Francis himself.

Immediately I composed a sort of verbal souvenir portrait. Now that, too, is years ago when aftermaths were not as yet in view.

This composer—whose music, like his life, shifted between the sophisticatedly bawdy, the vetivered nostalgic, and the genuinely moral and religious and sad (though never "depressed")—left in the wake of his dying a sort of chaos personally, and the grandest correction artistically. The day of his unexpected collapse, letters had all been answered, contracts signed, everything was in order.

On the one hand—according to the coincidence of hearsay—friends and family and (ironically) offspring suffered death, incarceration, and inheritance complications. On the other, while it is contrary to the "style" of newly deceased composers to be granted sudden fame (as opposed to painters whose market value by definition rises when they die), Poulenc nevertheless received an instantly belated quickening of appreciation. Indeed, ask the average Square, or Opera Queen, or Rock Lover, whom—outside his own specialty—he most digs from the present century, and the only name he's likely to come up with (besides Gershwin) is that of Francis Poulenc.

Why? For the same reason that everyone enjoys the Beatles. Such music makes us feel good, makes us cry, and we're no longer ashamed of these responses. Like the Beatles or like the novels of, say, James Purdy, which give the lie to the until-recently chic suggestion that criticism has supplanted fiction, the resuscitation of Poulenc de-intellectualizes the art of music in favor of kinetic response. Thank God he's good!

Another likeness to the Beatles, one that embarrasses: the "cute ending." Any number of Poulenc's pet works, especially shorter piano pieces (for instance, the first two *Mouvements perpetuels*), de-dignify themselves with a silly tail. Like "Strawberry Fields" or "All You Need Is Love." With these Beatles songs one blushes at the nuanced interpretations found in "culture mags." Transpose those interpretations to Poulenc and blush again, not so much at the critic as at the artist-as-apologist—as though he were saying: Don't take my lack of seriousness too seriously. (Gide had it both ways: "Don't be too quick to understand me.")

The dark afternoon in 1953, however, was far removed from the joy scene. Musical centuries have, since time began, switched themselves neatly from contrapuntal to harmonic and back again (otherwise stated: holy to unsacred, brainy to sexy, horizontal to vertical, inhibited to extrovert). Poulenc and the Beatles flow purely from harmony to heavenly harmony; and though the Beatles may profit fully, Poulenc can only smile from heaven. Because 1953 was the climax of a contrapuntal era, an era that continued through the year of his death.

The pupil swipes from—and surpasses—his master.

Like an inverted cuckoo, Francis Poulenc welcomed into his nest the eggs of many another songbird from past and present. Once hatched, the offspring took on the colors of their mother Francis, without (mysteriously) altering the least harmony of their various fathers—Couperin, Chopin, Mussorgsky, Fauré, Debussy, Stravinsky, Satie, Ravel.

Ravel's *Une barque sur l'océan* is a lesser work by a great composer. Poulenc's *Figure humaine* is a major work by a lesser composer—or one who used to be termed lesser. Yet one section from this major work, titled *Toi ma patiente*, is a note-for-note steal from *Une barque*; Poulenc doesn't even bother to change Ravel's key. Nevertheless his choral working-out is superior to Ravel's piano piece precisely because it *is* a work-ing-out.

In that game of if-you-were-on-a-desert-island-with-only-five-records, two of mine would surely be Ravel's *L'Enfant et les sortilèges* and Poulenc's *Stabat Mater*, because they comprise every aspect of the so-norous variables (sung words both solo and choral, and orchestra), and they do it à la française, which is my need. I might include *Figure humaine*; not, however, *La Voix humaine*, for, despite its beauty, it always relates the same story, whereas *Figure humaine* changes meaning with each hearing.

The day he won the Pulitzer for *Vanessa* Sam Barber came, along with me, to dine at Lee Hoiby's. "Have you heard," I asked, "that Poulenc's writing a monologue for Callas on *La Voix humaine*?"
    "Francis is opportunistic."
    "Still, it's a swell idea."
    "Because Maria's an opportunist—can't stand other singers onstage."
    "But still, it's a swell idea. Admit it."
    "You think so because you're an opportunist."
    "Yes, but still—wouldn't you have wanted her for *Vanessa*?"
    "All right. Puncture me where it hurts the most!"

But la Callas did not create the role.
    Jacques Bourgeois had already played me both recordings of *La Voix humaine*: Berthe Bovy's desperate "silent" version breathed onto wax back in the 1930s, and Poulenc's musicalization as realized by Denise Duval, who rivaled Callas as our greatest postwar singing actress.
    On Friday, September 15, 1961, Jacques took me to see (in Paris one goes to see opera, not hear it) Duval's performance in the half-empty hall *au Comique*. For forty minutes our attention could not quit this small woman, even as a few months ago we were riveted to Dietrich, Dietrich who scarcely moved but who, pernicious cobra, charmed us, mortal sparrows—the only difference being that Duval was a *vulnerable* cobra, striking our hearts while her own heart broke, so simply. So very simply, too she moved us during her five-minute walk-on in Dallapic-cola's *Vol de nuit*, co-billed that night with *La Voix humaine*. (*La Voix humaine*! And during the war years—years that the French call merely *l'occupation*—it was, on Éluard's verse, the massive a cappella *Figure*

humaine, dedicated appropriately, humanly, humanely, to André Dubois, who effected the Jewish exodus. Francis and all that was human
equals Francis and all that was selfish!) Who wept directly behind us?
The *maître* himself. Now at intermission he speaks:

"*Mon petit Ned, est-ce vraiment la première fois que tu l'aies enten-
due, ma Voix?*" For he tutoyéd me always, though I in return never
knew how to address the idol of my childhood—one so seldom talks
with statues. "Tonight's the fiftieth performance. The fiftieth! At every
one she interjects something new. You saw how she tore open that pack
of Gitanes, took out the cigarette, lit it, inhaled, all the time singing into
the receiver crooked under her chin! Never has she smoked before, la
Duval, nor should she. Nor should *you*, dear Ned, nor should you drink;
anything, *anything* that comes before your work is wrong. You look
terrible tonight, eyes wretched as the black hole of Calcutta." His own
orbs, staring into my features, were scarcely more lovely, surrounded in
all their abstinent glory of liver spots and moles. "You need air and sun
and a new view of France. Come tomorrow and spend the weekend in
Noizay with us, and we'll have two days of promenades and chocolate
soufflés."

Next morning at the Gare d'Austerlitz: "No, let's go second class,
the people are more fun to watch, thick smells, *les beaux gosses*" like
Colette he used 1920s' expressions, "heavenly banana peels, and dun-
garees—*des salopettes savoureuses. En deuxième* then to Tours, where
Raymond will pick us up. . . . What am I composing?" this loudly to
the whole carload "A pointilliste choral piece, pling, pung, just like
Boulez but all on white keys! Ah, Boulez—if only I were thirty years
younger! Yet I must continue on the road mapped out for me."

The weekend was quiet, quite bourgeois (I've described it elsewhere),
except for the formal beauty of Poulenc's miniature château and the
absolute richness of the Touraine landscape. During a decade in France
I'd known only Paris and Provence, a smattering of Bordeaux, and none
of the castle country with those valuable overall views of a passing
traveler. But now la Touraine! the expensive caves of green wine, a
thousand clusters of large yellow grapes plucked hot from the vine and
smeared juicily through the lips, the endless emerald landscape at the
end of summer, such formal gravel paths absent of poverty, wealthy
with conversation, and a sunset of accordions evoking those *Soirées de
Nazelles* of my host's faraway childhood.

We played our music for each other, he singing like a pregnant bugle his new *La Dame de Monte Carlo*, I phonographing Phyllis Curtin at song and Lenny Bernstein at my *Third Symphony*. The constantly re-iterated advice of Francis: "Stick with the orchestra, it's your true me-dium. La Curtin sings French *comme une française"* [he referred to my gymnastic *Jack l'Eventreur*], "but you don't write songs *comme un français*—and that's the only way. No, song is not your real nature, instruments are. *Reste donc chez l'orchestre."* Self-protectively I accept his motives as *his* self-protection.

Who will forget that voice, spoken or sung? The harmless venom, the malignant charity? His indiscriminate choice of friends, yet so discrim-inately faithful to a type: *la royauté des sergents de ville!*

A few days later as bread-and-butter gift I left a rare and fragrant package of Hindu joss sticks (purchased the previous month near Tan-gier's Xoco Chico) with the concierge of Poulenc's Paris apartment. On returning to New York the following week, I found a letter from Francis thanking me for the incense, which he hoped would light the way toward one of *les beaux flics* that roamed his neighborhood. The smoke, he said, weaved through his yellow plush armchairs, across the squeaking piano strings, and on out through the casements into the refracting sunlight of the Luxembourg Gardens, from whence it might float on the mist of his own song over the Atlantic to America where we would someday meet again. But we never did.

(1967)

POULENC'S
DIALOGUES

He is among the magic few. Without his art my world would weigh less. Any severities that now follow are the critiques of love.

If musical greatness, as Rimbaud claimed, is exclusive of innovation, then Francis Poulenc was a genius. If real artists, as Radiguet claimed, have their own voice and so need only to copy to prove their individuality, then Poulenc dignified the crime of plagiarism. And no composer of the past century, the only century in which originality was ever equated— by peasant and poet alike—with quality, was less concerned than Poulenc with originality.

Originality is a hollow virtue; everything's new under the sun. If to be novel were to be fresh and inventive and dramatic, Spohr would grab prizes from Wagner, Rebikov would drown Debussy in ninths, Schoenberg would expose Berg as an amateur theatricalist.

Poulenc was more than merely influenced: he rifled intact the treasure of others. This was once common practice (Bach-Vivaldi), and Poulenc revived the practice, a risky one for those few minor musicians who used him as model only to discover he was no model at all. For his practice was an end, not a beginning; like all strong artists he did not open doors but closed them.

He was a converse dybbuk. Using no mask, he sang through his own lips with other men's voices. His very lack of originality became the unabashed signature of unique glories.

The premise of unoriginality, it seems to me, must smooth the ground for any "original" assessment of Poulenc's current value. That ground, fertilized by music's five variables—melody, harmony, counterpoint, rhythm (the only component to exist by itself), and instrumentation— was plowed by the composer in his way, the way of pastiche that bloomed into personality.

Melody. Does that word recall him? In the purely Puccinian sense of soaring sweep, Poulenc was no melodist at all. Though his fame was largely vocal, and vocal supposedly means tuneful, offhand his only sweep that comes to mind is orchestral: the *2-Piano Concerto*'s second theme, the one that sounds like "Jeepers Creepers." And even those nine swooning notes, like Debussy's *fausses grandes lignes* (in contrast with the true long lines of, say, Ravel's *Daphnis*), dissolve before they evolve.

Singers never say "my voice," they say "the voice," as though that voice led its own life, which in a way it does. A voice's beauty and even its intelligence are not entirely related to the intelligence and beauty of the singer. When singers refer to "gracious writing for the voice," they don't always imply ecstatic Gregorian (Puccinian) flow, and this is something Poulenc realized more than any other voice writer. His prosody—in song, in chorus, in opera—is declamatory, one note to a syllable. Such little melisma as exists specifically within *Dialogues des Carmélites* is not in the French but in the Latin tongue, as at the start of the "Ave Maria." (In 1963, when Frank O'Hara and I collaborated on a song for a Poulenc memorial, my accompaniment was a literal quote from that "Ave Maria." Don't tell anyone.) If melodic meant poetic license—the stretching of a word beyond normal spoken length and thus beyond comprehension—then a Boulez would be more melodic than Poulenc. The latter may well be the most sung French composer of the past fifty years, but (or rather, because) his word settings are more verbal than vocal.

His tunes—usually they are true tunes, not recitations—stem from speech; he never squeezed verse into prewritten musical phrases. His concern for correct stress made even his lushest songs talky. Since most of those songs are composed on strict rhymed meter, and since the composer's instinctive language is diatonic, a formal squareness results that extends even to his opera recitatives on free prose. By further extension his instrumental pieces become, at heart, word settings from which the words are removed.

He liked to think of his prosodic excesses as perverse, though in fact they are superdescriptive. How wickedly pleased he felt, after hours of struggle, about a decision to distort and thereby to heighten the word *agonie* by agogically hitting the central syllable (although the French language, having no inherent tonic accent, would not call for such a stress) when Blanche, near the end of the second tableau, declares that were she to become a nun she would like to be named "soeur Blanche de l'Agonie du Christ!" This is the kind of detail that Francis Poulenc, the social man, with the catholicity of selection that total self-involvement seems to allow, used to recount not only to musical peers but to a countess or a concierge. And the countess and the concierge listened.

Take Chopin's dominant sevenths, Ravel's major sevenths, Fauré's straight triads, Debussy's minor ninths, Mussorgsky's augmented fourths. Filter them, as Satie did, through the added sixth chords of vaudeville (which the French call *le music-hall*), blend in a pint of Couperin to a quart Stravinsky, and you get the harmony of Poulenc.

Dialogues starts right out with what may be labeled Blanche's Theme, borrowed from Poulenc's own *Messe*, a work pure as holy water. With each reference to Blanche's father, whom she loves irreproachably, or when the father himself reflects upon his dutiful past, the theme flows through a chord sequence borrowed from Ravel's *L'Indifférent*, a work carnal as sweat.

Poulenc's dedication of *Dialogues* to Claude Debussy "who gave me the taste for writing music" may be precautionary. The Mother Superior's long allusion in prison to Christ in the olive grove is pitched over a chord sequence invented by Debussy for Saint Sebastian's long allusion to the wounded laurel.

Play the last twenty-nine bars of the first act, and ask someone to guess what Puccini opera they're from.

Counterpoint is no more an ingredient of Poulenc than of any French composer between 1900 and 1945. Only when compelled, as in unaccompanied choral works, does he concoct minor elaborations in the fifth species. But never even an abortive canon, much less a fugue. Exquisite and satisfying though his polyphony be, it always serves the means to a harmonic end.

Few of his time signatures denote other than a simple three or a simple four, and their metrical subdivisions contain no eccentricity. Yet he cannily bent those straight angles—circling the square, so to speak— through pulse.

Some French composers, for instance Duparc, write only what's inherently slow: their fast music is really slow music played fast. Others, for instance Honegger, write only what's inherently fast: their slow music is really fast music played slow. Still others, like Franck, write always moderato. Poulenc's music at all speeds seems born to its velocity, as though his very heartbeat, like a metronome, could readjust to several basic outlooks.

He enriched that plainest of all rhythmic devices, the ostinato. Observe "La Carpe," the last little song in the nineteen-year-old's first cycle, *Le Bestiaire*, based on quatrains of Apollinaire. "La Carpe's" ten limpid measures are as much a master's piece (if not a chef d'oeuvre) as the whole of *Fidelio*, since both are at once self-contained and infinite— they could go on forever. Two, and only two, chords, always displacing each other, are nonetheless welded by the once-stated melody in the voice, and their implicit monotony is made interesting by that slow-flipping tail in the left hand. Indeed, the accompaniment is not an ac-companiment but a piano solo with a vocal obbligato, endlessly repeated, a solo leading nowhere like those centenarian carp themselves, jewels with a single perfect facet, spawned under Louis XIV and still swimming at Versailles.

(As one idly ponders the vast lost branches from Djuna's *Nightwood* excised and discarded by T. S. Eliot, so one dreams of the castaway songs from *Le Bestiaire*. Once there were twelve. At the suggestion of Georges Auric, whose advice Poulenc sought regarding his every piece during forty years, six were scrapped. In 1955, for Marya Freud's birth-day, Poulenc did come up with another animal poem, "La Souris," from the Apollinaire collection. Was it new or a rewrite? Auric meanwhile had a more cultured but less adventuresome eye than his friend. The same eye he turned on Poulenc's music after the fact was turned on his own before the fact; intellect inhibited creativity. If Poulenc sometimes regretted giving forth, Auric regretted holding back.)

Ostinato was the one method, more than any other, that Poulenc used in order to make a piece go. It could be argued that he "thought ostinato" even when not actually employing it, which accounts for the unchromatic sameness of much of his work in all tempos. Ostinato colored his whole life, since he was born mature, never progressed or had periods, but spoke always the same musical language in both big and short forms. (His know-how predated his technique. The manuscript of *Le Bestiaire*, of all cycles the most sophisticated, was so naively notated—with triple flats and such—that the proofs had to be reengraved.)

His career ever more openly declared its derivations. One cannot quite put a finger on the source of "La Carpe," but the source of Poulenc's last great ostinato is thrillingly (I almost wrote disastrously) transparent. If the "Salve Regina" that frames the whole last scene of *Dialogues* did not exist, Stravinsky would have had to invent it—and did, thirty years earlier, for *Oedipus Rex*. Stravinsky's iterated triplets—three repeated notes that rise a minor third to three repeated notes that fall back a minor third that then rise again, then fall back, then rise, then fall, eternal, hypnotic—become, chez Poulenc, a series of duplets performing the same function, that of tensing a loose vocal line chanted by doomed comrades. Stravinsky's rhythmic *trouvaille* in its maddening simplicity is dangerously famous. But what exonerates his imitator from the charge of mere mimicry is this: whereas Stravinsky keeps his ground bass un-modulating and never doubles the "accompanying" tune, Poulenc slowly hauls the tonal center upward and adorns his melody with strings. "Salve Regina" becomes a French scaffold built from Russian wood, and the most affecting decor in all opera. Fifteen women move single file toward their death. With each horrendous crunch of the blade, one voice drops out and the music changes key until finally Constance intones the theme alone, perceives Blanche making her way through the crowd, smiles with faith, dies. Blanche herself then mounts the stairs and the opera ends.

So intense is the last moment that we ignore a plot defect: Blanche's name is not on the headsman's list. It is unlikely that a woman who elbows her way haphazardly to the block will get her head chopped off—and without missing a beat—just because she wants it that way. *N'est pas martyre qui veut.*

Some contend (the late Peter Yates among them) that the offstage guillotine distracts from the music, when precisely the guillotine *is* the music and far more integral than, say, the noise of Satie's typewriters in *Parade.*

In the game of pigeonholing composers by timbre—in which Chopin is identified as a piano, Bach a violin, Beethoven a string quartet, Debussy an orchestra with nothing doubled, Strauss an orchestra with everything doubled, Palestrina a choir, Hindemith a brass band, Stravinsky a drum with viola, Puccini a soprano with cello, Weber a white clarinet, Delius an amber bassoon, and Martinu (as Harold Clurman once described him) a Chinese nightclub under water—Poulenc turns into an oboe (although he looked like a trumpet). Why not a human voice? Because his nature is the oboe, a nature transferred to other mediums. Why not a piano? Because he composed so graciously for keyboard, the composition was weak, like much of Rachmaninoff's, which sounds less composed than improvised; and improvisation is a one-shot deal so far as lasting effect is concerned. It's only a game.

Yet demonstrably Poulenc was more at home with woodwinds than with brass or strings or percussion. He contributed nothing to the straight symphonic repertory. His ballets and concertos (except the one for organ) are seldom played. His orchestration, such as we hear it through the operas and the three chorus-and-orchestra pieces, is skillful and clean, always "sounds," always reinforces, but has no profile, runs no risks, never interferes. Like the pre-Romantics, his strings are mostly fill-in, his brass mostly fanfare, his battery all backup with no independence. Only his winds, which he treats (as Britten sometimes does) in the cantabile style that most composers reserve for bowed instruments, take on life of their own. But, among his chamber works, the sonatas for solo strings are hopelessly trite because he lives too close for comfort to the corn inherent in all strings. When he feeds this corn, at one remove, to winds, he finds his true milieu. Were you to object that his milieu is the human voice, I would agree, for he treats voices like woodwinds and woodwinds like voices. Were I a teacher I'd ask my Poulenc-singing pupils to emulate an oboe. Every song he ever wrote, with slight nudging here and there, "tells" on the instrument.

Neither of Poulenc's two most convincing vocal interpreters has a "real" voice of the kind that transports opera buffs. Yet Denise Duval was (except for Callas) the world's best postwar singing actress. Her greatness, like Pierre Bernac's, lay in intelligence. She contained the contagious vulnerability of all memorable performers; it wasn't the sound of her curving tunes but her *way* with curving tunes, her comprehension of words, her knowledge of her native language (the only one she ever sang in), and her eyes the size of Garbo's that could depict total innocence or total guilt. As for Bernac, his unlush voice can still sing rings around more lustrous stars. If you don't believe it, compare his homegrown versions of *C* or *Hôtel* with the touristy renditions by Farrell, Tourel, Kruysen, and even Souzay to see how he crawls inside the notes and inhabits the song.

Poulenc composed three operas. None were collaborations, their librettos being prewritten plays by French authors who were more or less his contemporaries.

The first, *Les Mamelles de Tirésias* (1944), was based on the two-act dadaist farce of Apollinaire, whom Poulenc never met, but who was the poet for his earliest song cycle, *Le Bestiaire* (1918). Concerning women's suffrage and featuring the incomparable Duval, it succeeded where many operas stumble—at filling the audience with true hilarity without compromising the music. Like French operetta of the nineteenth century, it was built of set numbers.

The third, *La Voix humaine* (1960), was based on the one-act realist monologue by Cocteau, who was Poulenc's dear friend and the poet for the composer's second song cycle, *Cocardes* (1918). Concerning a woman's suffering and again featuring the divine Duval, it worked where other operas collapse—at keeping recitative from flagging for forty-five minutes. Like no French lyric drama since *Pelléas*, it was built solely on speech patterns without set numbers.

Poulenc was faithful to his authors. He musicalized the words of Cocteau (like those of Éluard and Apollinaire) thoroughout his life, and the two artists died within months of each other.

Whether he ever knew Georges Bernanos I do not know. But between *Les Mamelles* and *La Voix humaine*, both very profane, brief, and up to date, Poulenc commenced in 1953 composition on that writer's very sacred, lengthy discourse about a tragedy of two centuries ago.

I never read *Last on the Scaffold* by Gertrud von le Fort. I did read and twice saw as a play *Dialogues des Carmélites*, which the very Catholic monarchist Bernanos concocted as a movie scenario from the German novel one year before his death in 1948. Bernanos himself did not see his work dramatized, for the movie was never made. But when *Dialogues* was transferred intact to the Paris stage in 1952, the author, who was hitherto known in France as in America mainly through the film of his *Diary of a Country Priest*, became a posthumous celebrity.

To me the play emitted a kind of antiseptic fervor. Protestant, I was both moved by and removed from the nonsexual concerns of the leading character. Blanche de la Force was a fictional aristocrat who, through morose and partly imaginary terror at life's ugliness, entered the convent of Compiègne, only to die an uglier death along with her sisters (actual historical characters) during the early months of the French Revolution. The drama is less about the revolt than about fear, fear in the absolute: Blanche's introverted hysteria is endemic to all time and place, and except for the melodramatic finish, it runs a motionless course. Her conversations and those of her mothers and sisters are largely abstract, a bit pietistic, hardly touching on love (except for Christ), much less on the amorousness that ignites nearly every workable opera in history, including *Parsifal* and *Suor Angelica*. Not, one might suppose, a text for the bon vivant Poulenc. Nor was it his idea.

But when Hervé Dugardin, on behalf of the Milanese house of Ricordi, approached the musician with the project of setting that particular drama to music to be optioned for a premiere at La Scala, Poulenc believed the commission to have been plotted in heaven. If his musical language (as pointed out) never changed syntax over a whole career, his format broadened increasingly. And if his choice of subject matter and medium alternated consciously between profane and sacred, instrumental and vocal, not since 1950 with *Stabat Mater* had he composed a religious work for voices. The time was ripe for what he felt would be his tragic masterpiece.

During those years of the early 1950s I intermittently visited his orange plush apartment, 5, rue de Médicis, overlooking the Luxembourg Gardens. After an ample slice of hot homemade mirabelle tart and a cup of chamomile tea garnished with gossip of high carnal vintage, Poulenc would seat himself at the blond-wood piano and bleat the most recent scenes from his work in progress. He sang, like all composers, abominably with zeal, and sounded as he looked: like a maimed cornet, a nasal ferret. But he was the best ensemble pianist I ever heard, his accompaniments for himself as for others being a rich exchange of equal rights. (His technique came from one master, Ricardo Viñes, who stressed the paradoxical, and very un-American, procedure of playing cleanly in a flood of pedal—*Le jeu de pédales, ce facteur essentiel de la musique moderne.*)

His interest in me was my interest in him, and I never let him down. Yet I would come away from these meetings with the kind of disappointment that I now recognize as that of the hero-worshiper who makes rules for his hero before the fact. Because Poulenc's most seductive traits had hitherto been those of harmonic opulence and ardent tune, traits utilized even in the pristine *Stabat*, I was bemused, resentful, that he should now forsake them for the new opera's spare, scrubbed texture. *Dialogues des Carmélites* is one of the very rare contemporary masterpieces—Britten's *Death in Venice* is another—whose value and viewpoint were not quickly apparent to me. Is that because I knew them first in a raw state?

The Paris premiere took place on June 21, 1957. The party afterward was at the Dugardins' comfortable mansion, rue de l'Université. There was a buffet for a hundred, though I recall only twenty or so heads—none of the cast—and a mood of cool civility. That was, incidentally, the last time I ever saw Cocteau, who stood aside with Dermit, singularly quiet. He asked me about my *Poet's Requiem* (a choral piece, using a text of his, which Margaret Hillis had conducted in New York the previous February), and I asked him about *Le Testament d'Orphée*, which he was preparing to film. But we did not speak of the opera we had just witnessed (nor, of course, of the fact that he would supply the book for Poulenc's next and final opera, *La Voix humaine*—unless you wish to call *La Dame de Monte Carlo*, a seven-minute monologue on still-another playlet of Cocteau's, his final opera). Indeed, no one spoke much of it, despite Poulenc's jocularity. Maybe the reason lay in the production, spartan and understated, in willful contrast with the overblown premiere in Italian four months earlier at La Scala. In any case, there was no feeling that history had just been made. Yet a month later *Dialogues* was mounted in German in Cologne, in English in San Francisco, and soon after in Rome, Lisbon, Vienna, and on New York television. During no season since then has it remained unperformed somewhere in the world. It is a fact of musical life.

Twenty years have passed since the Paris premiere and still I'm not sure what to make of *Dialogues*. I never hear it without crying, yet it bores me, which *Pelléas* does not. Flawed it surely is, as all beauty must be. Thus only the lesser, not the leading, characters state the salient points. (Mother Superior: "What God wishes to test is not your strength but your weakness . . ."—a reversible truism. Sister Constance: "We never die for ourselves but for each other, and sometimes in place of each other.") Thus Blanche, as stated earlier, is decapitated without a by-your-leave, while the fate of Mother Marie—she who coerced the nuns to take the martyr's vow—is not pursued. Thus, and especially (although Bernanos' text remains intact), it is in the three inserted Latin liturgies that the composer's muse soars to enter and break the listener's heart. The "Ave Maria," the "Ave Verum," and the "Salve Regina," extraneous to the play, are not only the summits of Poulenc's opera but of French choral music today. Beyond these set numbers there are no ensembles, no duos or trios, certainly no arias, not even for Blanche, although a couple of solos for the Second Mother Superior might be extracted and sung alone one day.

With all the recitative (and he will use still more of it in *La Voix humaine*) one longs for—and suspects that Poulenc may have longed for—a bit more schmaltz and a lot more wit. The play, though touching and even grand, is smug. Poulenc's innate style—that creamy pop-aristocratic style—runs counter to the "fearsome" plot, and at one brief mention of Paris, when sub rosa he quotes his own so-sly *Mamelles* about that city, we swoon. Poulenc is a tragic humorist, and that isn't always clear here. The Latin sections of *Dialogues* are musically more French than the French sections. The score, after all, is modern, and the text is modern, too, even though about the past. But the overall tone is, if not exactly dated, really quite old-fashioned, and so would seem to require more old-fashioned tricks of the opera trade.

In a sense Poulenc was too honest. The piece is filled with stuffing, albeit lean stuffing, which may be inspired, and perhaps even truly religious. But one waits and waits for it to pass so as to reach those lewd lush tiny tuneful seconds when he lets himself go.

These paragraphs, in a condensed and personal form, have tried to show that while Poulenc in any one aspect of his art was not unusual—and was sometimes even crassly derivative—when two or more aspects fused, sparks flew and life emerged. The "why" is hard to focus on. But the "what" and the "how" are tangible.

To recapitulate: Although he is the most performed French vocal composer of his generation, the long-hewn spacious air is far less characteristic of Poulenc's melody than is the straightforward tune. (The straightforward tune, what's more, seems the happy medium of all French composers, except for those few whose outright impressionism renders them melodically devious. I exclude Ravel, who had it both ways, and Franck, who was from another century—and Belgian.) Yet even his tunes, as the years rolled on, grew elliptical until, in *Dialogues des Carmélites* and all ensuing vocal works, the sung line became almost wholly recitative. Nevertheless this line, in whatever medium and however digested, seems to be the signature of Poulenc—the added ingredient that makes any robbed recipe his.

Thus stolen harmonies—lost chords—like objets trouvés become a personal brand by dint of the tune that binds them. Thus an assemblage of simple counterpoints conspires to form chords that vertically sound like someone else's but whose moving top voice chants pure Poulenc. Thus his rhythms (which like his tunes are quintessentially French in their foursquareness), although humdrum in themselves, present solid planks on which to build his special tunes.

Those tunes, like Ives's, all sprang from the town-band dance-hall memories of youth, seen through a glass darkly. If it could be argued that an artist is one who retrieves unbroken the fragility of his past, or that a child is "the musician beforehand," then Poulenc, as glimpsed through the bittersweet contagion of his vocal phrases, is the child-artist incarnate.

Inasmuch as this essay was composed apropos of a revival of his religious opera, it has not seemed urgent to stress the sensual human. Another time I may write of how Poulenc (whose name, please, rhymes with "tank") *became* his music while composing: how during the gestation of *Les Mamelles* he gaily cruised the boardwalk of Deauville, while during the birth pangs of *Dialogues* he developed stigmata and was confined to a Swiss clinic from where he wrote (premature) farewell letters. An essay could also be devoted to how his music became Poulenc: how all the more substantial works contain (oh, quite objectively) aspects of the composer's origins and tastes—the pell-mell elegant array of bourgeois and royalist and rough trade and holy water, of gourmand and esthete, pristine and maculate. If financial security (a fortune from Rhône-Poulenc pharmaceuticals) shaped his life, and therefore his music, a chaos of insecurity opened for those around him with his death. But I've said enough about this man whose memory and music I adore.

There are only a certain number of anecdotes, and I saw him only a certain number of times. When a catalog is closed by death, when potential stops, survivors can only rediscuss forever the same works, revive the same tales, until those tales and works begin to swerve, to shift their weight and their meaning as we too narrow our interests and reevaluate in the light of advancing shadows.

(*1976*)

POULENC'S CHAMBER
MUSIC FOR WINDS

Some well-known composers, when they die, become immediately less well known, enter a sort of limbo, and occasionally never reemerge. Of recent Europeans one thinks of Roussel, Vaughan Williams, Hindemith. Others are funneled rapidly into this or that repertory that retains a slight but rigorous portion of their oeuvre, usually works most popular during their lifetimes: Prokofiev, Milhaud, and (dare I suggest?) even Stravinsky. Still others overnight grow far more famous than during their lives. They are the rarest. Indeed, besides Bartók, is there anyone but Francis Poulenc? Yet three decades ago when the now-abandoned Honegger turned up on a French poll as the musician most likely to survive the millennium, Poulenc was not even an also-ran.

When he expired unexpectedly in the early afternoon of January 30, 1963, Poulenc at sixty-four was something of a has-been in the shade of the grasping serialists at home, while abroad he remained, immutably though always rather vaguely, the author of those three luscious *Mouvements perpetuels* and those three dozen fragrant *mélodies*. Despite the chic clamor around his every new work, he was still generally held as merry and superficial (how could attractive music be important?) by his peers; worse, Poulenc felt betrayed by that most desired of audiences: youth. He died unsatisfied.

Whereupon by some miracle his performances internationally broadened and soared. Today there is no cranny of Poulenc's spacious catalog that is ignored; his works in every category—chorus, opera, chamber pieces of every stripe, ballet, and naturally song—are played daily, and most are recorded in several versions. Why the posthumous upsurge? Because even in the face of such solemn monsters as *Stabat Mater* and *Dialogues des Carmélites*, he is still generally held as merry and superficial, but over the past twenty years the public has been permitted to claim, with a straight face, that superficiality is a profound attribute and thus to exonerate the composer. Everyone adored his music all along, but now intellectuals were allowed to admit it. There remains the merry stigma that (like superficiality) is attached by Anglo-Saxons to all things French.

Conventional wisdom is hard to dislodge. But if happy and sad are two sides of one coin, never has the metal been more unalloyed than when tossed in Poulenc's palm. Heads or tails, he is now almost always a winner, not, I contend, because he gladdens our hearts, but because the so contagiously seductive frivolity of his music is, like the man himself, fundamentally melancholy. Were this not so, it is doubtful that such giddy sounds could have so staunchly prevailed.

During his four productive decades he did not change his wardrobe with each new year, did not improve or grow worse, did not latch onto passing fads. He was excellent at the start and excellent at the end, and the excellence—the vocabulary (types of form, lengths, harmony, etc., as described above—never shifted: his thefts were ever from the same gods. The last works are not "realized" blossomings of young seeds, they are identical to those young seeds. A frenzied Presto or torpid Andante from 1918 are interchangeable with a torpid andante or frenzied presto from 1962.

A second piece of conventional wisdom (the first: superficiality is necessarily unimportant) claims that Poulenc's writing for strings is inferior to that for winds, and this wisdom is abetted by the composer's anecdote: "In 1947 when I heard a run-through of my string quartet, I kept thinking, This would be better on oboe, this on horn, this on clarinet. *Le quatuor à cordes n'est pas dans mes cordes.* I was so ashamed that I threw the score into a gutter of the Place Péreire." An unlikely story, except metaphorically. Composers are too thrifty to destroy, so dramatically and without witnesses, their own offspring. His shame was more plausibly a generic Gallic embarrassment at his usual ideas being evoked by strings (innately hot and German) than by reeds (innately cool and French). A discreet composer cannot "hide behind" the bowed instruments. Yet who, including the man himself, will decry Poulenc's string writing in the light of the suavely grand *Cello Sonata*; the piquantly characteristic *Violin Sonata*; the ever-popular *Organ Concerto*, whose featured instrument nests in a gleaming forest of strings from which emerges a solo viola more touching than Orpheus's (I mean Gluck's) flute; or the lustrously unaffected string writing in virtually all of his symphonic pieces? True, Manuel Rosenthal, one of the composer's wisest conductors, recently told me, and not in secret, that Poulenc in his aristocratic amateurism never felt at home with orchestration, often farming out his larger works to professionals like Elsa Barraine (which may account for the occasional overloading at precisely those moments where it's least called for—the timpani, for instance, during the "Ave Maria" in *Dialogues des Carmélites*). And true, Henri Hell, the composer's chief biographer, once showed me a collector's item, the salvaged first proofs of the early *Le Bestiaire* so incompetently notated that they were refused by the publisher. The fact remains that, whatever Poulenc's instrumental expertise, the composition itself in the abstract, like Bach's *Art of Fugue*, is irreproachable as to voice leading and economy of dialect: there is nary a note ill placed or too many. When the "concrete" encroaches—the human breath called inspiration—it is my impression that *all* his purely instrumental music, whether for strings or winds or brass or percussion, is less alive than his vocal music. Not inferior exactly, but lacking the excruciating rightness that rises from the voice. Poulenc was in his element only when setting words; the rest is, if not a substitution, at least a rehearsal. There is no *trouvaille* in his instrumental oeuvre that was not used to more telling effect in the vocal oeuvre.

Perhaps the foregoing theories can be corroborated by comparing the complete songs of Poulenc with his complete chamber music for winds. If it can be said that a composer always in some sense resembles his output, and that Poulenc looked like a trumpet and spoke with the nasal moan of an English horn, it might be added that the adolescent Poulenc and the adolescent Auden with their overripe lips, unlovely noses, ungainly bodies, and wisely humorous eyes (as pictured in recent biographies of both men), resembled each other like brothers. Yet Francis Poulenc, the quintessential Frenchman, probably never heard of Auden, while Wystan H. Auden, the quintessential Protestant, loathed all things French. Which allows for the displacing of a third piece of conventional wisdom: composers do not resemble their works. Still, although Poulenc, like most composers, could not sing, his best pieces, even the strictly instrumental ones, do, like all great music, sing.

The wind chamber pieces here discussed are arranged in no consecutive order but according to how comfortably they fit onto a disc side. Chronology is of no matter, since, as I've explained, the oeuvre doesn't grow;

and the works, even their separate movements, can be flung kaleido-scopically across the decades and resettled with no esthetic damage done. The repertory spans forty-four years, from 1918 to 1962.

The game of spot-the-origin seems as valid a mode as another for pinpointing the élan of a Poulenc piece. His three-movement *Sextet* for piano and wind instruments (flute, oboe, clarinet, bassoon, horn) starts with an upward sweep from Beethoven's *Third Piano Concerto* (as fil-tered through Stravinsky's *Oedipus Rex*), then melts downward into Prokofiev's *Third Piano Concerto*. The middle section, called Divertisse-ment, sounds like a pastiche of Raymond Scott's pastiche of Mozart's *Sonata*, K.545 played "with a beat" and retitled "From an Eighteenth-Century Drawing Room." (The *Sextet* dates from 1932 to 1939, the period of Scott's trend of "swinging the classics," which Poulenc may well have been on to.) The Finale returns to the insolent tone of the beginning, and the whole, formally neat as a Haydn romp, reflects, as so many of Poulenc's three-movement works reflect, the giddy violence of a country fair where you lose your money in the morning, your heart in the afternoon, and regain them both in the evening beneath a shower of stars.

The little *Sonata for Two Clarinets* (in B-flat and A) "comes out of the silence," wrote Cocteau, "and then returns to silence like a cuckoo in the clock." A cuckoo, yes, or a nightingale or a prophet bird. For what the piece owes to Stravinsky's *Rossignol* or Schumann's *Vogel als Prophet* is inestimable. The year was 1918, Poulenc was nineteen, and *Petrouchka* was eight. Yet was Poulenc's filching of Stravinsky's famous "*Petrouchka* sound"—a pair of clarinets in rapid close harmony—more sinful than Stravinsky's filching of that same device from Ravel's *Prélude à la nuit?*

Forty-four years later Poulenc penned the *Clarinet Sonata*, although to the ear of any musicologist it could have been a mere month later. Like Debussy at the end of his life, Poulenc projected a series of six sonatas for divers soloists, and like Debussy he lived to complete only three. Dedicated to the memory of Arthur Honegger, the first of *les Six* to die, the *Clarinet Sonata* is the *maître*'s own swan song, nor at his death was there found any rough draft for works to come. The post-humous premiere is listed by Henri Hell as occurring in Carnegie Hall on April 10, 1963, and performed by Benny Goodman and Leonard Bernstein (although Bernstein does not recall the event). The three move-ments are free in form, non-developmental, *triste*, clarinetistic yet without virtuosity, almost childlike. The "Prophet Bird" configuration from the two-clarinet sonata reappears here (as well as in the *Flute Sonata* and the *Oboe Sonata*).

The eight-minute *Sonata for Clarinet and Bassoon* (1922) is in style and content a twin of the two-clarinet piece—but a passive twin, duller in her frothy aims.

I find no data on the 1934 *Villanelle pour pipeau et piano*. *Larousse* defines *pipeau* as birdcall, lime-twig, or pipe. Pipe, meanwhile, seems to be a three-hole fipple flute (the piccolo is apt). Anyway, this delicious *sicilienne*, lasting all of ninety seconds, can be played a cappella or with an optional and luscious piano background. The *Villanelle* echoes the plaintive folkloric calls, so appealing to all of *les Six*, intoned in 6/8 time by harvesters at close of day, a hundred miles away, a hundred years ago.

The *Trio* (piano, oboe, bassoon) is a work dear to my heart, not least because I own the original score. Francis Poulenc, who dedicated the piece to Manuel de Falla in 1926, gave the manuscript to a childhood love, Raymonde Linoissier, who, just before her early death, gave it back to its author who gave it to Marie-Laure who gave it to me in 1951. The crumbling title page is bespeckled with everyone's faded handwriting. The quality? I am reminded of a character in an Albee play who says, in a quip about love versus sex, "But that was the jazz of a very special hotel, wasn't it?" The texture and dialect of absolutely all of Poulenc's music, whether it apotheosizes the Virgin Mary or the cop on the beat, is from a very special hotel in whose palm court his country-fair opuses sound as in-place as his sacred *Gloria*. The middle of the *Trio*'s three movements again uses Gluck's ballet music, very evocative among the dusky hallways.

Gluck haunts us too in the center of the *Flute Sonata* where he is joined by "Mother," a World War II ditty. This sonata was concocted at the Majestic Hotel in Cannes between December and March of 1956 and 1957, and instantly entered the repertory of Jean-Pierre Rampal and Robert Veyron-Lacroix. When I asked Veyron-Lacroix how the new sonata was, he replied, *Toujours la même chose*. And so it rather is.

But if none of these woodwind pieces are as touching as the songs and choruses, the *Elegy for Horn and Piano* is perhaps the most unusual in that it's of a single *souffle*, yet vastly varied, and tries, vaguely yet ploddingly, for atonality. Composed in the autumn of 1957 to commemorate the death, in an auto crash, of the British horn player Dennis

Brain, it seeks to depict that very crash through a recurring feverish Stravinskyan figure interspersed with portentous unison statements of twelve-tone rows. But the material is not mulled (certainly not in a Schoenbergian sense), and the melodies, though spacious and nostalgic and even gorgeous, are finally unsatisfactory by forever corralling the horn into its lower grumbling ranges.

If the *Elegy* is the most unusual, the *Sonata for Oboe and Piano* is, as such things can be judged, the "best" piece of the collection. Simultaneous with the *Clarinet Sonata*, and finished just weeks before Poulenc's demise, all the tricks of his trade are jelled into thirteen moving minutes. Although dedicated to the memory of Prokofiev (how many of even Poulenc's gayest works are obituaries!), that composer is evoked less than is Stravinsky's *Sacre*, peppered with quotes from Debussy's early *Danse* and Ravel's *Nahandove*. But the chief evocation is subliminal—that of the pianist Jacques Février, beloved of us all, who assisted at what the French call the *création* of this piece. Now Jacques too is dead, as are most of the friends cited in this essay.

With their deaths comes an altering of traditions on how music should or should not be composed and performed; prejudices and persuasions swerve, become secondhand, thirdhand, and Poulenc settles into new perspective. Hearing the woodwind catalog in one fell swoop forces me to realize that though each piece is foolproof, they are all the same. The sameness is stressed not because the language is ever unchanged (which it is—and so it was too with Chopin), but because there are no conversations, no argument, no strain. All players are in accord at all times. The two clarinets, the piano and oboe, the bassoon and horn, do not have separate personalities. They are clones nodding at each other. Is the sameness perhaps less trying in the vocal music where the tunes are quite simply more solid and more contagious? Still, he never changed his tune throughout his life.

(*1984*)

BERNAC AND
POULENC

Around twenty years ago, before the funeral bells of song began to toll, a very Parisian team, and the ultimate in their art, arrived in America for a first visit. They were composer-pianist Francis Poulenc with his longtime colleague Pierre Bernac, baritone-musician, and they had come to present a group of recitals in Town Hall. I can still remember the photograph used for their advance publicity: the two gentlemen were standing informally and gazing straight into the lens with daguerreotype Gallic grins as broad as Fernandel's. What a contrast to the still-standard American pose of an artist absorbed in a score that speaks to him of his serious craft! And what a promise of humor, sensuality, fresh air!

The general public over here didn't then know much of Poulenc's larger work; indeed not until after his premature death in 1963 did certain of our "big critics" conclude that, well, he wasn't all just perfume and frivolous frills. But if he was already famous through small piano pieces (especially, to his annoyance, the *Mouvements perpetuels*), his reputation had really preceded him across the ocean on wings of song. Poulenc was the undisputed master of the medium. Every qualified vocal teacher taught his *mélodies*, every imaginative American recitalist (there were several) sang them, every voice-minded composer learned them by heart, and every tasteful collector returned from a first postwar trip to France with records this pair had been producing since they joined forces in 1935. No wonder Town Hall was packed to the rafters on this occasion, and on subsequent ones for the next few years, with the international gold of that dusky *belle époque*: Povla Frijsh, Eva Gauthier, Maggie Teyte, the young Tourel, and local ladies like dear Nell Tangeman, Janet Fairbank, Mina Hager, with their hundreds of followers.

As a result of his world tours with Poulenc, Pierre Bernac quickly became *the* authority on French song and on the poetry to which it was set. If Americans, who usually specialize, are taught to sing (badly) every language but their own, Bernac, like all Europeans (usually general practitioners), mastered his own tongue first and foremost. To this day no student genuinely concerned with either *mélodies* or *chansons* (there aren't many left, *hélas*) can count himself equipped without a trip to the Avenue de la Motte-Piquet to coach with the master.

That master has never been famed for the gorgeousness of his voice— or rather, his *voices*, for primarily he is an actor, a multi-masked *diseur;* much of the vocality is actually faked (especially high notes), smoothed over with poignant suavity and with the tastefully earthy twang of Opéra Comique. Bernac's chief quality was, and is, that he knows what he's singing about, and how to persuade you that his version is definitive. He does this through a flawless if sometimes coy diction; he does it, so (literally) to speak, by *reciting* the verse as already re-etched in its lowest terms by Poulenc (or Gounod or Chabrier), not by interpreting—that is, adding to—it; and he does it by molding those economically near-literal repetitions in such manner that they are never twice the same. All of which, I suppose, is what makes French music French. (Although why French music should be deemed by those who don't need it—even by some who do—as nonphysical, as antiseptically formal, as sophisticatedly antisensual, seems incomprehensible. I, for one, truly swoon again and again over the tunes and harmonies of *Daphnis* or *Jeux*, of *Dialogues* or even *Socrate*.)

Similarly, Francis Poulenc knew what he was composing about. In the tradition of Satie out of Fauré (the first he adored, the second he loathed—perhaps because he saw himself too closely mirrored), he set words to music according to the dramatic dictates of the text, though without literalisms, and according to the century of the poet. His songs *spoke*, most often with a so-French note-to-note syllabification, as opposed to the more melismatic Italian style. He was probably the most eclectic composer who ever lived, borrowing undisguisedly from a hodgepodge of tried-and-true languages. Yet in speaking those languages with an accent instantly identifiable as his, he proved them far from exhausted.

As to his accompaniments, they are sometimes precisely that. More often the piano interweaves itself as a conversational filigree with the voice, Debussy-style, or plays along in unison, Schubert-style. His personal execution of these accompaniments was not in the self-effacing genre of the habitual hired pianist who puts down the soft pedal at the

concert's start and lets it up at the end. No, he shared, chattered, sometimes dominated. And his chattering domination was never so well matched
as when he concertized with Pierre Bernac.

In that already-faraway quarter century before 1960 during which
Poulenc and Bernac functioned as a professional team, they recorded
the composer's complete piano-vocal and chamber-vocal works (some
of them many times) as well as the main baritone (or more properly,
baryton martin) repertory of nineteenth-century Germany and of nine-
teenth- and twentieth-century France. Two recitals culled from the last
category have now been reissued (*Bernac and Poulenc: Mélodies* on
Pathé Records and *Recital* on Odyssey Records), and are the purpose
of this discussion.

The first recital was recorded over the beginning decade of their af-
filiation and contains a mixed bag from Gounod to Auric. There is no
condescension in the artists' approach to a non-Poulenc repertory: it
shines with both responsibility and love, and with the venerable elegance
that comes from possessing such music in throat, fingers, and heart since
childhood. Nevertheless, of nineteen songs by the ten composers represented, it becomes Poulenc's own "Montparnasse"—his realization of
Apollinaire's lonely words and Bernac's understanding of that realization—that most strikes home. (The composer once noted in his yet-
unpublished *Journal de mes mélodies* that this three-page song, composed over a period of four years, had cost him great strain. You'd never
know it!)

Other representations seem pale to me today, especially the Gounod
that tediously promises to hatch from its honeyed cocoon but never
does, and the Chausson, both words and music of which grow distant
in a way that no longer makes a difference. Chabrier, of course, is the
personal joy of all Frenchmen, a joy that (like Pushkin for Russians)
never bridged the frontiers. Three famous songs each by Fauré and
Duparc are included, and a pair by Roussel sounding a bit too close for
comfort like the gorgeous Ravel that follows. As for the Milhaud and
Auric contributions, they must have been chosen less out of malice than
charity for two partners in crime from the heyday of *les Six*.

The mechanical sound is far from perfect, and Bernac declared last
year that this disc's overall point of view didn't always jibe with his
current approach. Yet his voice was never to sound fresher, and certainly
Poulenc's pianism was exemplary, if occasionally too toned down.

His pianism is occasionally too toned up on the second record, but like most composers I rather approve. This recital is more successful, more inclusive (being two discs containing goodly slices of Debussy and Ravel, the father and mother of modern France, and three large cycles by Poulenc himself); the sound is closer to what we've grown accustomed to; and the performance represents the peak of the team's expressive powers in 1950 during the American successes.

The *Histoires naturelles* were performed in 1907 by their composer Maurice Ravel, with soprano Jane Bathori, who at least until recently was still living in Paris. No doubt Mme. Bathori passed on some pointers from the horse's mouth to M. Bernac. It is hard now to imagine this cycle as having a legitimate reading by anyone but him: from his impersonation of the pompous peacock to the giddy guinea hen, he literally inhabits the bird kingdom, from which he emerges with a startling new voice as a Jewish cantor in the same composer's *Hebrew Songs*.

Chabrier's *L'Île heureuse*, which adorned the other disc, is repeated here as an appetizer to five Debussy masterpieces and three winners by Satie. *Calligrammes*, a suite of seven Apollinaire poems as musicalized by Francis Poulenc, was premiered at those famous New York concerts. It is full of contrast and ingenuity, but glibber and less immediately opulent or theatrical than his two earlier cycles, *Banalités* and *Chansons villageoises*. In those, one's spine turns to glass at such music as "Sanglots" or "Le Mendiant," while songs like "C'est le joli printemps" or "Tu vois le feu du soir" will, thank God, still make us cry.

But our tears are the purging ones of release that ultimately melt into smiles as wide as those of these Frenchmen twenty years ago. Their smiles in retrospect have turned to a laugh, partly the bold laugh of two artists who said they'd been no less influenced by Chevalier than by Mary Garden, and partly the last laugh that symbolized both the end of one communicable epoch and the start of another wherein pleasure, as the word is generally understood, becomes a vanishing criterion.

(*1962*)

THREE

GERMANS, RUSSIANS, AND OTHER EUROPEANS

THE *ROSENKAVALIER*
DIARY

Have I a crying need to shed some private glow on Strauss? There lurks in his musical soul an element as repellent as it is alluring, like an overdose of Benzedrine, or like a ten-pound hummingbird, thrilling but useless, that never finds repose. The element simmers in even his calmest measures; scarcely a page is without continual shifts, unprepared modulations tilting the sonic axis this way or that, depending on which pivotal common tone rises up. The rising up is from a perpetual quicksand—at least that's the response of my metabolism, which craves the stable ground of France. Now French music, when contrasted with German, is often pegged as flighty, ironically the very ingredient I reproach in Strauss. Well, flightiness is where you find it, and so is stability, and by the advent of puberty I had come to terms with my tastes.

Flatteringly, Robert Jacobson has asked me once again to write for his magazine *Opera News*, proposing, as a switch from my habitual French bent, to try a hand at *Der Rosenkavalier*. Indeed, of the eighty or so articles I've penned on matters musical, none has been about a German work. But now for a week this sheet has been propped in the typewriter, blank. I have no viewpoint. Nor, until the above entry, did I realize I had no viewpoint.

"Look, Grace, look. See the little bird, Grace? See the little bird?"
 Pretending to read, I recited those phrases from my primer to any captive neighbor. Actually Mother had taught them to me by rote. One magic day I turned the page . . . and was able to go on! Separate letters merged into words, and without half trying I read. The book meant something.
 Likewise a musical education. Getting acquainted with a new piece

resembles the mastering of a new language. After long toil—or some-times no toil at all—suddenly there is a click and you are inside instead of out. You comprehend. Or else there is no click, and you never com-prehend.

I haven't yet quite gotten inside Strauss, nor even his scrumptious *Rosenkavalier* after forty years of trying. But finally I comprehend.

Tricks of fate, by the time I entered high school, had already versed me in *La Mer, Le Sacre*, and *Les Chansons madécasses*, though I knew not one so-called classic. Strauss, however, was said to be modern—our sole criterion—so when Bruce and Frazier (more sophisticated than I) said they were going to see, to hear, *Der Rosenkavalier*, I went, too, sitting alone in the Chicago Opera House's gallery. Next day, when they asked during gym if I didn't agree that the Presentation scene was the most divine moment in all art, I sensed sarcasm: they knew I'd sneaked out after Act One.

What were those women—so many, many women, upper-crust and overfed—whooping around like that for? It wasn't Modern; it was merely a mess.

French music, tersely defined, is: that which does not resemble Strauss.

To be un-German is to avoid counterpoint. Canons, rounds, and fugues form less a part of general French history than do simple songs. In opera the multivoiced set number, the trio or quartet wherein three or four personalities simultaneously express three or four distinct re-actions, is exceptional. With Stravinsky (that most French of Russians) seldom more than two things occur at once; with Poulenc, one. Nadia Boulanger's only recorded comment on *Rosenkavalier*: "Too many notes."

French tune is diatonic, conjunct, restricted to a tetrachord or occa-sionally to an octave; Straussian tune skips, soars, rocks.

Straussian harmony revolves around dominant and diminished sev-enths, and nothing in between; Ravelian harmony centers on major and minor sevenths that add that touch of—what is it?—sentimental citrus. Strauss changes key constantly, Ravel rarely.

Rhythm in France (that is, Ravel's rhythm, for Ravel and Debussy are the embodiment of early twentieth-century French esthetic as Strauss and Mahler are of German) is succinct (you always know where you are, as though the musician were making amends for no tonic accent in his spoken tongue), while Strauss's rhythm is ambivalent (you never know where you are). (For the record, in the two musics—sacred and profane, aristocrat and worker, classical and pop—that have flowed parallel toward us since the dawn of time, one has remained amorphous rhythmically, the other maintaining precise scansion. Gregorian chant does not emulate the sex act, but the chant of cotton bailers does.)

The French (or Ravelian) orchestration is based on pure line; you always hear which instrument is playing, and doublings are used less for thickening than for weight. Straussian orchestration, even at its softest, is seldom pure; two colors forever blend into a third, you're never sure who is doing what. Both Strauss and Ravel, with the affluence of pre–World War I, orchestrated for everything but the kitchen sink (and in *Sinfonia Domestica* and *L'Enfant et les sortilèges*, didn't they even use that?); yet chez Ravel the "everything" retains crystalline identity, while with Strauss it is lost in an undifferentiated whirlpool.

If I still laugh at those women whooping around, the point has been reached where I can elsewhere weep. That the tears are impelled by what I hear as his Frenchness would doubtless surprise Strauss. Not that he was anti-French, just un-French. There is no mention of Stravinsky nor indeed of any French composer (except Varèse, of all people, in a footnote) in the Hofmannsthal-Strauss letters, and Diaghilev is called only "the Russian"—despite that impresario's effort to deinsularize European art.

But did Debussy and Ravel in fact give much thought to Strauss?

Again for the record: As two simultaneous musics flow toward us through history, so at any point in that history we find pairs of composers representing flip sides of the same coin or, if you prefer, the melancholy and sanguine components of their country's nature: Bach and Handel, Ives and Ruggles, Bartók and Kodály, Debussy and Ravel, and, of course, Mahler and Strauss. Going one step further, one might contrast Debussy (rather than Ravel) with Strauss as the comico-tragic mask of European music. (Except that Debussy, France's sole impressionist, goes against his land's rhythmic precision by being as vague as Strauss in that domain.) But do not forget that resemblance and influence are not synonyms. A composer's received influences are what, when disguised by his personality, make him an artist. Of course, to disguise the things he has taken from others (and the ingredients of all aspects of Mahler's and Strauss's palettes were identical), he must first be conscious of those things; only second-raters proclaim their originality, blind to the origins bursting their seams. The creative act lies in reconditioning borrowed objects, in making them yours.

Tonight at a party I am chided about my game of spotting second-rate composers of first-rate works. I reply that Strauss, whatever my personal bias, is a first-rate opera composer (since to be second-rate means someone else is first-rate at the same game, and who out-Straussed Strauss? Mahler didn't write operas), but a second-rate songwriter.

Later I bump into Robert Jacobson and lie about how well these notes are going. I'm afraid to warn him that the piece seems to be cast in a diary format. But he doesn't flinch when I say that if *Rosenkavalier* were half the length it might be twice as good. Which is not to demean Strauss, since I say the same for Proust, my idol—Proust, for whom the mere word *rose* brought on allergies.

We hear not only according to the conditioning of our century but according to what we go against in our family. Not to mention simultaneous exposures! I hear Bach for his blue notes, Mozart for his lush suspensions. What I enjoy in Strauss has been strained through the Gallic sieve.

Dare I suggest to Mr. Strauss that the Knight's vocal moments commence in medias res (and I do mean *res*), with Octavian's supertonic "*Wie du warst!*" so reminiscent of Massenet's "*Il est doux*," which anticipates Ravel's "*Il est doux*" from Colette's *livret* for *L'Enfant*? Then might I ask Mr. Hofmannsthal if his *Rose* stemmed from Colette's *Chéri*?— or did *Chéri* come later?

Frenchness per se is not, of course, couched in the convention of nicknames, Bichette and Quinquin, nor in the fact that Hofmannsthal, seeking the mot juste, falls on the Parisian phrase, for these are conceits of the epoch. No, my tears fall with that falling major seventh—"*Ja, ja*"—as the tune, harmony, counterpoint, rhythm, and scoring all thin out à la française to revive the same acrid interval from two acts earlier— *Und Nachmittag*—evoking the gentlest of infidelities.

The Presentation scene ends with the "Meditation" from *Thais*. The Marschallin's soliloquy ends with the motionless moment after Poulenc's Prioress has expired. The *Orphan Trio* was cribbed by Menotti (via Prokofiev) for his *Trio* in *The Medium*. Poulenc took those rousing cries of "Papa, Papa!" for his *Mamelles*. Et cetera.

In *Humoresque* Joan Crawford, a rich toper, is bemused that John Garfield, an aspiring fiddler, doesn't care for martinis. She muses that "martinis are an acquired taste, like Ravel."

Are Strauss operas an acquired taste? Admittedly the taste can be acquired quickly by Teutonophiles, like gin for alcoholics. But to the Average American Music Lover, the prosy chirping in that jungle of strings is just noise. What can he hang on to beyond all that rich E-major, which no sooner comes than it goes? Most of those heaven-sent melodies are for orchestra embellished by voice, not the other way around.

Indeed, every Strauss opera is an orchestral tone poem to which the sung parts are attached like medals. That is fact, not judgment. But no amount of rehearing will resituate the genre, whereas *Pelléas* reveals bit by bit its classical formality: each vocal utterance is an aria in microcosm.

To liken Strauss to a prosifier, as opposed to a versifier, is not to slur him—I do the same for Debussy. Both were happiest, most themselves, when setting prose, which they dealt with *as prose*, not as verse. Hence their successful prosy operas. Their "poetic" songs were successful, too, but still prosy—talky, sprawling—not neatly stanzaic.

Because she has operatically portrayed both, I ask Evelyn Lear, "Is there a difference between portraying a lesbian countess and a straight count?" Philosophers, novelists, other composers, even music critics are no mystery to me, but actresses are. "Of course there's a difference," says Evelyn. "Geshwitz is a woman and Octavian's a man. It's not Geshwitz's sexuality, but her lack of it, which is the core of her portrayal. She adores Lulu spiritually; she is a martyr, not a toucher. Me, I love to touch beautiful things, including women. Geshwitz is close to my heart, but Octavian is closer to my bone."

Katherine Ciesinki, who has also sung both roles (including an Octavian to the catholic Lear's Marschallin), feels much the same. Judith Raskin, who has sung only Sophie, has had no "problems" with her assorted Octavians except perhaps with Francis Bible, who was "disconcerting." Kiri Te Kanawa is said to "dislike" the woman-to-woman exigencies in the Marschallin's role. Whether these notions abet or hinder or indeed bear noticeable weight on the soprano's ultimate rendition is unknowable to the listener.

Whether a composer's personal convictions ultimately bear weight on the quality of his language is also unknowable. Still, more interesting than the question of, say, how an evil man can create great art is the question of how a boring man can. For every colorful bastard like Wagner, Gesualdo, Beethoven (but are there many others, really?) there are the majestic bourgeoises, the standard cut of genius. But if Strauss would seem to have been Bavaria's most ordinary citizen, the women he brought to life were not. What would the composer have thought socially of his dead collaborator Oscar Wilde ("My genius is in my life; only my talent is in my work!")? Would Wilde have been relegated like Diaghilev, "the Russian," to a nationalistic definition? Did Strauss know Thomas Mann? Would he not have been tempted by a libretto on *Death in Venice*—so perfectly contemporaneous—or would he have found that a betrayal of his friend Mahler? Was Mahler his friend? Could Strauss only make operas about women?

Britten, born in 1913, was not even a twinkle in his father's eye when *Salomé* was composed or when *Death in Venice* first shocked a respectful world. Not until twenty years after Mann's death was Britten to make the first opera on a love that dare not speak its name. It is idle but somehow satisfying to speculate on what sort of piece Strauss could have made from the story, even as one laments that Poulenc ne'er set his hand to *Chéri* or *Madame Bovary*, or Copland to *Our Town*.

Bourgeois, maybe. But Strauss had been an official Hero for thirteen years (*Ein Heldenleben* dates from 1889) when *The Knight of the Rose* was born, and it was as the author of that opera that he identified himself when authorities knocked on his door during World War II. More than any of his other operas, the *Rose* was his choice as epitaph.

It also made the most money, although the considerable fortune he amassed through all of his music was as nothing to what John Williams is said to have earned through cinematic rewrites of Strauss's most popular tone poems.

Movie freaks not only collect comic dialogue from Crawford tragedies, they also catalog anachronisms (Jeanette MacDonald's wristwatch in *Naughty Marietta* or, in *On the Beach*, the seagull flying across the lens when all earthly life is supposed to have ceased), and so do opera buffs. A delicious anachronism is the Viennese waltz perfuming an eighteenth-century décor.

Less delicious is the Baron Ochs—the barren ox—who, if not exactly an anachronism, is inexpertly drawn. Yes, yes, I know he's *meant* to be a boor. But he's not *my* boor. Once during World War II I saw him disguised as Emanuel List. Boozy and startled by those third-act ghosts, he strode to the stage's apron and bellowed, "Hey baba rebop!" and "Hubba hubba hubba!"—ejaculations which, though apt to his coarseness, actually represented (for those who remember) not fear but a likable lust, like Sinatra's "Ring-a-ding-ding." Ochs's defenders, among them his librettist and composer who first named their comedy after him, defer to his lovability, as though he were Falstaff. But Ochs is obscene, and obscenity lacks the charm of grand vulgarity. Since I enjoy hardly a note of Ochs's vocality, and since Ochs has more to sing than anyone, there is much to dread in *Rosenkavalier.*

Ochs is inexpertly drawn because true nobility, no matter how cruelly rude and arrogantly insecure, never pulls rank, as witness Proust's Baron de Charlus. The largesse of noblesse oblige is taught in his childhood, so that even the dumbest of barons takes barony for granted. But if Charlus's bad manners spring from contempt, Ochs's spring from intimidation; the latter behaves more like the parvenu Faninal will eventually behave, or perhaps like Strauss's alter ego, than like one to the manor born.

If the sung parts lack remarkable melody in themselves, if they decorate the scoring rather than vice versa, and if the famous waltzes dominate the "accompanying" voice lines that wind about like stray vines, then are these voice lines—at once so disjunct and so cohesive—hard for performers to master? Schumann-Heink learned Clytemnestra by rote, but that was the trend of the times. The times did last into the 1940s when no less a diva than Lehmann, responding to a hint that she had mislearned a passage, said, "I used to sing the Marschallin under Strauss, and never got it right. It's too late now."

Such vocal parts as we listeners retain with love are few, and the same for all: the three-minute Italian air *Di rigori armato,* the nine-minute end of Act One, the eleven-minute Trio. What else? Vocally even these morsels are elaborations, not basics. Ochs has *not one tune,* though the orchestra does throw him some motives to toy with, notably the haunting mazurka *Mit mir.*

From its opening burst of four unison horns, compact and potent as a clove of garlic, to its closing spray of woodwinds, purposeful and poignant as uncorking a magnum, the opera's every melodic arch is designed by the orchestra, and so is most of the kinetic rhythm. By kinetic I mean, as stated earlier, a graspable, *succinct* beat telling us where we are by making our bodies react. But even the Italian Tenor Air, the one solo with a hearty ictus, was for decades heard by my ear as starting on the strong beat of a 2/4 meter. Now, knowing the score, I still can't hear it correctly as starting on the weak beat of a 3/4.

Speaking about Lehár, Strauss said, "Like him I can't write, for in a few bars of mine there is more music than in a whole Lehár operetta." But Hofmannsthal responded, "If it were possible, as a move toward a new style of expression, to reach the 'less-of-music,' a point where the lead would be given more to the voice, where the orchestra would be subordinated to the singers, then operetta might well yield up to this type of work its magic ring which conquers so completely the souls of the audience!"

Was Strauss so much better than Lehár? Yes, probably.

Music is the least carnal of the seven arts inasmuch as hearing, of the five senses, is the least involved in sexual intercourse. If operas are carnal, and especially one by Strauss, that is because opera is the impurest form of music, dealing as it does with visuals and books. Only the High Mass goes farther, being also danced and tasted and smelled. (The Church admonishes us to eschew the senses while seducing us with every one.) Strauss's characters, except for maybe Elektra, are not notably concerned with the state of the world, much less with making a better world.

Hofmannsthal, the librettist we all long for, being great, lacks the casual perfection of lesser mortals. Thus not only Ochs seems misdrawn.

To suspend disbelief is a given of most art and of all fairy tales. To suspend belief is more uncomfortable. The Marschallin's appearance in the last act has never been explained to me, but let it pass. Let it pass, too, that she neatly gets everyone off the legal hook by declaring to the Commissary that this is "merely a Viennese masquerade." But when, the Commissary having gone home, she thus reproaches Ochs (according to the exquisite translation in my vocal score), " 'Tis well for you it was not really Mariandel whom your villainous persuasions have misled," she lies. There is no Mariandel. If the Marschallin is not quite an accomplice to the villainous doings, she *is* hitting the man when he's down. Strauss in later years, coaxing Hofmannstal to develop the character of *Arabella* by way of explication here and there, claimed that, after all, "length never harmed *Rosenkavalier*." But length does harm *Rosen-*

kavalier. Trim down the padded high jinks of Ochs and use those squandered minutes for explication. (For example, what is the Marschallin's "cure" for Faninal's ailment, promised at the end?)

And *Arabella?* A perfect creation. Alas, unlike Frankenstein's creation, she was born dead. Despite undeniably inspired attempts to breathe life into her (some using "How dry I am," which has served repertory from Chopin's C-sharp minor *Scherzo* through *The Lovers Waltz* to Big Ben's motive in reverse, others sounding like Kurt Weill—for instance, the *Mein elemer*! sequence), she just plods on and on, hyperthyroid but spectral, empty, annoying. Perfection palls.

That which most defines a genre, if we like the genre, is what can most irritate us, too. Our loved ones' endearing mannerisms will sour, as will the best pâté or mousse. Like Debussy, indeed like any true composer, Strauss gave us more than a unique style and subject; he gave us the Strauss sound. Vocally that sound emerges from sopranos, all of them after *Salome.* But that enticingly high, clean, sweet, and swooping pianissimo curve effected by his well-off heroines has cloyed by the time it reaches *Arabella.* Yet to retrace the curve back to that adolescent night in Chicago is to hear now what I couldn't then; to hear, that is, from the viewpoint, or soundpoint, that I've now established. The Straussian sound has somehow joined the Debussyan sound—pure white, nonvibrating, sad. Thus, since I can accept Richard Strauss as a fact of life (though not necessarily of *my* life), were I asked to name one German opera that I like above all others, an opera that, weirdly, I can hear as I hear *Pelléas,* I would of course now answer: *Der Rosenkavalier.*

(*1982*)

A STRAUSS BIOGRAPHY

An artist, we are told, is a knot of seeming contradictions no philosopher from Socrates to Susanne Langer has ever been able to unravel. And we are told that, like everyone, artists struggle between disordered parts—sacred and profane, black and white, or whatever—and that their resolution of the struggle becomes a formal offering to the world. This offering might on one occasion be a requiem mass and on another an erotic ballet, expressions of split personality. (Or was the artist merely fulfilling the terms of a commission?) Yet who can prove, especially in wordless music, that there is any "expression" at all? Is art the mirror of its maker, or his magnetized shadow? Does it lead or follow him? Is it the chicken or the egg?

Must an artist's domestic life resemble, say, that of Debussy, whose cool sensuality drove women to near suicide while simultaneously defining the texture of his undeniably great music? Then what of D'Annunzio whose home life was similar but whose work was inferior? Or Byron? Or Bach, who despite twenty-two children was, as the saying goes, quite normal? (But that was in another time and country, and besides . . .) No, even Freud's conjectures on Leonardo or Dostoevsky are probably irrelevant, if only because in writing of artists he was writing art.

Novelists, along with philosophers and psychoanalysts, are tempted by these questions, especially as they relate to composers who, more than any other so-called creators, appear mysterious to laymen. (Does that afflatus issue from God or Satan? Can a musician really *hear* all those notes in his head?) Yet not even in those fictional essays of dear Romain Rolland or wise Thomas Mann does one find satisfactory clarifications of causal interrelationships between the social being and his silent greatness. Inspiration, which outsiders always want to hear about, is really beside the point, since we are all inspired but we are not all great. If an artist is like everyone else, but no one is like him, wherein lies the difference?

Certainly artists themselves have no answer, nor do biographers, although the latter after the fact assemble answers that are presumably relevant to something—assuming that any question worth asking has only one reply. No sooner is genuis defined than it is contradicted.

A case in point is Richard Strauss, whose only paradox was in his not being a paradox. Not at least in his private life, of which no known element possibly could satisfy a Hollywood concept of artist. He had few struggles, creative or financial, was neither lover nor wit, neither deviate nor jester, touching nor hateful. If for nearly half a century he was the world's most successful composer, he was not even a monster. Nor certainly was he in any sense a hero. Specifically Strauss's life as non-hero becomes the subject of George Marek's recent interesting biography: *Richard Strauss: The Life of a Non-Hero.*

Interesting biography of a dull man? How has Marek turned that trick in a book that is more on the person than his music? I suppose by having a sufficiently contagious admiration for the music to want to show the man's very ordinariness as extraordinary. Mr. Marek succeeds. He succeeds not so much by painting a portrait of his subject as a landscape from which that subject emerges: upper-middle-class Germany in the latter 1800s. During that period Strauss, although musically famous and fortunate, represented "modern" radicalism; none of his new works was then received without a success *de scandale* as well as *d'estime.* Today with the knowledge of hindsight we recognize his bombast to have been not of innovation but of agony—he wasn't a forerunner but a culminator. One proof might be that no younger composer of value can be pinpointed as having come out of Strauss as Strauss himself came out of Wagner. Indeed, should we continue to treasure him, author Marek feels it will be due to his role as the last of the romantics. Being the last of anything seems naturally nostalgic, but it is rather boring.

The Bavaria into which Richard Strauss was born is described as a properous mixture of nectar and beer, the nectar being exclusively German music that was judged as much for its moral as its artistic worth, and the beer being a certain weighted negligence such as Bülow's magnificent conducting of the *Eroica* without a rehearsal. Some of the nectar was poured by Wagner's gods who reigned over the cultural scene; and some of the beer, at least in Strauss's case, by his own mother, whose maiden name of Pschorr was that of Munich's most popular brand. Strauss's father, Franz, a great horn player under Wagner (whom he loathed) and a sweetly pleading man, was his son's first mentor, which he remained until his death in 1905. He supervised Richard's rapid rise with pride, apprehension, and floods of advice mostly unheeded.

Richard quite early shook off his father's anti-Wagnerism, adopting the Sage of Bayreuth, along with Mozart, as his most permanent spiritual influence until "Wagner lifted him from Wagner." He shook off less quickly a puerile adherence to his parents' anti-Semitism, a sentiment further quickened through alliance with the famous conductor Bülow. Bülow was not only the most singular sponsor of Strauss's young career, but such a powerful figure of the nineteenth century that he is granted a whole chapter. And the book springs to life. For Bülow's life was one of glittering aphorism and neurotic dedication, of abject devotion (to Wagner—to whom he relinquished his wife) and deadly rivalry. He was a strong champion of progressive causes. To him Strauss owed his first regular employment, that of conductor, a profession that nourished him throughout his life as extensively as his two other vocations of composer and (he hoped) of "gentleman genius."

Another conductor (and anti-Semite), Alexander Ritter, was soon to join Bülow in advancing our non-hero. It was Ritter's belief in "music as expression"—that is, containing extramusical ingredients—that doubtless turned Strauss to the tone poem. That form, if form it may be called, he all but monopolized, despite such previous non-verbal storytellers as Berlioz, who at heart was German. It is precisely this avowed or implied need to narrate that lends certain music that plodding quality definable as German, no matter who writes it. By the same token Mendelssohn was French in heart, descending from a line of tonal landscapists beginning with Couperin, climaxing in Debussy, and decaying with Respighi and Delius, both of whom must also be considered French.

In 1887 Strauss made the acquaintance of the gentle Gustav Mahler and of the termagant Pauline de Ahna. The former was to remain his faithful colleague although "their natures were antipodal. . . . Mahler was always telephoning to God, while Strauss had his eyes fixed on the world." Pauline was to remain his faithful wife although her viraginous presence forever proved the bane of all but her willingly henpecked husband's existence. She was his only love. To his biographer's admitted disappointment, Strauss was not personally erotic—he let it all out through the music. His abstinence was not *maladive* however, or "poetic" like, say, Chopin's; perhaps more than any other major composer Strauss lived in the world, his main nonmusical preoccupations being self-aggrandizement and money and a card game called Skat. His image was far more that of a performer than of a creator, although unlike performers his real-life sensual demands were small.

But his sexual, morbid, and heroic compensations through art were elephantine. By 1905 he had produced programmatic works on two Spanish legends, those of the lady-killer Don Juan and the *gaffeur* Don Quixote, another on death, and still another on a hero's life—presumably and ironically his own. He had also composed his third opera which when reduced to lowest terms becomes a pile of scraps, but which as a whole adds up to a compelling horror about one of the most unbalanced presences of all time: Salome. It is a masterpiece of civilized barbarity in which Strauss celebrates from afar the first in a series of very perverse ladies.

He had also by now met the first (and best) of his operatic collaborators, the Austrian Hugo von Hofmannsthal. During the next decade the two would invent at least three nearly first-rate dramas, of which certainly *Der Rosenkavalier* must go down in history (despite Stravinsky's delicious remark about it: "How well they go together, bad taste and vigor").

In his portrait of Hofmannsthal, Marek's prose again gains animation. The librettist—like many another subsidiary character—was simply more intriguing and complex than the leading man. Indeed it is the discussion of minor heroes surrounding Strauss, or politico-sociological depictions of the epochs, spanned by his life, that make the book readable. The composer was always in contact with people of quality, albeit of Teutonic vintage; artistically he seemed less stubborn than simply incapable of comprehending other than the German mentality, as his correspondence with Rolland would indicate, or his naive taste in contemporary music. (Taste, of course, like intelligence, is no prerequisite to creativity.)

With the first war came a hiatus of nearly a quarter century during which—at least as Marek sees it—the composer's ideas ebbed, faltered, and, after the death of Hofmannsthal, imitated themselves with other scenarists. He passed through phases more or less dry or fructuous, but never retrieved his early élan. His resurgence into genuine orginality came only as a kind of swan song after eighty. Assuming that the musical products are enough celebrated to need little elaboration, what then was the master's life during these periods?

Well, he went to America and was a great success. He collaborated with such world figures as Reinhardt, Zweig, Beecham, even Somerset

Maugham (who translated *Ariadne*), all most successfully . He discovered Jeritza and Lehmann, who were big successes. In fact, most of what he touched turned to success. He became a classic in his own time, lived a most comfortable life (though he did not seem capable of intimate friendships), and was never, never idle. He did good things, such as helping to found the powerful GEMA—which corresponds to our ASCAP—and becoming the active head for many years of the Vienna Opera. He did bad things, such as being—if not downright pro-Nazi— at least indifferent to the horrors. (He was heard to announce: "The Nazis were criminals. Imagine, they closed the theaters and my operas could not be given!" Though, in fairness he did once write to Zweig, and during dangerous times, on the subject of Jews: "For me there are only two categories of human beings, those who have talent, and those who have not.") He appeared to be quite avid for literary culture despite his manifest vulgarity. His parsimonious conceit was finally no more accentuated than many a lesser artist's. His rather dreary sanity nevertheless produced some thrillingly mad music, for as Marek points out, Strauss was bold. It is Marek's theme, however, that Strauss as a young composer promised greater genius than was ultimately forthcoming, the reason being that even as the man could not grasp the rhythms of changing eras, so the artist within the man could not survive them.

And even as that man's life palls, so in the end does his music. In my childhood I used to ask how such an untheatrical human could have penned such theatrical scores. Today I ask: Is that music so theatrical? Is all the huffing and puffing, endless explication, overthick orchestration really so engrossing? Could it be just a heavy reflection of a heavy soul rather than a fanciful contradiction of that soul?

George Marek, although more indulgent than I, does not, with all his just appraisal, unreservedly admire one single work of Strauss. And yet he did write the book. That he wrote it, I repeat, must be because he loved something in the music. What he has given in honor of that love is a fairly valuable sociological study, though he has come no closer than anyone else in demonstrating what makes a composer a composer.

(1967)

NOTES ON WEILL

PRELUDE. As I begin these lines I'm not sure where they'll take me, for although I despise disjointed prose (and music), my feelings about Kurt Weill over four decades have been so diverse, fluid, contradictory, that they inspire exhilarated confusion. Still, if a viable critic is he who rekindles into a contagious flame his reaction—good or bad—to previously experienced works of art, I'll aim here toward an impersonation of that creature. And since there would seem to remain no method but the personal précis for approaching the history and the catalog of so public and beloved a musician as Kurt Weill, I shall divide this essay into a suite of random souvenirs. Because one thing leads to another, with luck these souvenirs may guide me to a more orderly glance at the tangible components of any given Weill score.

DISCOVERIES. During the 1950s I lived in what was maybe the most marvelous house in Paris, chez la Vicomtesse de Noailles, known to everyone as Marie-Laure. Exactly twenty-one years my senior (having been born on Halloween in 1902), Marie-Laure was a woman of fame, fortune, intelligence, power, and of eccentric handsomeness in the style of—well, look at the portrait by Balthus from whence she gazes at you with the candor of a naughty feline and whose startlingly high forehead is framed by a Louis XIV coiffure. Herself a painter and poet of real gift, she was also no less an artist's patron than Misia, and much richer. With her spouse, Charles, Vicomte de Noailles, she was responsible during the late 1920s for, among other masterpieces, the movies of Dali and Buñuel. When, because of the young couple's sponsorship of *L'Age d'Or* the Vicomte was threatened with expulsion from not only the Holy Church but, far worse, from the Jockey Club, he decided to spend the rest of his days as a gentleman gardener, retaining Marie-Laure as fond friend and co-parent of two daughters but allowing her to lead her own—as he termed it—bohemian life.

Like so many visual and literary people Marie-Laure was not especially musical, but she loved, quite literally, musicians. How many major musical works would never have been heard but for Marie-Laure, works not only of the *petit cercle*—Poulenc, Auric, Markevitch, Sauguet—but of "foreigners," too! For instance, Kurt Weill.

In the spring of 1951, among the piles of inscribed scores by Britten, Rieti, Nabokov, et cetera, atop the white piano in Marie-Laure's ballroom, I found a dog-eared black-and-white piece called *Der Jasager* on the flyleaf on which appeared this phrase in india ink: "*Dem Grafen und der Gräfin de Noailles in Dankbarkeit für die ausgezeichnete aufführung 'Des Jasagers,'*" signed "Kurt Weill." I understood no word of this, nor of the text of the brief opera, which week after week I played on the white piano with love and awe. Few other pieces had struck me so fast and left me so long with their nourishing wounds—*Les Noces*, *L'Enfant*, *Socrate*, *Les Biches*, *La Mer*, what else? And *Jasager* alone among them was German. The music seemed sophisticated and savage, yes, but what was it *about*—children's games? Romantic love? War and hope? Indeed, is music, with or without words, "about" anything? I kept the score (coveted to this day), but it was not until 1953, when musicologist Marcel Schneider gave me a blow-by-blow translation into French, that I comprehended the hard-boiled parable, thus to admire further Weill's sly and touching setting.

Meanwhile Marie-Laure told me that in that very ballroom twenty years earlier she and Charles had hosted the first French performances of *Der Jasager* and the *Kleine Mahagonny*. Gosh. Weill during a fickle French season became the toast of the town, then was dropped—by all but Cocteau, with whom he composed a few pale songs and plotted an opera on Faust—to be replaced, in this wary milieu where the winds of Hitler already stirred, by less Germanic-sounding sounds. (Irony: When I interviewed old Florent Schmitt for the *Herald Tribune*, he recalled Kurt Weill without apology as merely *ce sale petit juif*.) Here now was I, thrilled to reside in daily proximity with the ghost of Weill. If for a dozen years the tunes of Weill on jukeboxes had been a fact of life, the fact of Weill had never before hit me.

Danny Kaye was, I suppose, my first connection, if not to Weill himself, at least to *Lady in the Dark*, with that crazy 78-rpm of "Jenny" and "Tchaikovsky" in 1940 when such canny upcoming composers as we in Chicago thought—how wrongly!—more about who performed than who wrote the music we were catching on to. Four years later when we had all relocated to the magic of Manhattan, it was still not so much to Weill as to Sono Osato dancing that I responded to *One Touch of Venus*. In 1944 Lys Bert (now Symonette), the first soprano ever to sing my songs in public, was working in *The Firebrand*, which she coaxed me to attend "because Lotte Lenya, who is married to the composer, is a wonderful singer and you have a lot to learn." But if the Black blues singers I'd been raised on had conditioned me to the straight vocal attacks that fan out into tearful vibratos, I was dismayed by Lenya's continual and suspiciously European glottal quiver. In high school we had accepted Marlene Dietrich's eerie baritone without flinching, but Lenya would take getting used to. Next year, Remo Allotta (now Kenneth Remo) had a solo in *Street Scene*, which I practiced with him. The little aria, with its predictable lowered thirds and sevenths—was this the only trick "they" knew for Americanizing their melody?—did not bowl me over. But if in 1946 Walter Huston's disc of "September Song" did seem very true, it was not until reaching Paris in 1949 and seeing the film *L'Opéra à quat' sous*, with Margot Lyon as Polly, that the composer began acquiring an identity beyond his oeuvre. By the time I reached *Der Jasager* I knew each *Threepenny* song by heart in French, the language that still seems most wildly right for them. And I realized that if we must side with these or those, I fell among the ones who favor early-European to late-American Weill.

In 1960 at Buffalo University I presented what may have been the first United States hearing of *Der Jasager*, as *He Who Says Yes*. In a piano-vocal version, myself at the keys, I used my American translation of Schneider's French translation of Brecht's German translation of Waley's English translation of a modern Japanese translation of the fifteenth-century Nō play called *Taniko*. If through all this Brecht's biting comment on pre-Nazi Germany rings true, is the comment less applicable to other totalitarian situations, and is Brecht the actual author of the comment? I wondered then as I do today why Brecht gets such acclaim: the dialogue, straightforward as children making it up as they go along, is so close to the original Nō as to leave little but a credit line for the German poet. But I no longer wonder about whether the "worth" of vocal art is determinable for those who can't speak the language. Great opera sounds less great in bad performance, but no opera is musically undermined by a misunderstood libretto.

FACTS AND GOSSIP. Weill took no interest in French music, and his library, bequeathed intact to the newly opened Weill Foundation,

contains no French literature. He was nonetheless close to Darius Milhaud, perhaps because both were Jewish expatriates in America. He was
proud of the long line of rabbinical ancestry in his family tree, the first
entry of which reads: "Juda um 1360—Weil d. Stadt." But like so many
refugees, Weill and Lenya spoke only English to each other ("Is here no
telephone?"), a tender respect forever passing between them despite the
fact that in America during her husband's lifetime Lenya was not allowed
to star. He was little more than five feet tall. Were there other women—
or men—in his life? No one will say for sure, but one hears rumors of
Dietrich (whom Lenya disliked) and the notion is pleasing; certain it is
that at least two of his early songs were designed for the German actress.

THE COSIMA COMPLEX.   Can a composer reach Valhalla
without promotion? Do great artists go begging? I used to think the
truth will out, just as I thought that bad performance cannot subvert
good music. Another misconception was that players with poor technique should stick to "simple" stuff, despite the evidence that a two-
part invention ill-played is more painful than an ill-played *Hammerklavier*. A dead composer, no matter how vast of scope, without some
sort of agent ends up unknown.

   An annoying but valuable race of fauna is The Composer's Widow,
usually a naturalized German-American who, though often a musician
herself, spends the declining years pushing her late husband's output. In
our mid-century there were the Mmes. Schillinger, Weigle, Itor Kahn,
de Hartmann, Berg. Lotte Lenya differed from them only in intensity,
and with the added appeal that with her husband's death her own career
soared. But that career thrived for thirty years almost solely on interpretations of Weill's music. If it is idle to gauge what Weill's current
status might be without the posthumous luck of a Lenya (Lenya, like
Garbo or Misia, became a legend on a single proper name), one can
safely conjecture that Weill's style, at least in the vocal music, will forever
be colored by Lenya's style.

LENYA'S STYLE.   We Americans have no history of popular
singers performing successfully in any language but their own. Nor,
unlike the English, have we any convincing bilingual actors. But the
Weimar Republic did produce three chanteuses (only the French have a
word for it) seemingly as much at home in English as in their native
tongue: Marlene Dietrich, Greta Keller, and Lenya. Since I don't know

German, I'm no final judge of these women as being actually stronger in their adopted language, like Conrad and Dinesen and Nabokov who lent new dimensions to English. I do know that I thrill to them more in their guttural Berlinese. Poulenc told me, after I proudly showed him a setting of Ronsard, "Stick to American and leave French to us. You have too much wonderful poetry to be dabbling in what we can do better." The advice sinks ever deeper as time flows by, and unlike Lenya, I was never obliged to praise the Lord in a strange land.

Even among classical singers there is probably no genuine multilinguality. But if in stance and diction classical singers have much to learn from pop singers (Bernac claimed to have gleaned more from Maurice Chevalier than from any "concert artist"; and I myself, because it was in the air, filched for my vocal writing the lilt and ebb of Billie Holiday's whine no less than the clean sweep of Schumann or Chabrier), God keep us from Grace Moore's hip descendants with a right to sing the blues—there is a difference *in kind*. And there is a difference in kind between overseas and home pop. When Lenya mouths the puns of Ira Gershwin, I cringe no less than when Balanchine stages the tunes of George Gershwin. To miss the point is not necessarily to be dumb, but Europeans don't swing.

Lenya had more voice than Dietrich, less than Keller, but of course none of them had the "trained" voice improper to their repertory. She could carry a tune, she could "interpret," and like the grandest pop singers—Piaf, for example, or even Peggy Lee—she could put over a song through understatement, standing there in a little black dress, projecting the words, the *words*, eyes closed, hardly moving, the way Chinese actors hardly move except to lift a hand slowly as a mountain crumbles.

Chinese is just how her pinched soprano sounded on the disc Marie-Laure played of "Alabama Song," and the 1929 orchestra too had a rickshaw tilt. Mosquito-ish was the international timbre of all chanteuses (canaries, they were called) until the torch song of the 1930s lowered their range by an octave. For the 1960 *Mahagonny* recording Lenya becomes an alto, though retaining her role of Jenny, while Gisela Litz as Begbick slides off pitch on every note. Is this more "authentic," or less, than the old days? Hear now the gorgeous English vocalists in the 1975 DG recording. Their expertise shocks. Yet their understatement in its control has come to sound more necessary than the German singers' randomness, bringing tears to the eyes through an instrumental ensemble possessing both higher brute force and tenderer nuance.

Sure, tradition spawns tradition. But recordings can also show the gradual corrosion of tradition that the greatest music seems to withstand. (Never mind that modern gesellschaft renditions might sound like Greek to Bach himself.) Lenya sings from the horse's mouth, and oh, the fresh air she lets into a song! Yet is she, even in German, forever perfection? Observe her attack on the last word *blau*—sounding as two syllables— in the *Matrosen-Song*, as though overstruck with the amateur's last-ditch doubt that she might not have "sold" the tune. Consult then the lyrics in the Columbia booklet and see that (as a cover-up?) the word is printed *blau-au*. That reemphasis is absent from DG's booklet where the same lyrics are reprinted for Meriel Dickinson. Dickinson *is* perfect. Her perfection is based on Lenya's imperfection.

Indeed, Lenya is the model against whom all female pretenders will be appraised. Teresa Stratas' voice is ravishing and wise, to be sure, but has nothing to do with Weill. The well-focused genteel subtleties contradict Weill's admonishment to his wife: "Don't study it, it will spoil your musicality."

The male Weill voice? (Tradition spawns tradition, etc.) Except for Sam Barber, who owned a true and cultivated baritone, has there ever breathed a classical composer, at least in America, who could put over a song without making you squirm? Only Marc Blitzstein, and he wasn't quite classical. Marc with his non-voice did not, exceptionally, sabotage his own music, and his winningly wheezy *sprechstimme* was the point of departure for every male member of *The Threepenny Opera*. The whole cast sounded like Marc Blitzstein, who sounded a bit like Walter Huston, who for all we know sounded like Weill himself, who, if he sounded like anything, was doubtless not unlike the very species of singing actors that the nature of his work engendered—as Wagner's work engendered the heldentenor—for the first time ever.

BRECHT. If I am of those who could live without him, it is not to underplay Brecht's final value (I could live without Berlioz too)—it's a question of taste. Yet Weill, whom I need, would not have been Weill without Brecht. Like Thomson with Stein or Sullivan with Gilbert, Weill with Brecht becomes more than the sum of his previous parts. His notes shed dew onto Brecht's sour books (music without words can never of itself convey sourness), and their collaborations, using no musically exploratory language, were and remain like nothing ever heard before.

What they lacked in humor was made up for in irony, and for the first time since *Don Giovanni*, horror was depicted by snappy tunes.

In his recent memoir *Voices*, Frederic Prokosch evokes the German poet in a Third Avenue bar during World War II. " 'America!' said Brecht. 'It was Kafka who really invented it, but they've taken the hint, and it's beginning to look like Kafka.' " Brecht had taken the hint too. His Florida, drawn for *Mahagonny* twenty years earlier, was (like Rimbaud's *"incroyables Florides/Mêlant aux fleurs des yeux de panthères à peaux/D'hommes"*) pure fancy, but a fancy robbed precisely from Kafka's daft 1912 portrayal of our fair land. Brecht liked to say things, claimed Prokosch, "that were blatantly untrue, as though to see whether his sly subversive charm could make them plausible. . . . His revolutionary posture seemed to be a playful gambit which provided his talent with novel and shocking attitudes."

Novel and shocking are not how I find the master's attitudes, but boring and dated. But then, many great works are boring, witness Beethoven's quartets from whose violent virtues we sometimes take refuge in wandering minds, and all great works are dated, for all are historically locatable: they date well or date badly. Yet Brecht's thesis that good men will always lose and that Authority will always convince the People that they're being killed for the best of reasons, though possibly true, causes in me a non-carthartic depression, possibly because those People are not people. The citizens of *Mahagonny* are sci-fi replicants programmed to indifference. Indeed they are (the author would contend) not unlike ourselves, programmed to ignore the humanity of other nations, and ultimately of each other.

Brecht's characters are forever generalities; only through Weill's art do they become particulars. Weill is bigger than Brecht for the pure reason that he can endow the playwright's symbols with vibrating flesh. It is the paradox of music that, while being itself abstract it lends humanity to all interpreters. No Claggart or Shylock or Iago or Jakob Schmidt remains entirely bereft of our compassion so long as he sings. I weep at Weill, I do not weep at Brecht. Brecht is less heightened than simply absorbed by Weill.

Brecht lamented that his pessimistic texts, as set by Weill, always left listeners feeling good. But isn't music's native property celebratory? Unlike certain literary works—one thinks of *Werther*—music never prods its hearers into killing themselves (despite the "Gloomy Sunday" legend). Song is the ultimate purgatory lending an inner glow to even the most

despondent poetry. And composers as a breed are less prone than painters and poets and He Who Says Yes to committing suicide.

INFLUENCE. I've listened to Weill's *Violin Concerto* on eight
successive days, but can't remember much about it between times except
what it owes to Stravinsky's *Octet*. Composed in 1924 (when Copland,
his exact contemporary, was still a student), it is a finished work in all
ways but the crucial one—it lacks identity. So do all Weill's other instrumental works. Yet from the start his vocal works, with their jazzy
derivations, had the Weill stamp. No one before had used the vernacular
in anywhere near that way.

When an Englishman paints with a Yankee stroke—as Peter Maxwell
Davies in part of his *Mad King*, Britten in *Grimes*, Tippett in *A Child
of Our Time*—Dixifying his palette with those rigid syncopations, any
midwesterner of my generation will lower his eyes in pain as when his
grandfather tried to dance the Big Apple. The embarrassment comes
from the Britisher's non-incorporation of the raw material, as opposed
to Ravel and Milhaud, Hindemith and Henze, Rota and Petrassi, all of
whom filtered their Americana through such local sieves as to render it
surrealistically personal, thus to be exported back to us as national
barter. Only Kurt Weill seems somehow autonomous.

If Weill did train an occasional lens on our fox-trots, much of his
"jazz" was, in fact, not derived from North America at all. Consider
his frequent use of Argentine tangos, Bohemian polkas, Viennese waltzes,
Sicilian siciliennes, and French javas, not to mention a balladic English-
ness evidenced so early in the seven sveltely adult *Frauentanz* songs of
1923.

In art the question of influence, or indeed of liberal uncredited helping
oneself to the ingredients of others (plagiarism), is endlessly engrossing
and endlessly irrelevant. Stature has little to do with originality. What
an artist steals, if he is an artist, melts—during the very act of being
stolen—into a new shape, as though in conspiracy with, but really despite, the artist. For instance, the form and tune and key of Ibert's "Little
White Donkey" owe everything to Debussy's "Girl with the Flaxen Hair,"
yet each piece's effect is independent of the other. In the penultimate
"motionless" movement of his two-hour *War Requiem* of 1961, how
much does Britten owe to Weill's twenty-minute *Berlin Requiem* of three
decades earlier, with those unmetered phrases for the Unknown Soldier's
soliloquy, like Weill's long solo over a Hammond organ? Wilfrid Owen's

compassion and Bertolt Brecht's bitterness seem to join in their composers' nearly unbearable inspirations. (Yes, I never used to think so, but there *can* be political statements in art, at least if the art has words, and if it's not change but reconfirmation you're after.)

How did Weill take to Marc Blitzstein, who—even as Eric Bentley became our shadow of Brecht—was something of our echo of Weill? A creator by nature both thrives on and mistrusts imitators. Weill was leery lest Marc steal the thunder, while Marc, only five years his junior, apotheosized Weill as a second father. They scarcely knew each other (although Lenya and Blitzstein, a decade after Weill's death, would become partners in both art and crime as the dollars rolled in from the Americanization of *Three-Penny*. But of all Weill's acolytes (they are not numerous) Marc is the only one who gets away with it, *if* he gets away with it. Blitzstein's glory came from another man's music, but a moratorium was placed on his own after his death in 1962 until the revival of *The Cradle Will Rock* in 1983. Which implies that for the moment the world is big enough for both men. Still, a pastiche of Weill is more treacherous than a pastiche of, say, Schoenberg, if only because Weill's pieces, like Poulenc's, are themselves pastiches, and because he recomposed the same four or five pieces over and over and over. Weill borrowed from himself, of course—what composer doesn't? ("Surabaya Johnny" is an unblushing spin-off of the "Moritat," unless it's the other way around)—but the frame for borrowing was narrow.

SHAPE AND RHYTHM. Such broad variety through such narrow channels! His means were as limited as Mozart's, his operas being segmented into set numbers, and the meter for these numbers being inevitably in only a square three or four or sometimes six. Kurt Weill, like Gershwin, almost never dipped into the eccentric time signatures permitted to his times—the jagged 7/16s of Stravinsky or the 5/8s of Copland. Only at the horrific moment of Joe's death in *Mahagonny* is the rhythm ambiguous, à la *Sacre* rather than à la *l'Octuor*. Nor is there a trace of the amorphousness of Wagner or Berg, and what he takes from America is jazz that has never been metrically complex. Yes, such broad variety. Considering that Weill's canvas was rapid (to mix a metaphor), his metabolism whirled. As Gabriel Fauré, for one, was temperamentally phlegmatic (his fast music is really slow music played fast), so Kurt Weill was by humor sanguinary (his slow music is really fast music played slow). Little of his music is intrinsically slow—that is, it sounds as good at twice the speed. And all of his operas function by virtue of headlong impulse; they work theatrically through acceleration. Four-fifths of *Mahagonny* is allegro molto—a driving, socko rapidity. Those rare moments of indigenous largo gain effect in part by geographical location. Would the duet about the cranes, extracted from context, pack as gentle a wallop if it weren't a safety island drifting among live volcanoes? As for the indigenous largos of *Der Jasager*, they may be slow as the metronome ticks but they carry no repose: those stilled moments before the key word *ja* are tense to the point of excruciation. And what of the deceptively casual, unbearable "Vom Ertrunkenen Mädchen" from *Berlin Requiem*? Curiously, the only "repose" I find in the pre-American Weill lies in allegretto moments, in "Lied der Fennimore," for instance, or in "Surabaya Johnny."

LINES, CHORDS, TUNES, HUES. So his beat is almost without exception symmetrical, his rhythmic splitting of that beat simple, his tempo for the rhythm fast, and his fastness of two sorts—the utter frenzy of atoms spinning ("Das Lied von der harten Nuss" from *Happy End*) and the utter stillness of atoms spinning (the question-and-answer duo from *Der Jasager*). Now what of the counterpoint, harmony, melody, and instrumental color supported by, sometimes even provoking, these beats?

Weill's Germany, notwithstanding the heritage of Bach, was no more contrapuntal than the France of *les Six*. There had been no true, worked-out linear constructions there since Wagner, or since Reger, if you must. (Hindemith, though of polyphonic bent, does not count: his fugues are chips fallen where they may.) Weill does sometimes try for sequences of "false" imitations during instrumental interludes, or for contrasting independent strands during big choral numbers; and while these strands and sequences are compelling as sheer sound, they don't dramatically "mean" anything or lead anywhere as, say, the sextet from *Lucia* means and leads.

To what does his harmony owe its singularly infectious lushness? To simplicity. To antique recipes that, as when realized by good cooks, suddenly taste new, who knows why—is it the wooden spoon, the earthen crockery? A common triad in first inversion, a secondary seventh in third inversion, take on a Weillian cast through being approached by an unprepared modulation (which we now hear as inevitable) and being quit with a hurtful flick of the wrist, but the chords in themselves are not novel.

The melodies atop those swerving ostinatos? As with all memorable music, the melodies are what make a composer a composer, for melody is the matriarch of sound. When we remember Kurt Weill it is tunes, *sung* tunes, that fill our brain. To say that they are generally intoned, like Verdi's, to an oom-pah accompaniment as distinct from being shared, like Debussy's, with an autonomous partner, and that a chief characteristic is the falling fifth, is to situate but not to evaluate them. They can serve as classroom models, but they are also breakthroughs in that Weill's casual turns on grim words set—or upset—the traditional notion of grim and casual, like the Lehár waltzes Nazis played to drown out their screaming martyrs. Yet who will define casual? Is there a sole "correct" setting for any one text? Is the mad scene mad?

"Do you do your own orchestration?" That question so often heard by composers would be insulting were it not so weird. Well, the Broadway or Hollywood composer must in fact, for union reasons, farm out his scoring, even if he himself knows how. Possibly because Weill was granted dispensation by Local 802, he became the only theatrical composer in America since Victor Herbert (nor have there been others—not Bernstein, not Sondheim—since Weill's death thirty-four years ago) to orchestrate his own shows, a fact that lends to his art an inimitable and, to the unwashed, an indefinable texture beyond the specialness of his tunes and chords and lines and beats.

The texture comes from brass and winds playing what our ears are programmed to hear from strings; from strings reduced to a minimum, if present at all, playing what the others more usually play; and from a battery that includes nice surprises like banjos, zithers, accordions, xylophones, and out-of-tune pianos all playing, not ragas but diatonic ditties as pretty as you please.

LOOSE ENDS. Would we know his music represented "injustice" if the libretto didn't tell us?

Weill did not write songs, strange as it seems. Not in the recital sense.

Do the absolutely American tunes of Kurt Weill, like those of the other chameleon, Vernon Duke, sound American to Europeans?

Does "Lied der Fennimore" foreshadow the Beatles' "She's Leaving Home"?

Though his impulse was toward short forms (only the early fiddle concerto is protracted and through-written), could not his talent for soldering them into long forms mean that he had an impulse toward long forms?

Of course scope doesn't guarantee greatness, or else Florent Schmitt would surpass Fauré.

To judge Lenya and Weill solely by the side-four Americana of the singer's 1957 album is to vote thumbs down. Yet Weill did not have periods (those pedantic conveniences) any more than any artist. The real fact is that the young pieces of any composer are always, at the very least, "as good as," as *alive* as, the old pieces.

If in America he had used her sparingly but regularly, as Fellini used Giullietta Masina, would his posthumous career have emerged otherwise? Well, Lenya the re-creator (unlike creators whose youth is "as good as") only grew into her myth with age, and her late timbre was more interesting than her early. Like Alice Toklas, Lenya needed widowhood to sanctify her love.

What is Weill's uniqueness, his value? His uniqueness, once again, is the gift to write whole operas that are real operas but woven as garlands, operas that rise and fall and rise again, are of a piece yet mantled like song cycles in which any small part is nonetheless extractable and self-contained. His value is in being better than others at the same game, a game worth playing.

E N V O I.   Although I saw Marie-Laure every day for a decade, I hardly recall ever discussing Kurt Weill with her. Unlike Lenya, she loathed thinking of herself as History. Had she lived longer than her sixty-seven years, she would doubtless eventually have wanted to "get it all down." Meanwhile she was obsessed with being up to date, loved for herself (whatever that self may be), eschewing the notorious collaborations with Charles while assuming that documentarians would take care of the facts. But where are the letters, the interviews, the diary she kept every night of her life? The "facts" of this famous woman are all but forgotten.

Marie-Laure died in 1970. The last time I was in Paris her marvelous house stood as it had for years, hollow and vast and dark in the Place des États-Unis, awaiting the wreckers. No wild Weillian strains wafted forth from the haunted casements, ah no! But Weill is heard ad nauseam all over Paris now, as he is heard around the world. I would like to believe that his popularity gained as much momentum from the early push of my dear friend as from Lenya, even though Weill is today in the position toward which all dead composers aspire, of being able to take care of himself.

(*1983*)

NABOKOV'S *BAGÁZH*

My gaudiest musical memory is from 1952 in Paris—that least musical of cities—when for thirty April nights a festival called "Masterpieces of the Twentieth Century" offered mixed pleasures to an international elite. One after another major revivals and massive premieres, by Stravinsky, Thomson, Berg, Britten, and scores of others, were conducted by Monteux, Markevich, or the composers themselves, all immaculately produced, and very, very costly. The funds came from the CIA, a fact then not known to the diasporic jack-of-all-artistic-trades who single-handedly launched the evenings, Nicolas Nabokov.

Nicolas Nabokov has never been a public name so much as a force behind public names. He has known everyone worth knowing in the world of music, and they have all known him. If, during the fifty years that he has engaged in unremunerative pursuits to benefit fellow artists, he has been less flamboyant than a Hurok, that is because he is more concerned with creators than with performers—more concerned with What than with How.

Promoting the What, Nabokov, after the Paris success, organized similar festivals in other world capitals. He has also been a professor (notably at St. John's College, where he overhauled the Great Books curriculum), U.S. cultural adviser in Berlin, political activist (he co-founded with Mary McCarthy the Red-baiting American Intellectuals for Freedom in 1949), commentator for "Voice of America," editor of a series of books on modern music, and a theater director and producer. Distinct from these various occupations, the man Nabokov has been continually a composer. His catalog is understandably short, but over the years since his 1928 ballet *Ode* for Diaghilev, the output has been serious and solid, with two full-scale operas, *Rasputin's End*, to a libretto by Spender, and *Love's Labour's Lost*, libretto by Auden.

Nicolas Nabokov is also an author. Twenty-five years ago he published *Old Friends and New Music*, and now on the same subject but in the form of memoirs comes a second book—despite the protest that he does not pretend to be a writer. Maybe the protest is a red herring, for to read the opening of *Bagázh* (Russian for "baggage," "peripatetic") is vaguely to reread the memoirs of Nicolas's famous cousin, the one who collects butterflies. Routines of those well-off cultured infants during the ancien régime were not unalike, and the intent of both was to evoke such routines solely through a trust in memory's capacity for truth. But for the musician the debris of dreams floats in less fragrant amber than for the novelist. *Bagázh* is well under way before sounds of music are heard, and only then does it take off on its own. For if Cousin Vladimir was not drawn to music (indeed, like so many great writers he was—is—unembarrassedly ignorant, even contemptuous of the art), for Nicolas music defined living, and hence his character.

His character emerged with the revolution when the Nabokov clan established itself in Berlin. Most Russian expatriates—Stravinsky, for instance, or Tchelitchev—were of Gallic inclination, but Nicolas's long German sojourn irrevocably stamped both his music and personality. It was there he began to hear concerts, mostly in attendance with an uncle who informally but finally was his most vital instructor. He became a reviewer for a Russian-language daily ("The only way to deal with a piece of music is to listen to it well and then bombard it with the best words one can find"), and began to have his own pieces performed. Prospects of other performances, or sometimes the mere need for proximity to other musicians, led him to France and finally to the United States. Candidly he discussed connections, even affections, but his income sources remain hazy, and never a word about his health, his romantic life (though he is much married), nor the romantic life of others. For this is what he calls "a book about friendship," and so it is.

About the content and shape of new music in general and the economics that surround it, Nabokov is clear-minded and farseeing. About his own music he is reticent. One short paragraph suffices for personal esthetic, which is that he has no esthetic beyond being tonal, nonexperimental, consistently tuneful, belonging unmindfully to his generation, and composing what "sounds Russian to foreign ears." However, the texture of Nabokov's briefly expressed concerns as a composer will come as news to lay readers who "love music." He does not extol the thrill of creativity; rather he underlines the horror of amateurism, of half-empty halls, of some crooked managers, in short revealing the vulnerability (instead of the smugness) deep-seated in all true artists. Nor does he talk much about performers. If an occasional vocalist is referred to, it is never by name.

Elsewhere names fly thick and fast. Maritain, Gershwin, Cocteau, Prokofiev, all are claimed as staunch acquaintances but never heard from again, while legends whom the author met but once and scarcely knew are recalled at length. Long pages devoted to the dilapidated Isadora tell only what we've heard a hundred times. Long pages devoted to the ailing Rilke relate only what the musician told the poet (how Lenin's upper-class accent contradicted what he said), not what the poet replied. Maybe Rilke wasn't talking.

Indeed, if one thing is frequently confirmed here, it is that great artists save their greatness for their art and don't squander it in conversations, even with each other. Lesser lights sometimes shine brighter—the grandmothers, for example. One, the traditional regal iceberg in black, admonished Nicolas for six pages: "Never stick your *pipiska* into a girl"; the other sums up a lost epoch when she chides her older son for flirting with his younger brother: "What are the servants for?" And there are grand portraits of bigger fish: Of his harmony teacher, the obese and original Rebikov, who froze to death at the end of the revolution, and whose unpublicized influence on Debussy possibly changed the flow of French music. Of Diaghilev, who, far more than a régisseur, was a wet nurse and matchmaker and always in debt. Of Stravinsky, whose social moeurs and compositional processes he analyzes much more deeply than his own. Of Harry Kessler, a German Charlus; of Pyotr Abrassimov, an enigmatic ambassador; and especially of Auden, whose dying days, though powerfully fructuous, seemed lonesome and cranky and filled with longings to end it all.

Nicolas Nabokov himself is never cranky, except about Soviet Russia. The political state provokes a nagging contempt, the country a physical loathing. Thus one would have welcomed more reaction to his chosen homeland, America—accounts, say, of the noted American composers known to be his friends. For he has done as much as any Russian since Koussevitzky toward putting American music on the map.

(*1975*)

STRAVINSKY
VIA CRAFT

Twenty-three years ago, conductor Robert Craft, now forty-eight, became and remained the person closest in proximity and confidence to Igor and Vera Stravinsky. From their first meeting in Washington in 1948 until the composer's funeral in Venice last year, Craft catalogued the relationship with Boswellian acuteness. Over the past thirteen years the catalog has become public in six books, three in the form of conversations, three others partly in the form of diaries. Now those diaries, along with some final entries, have been collected into a single volume named *Stravinsky: Chronicle of a Friendship*.

The distinguishing feature of a journal as opposed to a memoir is on-the-spot reaction, the writer's truth as he feels it, not as he felt it. If that truth is no more "truthful" for being in the first person, it does contain the defining character of immediacy. The intimate journal is a literary form used almost solely by the French. They keep it as a sideline, a book about how hard it is to write a book. Not only France's authors, from Rousseau and Baudelaire to Amiel and Green, but her other artists too, like Berlioz and Delacroix, de Gaulle and Poulenc, have made literature of their lives. The genre has never been popular with non-French continentals, still less with the British, who prefer autobiography; and it is virtually unpracticed by Americans, who, with all due liberation and collective carnality, do retain a decorum toward their personal selves. (We know more about the actual life of André Gide than we do about that of John Rechy.)

Robert Craft has therefore brought us something rare, no less for its singularity of device than for its superiorty of content. Avoiding the archetypical diarist's self-portrait painted in confessional tones, Robert Craft instead portrays a milieu—a milieu as experienced through a friend who happens to be the most influential musician of the twentieth century.

No such book has ever been written on a composer. No frank firsthand reports, certainly no literary ones, exist on, say, so tantalizing a personage as Maurice Ravel; to realize how recent yet how forever lost the human Ravel has become (or Debussy or Brahms or Schubert or Haydn or Bach) is to value Craft's diary the more. In a great man no detail is boring, be it about his art or about the quotidian society affecting that art. But perhaps a life, as distinct from a life's work, can be immortalized only when it has been largely public. If Ravel was a recluse, Igor Stravinsky was always most colorfully outward.

His outward color has long been on record, first in the autobiography *Chroniques de ma vie*, said to have been ghosted by the Franco-Russian musicologist Pierre Suvchinsky, and later in the lectures called *Poetics of Music*, said to have been ghosted by the French composer Roland-Manuel. The books exude the cultured wit we know still better through Robert Craft, himself a sometime ghostwriter for the master. That Craft authored many an interview credited to Stravinsky has long been common knowledge to the musical community, though lately the public has learned of it with outrage. Why outrage? Craft merely interpreted Stravinsky's intellectual thought in communicative English, even as he interpreted the composer's musical thought from the podium. To charge that words give new meaning to thoughts, and therefore that these thoughts became Craft's, is to assume that an interpreter can invent the thoughts of a creative man. We must assume only that a great musician need not be an equally great annotator, that Stravinsky was in fact a great talker, and that there may be more than one real version of how Stravinsky lived and loved. As to the present chronicle, there is current controversy regarding its authenticity too, as though authentic art were measured by fact. Since the choice of genre is authentic for Craft, and since Craft is an artist, the result must be authentic for us, because art speaks truth even in lies (witness the royal portraits by how many great painters!). Nor is there reason to think that Stravinsky himself did not sanction those minor adjustments of time and place, which is any illustrator's prerogative.

Read the book, then, as a guide to international intelligentsia, with snapshots of the Great in discussion with Stravinsky (often over alcoholic meals): Eliot, Genet, Borges, Khrushchev, Giacometti, Forster, Cocteau, Graham Greene, Saint-Jean Perse, plus an enlarged portrait of W. H. Auden and an X ray of Aldous Huxley. The chronical is also a travelogue through a dozen nations whose orchestral forces and audience responses are criticized, along with Stravinsky's reactions—gustatory and intes-tinal—to local menus. And his reactions to all flora, fauna, and ideas, most particulary expressed in the long account of his return after fifty years to his native Russia.

The book is a diary in the real sense of depicting Stravinsky's days of finicky order in his own work and of unflagging interests in other people's. The days bring continuous remembrance of Diaghilevian things past, enjoyment of the tangible present (high gossip or the nightly phono-graph recital), and apprehension about the future pressing ever more heavily on Stravinsky's weakening flesh.

The closing entries detail excruciatingly the decline and collapse of the great artist's body in which the brain continues inventive, then of its death and burial, complete with throngs and television cameras, in the lagoons of Italy.

In this warts-and-all portrayal of a famous family, no attitude seems too subtle for clarity, no emotion too private for exposure, no musical concept too complex for elucidation. So seamless is the design that it is almost a relief to discover a rare flaw in language (*"Elle a du chien"* means "She has class," never "She's a bitch"), a contradiction in view-point ("Stravinsky's genius is wrapped—for protection from musical data—in a vacuum," although the remainder of the book shows the contrary), or a misreading of camp (Auden's "You have ruined Mother's Day" should read ". . . mother's day").

Robert Craft himself remains aloof, all-knowing, while he involves the reader in the very textures of life—in champagne and sweat, in nocturnal anxiety and colored inks, and above all in the ever-present world of musical sound. Since he is able (yet it's impossible!) to evoke that world through words, he proves again that he is not only compas-sionate and sometimes quite wickedly funny, but the most readable and intelligent living writer on music.

(*1972*)

VARIATIONS ON
MUSSORGSKY

THEME. Mussorgsky! My instant response to those three syllables is not as tingling as to, say, Stravinsky, but it is nonetheless as entrenched. When he is there the air is rich. When he is gone I forget him. What is he made of?

ATTITUDES. As an opera composer he has no buffs, not in the sense that the Bel Canto boys have. Of course, buffs care less for opera than for who sings it; they want glamour, which stems from singers more than from song—female singers at that, the ones with high notes. Glamour, "an often illusory attractiveness" (*Webster's*), is artifice, maquillage, the prerogative of women. Not that such attractiveness in the specific world of song is forbidden to men; it is simply unattainable to them. Thus in that world (as distinct from the more general world of music), female singers demand and receive equal pay because they are irreplaceable by men—as distinct from female oboists or drummers. A male's vocal repertory tends to lie in his speaking range; any man in song seems more natural than a soprano whose tessitura lies higher than her daily speech. This highness makes her a Highness, which in all languages is feminine, unique (there's room for only one queen), and an object for buffs who eschew the natural—as art itself can be said to eschew the natural. Not that male voices are less artistic, just less flashy. *Boris Godunov* is a man's opera, and since its composer's entire oeuvre extends like tendrils toward or away from that masterpiece, Modest Mussorgsky is a man's composer.

Although male superstars today are almost entirely Mediterranean tenors who vie with divas, our concept of the male voice is as the inverse of the female, a focus that descends, resonates in the dark, is "masculine," not for buffs. (If the lowest vocal utterance comes out of the classic Russian basso, interestingly all of the basses in *Boris* hover around

189

middle-C, and none ever dips below the staff. The role of Boris himself *sounds* like a bass, and the true basses in the opera sound like *Russian* basses by virtue of being conceived in a land where even choral basses can hit a cello-C, though Mussorgsky never scores them that deeply.)

As an instrumental composer (admittedly the catalog is short, at least of finished pieces) he has no buffs either, not in the sense that even Charles Ives—the one musician of our times to whom Mussorgsky might be likened—has, Ives being posthumously the object of an international cult. Virgil Thomson, in whose recent *Reader* of nearly 600 pages one finds Mussorgsky's name mentioned only in passing and unlinked to a value judgment, writes of the extremely rare category of composer "who lives by nonmusical work. The chief mark of his work is its absence of professionalism. It is essentially naive. . . . He invents his own esthetic. When his work turns out to be not unplayable technically it often gives a useful kick to the professional tradition. The music of Modest Mussorgsky . . . did that vigorously indeed." Except that Mussorgsky was part of the so-called Five, whose other members, also musically nonprofessional, had technique to burn. Indeed Rimsky-Korsakov, a naval officer by trade (as Cui was a military engineer, Borodin a chemistry professor, and Balakirev a librarian), wrote an orchestration treatise that today remains a model of its kind.

Rimsky also spent untold thousands of hours "improving" the output of Mussorgsky after the latter's death. Rimsky, less gifted but more expert than his pupil—a pupil who was his senior by three years—was impelled not by jealousy but by a generosity that literally bequeathed us, for better or worse, the Mussorgsky we know.

What did Mussorgsky living think of Rimsky's own music? According to Rimsky, he was more or less indifferent, "and it could not have been otherwise. On the one hand his fastuous self-conceit and conviction that the path he had chosen in art was the only true path; on the other hand, complete decline, alcoholism, and, as a result, an ever-befogged mind."

"Mussorgsky cannot be classed with any existing group of musicians either by the character of his composition or by his musical views." So penned the man about himself in the last year of his life, words that could as readily apply to another musician, not yet sixteen, 2,000 kilometers away—Erik Satie. Now although every composer I know would be quick to apply the words to himself, are they truly pertinent to anyone of the last century except Satie and Mussorgsky? The work of these two men floats in a timeless modal limbo that for all we know echoes the sound of medieval Gaul or ancient Crete.

It's not that they are primitive (a composer, unlike painters or poets who deal in mediums available to any kindergartner, can never be a primitive: a special expertise is crucial to even his simplest jottings) so much as resistant to the conservatory. The resistance is not in itself unusual, except that in their case it paid off. Satie, like Rimbaud or Lautréamont or indeed like our Charles Ives, became posthumuously a cult figure, while Mussorgsky, strange as it may seem, became an establishment fixture.

TUNE AND WIT. All music worthy of the name is a sung expression, be it a tuba sonatina, a percussion improvisation, an electronic étude, or a quartet for keyboards tuned to a thirty-seven-tone scale. Inside every composer lurks a singer longing to get out, and this very frustration is what makes him create. Other than Samuel Barber, is there a single composer of modern times, with an agreeable voice? Poulenc could scarcely carry a tune. Yet it is his melodic élan—as it is with Machaut and Chopin and Griffes and anyone beautiful you can name (not just Schubert and Puccini)—that distinguishes him from less inspired colleagues. Thus Mussorgsky. From start to end his *Boris* is a cornucopia of melody, skilled and contagious, from which phrase after plangent phrase flows forth. Those tunes, often so astonishingly long and traced, like the meandering Urals or (a more proper comparison) like plainchant, are nonetheless—unlike plainchant—solidified, given a beat, jelled, as though the antipodes of folk song and lied were met. There's always been a difference in kind between song of church and state, of parlor and field. Music of the Gregorian aristocracy is the casually meterless noncarnal stream of unison male choruses; music of "the people"—music to labor by or to dance to—is the purposeful "hard-rhythmed" necessarily distracting regular throbs of sexual intercourse. Chez Mussorgsky these two musics, which by definition cannot be joined, are joined, if not in intent at least in effect. Follow, for example, the opening choirs of *Boris,* or the free yet businesslike "Promenade" that winds about the *Pictures at an Exhibition.*

Like all great composers he hits the melodic jackpot four times in five. But if the surging wealth of tune in *Boris* is almost continually thrilling, are his songs that good? (Good songwriters can't guarantee good operas and vice versa; otherwise the songs of Puccini and Verdi and Menotti would be common fare, as would the operas—but there really aren't any—of Schubert and Fauré and Mahler.) Tears well up when I play through the cycles *The Nursery* and *Songs and Dances of Death*, but do those tears spring from the sad ebb of the sounds themselves, or from the recall of the utterance of the sounds by a long-ago friend, Jennie Tourel? A third cycle, *Sunless*, which I've never heard sung, seems turgid and undistinguished. Undistinguished or not, the third song, "Vacation's End," is the source from which both Debussy and Stravinsky undisguisedly stole—yes, stole—eight measures intact for *Nuages* and *Le Rossignol*, pieces that although paradoxically superior to their origin, are so similar to each other as to bear no stamp of their makers' identities. The eight measures are made up of wide-spaced parallel octaves (actually parallel fifteenths and twenty-seconds) melting through sixths and thirds into what became Bartók's "Lake of Tears" forty-five years later. Similarly Puccini's Orientalisms of a generation later seem to derive less from the mysterious East than from *Boris*'s choruses.

Apropos of Puccini, this essay was initially to be on the Italian composer as well as on the Russian. Accordingly I began to hear resemblances rather than differences between the two. Yet the Russian's chief biographer, M. D. Calvocoressi, makes no mention of Puccini, while the single reference to Mussorgsky in Mosco Carner's 500 pages on the Italian resides in a footnote: "Puccini shared this quirk [a predilection for play on words, and neologisms] with Mussorgsky, who often introduced a fantastic element into his puns which is absent from Puccini's." Although given no example, we can suppose that the "fantastic element" is the temperament of Russia—the vastness and vodka, the sloe eyes and guttural tongue, the racial mix and low temperature—as opposed to that of Italy. To outsiders Italians seem to lack a sense of humor because they *are* humor incarnate: their every act seems funny, except to themselves. If Mussorgsky meanwhile appears quite without comedy as I understand it (we all have comedy, though mine isn't necessarily yours), he didn't lack the tragic sense, rougher and more vulgar than Tchaikovsky's suave *Pathétique*, but no less grand. He did have wit, especially in the non-vocal works, all of which are programmatic. In *Pictures at an Exhibition*, for instance, the mean sarcasm of "Shmule and Goldenberg" makes us smile, but only when we know the title. Context is all. The recurring "Promenade" is amusing with its bourgeois implication (we glide with the tourist across the museum parquet), yet the motive is derived from the supersolemn Coronation choirs of the previous decade. Who knows if the composer meant this as amusing; he was of a different time and place. However, so was Mozart, and *his* comic intent is clear. But I stray from the tune.

Puccini, twenty-three years old when Mussorgsky died in 1881, surely knew *Boris*. Scarpia's seductive rationale to Tosca derives from Rangoni's seductive rationale to Marina: same rises and falls, same oily chromatics (which meant "deception" in the nineteenth century), same meandering yet purposeful vocalizing, same meter and tempo, same true beauty. Meanwhile Marina's "Polonaise" is dull and mediocre, and so is her earlier E-flat arietta, "O Tsarevich, I implore you," although it provided one of the noble strains of *Swan Lake* so aped by 1930s movies about hospitals. Marina is not a nice person, nor does music lend her a vulnerable edge as it does to crueler villains such as, well, Rangoni again, as in his Arkel-like plea, "I am but a servant of God." Indeed women are to Mussorgsky's art as they are to Walt Whitman's: deferentially treated with rewardingly singable lines, but warm as only snow is warm, indifferent. Mussorgsky didn't care. If Tourel made an impression, it's because in singing the *Songs and Dances of Death* she took on male repertory.

All of his music is peasanty, yes, superimposed upon the modality of liturgical chant. Like Poulenc he invented his own folk tunes, and all his characters sing them; not just peasants but boyars and czars and princesses burst forth with hymns and arias and drinking songs you'd swear were transcribed in a dream from some ancient collection. The themes slide easily from class to class, as when the Idiot's plaint becomes the people's plaint, and the people's mode melts into the soldier's mode, which in turn slips clear out of one opera and into another, and even into the non-vocal works of every stripe. I love his tunes. Yet when walking down the street and whistling one, I'm never too sure where it's from—*Pictures? Bald Mountain? Khovanshchina?* When young Feodor sings the giddy "Parrot Song" to his anguished parent (a delicious minute often unaccountably cut), I am taken in memory—because of the play between mediant and subdominant over a tonic pedal like blue-and-white threads revolving on a silver spindle—across many a border to the France of Debussy's heather and Ravel's lentil gatherers, and of Madeleine Grey's Auvergne.

R H Y T H M. When needed, Mussorgsky could cut an ostinato as obstinately as Philip Glass a century later. Play those forty-two famous measures from the "Coronation Scene" for a minimalist freak who's never heard them, say they're by Glass, and you'll be believed. Indeed those measures, because unchanging in velocity as well as in harmony (the accumulative excitement comes strictly through a simple piling up of notes from bar to bar, first wholes, then halves, then quarters, then eighths, then sixteenths), are actually more "motionless" than Glass's chaconnes, because upon those chaconnes, sooner or later, a tune is laid, while Mussorgsky's pattern remains an accompaniment to nothing—a grandly stretched canvas without a picture. Still, if the measures seem richer than Glass's, it's that, although devised from but a pair of harmonies—the dominant seventh of D-flat and the dominant seventh of G—those chords, being an augmented fourth apart, are as distant as any two chords can be (their only common tone is C). Glass keeps his triadic arpeggios pretty much in one family, while Mussorgsky—or Boris anyway—is plagued by the very *diabolus* from which *West Side Story* and its family rivalry grow: the augmented fourth.

The "Coronation" meter is a square four, but elsewhere and often he was eccentric. A 5/4 signature, deemed so odd in the *Pathétique* of Tchaikovsky, was par for the course to the composer of *Boris Godunov* and recurs throughout his catalog. Twenty-five years before Tchaikovsky's swan song, Mussorgsky wrote something named *The Feast*, proudly drawing his teacher's attention to the 6/4 plus 5/4 meters as "constituting the whole *chic* of this little piece . . . both Russian and, I venture to say, musical." Like Satie he endlessly reiterated short motives, but unlike Satie's motives his were likely to be lopsided. Feodor's scrumptious arietta about the parrot, for example, was first drafted in 4/4 time, then recast to its true impulse, a continuing 3/4 plus 5/4. The opening song of *The Nursery* contains, in its fifty-one measures, twenty-five unsystematic changes of meter: 7/4 to 3/4 to 3/2 to 5/4 to 6/4, et cetera. Whims of a child.

Rhythmically he was the most unusual composer of his century. Not until *Petrouchka* in 1912 was there a score that in bar to bar irregularity even remotely looked like Mussorgsky's.

C H O R D A N D L I N E. There's not much to say about his harmony. As with all born melodists, his chords come out of his solo lines which are generally spacious (in contrast to composers sans gift of tune—

Beethoven, maybe, or Debussy—whose solo lines are generally spasmodic and derive from their harmony). Mussorgsky's accompaniments by themselves lack identity (as opposed to, for example, Richard Strauss's: *Rosenkavalier* is a gigantic orchestral self-contained Christmas tree upon which incidentally is strung some vocal tinsel). They are precisely that: accompaniments—often chromatic, more often modal, seldom dominant-tonic. In most of his music just one thing happens at a time; a voice—instrumental or vocal, alone or accompanied—expounds and may be answered, but there is seldom simultaneous conversation, let alone sextets or fugatos.

Nor is there much to say about his counterpoint, which runs counter to the chief esthetic of Mussorgsky as to that of all nineteenth-century composers (save Reger). Even his choral writing is chunky and vertical rather than imitative and linear.

H I M S E L F.   The early unbearded photographs show his lips to be—like Charles Laughton's or Alban Berg's or indeed like Sacher de Masoch's—sort of masochistic, overripe but weakly sagging, while his eyes, like those of goiter sufferers, tend toward protrusive hugeness. He also resembled Christian Bérard and Bette Davis.

Was he charming? Carl Van Vechten, in his 1922 biography of Rimsky-Korsakov, writes: "Of the Five, Mussorgsky . . . stands out, perhaps, as the most important figure that Russian music has yet produced, but he is not, in one sense, so typical a figure (certainly he is by no means as lovable a figure) as Rimsky-Korsakoff."

What of his domestic, his amorous, life? Putting my not-inexperienced instincts to use, and putting two and two together mainly from what his biographers obviously avoid, I'd say that Mussorgsky was homosexual, insofar as that term is apt eight generations later for a concept of behavior that now changes every year (the concept, not the behavior). I'd add that his homosexuality—unlike Tchaikovsky's, which was "realized" though tragic (a liaison with his nephew prompted Tchaikovsky's state-enforced suicide at the height of his productivity), was probably unfulfilled. Calvocoressi devotes exactly one paragraph to the touchy matter: "He was never interested in expressing in music the emotion of love . . . those emotions were foreign to him. [He had] a horror of marriage." Calvocoressi boosts vague rumors about an infatuation with a cousin, later with "a brilliant society woman," and later still about "a great love, probably platonic," for one Nadezhda Opochinina to whom after her death was composed an *Epitaph*, the "only one of Mussorgsky's works in which he expresses his true feelings. . . . Probably this love was the secret garden of his soul which he kept inviolate and would not reveal even to his intimates." More probably he was simply frustrated by a love that dare not speak its name, and the frustration led to his own form of suicide: alcohol. Calvocoressi, remember, was writing in 1909, and he was as naive about liquor (which he calls a habit, not a disease) as about sex. "In all likelihood, " he notes, "but for his father's having planned for him, as was usual in their class, a military career, [Mussorgsky] would never have become a dipsomaniac. . . . A nervous disorder in 1858 [was the] aftermath of the regimental hard drinking." We do not learn if the other soldiers of his regiment suffered aftermaths of "nervous disorder," or if indeed they ultimately died, as he did, in a brandy-soaked stupor. We do learn that "a native delicacy prevented his ever touching upon the subject [of love] in his letters or conversation . . . and he disliked certain coarse jokes." (Despite his regimental hard drinking?)

Mussorgsky's dear friend, art critic Vladimir Stassov (he who instigated the commemorative show of Viktor Hartmann's drawings, which served as models for *Pictures at an Exhibition*), recounts an incident that the composer told him, about the inspiration for a song to his own words:

> He was standing once by the window when he was impressed by something going on under his eyes. An unhappy idiot was declaring his love to a young woman who had attracted him; he was pleading with her, though ashamed of his unseemliness and his unhappy condition; he himself understood he could have nothing in the world— least of all the happiness of love. Mussorgsky was deeply impressed; the type and the scene were firmly imprinted on his soul; in a flash there occurred to him the peculiar forms and sounds of the embodiment of the images that were agitating him, but he did not write the song at that very moment.

Is this the same idiot who has the last word in *Boris*? Or is it the idiot savant dwelling within the repressed Modest (apt name) himself? Like other unmarried composers—like Ravel, Satie—he seemed at ease with children. He was himself a child: the *The Nursery* songs on his own giggly texts attest to this. Like *Wozzeck*, *Boris* closes on the chilling utterance of the simple creature. Such brief economy after such complex horror.

INFLUENCE AND ORIGINS. The sound of *Boris* has so raided the collective unconscious that its miraculous moments—there are dozens—now resemble imitations of *Boris*. *Boris* reminds me of Poulenc's *Dialogues des Carmélites*, not the reverse, and both operas, by some crazy overhauling of time (in music there is no time!), seem comfortably echoed in *Pelléas*. Those rebellious yet so-unaltered scales that clang throughout Mussorgsky's own "Gate at Kiev" seem to have influenced Mozart's scales supporting the Commendatore, which later stamped the descending cascades in the second movement of Falla's *Harpsichord Concerto*, which in turn turn up in *Boris*. Mere scales, yet leashes at that, restraining pets that acquire the traits of their masters whose traits resemble each other.

The sport of sound-alikes is, and is not, idle. Why is it that in Boris's Act II diatribe (Oxford edition: "I stand supreme in power. Five years and more my reign has been untroubled." Belwyne edition: "I have attained to power. Six years have pass'd since first I ruled o'er Russia"), the string quartet accompanying the seven measures about his daughter's unrealized marriage could have been inscribed by Fauré, so far as the eye is concerned, but to the ear it evokes the steppes of central Asia? Immediately after comes the lament in A-flat minor (C-flat major?), a key I have seen but once before, in Poulenc's song C. There is no proof, but the composer in me suggests that the lament (like C) was conceived in—*created* in—the more sensible key of A-minor, then, found to be a bit too high, was squeezed into the next-lowest tonality, G-sharp minor which, seeming too brassy, too acute, was renotated in the madness of seven flats.

That lament, before it found its final home in *Boris*, had figured intact in two early incomplete operas. (Like Handel, like *all* composers, Mussorgsky was not one to drop a good idea, and knew that musical trouvailles were not inevitable to only one setting.) Those unfinished works, *Oedipus in Athens* and *Salammbô*, are unlikely subjects for the rigorous nationalist Mussorgsky was to become.

In Russia there was no so-called art music prior to 1840 (which accounts for the nonprofessional status of the Five and of their immediate predecessors). Unlike Germany and France where folk song and art song had been intermixed with the very blood of the land for at least three centuries, Russia, when her "classical" music was born full-grown into the romantic era, was more self-conscious about distinctions. The formal music of mid-nineteenth-century Western Europe could not revert to folk song for new nourishment, for it had never really left folk song. But Russian composers, whose classical training came from the West, found the eccentric simplicity of their native songs and dances a novel and inexhaustible inspiration. Although Balakirev was the leader of the progressive-nationalist group, it was Mussorgsky who, like our Aaron Copland seventy-five years later, became the most vociferous spokesman for establishing identity through use of homegrown goods. "Today my desire is to prophesy," he wrote to a friend, "and what I foretell is the melody of life, not the melody of classicism. I am at work on human speech. With great pains I have achieved a type of melody evolved from it. I have succeeded in incorporating recitative into melody."

WHAT MAKES RUSSIAN MUSIC RUSSIAN? Immersed for a week in a recording of *Boris Godunov*, I spent this morning by way of antidote with Shostakovich's *Fourteenth Symphony* (the symphony with soprano and bass solos). But just as after seeing a vampire movie one emerges onto the street where each passerby suddenly looks like a vampire, so Shostakovich reeked of Mussorgsky. Still, it wasn't as though I'd put on something by, say, Quincy Porter or Cole Porter; the two Russians *do* have an affinity, at least to American ears, and not just because of their use of the "Dies Irae" and pentatonic modes and shards of liturgical chant. The affinity is their spoken tongue. Although Shostakovich for his text takes verses from three poets (García Lorca, Rilke, Apollinaire) who couldn't be farther from his native soil, he takes them *in translation*. So powerful is the fact of language, as opposed to what is said in a language, that these poets lose their national identities and become Russian, more akin to Mussorgsky and to Pushkin than to the poets' homelands.

What makes Russian music Russian? The same thing that makes Italian music Italian, as distinct from Romanian or even from Catalan, that makes Japanese music Japanese, as distinct from Chinese or even Korean: the prosodic lilts and declamatory stresses, the highs and lows and softs and louds of the composer's spoken tongue. A Beethoven symphony, with its "guttural" outbursts, emphatic accents, and profound fermatas, is as much in the German language as a Debussy tone poem, with its ambiguous downbeats, frustrated climaxes, and *nasillard* scoring (for example, oboe where Wagner would use clarinet), is in the French language. Indeed French, being the only Western language without tonic accent (without one syllable's being favored over another in a multisyllabic word), is itself the impulse for impressionism, the school of suggestion. Because French by its very nature lacks rhythmic emphasis, only a Frenchman could have composed *Boléro*—that most doggedly rhythmic of exercises—because only a Frenchman would have felt the need. Despite his obsession with Spain, Ravel's instrumental portraits of that country are in French argot—they seem to lop off a habañera's final "vowel." Somehow a great artist is great by virtue of being incapable of covering his tracks. His tracks, the visible but involuntary traces of his thefts, comprise his individuality. Thus Poulenc, the most plagiaristic of modern musicians, sounds like himself even when he borrows intact from *Boris Godunov*. And thus Debussy, filching from *Sunless*, is the embodiment of that most notorious of Borges' characters, Pierre Menard, who didn't rewrite, he wrote *Don Quixote*, by the mere act of transcribing it.

If the foregoing holds true for instrumental music, how much more so for vocal settings that, no matter how ill written, reflect a composer's national language in spite of himself. You are what you speak. But I don't know Russian; I don't even know it as I know Spanish, just well enough to miss the point, let alone to judge Mussorgsky's knack for setting Pushkin's verse to music. Yet isn't a knowledge of how a composer sets his native tongue to music crucial to an assessment of that composer's output?

To my childhood Russia represented some halfway mark between the reality of Chicago and the fantasy of Cathay. I knew Mussorgsky some, but had never studied him, and had never really heard his language, until at eighteen I went to Curtis Institute where suddenly the parents of all the pupils seemed to speak only Russian. In 1946, when Tanglewood reopened after the war, Julius Katchen dazzled us with his *Pictures at an Exhibition*. Four years later I went with him on a tour of the Netherlands where he played *Pictures* (along with my *Second Sonata*) on every program. The music became second nature, and by extension the sound of the language was heard in the land. But only the sound. My copy, dated Paris, May 1950, of *Enfantines* (the *Nursery* cycle) boasts a French translation above the Cyrillic characters, a translation so obtuse in its misaccentuation that it belies my theory about how, in sung French, stresses may legitimately fall where they may. Yet if French is the language in which I memorized the songs, perverse as grafting a Siberian birch with a Provençal *olivier*, the result bore fruit: I learned all of Mussorgsky—though I learned nothing of Russian, which may be like caviar without vodka. At least that's what Russians tell you, they being conscious of their language as an artistic implement even more than Germans are of theirs. How they roll their eyes in ecstatic complicity at the mere name of Pushkin, and in impatient sympathy at our inability to seize such ineffability! Pushkin, who is Heine and Apollinaire—indeed Shakespeare—to all Russian composers!

I wrote to Simon Karlinsky, the only person I know who knows both music and Russian: "I want to write about Mussorgsky's setting of words, which musicologists say is 'new' and 'natural' and in keeping with the spoken tongue. But what do I (or most of them) know of the Russian language? To what extent did Mussorgsky stick to the text of Pushkin? Is Pushkin, too, 'new' and 'natural'? What are his metrics? Do they change from *Boris* to *Onegin*? Does Mussorgsky observe the metrics, or veer from them? Some critics say Pushkin used Blank Verse—but what does that mean in Russian? You alone can help me."

"Very briefly," answered Simon, "Mussorgsky got his 'natural' (conversational) manner of setting verse to music from Dargomzhsky's art songs, based on *prose* texts. Compared to Pushkin's original, the text in the opera is very much rewritten and altered, mixing Pushkin's verses with amateurish doggerel (just as Tchaikovsky did in *Eugene Onegin*). Pushkin's *Boris Godunov* was written mostly in iambic pentameter, unrhymed, in imitation of Shakespeare. But some scenes are in prose and there are also passages in rhymed verse. Much of the text was altered for the opera. *Eugene Onegin* is a different kettle of fish: it's in rhymed 14-line stanzas, set in a pattern which you can find in the easily available rhymed translations into English by Walter Arndt or Sir Charles Johnson."

Russia appears to possess the same rich variety of meter as America, unlike France where the concierge without even trying gossips in continual alexandrines. If Rimsky-Korsakov retouched virtually all of Mussorgsky's works, Calvocoressi has an amusing footnote apropos of Mussorgsky's setting of a poem by one Koltsov: "Or rather the mangled remains of Koltsov's poem as Mussorgsky left them. Rimsky-Korsakov never maltreated Mussorgsky worse than Mussorgsky maltreated his poets."

There are no coincidences for people who experience them frequently; it's just that such people's antennae are finely tuned according to circumstance. Thus the following words from a 1953 letter by the all-knowing Janet Flanner (who nonetheless knew nothing about music except what she liked) might not have caught my eye had I not just finished writing the preceding section: "... language certainly is what makes for *kinds* of singing, national singing, not singing methods that make the different kinds of voices, I think. The Russian language produces a kind of voice, especially in males. ... An Italian voice is not merely bel canto training, it is the singing of the Italian language, the same for the Wagnerian or lieder voice, the French nasal tenor, the bland white British voice."

Pasternak now speaks of the approach of inspiration: "The dominant thing is no longer the state of mind the artist seeks to express but the language in which he wants to express it. Language, the home and receptacle of beauty and meaning, itself begins to think and speak for men and turns wholly into music, not in terms of sonority but in terms of the impetuousness and power of its inward flow."

Poets are much more mystified by music than musicians are by poetry.

COLOR AND KHOVANSHCHINA. What do I hear when I hear *Do I Hear a Waltz?* or *Rhapsody in Blue* or *West Side Story* or in fact every single rock-and-roll hit that shrieks across the airways? Largely a coloristic afterthought, the garment, the *integument*—as the crossword puzzles say—of the organism. If the now-classic Broadway tunes of Sondheim and Gershwin and Bernstein survive by being precisely what they are—tune—the tune owes much to the enterprising garnishment of Jonathan Tunick and Ferde Grofé and Hershy Kay. What do I hear when I hear *Boris Godunov?* Tune, yes, but tune clad in the glitteringly impeccable coloristic afterthought of Rimsky-Korsakov. Now, the afterthought here is more pernicious than with the Broadway boys whose original works are, with their permission and according to union regulations, scored by elegant hacks. (That noun has become debased, but in truth a *hack* is an experienced hireling who knows orchestration like no one else.) A maze of camouflage rises between more than merely the scoring (the integument) of Mussorgsky's pieces and our ears; the very shapes and harmonies of even his tiniest songs have been tampered with by foreign hands. To whom do we owe the *sound*? Although every ballerina makes of, say, *Giselle* a unique message while nevertheless donning the unchanging garb of Adam's score, we can still know the dancer from the dance. But is there a wider discrepancy between the Borises of Melnikov, Chaliapin, Christoph, and Ghiarov than between the instrumentations of Rimsky and of Mussorgsky himself?

Someone more scholarly than I will have to find that answer. Questions about the scoring of *Boris* have been posed ever since I can recall—"Don't you think Rimsky's version is weaker?" "Don't you think Mussorgsky's version's too raw?" "Rimsky's finally more telling and more gorgeous?" "Mussorgsky's more savage and more true?"—as though everyone had the benefit of practical comparison. Well, the most recherché music *was* once instantly buyable in any one of a dozen shops, but today even Patelson's doesn't stock many a standard opus.

Mussorgsky is hardly an unknown quantity; yet there is no study score of Rimsky's version of *Boris*, much less of *Khovanshchina*, as there is of Wagner and Verdi operas. And there are no printed scores at all of Mussorgsky's own version of his operas, much less of his songs and orchestral works. References to Mussorgsky's "rougher" orchestration (and to Shostakovich's—for he too revamped *Boris*) abound in biographies, and there would seem to be as much extant documentation on him as on Beethoven or even Elgar. Where does a mere mortal procure this? (Mussorgsky has no buffs.) Schirmer's did kindly lend me their sole remaining full score of *Khovanshchina*, a forty-pound ink copy in Russian with a stilted French transliteration. Like all available printed music by the composer, this is not free of bowdlerization. Thus opinion as to the true colors must be based—at least for me, since I'm not a researcher—on tact, taste, a sixth sense.

Orchestration is a craft, anyone can learn it. Obviously it plays a part in certain compositions, but orchestration is not composition. No orchestral work, no matter how hugely and indigenously instrumental, is entirely betrayed in smaller arrangements, not even Ravel's *Daphnis* or Stravinsky's *Sacre*, which still "speak" in the piano reductions concocted by the authors themselves. No piano work, no matter how economically "made for the hand" (as virtuosos put it), is entirely betrayed by instrumental arrangements, as witness Chopin's *Sylphides* or indeed Mussorgsky's own wildly pianistic *Pictures at an Exhibition* as orchestrated by a half dozen admirers, most notably Ravel. Georges Auric once told me that Ravel, the most expert orchestrater who ever lived, had plans to write about the craft in the manner of Rimsky's treatise. But whereas

Rimsky had used extracts from only his own works as models to adopt, these models having proved successful through trial and error, Ravel would use examples from *his* own music wherein his intentions had failed. He never wrote the book, how could he? But his orchestration of *Pictures* is a lesson in how, by a quiet change of wardrobe, the character of a work may be altered without its integrity being damaged. In its rich simplicity, its avoidance of percussion and of doublings, the scoring reminds one of Rimsky's own, except for the use of what seems the inevitable find: an alto saxophone, which would have been unknown in old Russia. I, for one, am not much troubled about who toyed with what in Mussorgsky's catalog any more than in Bach's.

What is one to make of the unfinished *Khovanshchina*? It is not easily recalled, and then in a blur. From the outset details seem familiar yet borrowed—airs and effects we've always held dear but never labeled, like themes from old radio plays. Are those birdcalls from *Siegfried*? From Respighi? Or maybe from MacDowell? Why, they must be from Mussorgsky, because now come the Coronation outbursts—except shouldn't they be in *Boris*? Or am I hearing a *Peter Grimes* interlude, or the close of *Tosca*'s first act? Is that the "clock music" from *Rosenkavalier* or from *Boris* or from *L'Heure espagnole*? And Marfa's little air: isn't she quoting Franck's *Prelude, Aria and Finale*? The opening of the fifth act, with its descending bass, oboe fioritura, and similar prose text, resembles—but is somehow less convincing than—its offspring: the long prison solo from Poulenc's *Dialogues*. The pompous entry of Khovansky is very *Turandot*, while all those girls' choruses hint at *Prince Igor* even as the dance numbers hint at (were perhaps written by) Rimsky-Korsakov.

Judging by comparison, especially by comparison with other works of the same composer, is of course facile and usually uninstructive. Except that in the present case its very derivations—its point of comparison—form the framework for the piece, and that piece must sink or swim accordingly. Not that Mussorgsky is unoriginal; rather, at least in *Khovanshchina*, when he is not influenced by his own unprecedented past he is paradoxically influenced by the future—by artists who robbed him, then put their booty to more beautiful use.

There is nothing in *Khovanshchina* that is not better in *Boris*. The music may be "as good as" *Boris*'s without the mystery; but the story, despite its ambition and ultimate horror, lacks purpose, vitality, and above all, unity. Everything's too big: overstated fanfares, routine marches;

indeed each personal utterance is a Bolshoi utterance. There is a good deal more female sound in *Khovanshchina* than in *Boris*, and the roles of Emma and Marfa (only two, as against eleven male roles, but they account for more than a quarter of the evening's singing) are more likable, and even more lovely, than the vaguely nasty and, yes, melodically dull Marina. But the singing never takes off, never soars, does not harbor that wild virus of wit and folly that every great, or at least grand, work contains to some extent.

MARGINALIA. Like Virgil Thomson, Glenn Gould in *his* recent *Reader* speaks of Mussorgsky only in passing but does add value judgments, mainly through the use of the word *awkward* in some form five times in as many sentences. He states: ". . . uninhibited by considerations of technique . . . for all the unashamed awkwardness of his style, Mussorgsky was Russia's musical coming-of-age . . . his bass lines are almost inevitably an awkward duplication of whatever the melodic germ of the upper voices happens to be. . . . He knew little of the French lucidity of form. . . . But somehow Mussorgsky captures, in his own awkward manner, the troubled, mournful presence of Russian belief. . . . His harmonic effects, perhaps because of their mammoth awkwardness, are strangely believable and human . . . those contemptuously original masterpieces of Mussorgsky with their deliberately awkward harmony, their ruthless simplicity cloaking a high complexity, their disdain for the worldly temptation of the salon success."

What are those "considerations of technique" he so eschewed, since it's impossible to come by first editions? It's like the usual refrain about Billie Holiday: "She broke all the rules, and listeners were shocked, but they came to realize . . ." What *are* the rules of jazz singing? Jazz is nothing if not a broken rule. But there are no rules, much less laws, and technique is whatever you can get away with. As for those bass-line duplications of the melodic germ, aren't Bach's bass lines—and not just in the fugues—sometimes duplications, awkward or not, of his melodic germs? And what is the "French lucidity of form" one hears so much about? Did Debussy have it? Or Satie? Or, to name an exact contempoary of Mussorgsky, Bizet? Is *Carmen* so much tighter than *Boris*?

One of Calvocoressi's more comic observations: "In the light of the composer's great love and understanding of the people, a few biographers ascribe importance to the fact that a proportion of peasant blood flowed in his veins." Still, doesn't it make a certain sense to describe Mussorgsky's music as *innocent*? All those endless repeats of modal melodies—as though *Boris Godunov* had been composed in the time of Boris Godunov!

The famous low Russian basso is in neither of these operas. There are no true low notes for either men or women.

Boris is extravagant as all opera must be. In its madness, especially as recorded by Ghiaurov and Visnevskaya who sing any old notes in any old rhythm, it sometimes sounds like a parody of Kenneth Koch's *Bertha*, itself a parody of *Boris*.

Like Shostakovich, he was attracted to Hebrew subject matter for his texts. Unlike Shostakovich he was anti-Semitic.

In the operas the orchestra seldom plays alone and the voices seldom sing alone, yet the instruments sound crystalline and the soloists are always comprehensible. That is, in theater composing, the height of professionalism.

The chorus too, as in Greek tragedy, is a major personage, and always comprehensible.

He wrote political music. *Boris* works because we care for the individual. *Khovanshchina* fails because there is no individual. In *Boris*'s cast there is unceasing action. In *Khovanshchina* there is not even passion, not even in the final ridiculous flames.

He wrote no chamber music, and no "absolute" music.

S T R E T T O.   His fans are not groupies because he did not compose for female voices, much less for high female voices, but like a pessimist he thought downward. He was a primitive, insofar as that term can apply to a musician; nevertheless, in contradiction to the only other two primitives that music has produced, Ives and Satie, he was capable of large-scale works that cohered. He had wit but not much humor as an American understands it. His greatest glory, as with all major composers, was his sense of melody; yet his vocal writing was, even with choruses, mostly syllabic. Again in contradiction to the only two other great vocal writers who were also syllabic, Poulenc and Debussy, his line gave the impression of melisma. (Is this because it stemmed from Russian Orthodox liturgy?) His syncopation and asymmetrical time signatures made for rhythms more daring than any heard before. His harmony, more like organum (again Satie) than like four-part chorales, at least in sadder moments, was like his counterpoint not special, but could be, when stretched into ninths and elevenths, eminently satisfying. Inasmuch as he was, as I hear it, Debussy's chief influence, he was by extension the biggest influence from the past century upon the present.

(*1985*)

RUBINSTEIN AT
THE MOVIES

François Reichenbach's documentary movie, *Artur Rubinstein*: *A Love of Life*, has nothing to do with music and everything to do with a musical personality. During ninety minutes not one piece is played through, and those samplings lasting more than thirty seconds are accompanied—lest we get bored—by melancholy landscapes or by physiognomies deep in thought. (In *Wuthering Heights*, a movie in no way about music, Landowska was allowed to play the whole of Mozart's "Turkish March" uninterrupted.) These predigested snippets glorify the performer over what is performed. Still, the film is likable because it's an honest portrait of an honest man who is bigger than life without being aloof.

Is it coincidence—Rubinstein's physical resemblance to Cocteau? More than any "celebrities" of recent generations, these two have seemed genuinely interested in other people. It's their gift of instant friendship, of making you feel you're the only person in the world. The gift can't be traded and it can't be faked. But it *can* be transferred to the silver screen, which quite melts into gold through Rubinstein's warmth and flows like sunbeams into the audience. That audience loves the hero not because he's a great musician but because he's a great actor—a pianist who also plays the role of pianist.

The film's all him; he dominates each frame. We're never sure to whom, off camera, he's addressing those clichés about the soul, about death, about life and love and the pursuit of happiness. But the clichés ring true and are sometimes even touching because, though the pianist may be a ham, he delivers the goods. Although no artist, creative or interpretive, can ever make decent verbal replies to questions about greatness, we forgive the bromides Rubinstein utters with his lips because he proves himself with his hands. We don't weary of his standard enthusiasm for standard works when his homely features crinkle into that infant grin.

As a cinematographer François Reichenbach is capable of only two stances: total anonymity, or total personality. The series he made fifteen years ago in an American marine boot camp was like a slaughterhouse documentary: individuals became symbols of the nonindividualistic military nucleus, and by extension of America as a whole. When Reichenbach attempts to fuse these stances, as in his pornographic home movies of the 1950s, he fails, for he takes protagonists from among people we know, and that leaves nothing to the imagination. The result is neither prurient nor informative.

He is not musical in private life but that's no disadvantage, at least in his dealings with a performing artist. (The best opera directors are laymen who realize that if action is properly spaced, music takes care of itself.)

Still, I shudder at how he might deal with a composer. What I deplore is not the film but the fact of the film. Except for Hollywood fantasies of yore or for rare documentaries (notably Madeleine Tourtelot's 16-mm examination in 1958 of Harry Partch's musical instruments, or the CBS television special in 1965 of Stravinsky as public figure), serious actual musicians canonized on film are always performers, never composers. A century ago, when executant and creator stopped being embodied in the same person, the creator lost out to the executant in both fame and fortune. Fame and fortune today do not lie in contemporary music. Performers who have movies made about them specialize in the past—Casals, for example, or Antonia Brico. A composer like Bernstein is filmed, yes, but always in his role as conductor or educator. It follows that Reichenbach should, and did, overlook one precious dimension of his subject: Rubinstein's service to living composers during the 1920s when he premiered works by Falla, Albéniz, Granados, Ravel, Milhaud, Poulenc, Prokofiev, Stravinsky.

Could one really film a composer *as* composer (the way Clouzot filmed Picasso in the act of painting)? Composing, finally, is a silent affair, forever hit-or-miss, boringly intimate, and not one bit visual.

A Love of Life plays to a far different public today in New York than when I first saw it six years ago in Paris. Then it showed simultaneously in several theaters with long queues of young people waiting. Here it shows in one theater sparsely filled with immigrant septuagenarians.

(*1975*)

ABOUT TOSCANINI

Hero worship is undisciplined, monotonous, seldom instructive. What is worse, it has, in musical circles of the past century, been turned from so-called creative efforts toward the interpretive, until today finally the mystique centers around the extra musical aura of a Casals rather than the strictly musical output of a Stravinsky. It seems one does not sanctify intelligence, or even creation if the latter is contemporary. A composer may occasionally resort to sanctifying himself through none-too-widely-read volumes on esthetics. Platitudinous nostalgia, however, furnishes the much broader propaganda that deifies performers (performers who owe their very existence to the composer). B. H. Haggin's book *The Toscanini Musicians Knew* is no exception.

Inasmuch as it succeeds in its aim, the book fails not only as literature (which it doesn't really claim to be) but as well-rounded documentation (which it does). The aim was to compile some seventeen taped statements by musicians who had performed under Toscanini, thus to give future generations a correct idea of that maestro's genius. Not a single composer is represented, no member of either Toscanini's general public or family, or even anyone who apparently knew him well socially.

Five or six of the monologues are by "name" soloists of the 1940s; all the rest come from that special breed called "the orchestra man," one who ultimately loses his identity in the necessary dictatorship of the symphony. Neither group is known for its subtlety of appraisal (let alone literary wit), although the soloists emerge more forcefully if only because they have stronger egos than the orchestra men. These last, having borne a more or less undifferentiated relationship to the Old Man (as they call him) when he conducted the Philharmonic, or later the NBC orchestra, tend to speak with one voice. The voice is rarely disrespectful; retrospect, of course, lowers tension and heightens sentiment: mostly the past is golden. (Toscanini, who has been dead a decade, would have been a hundred this year.) Sometimes, though, the voice splits apologetically by mentioning those notorious tantrums: some of the men felt that the constant apprehensive fear of the maestro kept them from functioning at maximum capacity, others that it caused them to function at their best.

Performers love anecdotes and are less oriented toward ideas than facts. Certain of their nearly unanimous and reiterated utterances are that the conductor had an extraordinary memory; that he was verbally inarticulate; that his rehearsals were more thrilling than his records or public concerts; that he was totally "honest" and refused to be "blinded by the glare of his own halo," especially in his desire for fidelity to a composer's intentions (though music notation is at best approximate); that his famous clarity was achieved through stressing the linear cantabile rather than the vertical aspects of his art; that Cantelli, had he survived, might have been the sole deserving inheritor of Toscanini's mantle.

Everyone speaks of his dynamism, but just one person (significantly the only woman interviewed, Jennie Tourel) mentions his physical beauty, reconfirmed by the inclusion of Robert Hupka's eight close-ups. Everyone speaks of his piano playing, but just one person (Alexander Kipnis) mentions how it sounded: "definitely not the playing of a pianist." Everyone speaks of his kindness (underlings always display surprised approbation when the Great do something "human"—that is, ordinary—like showing a touch of compassion or even playing golf), but just one person, a bassoonist from foreign territory (Philadelphia), mentions that Toscanini may not have been all *that* holy—and this very dissension ("the way he demolished people") makes one examination more revealing than others.

Assuming the whole group of statements to be faithful (I don't question their sincerity), most are so interchangeable in style and content as to be dispensable. Both individually and collectively they lack contrast and climax, and ultimately illustrate little not already known.

Certainly Toscanini was an artist of uncanny ear and impeccable, if limited, taste; indeed, my adolescence was revolutionized by his version of *La Mer* which seemed correctly icy and grand and unreal, but it was Debussy and not Toscanini who provoked the revolution. Perhaps, for all I know and as certain of his witnesses profess, he *was* a god come down to earth; but as such he was only a conducting god, and from the living composer's standpoint he was much less significant than, say, Koussevitzky or Mitropoulos. (Tourel: "He wasn't in favor of my singing contemporary music: he said it's not very good for the voice.")

One gets the impression—though this would be hard to prove—that many of the declarations of Haggin's book grew out of loaded questions, questions geared for favorable replies. ("Did we feel the force of his presence? Always—always!") Haggin explains that the impetus for his anthology sprang from a friend's idea for a book to be made up of what those who had known Freud recalled of their experiences. The tone of such a book would naturally depend largely on who was interviewed.

By the same token a series of comments by cultured nonexecutant musicians—composers and musicologists—whose acquaintance with Toscanini was as thorough but less abject than so many of those included here, might have combined to form a more instructive document. Meanwhile the title, because incomplete, is misleading. And the content, because redundant and one-sided, is boring.

(1967)

BRITTEN'S
DEATH IN VENICE

For two centuries after the death of Henry Purcell in 1695, England produced no music of great consequence. With Benjamin Britten's birth in 1913, the land awoke like Sleeping Beauty and picked up where she had left off. As though reincarnated, Purcell himself was Britten's main influence and love.

Britten in turn is the main influence if not love of English musicians today. Like a huge magnetic tuning fork his conservatism sets their tone: some resist, but by that resistance acknowledge that tone, which they cannot shut out long enough to move toward other fields of attraction. In a sense Britten even influenced his immediate predecessors (Vaughan Williams, Berkeley, Tippett, Holst, Walton, Bax, forever awash in the so-called modes of Hellenism and of Renaissance Albion), since he bettered them at their game and they knew it.

He is the utter eclectic. Not conventional so much as traditional, he does not fall back on the set grammar but pulls it up into his special syntax. It would be difficult to find in Britten's catalog any measure not somehow attributable to another composer, yet each measure is stamped with his technical trademarks just as each overall work is redolent of his human fixations.

His trademarks are metaphors. Like all artists, Britten does the undoable. In giving nonvocal music a recognizable meaning beyond its abstract meaning he becomes, more literally than Debussy ever dreamt of being, an impressionist, a metaphorist rather than a similist. This he manages through orchestrational tours de force and through obsessional rhythmic patterns. (In his new opera, *Death in Venice*, for example, his brushed drums *are* what you hear—not *like* what you hear—from vaporetto motors; his dipping viola patterns *are* what you hear from dripping gondola paddles.) His vocal music, too, is metaphoric. He treats speech values more eccentrically, investing them with the personal pulse of tension and release, convincingly filling the empty areas of pure music with the impurities of literature.

His human fixations are chiefly aquaphilic and pedophilic. Not only is water more than mere decor in operas like *Peter Grimes*, *Billy Budd*, and the first Church Parable, *Curlew River*, but a case could be made for the warm melancholy of water submerging his nontheater vocal works like *Holiday Diary* and *Friday Afternoons*, as well as the songs in *Nocturne*, *Lacrymae*, and *On This Island*. Young males are the raison d'être of such operas as *Peter Grimes*, *Billy Budd*, and *The Turn of the Screw*; they cast a central glow over some chamber and choral works (*Canticle 2*, *Saint Nicholas*, *Spring Symphony* and *A Boy Was Born*) and, by Freudian extension, upon some strictly instrumental pieces too, like the *Young Person's Guide to the Orchestra*. Britten has never set a drama on urban ground, nor on a theme of romantic love between man and woman.

For an eclectic rather than an innovator to dominate a country's art is fruitless: his followers in aping mere manner lack the verve of outright thieves. England's youngish explorers, such as Birtwistle and Maxwell Davies, seem not to possess the force of true discovery and so have remained in the shade of the old.

Suddenly the shade starts to shimmer with new slants. Music's recent global style of willful opaqueness is clearing away. A modernistic brand of ugliness that everyone hated without admitting it is no longer being manufactured with the hope of being unpopular. The pendulum swings back to the right. Since Britain, thanks to Britten, always *was* Right, British conservatism ironically is becoming the current avant-garde and is represented by the "representational" scores of Bennett and Maw, who are in no way revolutionary or even resistant. They sprang full blown and affectionate from the head of their foster parent, Sleeping Beauty. That parent meanwhile continues producing children of its own.

Benjamin Britten's musical language, cold for some, for me had always seemed warm and contagious, open to every dialect of mind and soul. But I was miffed at first by Britten's latest work, *Death in Venice*.

In preparation for the dress rehearsal I dutifully pondered the vocal score and couldn't make much of it. It did stress the trademarks and fixations—sea, youth, "forbidden" love—more candidly than ever, the metaphors turning psychoanalytically, if not musically, verbose as though the composer were forcing his dead collaborator's Germanisms onto his own native restraint. But the aftermath, at least on paper, looked sterile, padded, colorless, simplistic, and yes, lazy, with endless recitative on neumelike signs speckling an overextended text. However, since this was a reduced blueprint (even Britten's full scores don't readily yield their secrets in print) by a musical dramatist who was nothing if not experienced, probably there was method in his drabness.

Sure enough, at the rehearsal the hall brimmed with noises of skill and beauty. What for the eye was a skeleton became for the ear—when fleshed out by an orchestra—a wealth of *trouvailles* that unexpectedly shined up the dusty narrative.

Since then I've returned often to both live performance and to the score, and realized I'd originally missed some basic points (a reader's speed is never precise). Each verbal phrase, regenerated through live performance, exemplifies and redefines Britten's claim as the world's supreme melodist. If that claim was not immediately obvious in *Death in Venice* it was because the tunes were honed to microcosms. Those recitatives weren't recitatives at all, but total melodies refined to lowest terms. The elaborate book, filled with logical contradictions, could thus be imparted without sounding silly. If this music never "opens up" in the usual sense, it does so in reverse, like explosions in some galaxy seen through a microscope.

Melodists are those who flow rather than build, who let happen rather than make happen, who write tunes rather than figures—arched lines that feel singable rather than playable, lines that sound *sung*, whether planned for human voice or for mechanical instruments. Melody is the surf in which Puccini bathed, as did Ravel and even Hindemith, breathing passively, propelled by nature more than by calculation.

Fragmentists whittle more artificial, more *complex* pieces, since fragments, like cells, innately lend themselves to rearrangement and self-renewal.

Thus Chopin, who never composed for singers, was a melodist; Beethoven was not. Mahler, primarily an orchestral composer, was a melodist; Debussy, so happy with voices, was not. Thus Webern too was a melodist, not because his pieces aren't compact like Beethoven's (they are), but because his material is not reworked and developed.

(Who, finally, is more economical, the melodist or the fragmentist? A motive is a perennial that reblossoms in endless shapes, a piece of glass in a kaleidoscope. A melody can be heard a single time, spacious and inevitable, before, like a cereus, it dies.)

Benjamin Britten is the only living composer equally skilled at melody and fragment, whether writing opera, small songs, or "pure" instrumental works of every shape. He merges these assets in combination.

Like Mozart, Britten has a knack for making mere scales more than mere. Consider the questioning dream before the phantasmagoria in Act Two wherein four E-major modes set forth diatonically from low pitches, separate and float at different speeds to four unstable branches, alight, turn to solid silver and glitter fixedly, a frozen harmony derived from liquid counterpoints, a static plate upon which a roaming soliloquy is now etched. Again the modes ascend, and still again, each time climbing higher on the same common tones, each time arresting to form frames for the nervous words.

This simultaneity—this doing of more than one version of the same thing at the same time (literally the same thing, not variations, like a canon at the unison unfocused from too closely staggered entrances)—is Britten's metaphor at its most eloquent. Listen again to the scene in San Marco where the identical litany is chanted at two tempos evoking not only the cathedral's echoing walls but a different (though simultaneous) viewpoint, or soundpoint, in the minds of Aschenbach and Tadzio. With traditionalists newness plays no part; novelty lies in perception more than in what is perceived. In *Death in Venice* Thomas Mann (also a traditionalist, carrying on rather than breaking through, so that, like Britten, he seemed to predate certain of his elders) did not tell what had never been seen, but what had always been seen and not noticed. In his opera Britten, by telling what we've always heard without listening, revirginates our ears. Such perception is a thrilling and dangerous gift, a gift that both the novelist and the composer "lend" to their respective vision of Aschenbach, and that kills him.

The transfer of Thomas Mann's self-contained and well-known story into another medium could have been, at the very least, superfluous. Britten almost turns the trick because he has *framed* the text. Retaining intact the famous words, he has focused private colors on them from all around, and transported the finished tableaux for us to see and hear upon a stage. What we experience is a kind of masterpiece, although I'm not sure why, beyond the fact that it was composed with a marvelous ear for taste and tension. Nonetheless, two extraneous elements help to explain the specialness.

First is the well-timed collaboration of a dead and a living artist. Although Thomas Mann, whose hundredth birthday will soon be celebrated, was the first novelist to write with sensible intelligence (as opposed to emotional intelligence—for there was Proust, after all) about the musical creative process, none of his contemporaries ever set his fictions to music. Although ostensibly about the pull between a creator's sacred duties and profane desire or, as Mann put it, between Apollo and Dionysius, the subject is the waning of productivity as symbolized by the "mystery" of pederasty. Britten is the only composer ever to depict that matter centrally in opera. The matter needs his British understatement, not because homosexuality is the bizarre vice it seemed in 1912, but because today it is so very normal. We go along with myths like *Tristan* or *Turandot*, but stigmas of the not-too-distant past remain ticklishly close to our nominal magnanimity. Who any longer, when so openly all is said and sung, could possibly utter, and get away with it, the words of an old man suffering from a love that dare not speak its name?

Which brings up the second extraneous element: Peter Pears, the English tenor and Britten's lifelong friend, in the role of Aschenbach. Pears, who has realized most of the composer's vocal works in Europe, is now, at sixty-five, making his Metropolitan Opera debut. For 140 minutes he does not leave our view or our attention span. What some call his lack of opulence paradoxically lends his nonvoice a dimension of expressivity unknown to more standard tenors. His sentences are intoned with enviable clarity as though invented on the spot. For Pears is a thread of the score's very fabric: he appears to belong to the composer's living concept, and to the dead author's too, so serious and touching is his portrayal. To imagine another in the role is to imagine a harpsichord piece played on an organ.

Myfanwy Piper's adaption is faithful to a fault. She includes in the libretto nothing not in the novella, down to the last subnotion and symbolic echo. With transposition from art to art certain weights, while keeping balance, switch emphasis. A strawberry vendor, ominously recurrent in the story, becomes onstage an airy *refraineuse* risking comparison to another in *Porgy and Bess*.

Riskier still is Tadzio's realization. To make flesh of the ineffable is always a miscalculation. The success of parables like *Parsifal* or *Suddenly*

Last Summer, or of characterizations like Kafka's petty-bourgeois K or Auden's great poet Mittenhoffer, lies in the invisible ideal. Tadzio inhabits our fantasy no less than Aschenbach's. To find him now in person, a *dancer*, is to find a perfectionist intent on selling his craft. Observed as a ballet sans text (which the opera is for anyone ignorant of English), *Death in Venice* becomes the saga of a flirty boy who lusts for an old man but whose mother interferes so he drowns himself.

If the Silent Ideal must be depicted within a medium whose very purpose is noise, then mime, while a bit illegal, is probably the only solution; indeed, Britten has effectively based at least one previous opera around a mute but visible child. But actually to choreograph vast portions of the piece, as Frederick Ashton was hired to do, in the set-number style of Rameau is deadening for a modern mood piece; and when the Silent Ideal is rendered as a champion athlete, the careful craft of Thomas Mann, without a word changed, is utterly violated. Mann's Tadzio is no winner, but the passive recipient of everyone's love earned not through excellence but through innocence and beauty.

(*1974*)

FOUR

POPULAR
MUSIC

ANITA ELLIS AND BARBRA STREISAND

Potential in and of itself interests me not at all (the finished work is everything!). Likewise the artists or performers who, after staggeringly impressive early work, refuse for whatever reason to continue to provide the proof of their reputations leave their fans holding the bag. Fortunately the Rare Gift is usually given to one with the drive to turn that gift into public acclaim. There are no mute and inglorious Miltons in these cold and practical times. But even the exceptions that prove the rule have their minuscule cult following and often wield a powerful influence on others in their fields who *do* achieve deserved star status.

For the last twenty or so years, those who spoke of the wondrous voice of Anita Ellis had only a single album issued long ago (now impossible to obtain) to support their claims of her way with a song. Or, as if greatness can be discerned in the performances of a single work, they would suggest going to see the movie *Gilda* and closing the eyes to Rita Hayworth's visual beauty during her miming of "Put the Blame on Mame," the better to hear Ellis's aural magic on the sound track.

After years of very private living, Anita Ellis is again before her public. By pop standards her nightly concert at the Birdcage is old-fashioned, and so is her vocal style. But everyone loves her because what she does is rare, and she does it better even today than anyone.

Her platform manner is without manner. She stands there and sings, in basic black. For occasional emphasis she'll raise a hand like Lenya, close her eyes like Billie, or throw back her head like Piaf, but no histrionics, no sequins, no flailing arms. She's motionless, but what emerges is hot with action. She can shift from a whisper to a roar and back again in the space of three notes and not sound wrong; or hit and hold onto a tone, making it melt from an icicle into a tear merely by increasing her vibrato. The trick echoes Barbra Streisand and Judy Garland, but Ellis was *their* big influence: she coined hysteria as a vocal art.

She herself claims to being influenced by, of all people, Fischer-Dieskau. One does detect more than a residue of black women, though all her material is by white men. (Ellis is white, Jewish, and well off.) The selection is small (she's been doing the same twenty songs for thirty years) but classy: handpicked bonbons from the stores of Kern, Arlen, Wilder, Weill, or from sound tracks of those movies she dubbed for Rita Hayworth.

If the repertory of Anna Moffo is deeper than Anita's, Anita is not necessarily the lesser artist. American opera stars could learn a lot about English diction from her. Pop singers do have it easier than concert singers: their vocal range is narrow, they profit from the intimacy of microphones, and their words—"lyrics"—are simpler than the poetry of recitalists. But recitalists too often rely on beauty of voice at the expense of projection of their not-simple poetry. To need to stress that Anita knows what she's singing about is to decry the absence of what would seem to be the obvious goal of singers in any category. (Rock singers have nothing to do with singing, but with recording.)

With pop singers it's not the song but their way with it. The difference between pop and classical is the difference between playing and what's played. Jazz is a performer's art, classical a composer's art. With vocal jazz, pleasure lies less in what's sung than in how it's sung. True, Billie Holiday did certain good songs often, but she also had a knack of making trash good, for bending tones until the tune became hers. We have *arrangements* by the thousands of pop songs, while songs by Schumann or Poulenc can't be "arranged" and still retain identity. Pop is variable, classical invariable. A classical piece exists in a unique state; there is no question of fooling around. Insofar as a singer takes liberties with a classical song, its composer is betrayed. (Insofar as a coloratura *colors* a bel canto aria by inventing ornaments to hang on the written phrases, she steals the music, as jazz artists do, and sometimes improves it.)

I've never heard a singer, no matter how proficient, who was convincing in both kinds of music—pop and classical. Opera divas have enough trouble scaling down to Schubert songs without adding their rolled *r*'s to Gershwin tunes. As to whether Anita Ellis could handle an opera role is beside the point; that which is *hers*—the crooning purr, the world as cameo—has nothing to do with arias.

———

Coincidence this morning delivered the disc *Classical Barbra*. Once I wrote that Streisand could handle certain arias if she wished, but her timbre is geared in other directions. (By the reverse token Grace Moore, more recently Eileen Farrell, just never had it when trying to swing.) The point now is demonstrated by this record, starting with the title. Except for the Handel, none of her "numbers" are classical—they are what *l'homme moyen sensuel* thinks of as classical. Streisand's error is to aim at the mass public rather than to put out an edition for just a few thousand dear friends.

The program note boasts that "only one song in the collection is sung in English," as though classical meant foreign. Now, these songs contain a wider expressive range than pop songs, both in tune and text, yet Streisand feels that's exactly what classical songs don't contain, for classical means restraint. (Respect without comprehension. No language talent. No musicality, considering how musical she elsewhere is. Et cetera.)

The fact remains that in our century, although some instrumentalists live by playing in jazz bands at night and symphonies by day, and some classical vocalists can skillfully warble pop, pop singers simply haven't the tools for classical. (Imagine Billie Holiday or Bessie Smith or Peggy Lee convincingly faking even the dumbest Donizetti, let alone Schubert or Poulenc or Christmas carols.) Those with technical equipment miss the point, like Streisand.

(*1975*)

AFTERTHOUGHTS ON
THE BEATLES

Dear Sir:

The two major (there are innumerable minor) flaws in Richard Goldstein's criticism of the Beatles—and which render it undependable as well as (what's worse) square, despite his hip style—are condemnation by comparison, and inability to get to the point.

To state that one Beatles record is historically superior to another is both premature and irrelevant; each is self-contained and must now be judged as such. The judgment will not be consideration of side issues like instrumentation or, yes, even words, but consideration of the essential: the tune.

One example will suffice. For Goldstein to disparage "She's Leaving Home" as an imitation of "Eleanor Rigby" is unfair: the songs are independent, incomparable. If one *must* compare them, the *point* is that "Eleanor Rigby," though set to a poem of touchingly original and quasi surrealist winsomeness, is a tune predictable and banal as the average Kentucky carol. "She's Leaving Home," while set to less compelling verse, is a mazurka equal in melancholy and melodic distinction to any of Chopin's. Real musicians, and history too, judge music by musical standards.

Ned Rorem

That letter was addressed to the *Village Voice*, which published it in July 1967. As a result the *New York Review of Books* commissioned my first Beatles article. During its composition I learned a good deal more about the Beatles than I cared to know. I also thought about music in general, which hadn't much obsessed me for years. What follows here, then, is a random series of deletions and postscripts to that initial effort. Because, like most composers, my thoughts go in and out of focus, shift, vanish like slippery prize fish that return as worthless guppies. But one grows attached even as opinions sicken and metamorphose. It's hard to clean house.

When observing careers in the making, a conflict arises in both enthusiasts and detractors: they get so concerned with what *should* be developing that they grow blind to what *is* developing; they aggrandize themselves by showing what *they* would have done, while neatly ignoring what in fact was done. If we can already situate in retrospective our homegrown performing talents like Maria Callas and Ava Gardner, or creative ones like Tennessee Williams and Jerome Robbins, we are still witnessing the unfolding gifts of, say, Alfred Chester or Andy Warhol, whose works are not sufficiently distant for us to sort the wheat from their chaff. We are cruel to shrink an artistic generation to a five-year span, and to demand always something novel from our artists without allowing them to crib even from themselves. As though any artist ever really "said" more than two or three things in his whole life! He repeats himself continually, perhaps with varied colors and formats, but with the same recurring obsessions.

We've grown intimidated by bright critics, who in turn have been brainwashed by that breed I name "suspiciously articulate composers." Suspicious, because they place understanding before feeling. (Paradoxically, understanding has never before been a prerequisite of art appreciation any more than of love; in fact, once we *understand* our love—once its mystery is clarified—that love ironically evaporates. But then, love is no longer a question in art either.)

The bright critics meanwhile, to avenge their intimidation, vow to not let an artist get too big for his britches.

They speak of the artist's responsiblity. But he has none, even to himself. Responsibility's a moral question, art isn't. Unlike ethics, art doesn't seek to change so much as confirm: art renders us more so. Should it manage to change us, it would fail as art, nor could it even succeed so well as philosophic propaganda—the lucid logic of words and deeds. Ritual, being narcotic, changes us; art, being a cleanser, establishes us. The Beatles know that art evolves from ritual, but they do not confuse art with ritual, as do the inferior popsters. Politics rise and fall, but the work of art presumably goes on forever (it may change meaning from age to age, but not shape: the *fact* of it is stationary).

Responsibility? Artists will feel no guilt about not giving the public what it wants, though they may feel guilty about giving the public what it *does* want (i.e., what it expects), about being coerced, entertaining, condescending. Artists, after all, are the makers of manners. The performer may have a responsibility toward the composer, but the composer has none toward the performer beyond the practical one of making his music performable on some terms. Since with the Beatles composer and performer are one (or four, shall we say), that particular rift is bridged. Indeed, if for the bourgeois the word *artist* now means so much it means nothing, for youth—which dictates the tone of any generation—the words *art* and *artist* are no longer capitalized: art is where they find it, in museums or mountains, Buxtehude or the Beatles, formed by what they call "the environment" rather than by one ego signed in large letters. The youth-public itself has come to be less judge than participant in what is no longer good and bad art, just good and bad.

Lolita? Coincidentally, are not the Beatles, at first sound, like a choir of male nymphets? Like the long-silent castrati of Handel's day, evolving through Tom Sawyer via Balthus? Like Tchelitchev's leaf-children come to life with androgynous cries echoing all through the tree of hide-and-seek, not asking but forcing us to listen again?

Reaction to "intellectualism" came in the 1950s through the purple pleasure of nearly all painters retreating from methods of obscurantism by no longer avoiding "communication" as a dirty word (the same painters who now eschew the easel in favor of filmmaking and choreography), through the poems of Ginsberg and Kenneth Koch, and through the novels of Durrell and Nabokov. Music, as always, lagged behind like an abandoned child, a lost but pompous Fauntleroy nobody cared about anymore.

No, Europe never took American "serious" music very seriously. France still doesn't, but that makes little difference since France has surrendered to Germany her role as musical tastemaker. Of course today the only music taken seriously by anyone serious anywhere is that of the Beatles.

Yes, the revitalization of dodecaphonism recommenced not in Germany but in France. One doesn't think of France as latching onto "systems"— schools, perhaps (impressionism, surrealism, dada), but not systems.

Though, of course, it is not countries but individuals who make rules in art.

The Beatles indicate. The pendulum will not swing back, but it may swing all the way around (if the world lasts), at which time music will quit the artificial confines of concert halls and again become what it was before the Industrial Revolution—an art for what sounds like a contradiction in terms: the aristocratic populace.

What is their genre?

In *Music from Inside Out* I distinguished France from America as follows. The French popular song has triple meter with narrational subject matter in *a-b-c* form. The American popular song has duple meter with static subject matter in *a-b-a* form. Americans relate a state of mind, the French a state of body. The difference between America and France is, in the largest sense, the difference between Protestant specialists and Catholic non-specialists.

The Beatles, being English, straddle the ocean by describing little situations, or storylets, which develop, which "happen" (but which are certainly less than Piaf-type sagas), and they do it in both duple and triple meter. (True, "All You Need Is Love" starts out in 7/4, but that comes off as a gimmick no more adventuresome than Tchaikovsky, and anyway, it doesn't relate a story.)

The genre is semi-narrational.

Their autonomy seems no longer required for their success, or even for their personality. The much-publicized branching out is indicative, because clearly good, though as yet uncertain.

Paul McCartney's score to *The Family Way* might have been on a par with Satie's *Entr'acte* or Copland's *Of Mice and Men*; like them it was not a flow of Wagnerian molasses shadowing the action, but a series of functional set numbers (three, I think, if a single hearing could judge) as neat as those in a Purcell opera. Might have been—but was not. It seemed clear that although the young composer provided an uncut jewel of highest quality, it remained for some "professional" to polish, shatter, and set that jewel. The music was disseminated throughout the film with a gratuitously psychological "rightness," sometimes omitted where most needed (when the hero upstairs ponders while downstairs a contrasting bewilderment occurs—a duet situation Copland dealt with so touchingly in *The Heiress*), sometimes decorative where least needed, as in the tasteless finale. Had the dirty work (i.e, arrangement, orchestration, and dramatic juxtaposition of raw material) been left to McCartney, it is tempting to speculate on his ingenuity; for if music can't actually ruin a movie (though in *Doctor Zhivago*, say, or *Baby Jane*, it tries hard) it *can* enhance or radically alter a movie's complexion, or even a movie's intent (as in *The Blood of a Poet*). However clever McCartney's inventions may have turned out—given his technical compositional know-how—the ultimate result would still have proved nothing beyond his instinct for fine points of theater. How much, anyway, should a composer *know*? Some of our greatest show tunes were composed by the likes of Irving Berlin or Noël Coward, proud of their ignorance of even musical shorthand. Such presumption, if such it may be called, now pervades the long-hair world forcing definitions to change at breakneck speed. As to the age-old query about who enjoys music more, the professional or the amateur, that must remain as insoluble as who has more fun in lovemaking, man or woman—at least until an auditory Teresias shows up. For myself, I no longer hear new music except visually: if it pleases me, I inscribe it on a staff in the brain; photograph that notation; take it home, and develop the film which can be preserved indefinitely. This manner of musical recall is not, I think, unusual to many composers.

How soon will these words be dated? How soon, indeed, will anyone's! Or my diaries, for that matter? Or myself? Or this universe?

The fact is, I'm already wearying of the Beatles, resenting the pompous elation their efforts effect in the hearts of my friends. Already wearying, true to my times, as one gets with anything that becomes too "in." And I'm needing to return toward that hermitage, again to meditate upon, and then compose, something of my own.

(*1968*)

AGAINST ROCK

As social phenomenon rock is ever more intriguing, though as musical experience it is now virtually nil. Writings around the subject thus prove more provoking than the subject itself, being embroidery on bright fancy more than on dull fact. Yet when such writings pose as criticism, even as sociology, they usually fail. They fail because they concentrate on the "layers" of meaning in the sappy poesy rather than on the basic music, or because when concentrating on the basic they do not judge or even appraise, but describe mere sensual experience. Not that such experience is only "mere," but it *is* rather undifferentiated, sensuality being anyone's property.

These critical matters are growing more critical. For example, the Rolling Stones' "Sympathy for the Devil" has lately received the same psychoanalysis that the Beatles' "A Day in the Life" got three years ago. Whereas "A Day in the Life" will remain a landmark in the literature of great song, "Sympathy for the Devil" is terrible music with terrible words, terribly performed. To poets or musicians worthy of the name, that contention would seem too self-evident for further elaboration. For them this chapter ends here.

The music fails at the age-old device of imposing its matter through insistence rather than nuance, that is, through literal repetition rather than development. As with all unsophisticated techniques, only high quality can sustain it, which explains the staying power of monotone Moroccan chants, Kentucky mountain tunes, Ravel's *Boléro*, the Beatles "Hey Jude." When quality is low, the effect is like that of a child's tantrum drowning error in noise, which explains why so much pop (so much anything) evaporates without residue. True ease is hard; the gift to be simple is not freely offered to just anyone. The Stones are fake-simple, without gift. The design of their "Devil" lacks arch, the sonic element is without sensibility, much less invention, and the primary harmonies are not simple but simplistic. Neither does the melody flow anywhere, nor does its stasis invite hypnotism rather than boredom.

Misfired simplicity, then, makes this music bad.

The words, too, pretend. Since "now" becomes instantly "then," their timeliness is feigned, while timelessness remains beyond their control. Mick Jagger's presumably guilt-inspiring whine of "who killed the Kennedys?" is cheap Brecht, just as the Doors' Jim Morrison's apparently gasp-making declaration "Father, I want to kill you, Mother I want to——" is pseudo-Freud. So what else is new?

How many outrages are today indulged in the name of relevance! That a man is concerned with justice—is engaged, as the saying goes—doesn't make him an artist, since art may be truth, but truth alone is not art. *Guernica* is great not because it's political but because it's Picasso. Billie Holiday didn't need "meaningful" lyrics to grab your heart; her one strange fruit came from a basket of familiar corn, much of it rotten but which, on her Midas tongue, turned gold. Her repertory was of nonprotest staples by, at best, Kern and Gershwin. I suspect but can't prove (nor can you disprove) that what we now detect as her black resentment was actually the tone of private love affairs turned sour. Her words weren't bad because they weren't "good": they didn't aim to be "with it" on every level.

What makes Jagger's lyrics bad is their commercial up-to-date before-the-fact intent.

The vocal performance is doubly false, for the diction and timbre emulate the negroidistic accents of Bob Dylan, himself an ersatz Billie. Imitation is no sin: even the most innovative art is inherited; through rejection we still seek our parents—but we *choose* the parents we seek. Yet for artists, choice grows more selective than for Cordon Bleu cooks. Primary rule: Pick prudently those from whom you steal.

Jaggers's inability to revamp plagiarism into personal style because of superficial (even dishonest: he's a white Englishman) instinct for choice makes his performance bad.

Terrible music performed terribly: hardly a rarity, after all. Yet if I do not cite fifty other cases, that's because indignation is matched only by overratedness, overratedness growing more out of hand than the very artists themselves like, say, Albert Schweitzer or Barbra Streisand (though the latter has proved rather more professional than the former), characters simply not up to their overblown image. My resentment only flowers in inverse proportion to misplaced adulation.

To balance the record there exists, of course, terrible music beautifully performed: Miss Holiday proved this with a hundred songs, as do many concert pianists now digging up nineteenth-century camp, supposedly to counteract the coldness of "our times." As for beautiful music beautifully performed, this seems so rare that we each possess our small treasure of examples, while beautiful music badly performed seems so common as to require no examples at all.

If most rock is such terrible music, why its popularity not only with the great unwashed but with every level of journalism? Is it because most of us, not being "poets and musicians worthy of the name," settle for the mediocre? Or more likely, because rock is not heard essentially *as music*? Quality has certainly never been a prerequisite for popularity, though publicity has, and today publicity concerns itself strictly with the crest of the wave that soaks literally everyone. Some who put down Louis Armstrong (try with closed eyes to distinquish him from Jagger!) enjoy the Stones because they're "now," a criterion identical to the mid-1930s left-wing right-for-the-wrong-reason veneration of Shostakovich and John Jacob Niles. Folk song and Soviet symphonies are almost invariably liked for extra-musical reasons, for what liking them *means*. But since rock doesn't mean anything as either high poetry or persuasive politics, can we like it for the music? As the musical value is low, we must hope its medicinal impact lies in its stimulation of mass camaraderie, a stimulation that comes more from the mere fact of rock's existence than from the sound. Woodstock's 1969 Rock Festival is a case in question: most of the kids didn't even hear the music. But they proved other points of value. Which is fine, but not art.

The conclusion that finally we have "art for the people" (indeed Great Art, since it speaks to all) insults both art and "the people." The conclusion presumes art must be denuded of subtlety, must spell out the obvious for common needs. Anyway, what people? The bathetic stanzas of Mary Baker Eddy, promoted and functioning precisely like rock, are as effectively persuasive to another large group. But does that group's maintaining such verse is art make it art?

Pop critics are spokesmen of, rather than reporters for, the people. They tell me my preconceptions prevent my grooving with the Stones—"You've got to *feel* that sound"—as though feeling were not a question in Debussy and Bach as well. This is hardly reliable commentary, much less criticism, nor is it relevant. Who cares how pop critics groove? If the New Criticism's visceral, anyone's a critic: we all groove more or less the same. Who are these scribblers that we should prefer their physical reactions (just a reconfirmation of our own) to their perceptions of a piece of music? Must they take literally Ortega's motto Against Interpretation? Who are they that we regard their hallucinations more than our own, though theirs and ours are provoked by the same circumstance?

They are, of course, the Richard Goldsteins of this world, illegitimate offshoots of the already dubious "music appreciation racket." In stating that a critic's function isn't to "tell us what's good or bad anymore," Goldstein renounces responsible standards, substituting hyperpersonal bodily impressions; why should he claim to "know," art now being so ephemeral? Why then bother to notate his impressions, even to collect them in a book, *Goldstein's Greatest Hits*, captured for posterity, a posterity that will hardly be "now"? The new critics' prose, the Goldstein syndrome, stems from the unrevised stream-of-consciousness inspirations most frequently submitted in freshman composition. It is a kind of rambling poetry that, since its subject matter also is poetry (the fact of rock is nothing if not poetic), defeats its own purpose, like defining a word by using the word or depicting disorder in an undisciplined style—chaos cannot symbolize chaos. Such vagaries represent to professional criticism what most rock represents to the musical world: calculated improvisation, self-promotional and indiscriminate. Of course it sells. Like rock.

Rock sells to a gigantic audience. Clarity therefore is no more required of its defenders than it is of Hollywood advertisers. One message nonetheless shines through: coexistence is taboo—coexistence with the musical past or with other exponents of the musical present. This intolerance (read: ignorance) of nonrock music corresponds to the so-called avant-garde composers' intolerance of so-called traditionalists. A contradictory attitude, since rock freaks nominally are of compassionate natures. When they admit to being fed up sometimes with much current discography and wonder where to turn, does it never occur to them to hear *L'Enfant et les sortiléges*? Do they know what it is? Is relevance only today? When is today? Can they be turned on just by rhythm, not by tune? Do they know *Le Sacre du printemps*, or even who composed it? *Sacre* does have heavenly tunes, and one can hardly say it lacks a beat. But it *is* twice thirty years old.

Their patronizing of their elders is not hip, but old as youth itself, and about as intelligent as anti-Semitism. To "think young" implies, paradoxically, that one is no longer young.

Criticism as pure enthusiasm, with its resulting incoherence, its art-is-whatever-I-say-it-is obsession, ironically resembles the stance of the forementioned avant-gardists. Inasmuch as the works of Stockhausen or Babbitt are not kinetic or sensuous, their literary defenses are not musical so much as philosophical. Grooving is not involved: one doesn't *enjoy* their music any more than one "enjoys" Kant or Aquinas. So the explicative prose of a brainy Pierre Boulez or of a brainwashed Joan Peyser deals less in mind-splitting trips than in mindful logic. In extreme forms, as in the quarterly *Perspectives of New Music*, such prose can be as funny as its opposite number in the *Village Voice*. Or in a sheet like the new *Contemporary News Letter* where one reviewer confesses his inability to "say more" because lack of a score precluded analytic notation.

Certain high circles claim criticism as *the* literary form today. Still, no matter how constructive, criticism is not self-nourishing like the novel or the sonata, but a predominantly parasitic category (which includes, of course, the present essay). The category contains highs: Auden and Sontag, Thomson and Stravinsky, all creative artists speaking from the horse's mouth. The category contains lows, and the best example of the worst that's happening in the new visceral criticism is Richard Goldstein, because he imparts no appropriate information: he does not illuminate the music but offers only his reaction to the music. His is the tone for them all, though none is so brash as Goldstein in his transparent longing to at once chastise and be embraced by the establishment.

The new critic has become a built-in part of rock itself. Seeing the scene from inside out, he lacks a legitimate reviewer's objective vantage point.

If rock is really a polemical environment, like Woodstock, it can't be reviewed as music, since music's function is not to persuade by stating social truths. Yet if rock does present itself as music, preempting the location of classics in the culture of the young, it needs literate defense. Such defense is nowhere forthcoming. So the young swallow the falseness of rock's promotion as unquestioningly as others swallow Madison Avenue, which is no more expensive and false. The pity is that the promoters, in concentrating on rock as the sole art of today, no longer bother to resent all other art, because for them no other even exists.

(*1969*)

GREAT SONGS
OF THE SIXTIES
A BOOK REVIEW

Here is a book that should interest our vice-president, whose recent attacks on today's popular music have made headlines. This anthology of eighty-two songs which "ignited" our youth during the past decade offers a heady mixture of commercial exploitation and cultural documentation.

The music, attractively engraved on high-quality stock, is prefaced with an analysis of 1960s popular song by editor Milton Okun, introduced with an essay by Tom Wicker, and visually enhanced with eighty-four pictures of Sixties people and events, the whole sturdily bound in a loose-leaf plastic binder. Such a classy product, clearly aimed at the mass market (an affluent one, judging by the high price), should appeal primarily to an older generation that both reads a little piano and likes some of the tunes, yet found the Sixties sound mostly unpalatable.

Tom Wicker's introductory essay juxtaposes the various stresses and moods of the past decade with compassionate intelligence. He feels that the governing principle of the 1960s was change, often of a violent kind. Since change touched every socio-cultural aspect of that period (technological and economic developments having revolutionized man's basic processes), it necessarily touched the arts. Wicker's observations that "much of the music of the Sixties hangs on some aspect of change," and that Agnew saw "the 'revolution' of the Sixties as a menace to American traditions, democratic ideals, and property values," go far in explaining the underlying anger of the vice-president toward this music. But it is Wicker's discussion of the contradictions of the Sixties, and not of the music (or rather the lyrics) to which he only passingly refers, that makes his essay valuable.

Unfortunately, Milton Okun's preface is not only too extravagant for value ("The songs of Dylan in this collection include the two most important political statements of the decade") but largely consists of false comparisons at the expense of pre-Sixties pop song. For example, he states that while the music of the Sixties reverberated with genius and talent as never before, "craftsmen like the Gershwins, Porter, Kern, Hammerstein, Rodgers and Hart, Harburg, and Berlin . . . dealt with a single emotion—romantic love—in a way that seems superficial and impersonal. The young Sixties generation, on the other hand, was desperately concerned with the quality of life—and this concern marked the departure of popular music from sentimentality to hard reality."

But even as songs of the 1960s expressed many concerns, for each "hard reality" song like "The Times They Are A-Changin' " any buff can recite "My Forgotten Man," "Love for Sale," or "Brother Can You Spare a Dime?" not to mention Weill and Brecht or Woody Guthrie. And numerous examples abound in the music of those "craftsmen" that show them as concerned with the "quality of life" in their time as is Dylan in his. If most of the songs of the past dealt with "romantic love" (excluding the "My Heart Belongs to Daddy" variety), a peek at the table of contents of this collection reveals listings for several dozen oozing with the same sentimentality Okun professes to scorn.

He also reports that the most important influence on song of that decade was Negro music, "previously outside the ken of popular song." Forget all blues, all jazz, Bessie Smith and Ethel Waters, even Al Jolson, whose singing was no less a caricature of black sound than is Mick Jagger's. Finally, with the statement that only in the Sixties did people sing "as they really felt" (were Billie Holiday, Judy Garland, Mahalia Jackson, Louis Armstrong, even Peggy Lee mere automatons?), Okun resembles the huckster who disclaims the ingredients of any product not his own.

But it is "great songs" rather than prose that cover the more than 300 pages of this volume. Now to suggest that eighty-two of anything from any decade can be great, let alone from the still-warm Sixties, is risky. As used here, *great* denotes the editor's preferences rather than signaling any special quality or even popularity, since hits from *Hello Dolly!* or by the Jefferson Airplane aren't included.

Nor is there a single example of art song, certainly a major genre. A songbook with so grand a claim, yet which excludes an entire category from consideration, might compare with a book called *Great Singers of the Sixties* that omits any reference to Callas. Even though pop culture is more in evidence than ever before (richer, too, especially financially), this visibility too often leads pop purveyors into smug preemption.

If we accept this assemblage, then, as a selection of fairly recent pop tunes, a high proportion—around 15 percent—retains freshness after repeated exposure. This is a track record any decade might envy for any category, and suggests that the truly differentiating aspect of 1960s popular song from the two previous decades was one of quality: the Sixties songs were simply better. Not more relevant, not more concerned with life quality, not more meaningful, but simpler, more imaginative, more joyous. Better.

A technical explanation for this phenomenon would start with the rock explosions of the 1950s (Presley in America, Bill Haley in England) that temporarily reduced music to an elemental beat. Rock then coexisted for several years with the folk-song revival, finally to conjoin with these simpler melodies in time for us to discover the Beatles.

As for the whole song (music and words), high points defy technical explanations: the best lyrics aren't necessarily linked with the best melodies. For example, in "Alfie" Burt Bacharach, as usual, builds gorgeous vocal towers over a quagmire of verse, as also occurs to a lesser degree in Harvey Schmidt's "Try to Remember," Bobby Scott's "A Taste of Honey," or Jule Styne's "People." On the other hand, while Paul Simon's words can stand independently as poems, they are attached to predictable tunes, which also happens to certain poetry of Pete Seeger, Leonard Cohen, Joni Mitchell.

As for meetings of equals, the two most beautiful examples are wildly different: "Moon River" and "Eleanor Rigby." Yet other instances of words and music which, taken separately, would appear to breed frightful mutations, somehow produce healthy offspring when united: "I Think I'm Going Out of My Mind," "Society's Child," "By the Time I Get to Phoenix." If prizes were offered, they might go to Simon for lyrics, Bacharach for tunes. But can you imagine them working together?

In his preface Okun states: "The music of the Sixties was sound as much as song." May this serve as a warning to purchasers. *Great Songs of the Sixties* contains no echo chambers, multitrack channels, voiceovers, nor any of the other apparatus the sleek Streisands and jaded Jaggers used to excite our bodies, whose reaction was the sole criterion upon which this music was to be judged (if we believe the Sixties pop critics). In this book the songs are stripped to their bare essentials—a skeleton of melody and harmony. That so many of them survive such vivisection testifies to the robust health of popular music during that decade.

(*1970*)

JESUS CHRIST
SUPERSTAR

This would-be masterpiece which calls itself a rock opera contains two ingredients necessary to most lasting religious works: frenzy and clarity. The frenzy lies in the "colors" chosen to represent that most famous of agonies, the betrayal, trial, and crucifixion of Christ. The clarity lies in the straightforwardness of structure and idea that controls these colors. The combination results in eighty-eight minutes of theatricality that, though uneven, is never boring.

The piece is neither rock nor opera, although the reason for these labels seems clear: to pop promoters rock spells money, while opera spells the most intimidating word from the "classical" world—the world to be conquered. The piece is a pastiche from Palestrina through Percy Faith to Penderecki presented as straight oratorio in *Saint Matthew Passion* tradition. If it misses greatness, it does not lack for skill and honesty.

The two young creators of *Jesus Christ Superstar* differ from standard rock Cinderellas by being formally educated professionals. Their personal competence glows from each particular of versification and orchestration; one does not sense a producer's mastermind. Composer Andrew Webber comes from a certain culture, his father being director of a London music school, himself a graduate of the Royal College of Music. Lyricist Tim Rice had just completed a serious history of pop when he and Webber met and undertook their collaboration. *Superstar* was years in the making, and the craftsmanship no less than the raw talent surely supplies one hidden level of its wide appeal. Previous "large-scale" pop works, from Ellington's purely instrumental rhapsodies to The Who's opera *Tommy*, have not been intrinsically large scale at all but medleys of small ideas. *Superstar* has organic length: from start to finish it flows inexorably.

In current vernacular Tim Rice's libretto retells the final days of Christ. His wryest angle is to justify Judas Iscariot's motivations which he expounds more sensibly than does the New Testament. Like playwright Jack Richardson, who in *The Prodigal* represents the traditionally monstrous Clytemnestra as a logical being in a sea of ineptitude, Tim Rice shows us a rational Judas anguished that God should have created him only to act as Jesus' betrayer. "Judas had no reason to suppose," explains the writer, "that the man he was working for was anything other than a remarkable person and he was concerned that Christ was getting them all in trouble by going too far." Christ, meanwhile, is portrayed as the fanatic he was, given to tantrums not unlike those of the protagonist in Bernstein's *Kaddish*, to infantile poeticizing, to both surface and depth, and to the complete self-involvement of one who believes his own publicity. In short, a superstar. His death issues from stardom as a sacrifice, a suicide, an assassination, a dissolution. He is at once Marilyn Monroe, Yukio Mishima, the Kennedy brothers, the Beatles.

To say that the libretto holds up pretty well when read alone is to say a lot. Librettos being skeletons awaiting the flesh of music, few are without a touch of silliness when standing by themselves. Fewer still are works of art, although those laying claim to literature are usually built on original subjects rather than adaptations. (The works of Colette, of Gertrude Stein, and of Auden in the operatic realm are certainly finer, by this defnition, than those of Wedekind, Slater, or E. M. Forster.) Of course, if *Jesus Christ Superstar* isn't really an opera, then its text can't be properly called a libretto but a suite of poems. As poems they are not adaptations, yet, linked plotwise, they are hardly far enough from their source to be considered original. If Tim Rice, religious poet, is more comprehensible than the King James Bible, he is not up to the style of the New English version, nor as fantasist is he even up to the grammar-school versifiers from Kenneth Koch's famous class. What his words do have that is missing from other so-called rock spectacles is believability. His religiosity is neither maudlin nor "with it" but sturdy and genuine. It may not bring young people to the fold any more than Bach brought their ancestors, but it will bring them to *Superstar* for all it is worth.

The expository pattern maintained by Rice is the formal Passion treatment of set numbers. Each character (including the mob) has his say, and each is granted his more or less differentiated stanzas. These stanzas range unembarrassedly from the sublime to the ridiculous, passing through the touching (*"Christ you know I love you/Did you see I waved"*), the tacky (*"Tell the rabble to be quiet/We anticipate a riot"*), the coy (*"Hosanna Heysanna Sanna Sanna Ho"*), the Brechtian (*"To conquer death you have only to die"*), the upsetting (*"Tell me Christ how you feel tonight/Do you plan to put up a fight"*), the pop-bathetic (*"He's a man he's just a man/And I've seen many men before"*), the folksy (*"I dreamed I met a Galilean/A most amazing man/He had that look you rarely find/The haunting hunted kind"*), the glee club (*"When we retire we can write the gospels/So they'll still talk about us when we've died"*), and the cynically apocalyptic (*"Did you mean to die like that? Was that a mistake or/Did you know your messy death would be a record-breaker?"*).

As images the verses lack distinction; as drama they work like charms.

Andrew Webber's score derives totally from the music of others, but eclecticism is no sin and greater than he have fed off what's around. The true artist has never avoided stealing outrageously, stamping the theft with his own brand, and reselling it. If he gets no buyers he is no artist.

The whole overture belies the fact that we are to hear a rock opera. Within three minutes, and before any solo voice is heard, composer Webber has treated his listener to a nearly indigestible stew of Hindu ragas, of Rodgers's *Slaughter on Tenth Avenue*, Prokofiev's *Age of Steel*, Strouse's *Bye Bye Birdie*, Honegger's *Pacific 231*, Bernstein's *Fancy Free*, Copland's *Rodeo*, Grieg's *Piano Concerto*, and the "heavenly choirs" of *Lost Horizon* that blur into Ligeti's choirs stolen for *2001*. Yet within those same three minutes a personal energy has been established that will crackle for the next hour and a half.

Much of the recipe is accented with jagged 5/4 and 7/8 meters favored by America in the 1940s. Here too is Kurt Weill of the 1930s (in the "Hosanna" number, for example, or Jesus' solo about "The End"), and Bacharach of the 1960s ("I Don't Know How to Love Him"), and Gershwin of the 1920s (especially in those well-rehearsed cross rhythms in the big choral affairs), and even Tchaikovsky of the 1890s (hear those three *Nutcracker* flutes at the start of the section called "Tuesday," not to mention the entire Epilogue). There is Charles Ives, too, and Richard Strauss; indeed, those two composers are superimposed in the final chords.

Why the emphasis on influences? Because there are so many. Young composers often labor in the shadow of older ones, but Andrew Webber is almost as blacked out by the abundance of his heroes as Anna Russell when, in a hysterical mishmash of arias, she demonstrates how operas are made. (Curiously he diplays little trace of his British lineage, and none at all of Debussy and Ravel, the two Frenchmen who for generations were the chief long-hair lenders to the jazz world.) Where then lies Webber's originality? What is his "color"?

His originality, like anyone's, lies in the ability to take a chance and win. His color is the color of speed. The risk he ran here, whether by contrivance or by adrenergic dictates, was to use nearly all fast tempos. If one can assert that the most touching portion from the great classical cantatas are slow and introspective, then *Superstar*'s grandeur owes nothing to the past. Webber's music loses effectiveness in proportion as it quiets down; the somber moments, few though they be, are the least compelling. Where the text would indicate to anyone but Webber a reflective pause, a hush, he goes hog-wild. His color then is the maintenance of fever pulse, a *trouvaille* utterly appropriate to the story's tension, and reminiscent only of itself.

The male singers, mostly young Englishmen and all of them white, perform as is customary like the stereotype of preadolescent black Americans. The style comes to us twice filtered through the Beatles and the Stones, though the personalities of *Superstar* exude more carnality than Lennon and less snottiness than Jagger. The histrionics of Murray Head as Judas are hair-raising, while the Jesus of Ian Gillian comes off nicely as a revivalist imitating Judy Garland. Also notable are the Rex Harrisonish interpretation of Pilate by Chicagoan Barry Dennen and the dapper Herod of Mike d'Abo, who ticks off the one showstopper, a very funny, very cruel, Tom Lehrer—type soft-shoe number: "So you are the Christ you're the great Jesus Christ/ Prove to me that you're no fool walk across my swimming pool." None of these soloists has a "real" voice, not even in the Sinatra sense, yet paradoxically all are virtuosos, being disciplined actors able to carry the simple tunes assigned them.

The main female singer is Yvonne Ellimann, who, as groupie Mary Magdalene, combines the weaker points of Baez, Streisand, and the late Gladys Swarthout. Her tainted purity becomes insipidity, her emotionality a whine, while her idea of a persuasive mannerism is the glottal stop. Yet somehow she brings it off, she *works*, in a pop-stylist sort of way. Her songs end when they end.

In fact everything works, even the chorus which at best is very Southern Gospel, as in "Christ You Know I Love You," and at worst performs with the musicality of an exhausted hockey team, as in "Look at All My Trials"—the trashiest of a fair bit of trashy stuff. The instrumentation works too, the whole event being garnished by a chamber ensemble with solo guitars, by a children's choir as well as the large chorus (plus a special group named the Trinidad Singers), by an up-to-date Moog synthesizer, and finally by a full symphony orchestra (because of its identity with the classical world? But composers of that world now write mostly for the small combos formerly associated with pop). The workability of the whole concept, from foolproof title to last detail of liaison, stems not primarily from rare class but from an absolutely professional continuity. And the brashness is more moving than the art; the highest points of all this fervor do not equal the simplest Beatles love song.

The critical material thus far published on this best-selling enterprise deals with the "breakthrough," the message, the daring, the sociological value. There has been no assessment of the artistry of the text, much less of the music. This same situation existed two years ago around the Rolling Stones, and around the Beatles of the mid-1960s when their style began to be extolled as serious art by a new breed of critics. Not being trained musicians so much as self-appointed spokesmen for the youth market, pop critics dealt with musical matters in an extramusical manner: If the lyrics hit the nail on the head they made music.

Now, however, America and England (the only countries where these matters matter on a high plane), having learned that art is where you find it, anticipate the paid critics by crying *masterpiece*! Not only swinging preachers but middlebrow clerics join the throng, quick to find *Superstar* an antidote to almost everything bad: acid, obscenity, and the antics of Virgil Fox.

The piece's political powers being assured, this essay has tried to investigate the more delicate elements. It will be interesting to see how the projected Broadway production fares. Somehow the available version seems so ideally suited to the recording medium that a visual approach could gild the lily. Still, when *Saint Matthew Passion* has been announced for staging next season, it is only for *Superstar*'s producers to try their luck. The big sell is part and parcel of such a venture; if we apply *Superstar*'s moral to the fact of its current acclaim, then by its own definition it will suffer derision and misunderstanding. Meanwhile the oratorio, though not solid nourishment in our time of famine, is welcome as champagne during a drought.

(*1971*)

LAST THOUGHTS ON
THE BEATLES

The French have said America is the only country in history that passed from barbarism to decadence without an intervening civilization. One could appraise the Beatles with a twist on that bon mot: they are the only autonomous musical entity of this generation to have passed from barbarism through decadence and ended up thoroughly civilized.

Barbarism, in my definition, means health as expressed through the needs of childliness. All artists are children, and inasmuch as they grow up (i.e., intellectualize themselves) they cease to be artists. The first Beatles songs represent a violent physical reaction to those sophisticated cerebrations of the largely non-vocal, non-danceable music, both jazz and "serious," of the 1950s. Their sound (let us forget their lyrics for the moment) excited the body more than the mind for the first time since the war, and corporal stimulation was always music's function. This function they reestablished by the most ancient and simplest of fashions: by giving us tunes well wrought and instantly memorable—the tunes of spontaneous aborigines—though as yet unstamped with their now quickly recognizable individuality.

Decadence, as I understand the term, is the appeal of corruption, an attracting emergence from the beginnings of decay: in a word, art, art that achieves its highest pinnacle on the eve of an essentially non-artistic organization's downfall. For, as we know, art does not nourish or even instruct; it reflects. Therefore by definition art comes at the end, to oppose, as in a mirror. When art grows too ornamental—that is, too self-imitative or unrelated to the outside—it also suffers the decay it has reflected, and putrifies in its turn. Inasmuch as decadence, then, possesses non-negative connotations, the second of the Beatles' "phases," as represented by *Rubber Soul*, *Revolver*, and *Sgt. Pepper*, is decadent. These recordings have been so often shown, by literary critics, as climactic in our world's culture, both sociological and artistic, that they require little re-emphasis here. But they depict the group at the height of its orginality.

Civilization, to my way of thinking, implies boredom. It is a phenomenon that does not precede but *succeeds* decadence, which occurs, so to speak, after the fall, and which signifies a torturous rebuilding that must of necessity forgo the healthy abandon of both barbarism and decadence. Ironic and contradictory though this may seem, the *Magical Mystery Tour* lacks both mystery and magic and becomes a tour back to the tameness of civilization, a civilization where adults unconvincingly play at being children.

When I call the Beatles "an autonomous musical entity" I mean that, like Stravinsky, they are a self-contained creative unit. (I am less concerned with them here as performers—or at best must classify them as composer-performers, since that reconciliation seems to be the mode today.) When I speak of their "phases" I mean that, like Stravinsky, they have already gone through periods distant enough to be judged in retrospect. Yet when I mention "this generation" I mean less the literal span between the birth of parents and the birth of their offspring, than the current psychological span of an art craze—about four years. The present generation is therefore the one that has revived sheer fun as opposed, say, to Susan Sontag's already vanishing *new art* which she maintained "precludes pleasure in the familiar sense—the pleasure of a melody that one can hum after leaving the concert hall."

So much for definitions.

Only five of the eleven songs on the Beatles' new *Magical Mystery Tour* album are new. Two of the others, "Penny Lane" and "Strawberry Fields Forever," predate the famous *Sgt. Pepper* release, and each is a Schubertian gem of highest polish. The four remaining pieces were issued as singles over the past months; two of those sound like postscripts: their mood is the same as, but their quality is lower than, the colorful message of *Sgt. Pepper*. "Baby You're a Rich Man" has a contagiously clever melody and quite funny words. But "All You Need Is Love" is pretentious without charm: the preface in "bold" 7/4 meter, the interpolations of "La Marseillaise" and "Greensleeves," the superfluous cute ending (like that of "Strawberry Fields," which almost cancels out, or at least apologizes for, the genuine expressivity that precedes it, just as the icon-oclastic French composers of the 1920s would ruin perfectly straight-forward pieces with campy nose-thumbing swirls at the finish)—such devices, which are all too transparent, one finds analyzed by presumably intelligent reviewers for their "deeper meaning."

The other two singles foreshadow the substance of the latest songs. "Hello Goodbye" is both corny and tiresome; corny because it used old-hat harmonies (in this case the Neapolitan Sixth) with no unusual point of view, tiresome because of its self-confident insistence on a bad tune as though it were good. "I Am the Walrus" is classier and has even become something of a hit on jukeboxes. Musically, however, it is built from watered-down Old English modality, given a "beat," drenched in exotic orchestration, and passed off as new. As for the words, I await their interpretation in our learned reviews. Certainly they have convo-luted "in" references (to "Lucy in the Sky," for example). Mostly they are whimsical in Lewis Carroll style, and quite serviceable to the needs of song, being syllables that impel the voice to rise and fall. If, however, they contain a philosophy of today's despair, this intention escapes me. But then, of course, I'm over thirty. (Parenthetically, I often wonder if John Lennon smiles bemusedly at the serious diagnoses of his verse. It's always seemed to me that it is the critics who think of a "meaning," then write it down. The poet writes "it" down, then thinks of a meaning. The *meaning*s written down by critics are usually drawn from the poets who, if they were to read the multi-convoluted ramifications credited to their works, would turn over in their already unquiet graves. The most recent grave is that pictured on the *Sgt. Pepper* album cover, a rictus amazed at the wise essays "interpreting" it.)

The album cover of *Magical Mystery Tour* pictures the young musicians in fantastical garb, one nice walrus, and three less identifiable furry creatures. Inside is a twenty-four-page "full-color picture book" con-taining stills from their forthcoming television extravaganza and a series of comic strips narrating the (I guess) story of the film. Of the film's five new songs the least interesting (the most "civilized") is that title tune, a de-energized replica of *Sgt. Pepper*'s title tune. In both, the singers impersonate fairground barkers seducing us with their delicious cockney into new dimensions of adventure. But while we might be tempted by *Sgt. Pepper's Lonely Hearts Club Band*, whose words and music are poignant and witty, the *Magical Mystery Tour* declaims a tune of slight character set to rhymes as trite as a Cook's Travel Service brochure ("I've got an invitation/To make a reservation").

"The Fool on the Hill," if we want to make comparisons (and who doesn't), corresponds to the previous collection's "She's Leaving Home," or to the still earlier "Eleanor Rigby." Meaning that an exquisite melody—called ballad in pop parlance—illustrates bittersweet words with moral overtones. In this case the subject matter (as with "Michelle") is less narrational, more situational: unlike the other two songs "The Fool on the Hill" describes a state of mind rather than a state of body. The Fool is the misunderstood poet, unloved and dull on the surface, sensitive and philosophic at heart, like the idiot in *Boris Godunov*. The melody sweeps upward with gentle grace, and the interludes come sweetly garlanded with an icing of flutes and recorders. Yet despite the pleasant taste a certain willfulness keeps the piece from digestibility, as though McCartney, in deciding to go himself one better in nostalgia, self-consciously goes himself one worse.

By the same token "Your Mother Should Know," in emulating "When I'm Sixty-four," fails. As for "Flying," this is not, properly speaking, a song so much as a *romance sans paroles* in the Mendelssohnian sense, which still does not render it interesting as to texture, style, or content.

"Blue Jay Way," however, is not only the album's finest offering, it's George Harrison's best song by far. Reduced to lowest terms, Harrison's tunes have hitherto been as well shaped and lovely as most of the other utterly Western tunes of the group. But I always long to hear a non-Hindu tailoring intoned by maybe Sarah Vaughan. My own childhood goes back to the 1930s when Victor released the music of Shan Kar's troupe, a music that spellbound us long before Zen and acid were toyed with. Yet how do we *hear* it? Surely not with Indian ears! Nor were there words. Yet it spoke. But is there a point in attempting to translate such speech? No. And now with "Blue Jay Way" Harrison seems to have renounced such attempts at translation, which is certainly the wisest thing he may have learned from the foxy Maharishi.

If, as I declared earlier, "Hello Goodbye" employs old-hat harmonies with no special viewpoint, "Blue Jay Way" employs such harmonies with an astonishing freshness. In the 1820s Weber's use of the diminished triad sent chills up the spine; by 1900 that use had grown laughably hackneyed. Who would believe that today a composer could take that old triad to design a vocal line of such uncomplicated subtlety that it not only works, but works in the same freezing manner as it worked a century ago? Of the five novelties, then, this one alone (though it's certainly no "Day in the Life") makes the whole album worth the price.

Newness per se has never been the basis—or even especially an ingredient—of the Beatles' work. On the contrary, they have revitalized music's basics (harmony, counterpoint, rhythm, melody) by using them again in the simplest manner, a manner directed away from intellectualism and toward the heart. The intelligentsia, what's more (except specialists), now eschews the "modern music concert," only too glad to embrace the Beatles instead: to react, have fun, cry a little, get scared. The Beatles' instrumentation may superficially sound far-out, but it apes the flashier element of electronic background no more advanced than the echo-chamber sound tracks of 1930s horror movies. Their "newest" thing is probably a kind of prosodic liberty; their rendition—their *realization*—often sounds contrary to the verses' predictable look on paper. Yet even at that, are they much different from our definitive songwriters of the past? From Purcell, say, or Debussy? It is not in their difference but in their betterness that their superiority lies.

But their betterness is not always apparent. Again, like Stravinsky, they are already classifiable with retrospective periods. Inasmuch as they try to surpass or even consciously to redefine themselves with each period, they fail, as they mostly have with their *Magical Mystery Tour*. This isn't surprising with persons so public and hence so vulnerable. But where, from this almost complacent "civilization," can they go from here?

Well, where does any artist go? Merely on. Still, it should now be clear that they are not the sum of their parts, but four distinct entities. Paul, I guess, is a genius with tunes; though what, finally, is genius without training? John, it seems, is no less clever than James Joyce; though where, ultimately, can that lead, when he is no *more* clever? George, they say, has brought East to West; but what, really, can that prove, when even Kipling realized it's not the twain of deeds but of concepts which never seem to meet? And Ringo, to at least one taste, is cute as a bug; though anyone, actually, can learn quick to play percussion, as our own George Plimpton now is demonstrating.

We've become so hung up on what they *mean*, we can no longer hear what they're performing. Nor was Beethoven ever so Freudianized.

Just as twenty years ago one found oneself reading more books about Kafka than reading Kafka himself, so today one gets embarrassed at being overheard in deep discussion of the Beatles. I love them. But I love them not as symbolic layers of "the scene" (or whatever it's called), and even less as caricatures of themselves (which, like Mae West, they're inclined to become). I love them as the hearty barbaric troubadours they essentially are. As such I hope they will continue to develop, together or apart, for they represent the most invigorating music of an era so civilized that it risks extinction less from fallout than from boredom.

(*1968*)

THE MORE THINGS
CHANGE

Notes on French Popular Song

The French are not a musical people. They are more geared to the eye than to the ear. We too, when thinking of France, usually think less of her sound than her look: her painting and elegant clothes; even her grocery displays delight us. And we also think of her conversation—her exquisitely economical literary wit (not to mention her taste and smell, her cuisine and perfume).

Which is not to say France never produced great musicians: from Machaut to Messiaen, from Adam de la Halle to Jacques Brel, her composers equal any our world has known. But France—the France, that is, of post-World War II—possesses no hard-core musical public; her most adventuresome musicians must cross the border to earn their keep, at least those (composer and performer alike) who make so-called serious music. So-called popular musicians, being less adventuresome, seldom stray; they have always been nourished at home by an audience more concerned with the "visual literature" of their lyrics than with the fairly conventional tunes illustrating those lyrics.

If the general French public is not musical especially, specialists within the specialty—doubtless from resultant economic requirements—have always been less specialized, more "renaissancy," than their American counterparts. A very serious composer like Poulenc, or Henri Sauguet, will one day compose a strong Mass for chorus and orchestra, next day a fragile waltz for Yvonne Printemps. He thus follows the practice of Satie before him, of Reynaldo Hahn before Satie, of Messager before Reynaldo Hahn, Chabrier before Messager, and so on back. Or take Georges Auric who, after years of creating obscure ballets for Diaghilev, or of writing sonatas and such along with some thirty film scores nobody ever listened to, finally struck it really rich with the ditty *"Moulin Rouge."*

As for executants, consider Jeanne Moreau. She began in the 1940s as a bilingual (her mother was English) vocalist with Ray Ventura's band before going straight as an actress in Vilar's left-wing troupe, from whence she graduated into everyone's favorite neurotic movie star— who still records unneurotic songs, mostly by the innocuous Cyrus Bassiak. Meanwhile casual balladeers like Brel, drunk with success, branch into oratorio (with less success), while chansonnier Yves Montand has largely renounced singing to become one of his country's major stage and screen actors. Actor Serge Reggiani reverses Montand's route by now offering pleasant recitals in vaudeville. Jean Marais does that too, and so does Bardot. (The French, by the way, never use our word *vaudeville*—that form of entertainment extinct here but vital in Paris where ironically it's called *le music-hall*.)

Fluid states of mind are what French popular songs portray: they have always told stories that develop in a straight line, *a-b-c*, toward a delicious or catastrophic resolution. Which is why their words haunt us more than their melodies. French song is thus not bound to set forms: the subject imposes the pattern. Often the meter shifts to (or is entirely within) a regular 3/4—the dance of experience.

In storytelling lies the key to France's musical variety, from the trouvères to the modern minstrels. If from Ronsard to Éluard her great bards have not always been composers in their own right, modern composers— classical and popular—have always used their poetry. But they write their own, too. That typically Gallic phenomenon called *auteur compositeur* is as persuasive today as the new *auteurs cinéastes* who invent films in transit. Like Elizabethan playwrights they sell to every public; not for nothing does the prestigious series *Poètes d'Aujourd'hui* publish as pure poetry the lyrics of vulgar songsters like Brassens, Aznavour, or even Charles Trenet, alongside Mallarmé, Pasternak, or Paul Claudel.

Those pedagogical opinions were determined, rightly or otherwise, during a decade abroad. Opinions shift with the times, harden to conclusions or melt into reflections, then finally change. But change? *Plus ça change, plus c'est la même chose*, as the French are the first to observe: the more things change, the more they revolve back to their starting point. Revolution (as opposed to revolt) is everywhere traditional; my musical opinions, after a long flow of learning, now return on the wings of unaltered taste to when I was learning firsthand about Paris.

I arrived there nineteen years ago, the day world boxing champion Marcel Cerdan was killed in a plane crash. The same crash claimed violinist Ginette Neveu, and these two idols, different as night from day, were mourned together.

The French love their intellectual and popular heroes, and are loyal to both without distinguishing much between them. The humblest concierge, while he may identify more with the sagas of Fernandel, is proud to cite Debussy or Balzac; he may not know their works but he'll name a street for them. Culture was never a dirty word in Europe; in America the rare genuinely accepted culture heroes, as embodied in a Hemingway or an Orson Welles, were known for their *bon vivantisme* and not for what their art represented. In those good old 1940s, as in the days of Louis Quatorze, all France was aware of the privacy of her most public citizens. When Americans were not allowed then to consider their statesmen as having mistresses (or worse), the French followed with relish and approbation the anxieties and bedroom triumphs of the great. (Today, with de Gaulle and the Kennedys, the situation is somewhat reversed.)

So two masters, one of the boxing ring, the other of the concert stage, were conjointly lamented, as later Colette and Mistinguett would be, Gide and Louis Jouvet, Poulenc and Gérard Philipe. And on that awful October Friday of 1963 when Jean Cocteau and Edith Piaf fell dead, hand in hand so to speak, the rule was ironically reaffirmed. Cocteau, a jack-of-all-higher-trades, had been the esoteric darling of the elite. Piaf, a specialist of commoner emotions, had been the pathetic oracle of the workingman. Yet Cocteau had composed monologues for Piaf who, in turn, was Cerdan's mistress at the time of the boxer's death. Which brought the unhappy family about full circle.

At the time of my arrival Piaf was becoming her country's official widow. Humor, never her strong point, now utterly quit the repertory as her every private moan swelled into a public dirge, a culminating dirge of such importance that I'd like, before discussing other past and present French singers, to set their stage with this particular woman, my first and longest continental infatuation: *la môme* (as her countrymen called her), the little sparrow.

She was the greatest popular singer produced by France in this century.

Of the genre she became an apex, and as such proved—while remaining utterly French—an exception to the French practice of nonspecialization.

The genre, of course, was the troubadour epic which ultimately evolved into the naturalistic fin de siècle café-concert narrations of Yvette Guilbert, a sort of contralto whose piquant physique was glorified by Lautrec as early as 1890, and whose bizarre vocality she herself engraved on wax as late as the mid-1930s. (She died in only 1944, seven years after our Bessie Smith. Why, some of us could have known her!)

Piaf stemmed directly from Guilbert, through Damia, and like those ladies used song successfully—at least for a time—as a weapon against life. Sharpening their best qualities into a perfect arrow, she pierced the hearts of all ensuing Parisian stylists, female and male, except maybe the late French rock crop who aren't really very French.

The utter Frenchness of Piaf came, negatively, through avoidance of Americanisms. If her accompaniments sometimes did insist on a Harlemesque beat plus an occasional saxophone (though let's not forget: the saxophone was invented in France a century ago), mostly her orchestrations emulated the oh-so-Latin accordions of the neighborhood *bal musette*. (Incidentally, France's serious composers, who always deemed Negro jazz the sole American product worth acknowledging, never managed, from Ravel to Milhaud, more than a translation of the outer trappings into their pristine counterfeits. But then in turn, we never found the key to their kitchen. Like cooking, music is not a universal language.) More positively, Edith Piaf's Frenchness came through the kind of tale she told. If Chevalier at eighty is still (understandably) his nation's official optimist, Piaf, during her forty-four brief years of consoling the urban underdog, represented the *grande pathétique*. Her verses spoke of love fermenting into murder, then of redemption and of love's return in heaven. They spoke of Sunday fairs in the squalid Vincennes park as reward for the barmaid's six-day week. They spoke of injustice in Pigalle's underworld—what Parisians call *le milieu*. They told also, like Jerome Kern's song "Bill," of life sustained through fidelity to the unfaithful, but, unlike "Bill," that life was prolonged more through words than music. More as *littérateuse* than as *musicienne* is the sparrow recalled today, as she was applauded in her prime.

As for evading the role of nonspecialist, Piaf was indeed forever one-track-minded. The concentration made her unique. No *auteur compositeur*, she executed what others (mainly her friend Marguerite Monnot) created so accurately from her private experience of resigned—and not-so-resigned—distress. This she re-experienced publicly through the chanson, an art traditionally depicting city rather than rural problems through a form as valid as (and older than) the recital song as realized by Duparc. Of course, being famous, she was frequently called upon to reenact her number within trumped-up tales for theater and screen, though she never brought it off. Whatever her number, it was not versatility.

This morning I played some early Ethel Merman records, alternating them with Piaf and with another old and faithful love, Billie Holiday.

Merman belted solely as a technique: she was objective where Piaf was personal. Piaf could belt like Merman, but she melted Merman's brass into the pathos of Holiday.

In more ways than one Edith paralleled Billie. Professionally, though highly mannered vocally (manners, after all, are what make the Great great, great being the quality of the inimitably imitable), neither had the least *mannerism* in stage comportment. They just stood there and sang, each in her invariable costume: for Billie the coiffed gardenia, for Edith the simple black dress. Oh, in moments of high emphasis Holiday might close her eyes, while Piaf would slightly raise an arm, as Lenya does; beyond that, nothing—nothing but the immutability of projection. They never "put over" a song other than through the song itself, a lesson our Tony Bennett or Johnny Mathis—to name but two—could nicely heed, inasmuch as they've learned more from women vocalists than from men.

Their personal lives intertwined as well, like Baudelaire's with Poe's, though they may never have heard of each other. Both emerged from the *bas fonds*, Piaf as blind adolescent crooning for pennies in suburban alleys, Holiday as pubescent Baltimore Oriole working the bars of Lenox Avenue. Both their repertories forever featured those youthful and apparently continuing hardships, though Billie had a fortune slip through her fingers and Edith's eventual bridesmaid was Marlene Dietrich. From first to last, though sometimes wealthy and all times beloved, both were victimized and exploited, as is ever the case with simple addicted geniuses whose hearts rule their heads. Both sank back into publicized poverty. Then both perished, early and accidentally, in the icy light of abject stardom.

Returning to the Paris of '49 where Piaf reigned supreme, we find certain gentlemen and ladies-in-waiting, no longer waiting.

I asked about suave Jean Sablon, and was told he was passé. (Though just now in 1968 he's made another record: the French *are* faithful to their heroes!) But the very young and strangely gorgeous Juliette Gréco, yard-long tresses trailing over her slacks, was philosophizing in a Dietrich-like baritone about growing old, on words of Queneau and music of Kosma. Gréco's obsession echoed through the boîtes of Saint-Germain where she was crowned high priestess of a superficial existentialism—to Sartre's dismay. Not to be outdone, Cocteau took her up as he had Piaf, and cast her as a fury in his movie *Orphée*. Then, publicizing the alteration of her handsome nose by stylish Docteur Claoué, she proceeded (still gorgeous though less strange) toward a more standard film career, toward two or three marriages, an affair with Darryl Zanuck whose promotion of her never caught on internationally, a waning of acting demands, and a return to the clubs—this time interpreting material written for her by the rising Françoise Sagan.

I also asked about famous-legged Mistinguett, first mentor and mistress of Maurice Chevalier, and learned she was running a zoo—a *zoo*!—on the route to Saint-Tropez. (Though a few years later, well into her seventies, she made a gala comeback: "Her voice still tintinnabulates on pitch like a nice weathered sheep bell," wrote Janet Flanner.) But the very robust and juvenile Yves Montand, a protégé of Madame Piaf, was packing them in at the Théâtre Wagram (since torn down) with lyrical recitations debonair and earthy on words by all from Rimbaud to Trenet—and naturally himself. He grew more somber, more political (left), on wedding Simone Signoret with whom he starred in Sartre's adaptation of *The Crucible* after triumphing in his first nonsinging screen role, *The Wages of Fear*.

Around Montparnasse the legendary diseuse, Marianne Oswald still gave lectures on surrealism, acted in art movies like Kenneth Anger's never-finished *Maldoror*, and sang in a voice that made Marlene's sound like Tebaldi.

Up in Montmartre, Patachou, another old girlfriend of Chevalier, held forth at a special club. In a gentle voice she interpreted poetry of a compassionate nature, while wielding a pair of scissors that snipped off the ties of all male guests (and we know what *that* means). Next door in her own shop, Geneviève, with an impact at once tough and tender, declaimed poems antiwar and pro-love, healthier by bourgeois standards than the pro-death eulogies heard in left bank lesbian boîtes.

In the mid-1950s younger women such as Mike Michelle sailed briefly into sight on the reputation of a single song (like our Bobbie Gentry), then faded out again.

Younger men lasted longer. And they were blooming all over, fresh and inventive, composing songs for themselves and for each other, on words by the classic French poets or by themselves or by each other. (Stung by the bug, I even wrote a few myself, on the Prévert-oriented poetry of actor Daniel Gélin for Algerian *chanteur* Mouloudji—who never sang them.)

Their tunes mostly leaned toward folk song as synthesized by hotel bands of the 1930s. In beauty of curve few could compare to Richard Rodgers or to the best of the Beatles today. But their words were exhilarating, timely, personal. They sang of their First Communion; of sensual discovery during military service in Indochina; of fantasies— like those of Kafka, Buzzati, Cavafy—about barbarian invasions of Paris streets. Paris streets, down to the last cranny, have always been extolled by their inhabitants with affection or loathing, something seldom done musically for the byways of New York.

In vocal delivery they tended to imitate each other (as Dean Martin and Sammy Davis logically do) or their immediate forerunners, like Georges Brassens and Leo Ferré on one hand, Sablon and Trenet on the other. These men were no chickens (neither are Martin and Davis today), though they remained fairly active and very influential. Trenet and Sablon were Crosby-type crooners, while Ferré and Brassens, though doubtless self-styled as "naturalists," had both inherited by osmosis the excruciating nasal vibrato considered elegant by French opera stars. All were troubadours, terribly subjective and quite healthily masculine, endowed with aggressivity and wit, though necessarily short on morbidity and camp.

Who were they? Charles Aznavour, Jacques Brel of course, and the young Gilbert Bécaud. Also youths like Sammy Frey, Sascha Distel, and a whimsical quartet called the Frères Jacques.

The late 1950s saw the distaff side regaining hold with Jacquéline François, Barbara, and the dynamic Germaine Montéro who imposed the raw tint of her native Spain onto the blasé molds of café song.

By 1960 Elvis Presley had so disarmed the rest of the world that France, seldom acquiescent in matters experimental, did open her gates to *le rock-n-roll*, albeit an ersatz version later called Yé Yé. As exemplified in Johnny Halliday this version momentarily immunized Paris against all other music.

In November 1961, the evening before I left France, Nora Auric (Georges' bright wife) took me to hear Johnny at the Olympia. Still ignorant of Presley—of Presley's *art*, if you will—I was skeptical about meeting it secondhand. Yet from the moment that handsome kid appeared and for the solid hour of his gyrations, Nora and I were as drugged by the mass hysteria loosened by his superbly whorish musicality as were the five thousand adolescents that jammed the hall.

Since then at least one serious novel has been devoted to Halliday, and a good deal of intellectual criticism. I believe he married his vapid colleague, Sylvie Vartan, then took up with Brigitte Bardot—old enough to be at least his sister. But of these and other things Parisian, most of what I now know I read in women's magazines.

This afternoon a responsibility for being au courant dragged me through the furnace of Manhattan to the Discophile where I purchased no less than seventeen newish French records. In a single sweaty séance I listened carefully, and with very mixed reactions, to each and every one. Judging from just these discs, my premise is reconfirmed: the tone of France's 1940s remains inviolable.

It's sort of comfortable—the realization that in our animated epoch France preserves a snug, almost smug, status quo. She never really did export her art; what we liked of it we robbed, kept provisionally, and gave back. If sometimes the Waldorf or Plaza did extend formal invitations to Gréco or Geneviève, their special impact never "took"; their language lacked that Esperanto appeal of our Westerns ever popular at Champs-Elysées cinemas. Conversely, expatriate Negroes of the 1950s never took, as Josephine Baker had in the 1920s, because they were doing an American thing, while Baker had literally translated her whole being into French. The French did love Negroes as novelty—not as U.S. exports like Billie Holiday, but as African stylists like Katherine Dunham.

In her isolation France has kept pure. Or almost. She may be different from the United States, but over the years she doesn't grow too different from herself: the fatigue of homogeneity vaguely contaminates her popular music now. Half of it is recorded live in music halls, complete with the detestable practice of incorporating the applause. All of it of course is vocal, expressing the good old Gallic themes of putting down the church (yet concerned that if Christ were recrucified today he would pass unnoticed), of putting down the upper classes (to the delight of the chief public, a solvent bourgeoisie), and of putting down old age (though isn't it we Americans who are supposed to be notorious youth worshipers?). They do still hold love high, and that is a blessing, a blessing of the strictly one-to-one male-female ratio, sometimes garnished with the complacence of longevity, more often with the anxiety of impermanence. Not for Frenchmen the checkerboard possibilities of a tribal love-in! They reiterate comparatively simplistic problems, old-fashioned, I suppose, next to which Anglo-Saxon rock comes off as actually sophisticated. (How long rock will remain sophisticated before sounding old-fashioned is an open question.)

Meanwhile the themes, as uttered on these records, do not activate the present—at least not for me. They reactivate the past.

I used never to weep at Great Art, at Couperin or Kierkegaard, maintaining it was too multidimensional for the specific of tears. I wept at the rapid associative revelations of a Piaf, or at Lana Turner's soapy dilemmas. Crying was caused hence by entertainment, not masterworks.

Today tears dictate my first judgment of any works, their levels be damned. What counts is to be kinetically moved. And who says Edith and Lana aren't art—or, if they are, that Kierkegaard is more so? My criterion is no longer analytical.

None of these records makes me weep. They all project a certain hardness, even in heartbreak, which I never used to notice. Maybe their strong levelheadedness, compared with our distracted neuroses, goes against the American grain. More likely it's their persistent cliché.

Not one French popular singer of either sex has a real voice, in the sense that our Sinatras or Streisands are real baritones or mezzos. They still "talk" their tunes, beguiling through anecdote rather than through a formal development of sound. Thus their orchestral arrangements strike us as outmoded, naive. For example, when working toward a climax (and most French songs, being stories, have marked climaxes), they all employ one and only one device: the obvious modulation upward by half-step with each stanza, gaining momentum not through musical invention but by yelling louder. This is as true of the artists of 1968 as of those from 1949, the majority of whom are the same.

Juliette Gréco is still very much about, still admired for her philosophic laments, still handsome in her forties while intoning the hit that launched her two decades ago, "Si tu t'imagines," about youth that can't last. Meanwhile Barbara recounts an older woman's anguish in falling for an adolescent boy. That boy may be Reggiani (now forty-fivish) singing about the "older" woman in his bed, while at other times his frightful touching tenor relates his own problems of aging, put into words by Boris Vian, Apollinaire, and yes, even Baudelaire. Patachou, newly blonde and more than slightly wrinkled, still ingratiates with that calm and not unpleasant hum.

They say Brassens is getting old—a breathing monument—but he still charms devotees with a vocal monochrome (to me, charmless) whose chief idiosyncrasy remains its lack of idiosyncrasy. And still growing strong in their middle years are Brel and Aznavour; so is Bécaud in his advancing youth.

Of course Aznavour, like Jeanne Moreau, has been internationally immortalized as an actor by new-wave genius François Truffaut. But he sure keeps on singing, or rather, non-singing in his torturous tremolo, forcing the Big Sell as cymbals crash and audience shrieks. Bécaud too continues his non-singing, equally "beloved" (I cringe when, like Mitch Miller, he invites us fans to join in), and creating grand numbers of which at least one became a hit here last year under the quaintly mis-construed title "It Must Be Him."

As for Brel, his work too has lately satisfied a certain New York audience, thanks to that curious miscalculation over on Bleecker Street—a disparate black-and-white version of Brel's own technicolor rendition of his tunes. Those tunes, like virtually all these French ones I've been listening to, are undistinguished, their instrumental adornments ever more vulgar—meaning literal: they mickey-mouse the words. The words of Brel I find pretentious because, in deriving from Villon via Weill and Brecht (in themselves quite noble influences), he takes their sense without their sensitivity, their surface passion without their understatement. Good intentions, honesty, a no-nonsense attitude are not enough for a good song.

The no-nonsense syndrome is all too characteristic of the virile French. They do have guts, if you like guts; but the Brel-Bécaud-Aznavour sound of the confident belligerent male is in complete opposition to the current pop Anglo-American sympathetic adorable sexless cool sound of the Beatles or Tiny Tim. If the French individual extroverts direct their message toward the opposite sex in particular, our collective narcissists direct theirs toward people in general. Americans don't tell stories be-cause gangs don't tell stories, they sing hymns. Stories are what McLuhan would call a hot medium for single singers.

A new record of old Ferré enforces the syndrome. Nonetheless one of his songs nearly made me cry tonight. "Vingt Ans" examines the same insouciant virtues of youth that Gréco mourns, but where Gréco retains an urbane sangfroid, poor Ferré collapses with a contagious spasm. In another, "Y'en a marre," the verses hysterically lacerate that same Tax Man the Beatles disdain with a dead pan. Its harmonies, by the way, are right out of Golaud's lament in the last act of *Pelléas* (or Rodolfo's in act three of *Bohème*, which is the same thing), thereby emphasizing a predictable allegiance to an Opéra Comique past rather than to an off-Broadway future. And why not?

Elbowing their way beyond these established rocks into the ebbing starlight of Johnny Halliday's pseudo-rock are younger boys like Adamo, Antoine, Guy Béart. Cute Sylvie Vartan may still be around—I wouldn't know—but not in competition with post-Piaf kids like Eva, Gribouille, or Mireille Matthieu, assertive little screamers indistinguishable from their predecessor in all but quality.

From far away my impression is that this youthful clan is less a pastiche of foreign trends than a parasite of the firmly entrenched middle-aged raconteurs. In itself the clan amounts to little, and is certainly not "new." The new in France lies, as always, in tradition: in a refurbishing of the old.

(*1968*)

FIVE

THREE LANDSCAPES WITH FIGURES

WHERE IS OUR
MUSIC GOING?
(1968)

PROLOGUE

More than ever in history, laymen and practitioners today show concern
with the directions music is taking. Where on earth is it leading us? How
should we listen? Could it be that music's current incomprehensibility,
like that of all the arts, indicates a massive hoax perpetrated by a new
society of amateurs impuniously calling themselves artists? Are not these
amateurs nevertheless serious in declaring our world so paralyzed by
the increasing victories of matter over mind that nothing makes a difference? Or could such incomprehensibility signify a final clarification
for the soul as opposed to merely ear or eye, the courage of the irrational,
the last of mimetic subservience, the first clean air exhaled by creators
since the Industrial Revolution—and everything makes a difference?

Replies depend, as they always have, on how old you are, where you
stand, your political sympathies, and your overall suppleness; in short,
on considerations not directly related to artistic taste.

Some things do appear certain. American artists in the past decade
have grown diversified. Unlike family doctors who are perishing in ever
more specialized arenas, serious composers, who once kept company
with only each other, are thriving everywhere because they're now working for every medium, including that of providing background sounds
to look at pictures by, and all seem articulate as can be.

Articulate, yes. Or so I had imagined. Verbal, at least: certainly more
so than their prewar image. For this reason—and because there seemed
no longer a clear line between the arts—I had felt that rather than myself
composing an essay on the intriguing problem of where music is going,
it would be more original to solicit reactions from a number of acquaintances. My plan was to select and compare opinions from young
and old, right and left, from all categories of artist including both the

elite and general publics'. Like Professor Kinsey I would have access only to Americans, a necessary consideration despite the increasingly homogenized world culture.

Well, the project landed me at a dead end. For instance, I began on top by visiting an old acquaintance and sometime teacher, Aaron Copland: he, if anyone, would have authoritative opinions as to music's future. At his rambling home near Croton we passed an evening tête-à-tête, beginning over a succulent platterful of perch fillets and ending with an audition of tapes by Conlon Nancarrow, an American reclused in Mexico where since the 1930s he has composed painstakingly for pianola rolls with flabbergasting results. Meanwhile I attempted to draw out my host on matters prophetic.

But he was not easy to pin down. "I don't get around much anymore," said Aaron Copland, "except to conduct my own concerts. Besides, what with guys like Cage on the one hand and Babbitt on the other, it's hard to know just where it will all lead. . . . Yes, we did have rival groups in the twenties, but there was nothing that resembled the scene in today's universities. Why, universities used to be hotbeds of conservatism! Suddenly now—and strangely—schools want to get in on the act. The 'act,' as they see it, is the avant-garde; and the farthest-out composers have quite comfortable jobs. Look at this magazine, for instance."

From a slick pile of new musical periodicals he drew forth *Source*, a luxuriant review edited by Larry Austin at Davis in California. It brimmed with speckled graphs of such intimidating complexity that we both chuckled with defensive amazement. (*Modern Music*, which closed shop in 1946, had been the last magazine devoted to "the cause." But the cause then was multileveled. The recent music magazine revival was perpetrated by subsidized groups, each with a specialized ax to grind.)

"The word 'musical' *does* seem now to have less urgency than 'ingenious,' " he went on. "I'd never have guessed this would all come about. Certainly the symphony orchestra situation is not encouraging, as Lenny points out." He was referring to Bernstein's recent question in the *Times*. ("Are symphonies a thing of the past? No, since they are still being written. But yes, in the sense that the classical concept of a symphony *is* a thing of the past.") He was referring also to the lack of enthusiasm most name conductors have for new music, not so much because it's new as because it's become just too difficult for their allotted rehearsal time; hence the switch from professional concert halls to university gymnasiums as the seat of new trends—trends, what's more, now scaled to small ensembles-in-residence backed by Fromm or similar private foundations.

Diplomatically I asked Copland if today's young liked, took seriously, his most popular repertory works like *Appalachian Spring* or *Quiet City*. (My unspoken intent was to learn whether he was troubled at having been, so to speak, replaced as Leader of American Music—at least for camp-following Young Turks—by more complex composers like Elliott Carter.) "Good Lord, no," he answered. "Kids no longer can admire a *successful* piece. They want to hear my *Connotations* or *Inscape*. But music that's 'accepted,' that makes money, is automatically suspect. . . . Whom *do* they respect of the recent past? Certainly Varèse more than Ives, because Varèse never *was* accepted by the general public. Even Webern now is almost a 'safe' musician."

And whom, I wondered, did *he* like today, especially among our countrymen? "*Like* is a dubious emotion, assuming it's still a consideration. But I listen willingly, if not always pleasurably, to—hmmm—Xenakis, or, well maybe—Takemitsu. Of course, they're not Americans." Whereupon he mentioned, off the record, a few young U.S. composers he sometimes listened to "willingly."

For the most part Aaron Copland did not venture past the first paragraph of a reply to my queries. He had his reasons. Toward midnight, while driving to the train that would deliver me back to Manhattan, he announced the imminent publication of a revision of his 1941 best-seller *Our New Music*, now named *The New Music*. Since he had (significantly!) depersonalized his title, I've appropriated his possessive pronoun here for this essay, originally called simply "Where Is Music Going?" That's as much as I got out of Copland.

Big shots, I realized, would hesitate at releasing their theories since they have articles of their own to write. (Virgil Thomson frankly declared: "I am less interested in where music is going than in where it has just been," though I'm not sure how he means this.) As for littler shots, I'd planned to interview those from my generation of friends who were either composers themselves or performers or plain music lovers, asking them in particular what music since 1940 they really enjoyed hearing: did they retain today the same energetic curiosity they once felt toward "modern music"? I talked, for example, with Robert Phelps, a novelist in his mid-forties, a Francophile, a wry and pithy book critic, and husband to the painter Rosemarie Beck, herself an amateur violinist.

"It was, in fact, twenty years ago," said he, "that I discovered Modern Music and improvised a little festival in Woodstock—with Henry Cowell, Arthur and Esther Berger, and Robert Palmer. Now I settle for what makes me cry—Poulenc, Cole Porter, player-piano rolls from my childhood, the *Chansons de Bilitis*."

These words, of course, expressed pure reaction rather than the desired opinion, as did those I received from another friend, John Gruen, composer of a wee but pungent sheaf of songs, music and art critic turned interviewer, and husband to the painter Jane Wilson, herself an amateur pianist. Like Paul and Jane Bowles in the early 1940s, this young couple is something of a pacesetter for the 1960s, proposing tastes and reflecting moods of the witless but talented peacocks on seesaws. "Where it all will end I wouldn't know," Gruen sighed. "I only wonder where it *can* end. Anyway, the whole scene's exposed in my *The New Bohemia*. But as far as my own music's concerned: what difference can it possibly make in the total assault of noise that now surrounds us!"

As for my onetime schoolmate, pianist Eugene Istomin, when his opinion was sought he merely went to the phonograph and turned on *Das Lied von der Erde*. "I want beauty," he announced. "Are they today composing out of the same *need* as Mahler? Does that need still exist? Do they *hear* what we heard when we were at Curtis? Do composers want to *communicate*, or merely to distinguish themselves—assuming there's a difference? Myself, I can only perform on the keyboard that which I feel requires reinterpretation. When the Ford Foundation asked me to commission a composer of my choice, I could think of no one who might write today what Chopin or Rachmaninoff hadn't written better yesterday. So I went to Roger Sessions, just because his music was problematic: in going against my senses, it went against them *with strength*. I've always loved problems. Yet though I may never play his piece (it would take six months to digest), I'll supervise the rehearsals of whoever does, because I admire Sessions unqualifiedly."

Conversation with old friends is often unproblematical precisely because it is with old friends: the attitudes have become predictable. Like lovers, friends result from involuntary choice, though unlike lovers we accept them because essentially they agree with us. The same holds true for professional colleagues, rivals though they be. Accordingly we acknowledge their conjectures in good faith: we long for them to be right because it makes life easier. But our—and their—good faith is not by definition representative of an inclusive scene: there is always an enemy camp with a view to be considered. Now, for the individual artist an enemy camp is, of necessity, wrong; artists are artists by virtue of being categorically right, by virtue of their nonmagnanimous aristocracy. Most of them do keep their eyes—or, in the case of composers, their ears—open to the tone of the times, if only to avoid what not to do. But inasmuch as they write papers like this one, they must momentarily cease being artists and become objective appraisers. Objectivity is not easy, least of all for an artist turned sociologist; and to conduct appraising interviews with the enemy camp takes time, time better employed in making art.

As a result I have decided, after misfiring my initial project, to forget both friends and foes and, for better or worse, to render this article as a personal précis. This I shall now do—I, the musician Ned Rorem—by airing the biases any composer does and must possess from conviction and for armor. These biases will be involuntarily submitted through descriptions of music's shiftings over the recent past, within our mercurial present, and through an uncertain future. About what music was and what it has become I have reached conclusions. About where it resultingly might travel I am as vague as the next one.

WHAT IT WAS

From just after the last war until 1960 the musical world was split into three categories, each with its own audience and aim of expression. These categories were jazz, experimental, conservative. In that order I'll define them.

For lack of a clearer cover-all term, jazz here applies less to the specific Louisiana-Chicago phenomenon than to that music also known as popular—as distinct from classical. Classical is equally imprecise ("longhair" would be better), since it really obtains to a historic era and unreally implies a superior intent rather than content. Certainly popular music is now history, a history not quickly proven to be less "significant" than classical music's. So I shall retain the word jazz, assured that most people understand it as I do.

Prewar jazz was lavish and immense, exemplified by the big bands of Duke Ellington or Artie Shaw that performed through-composed, meaning non-improvised, orchestrations. These were arrangements of so-called standards, sumptuous in sound yet rigorous in rhythm, fulfilling the double need for Hollywoodian fantasy and for supporting dance crazes. The arrangements *swung*—with a careful exoticism. Often as not they accompanied vocal stylists like Doris Day or Peggy Lee, equally strict and equally glamorous, who crooned sentimental verse in tune with the casual poignance of that epoch's younger generation. The largeness of the period was occasionally counterbalanced by intimate groups-within-the-group (Benny Goodman's trio, for example), but these were more a quaint indulgence than a necessary antidote. The antidote to the ultimate elephantiasis came with the financial restrictions of World War II. Similarly, a quarter century earlier, another war had reduced Diaghilevian grandiosities to chamber dimension, hence altering—through economics, not esthetics—the whole nature of musical composition.

Probably economy rather than esthetics also produced our little post-war groups of progressive jazz, although the Brubecks and Mulligans of that decade could hardly be called uncommitted. Commitment in music, however, is pinpointed through lyrics rather than tunes (could we truly get Weill's "message" without Brecht's texts?), and the new cool movement was wordless. Commitment, as it had been championed in the depressed 1930s, was "out" in the fighting 1940s (except for such harmless horrors as "He's A-1 in the Army and He's A-1 in My Heart"), not to return until our thoughtful 1960s. Gone with the war was the oral lament of "At Least You Could Say Hello," the dizzying nonsense of "The Music Goes Round and Round." Gone was the kinetic impulse of Gene Krupa and twenty gold trumpets. And gone too was the Negro aristocracy—the Dukes, Kings, Counts—who had dictated the tone of our first half-century.

Here to stay, or so it seemed, was a breed of swinging Wasp bred into "tolerant" milieus, weaned at the conservatory, and launched through clubs that served sodas to an intellectual public. That public, in forgoing dance and song and alcohol, encouraged the growth of a jazz that was improvisational in structure, pseudo-atonal in texture, and eccentric in beat. A few old-time vocalists like Billie Holiday remained stylish, but were heard now, head in hands, as recitalists accompanied by "artists" such as Lester Young. The core of jazz, which like all music had been formed from words that are more than words, was changing from a verbal into an instrumental utterance, an utterance by nature more sophisticated, more artificial, diffuse, "abstract." Such a change presupposed more rambling forms; and if an old-timer like Louis Armstrong today still "sings" through his trumpet, the trumpet of Ornette Coleman and his white imitators during the 1950s soared higher than human and longer than freedom.

With the education resulting from a racial integration of jazz performers, it became only logical that experiments be tried. What Gunther Schuller named Third Stream showed attempts at conjoining jazz and classical. The attempts were manifest in the classy, moodily elegant and presumably Schoenbergian but actually Ravelian musings of esoteric combos (like bass flute, vibes, celesta, solo fiddle); in the pitting of a soloist like Maynard Ferguson against a through-written piece for philharmonic as in Bill Russo's slick *Second Symphony*; or in the setting of an improvisatory microcosm among a "strict" orchestra as in some of Schuller's own pieces.

The Third Stream flowed with oil and water, never merging but diverging as undirected tributaries that dribbled into limbo by 1960, when jazz finally lost its definition both as a players' art and as a solid compositional medium. It was then—meaning now—that the art of song, for twenty years dormant, was revitalized. Revitalized, not by soloists but by groups; the Andrews Sisters of yore were paralleled most noticeably in the advent of the Beatles.

The division called Experimental is a music that in turn may be split into three factions: serial, electronic, chance.

Serial composers are the inheritors of Schoenberg's twelve-tone formula as filtered through Webern, then recodified by Boulez in Paris and Babbitt at Princeton. Integral serialism, as the recodification is known, presents the predetermined systemization not only of pitch or tone but of all musical variables: rhythm, dynamics, silence, et cetera. In opposition to the built-in opulence of jazz—a pleasure in sound for sound— integral serialism was not geared to seduce the senses, having other fish to fry.

Fish is a brain food, never the basic diet of artists from prehistory until World War II. During those millennia the making of music was the making of romance insofar as romance means evasion of reality, or rather, heightened reality, concentration of emotion as against logic, controlled fantasy of self-expression; in short, art: art as expounded by Tolstoy or Freud but never truly defined except through itself. When the atomic age reared its ugly clouds, however, that rising generation who earlier would have been impelled toward art was deflected toward science. Trips to the moon, to inner space, or to death by holocaust, were now practicable voyages, and romance switched from bass clefs to test tubes. Art's function, of course, is not to clear away clouds. Art mirrors, proposes questions, sometimes alternatives, but never answers. More than ever art now seemed a follower, and often those few young talents who inclined toward art necessarily reflected science; their music grew into a demonstration of logic for its own sake rather than for that of "romance."

Serial music, then, was made by brains and performed for brains— when it was performed at all. For performance appeared less and less a prerequisite to the notes (were they still notes?) so exquisitely inscribed as an end in themselves on graph paper, while the joys and terrors of the ear (not to mention the soul) became a negligible, even embarrassing, consideration. Public auditions, such as they were, had mostly left urban concert halls for subsidized campuses. Attraction to such music was nil, since suddenly it could not be heard as we are conditioned to hear— that is, with reference to the past. The organized music of the 1950s, although true to that iconoclasm Thomson names "the tradition of constant change," had evolved by obliterating its heritage.

And so by 1960 the purist audience for integral serialism—a music more seen than heard—had nearly atrophied from hemophilia: one week's public became next week's performers for an incestuous minority par- adoxically claiming some of the decade's healthiest brains.

Meanwhile the more generalized elite of music fans was staring around in a daze. After all, they couldn't listen to Donizetti forever; they wanted to show goodwill toward modern music, yet shunned those recitals where the only scandal would be tedium. In 1960 it was still low class to admit being bored.

Electronic music means the mechanical fabrication of hitherto un- heard sonorities and their formal combination. The initial experiments during the war years were most noticeably credited to Frenchman Pierre Schaeffer's musique concrète, so-called as distinct from abstract music. Schaeffer's new sound fusions and those of Blomdahl, Badings, Krenek, and others, resulted from taping "normal" instruments distorted through unusual speeds and eccentric juxtapositions. The psychological outcome was nevertheless, when reduced to lowest terms (disentangled from its novel verbiage), often one of standard concepts made to "sound funny." Certain American works—for instance, those of Luening—came off as diatonic ballads heard from under water miles away.

Younger pioneers like our Richard Maxfield and Morton Subotnick, or Cologne's Stockhausen and Venice's Nono, dispensed with instruments altogether and dreamed up strictly electronic collages that by their nature presupposed new structures. Such mechanical essays were, to be sure, not wholly new, deriving as they did from the percussional forays of Varèse and Cowell a half century earlier. But the total artifice did represent an advance if one assumes, like Stravinsky, that advance means "retrogressing faster." The musician as individual performer had, after all, been disposed of.

By 1960 several universities had set up costly electronic laboratories plus courses in their use. Yet the music seemed still incomplete, not something one could just sit down and listen to. The medium cried out for superimposition on visuals; it succeeded commercially as background for science-fiction movies, noncommercially as accompaniment to modern dance or even to the classical ballet of Balanchine. But it did not yet succeed alone.

If electronic phenomena were of diverse foreign origin, the "music of chance" evolved specifically in America through a single man. John Cage had long been not only a musician but a philosopher of original wit. From his very beginnings he needed for composition to derive not just from its own past, nor even just from the sister arts, but also from points of view and of feeling, from city sounds, the earth itself, mushrooms. He took from—or rather merged with—the vast realm of our world's noise, striving toward an "emancipation of music from its notes."

The emancipation was arrived at through what inevitably became "accidental" operations originating from the *I-Ching*, the Chinese *Book of Changes*. The resultant "chance music" has been more fancily labeled Indeterminate; indeed, *Indeterminacy* is the title of a recorded lecture by Cage. The lecture itself is, if you will, a piece of music, for like so many contemporary musicians Cage has been no less influenced by composers than by writers, not the least of whom is Gertrude Stein. Still, the influence is as much through writers' sound or their look on paper as through their meaning. "I don't give these lectures to surprise people, but out of a need for poetry," explains Cage. "Poetry is not prose simply because poetry is one way or another formalized. It is not poetry by reason of its content or ambiguity but by reason of allowing musical elements (time, sound) to be introduced into the world of words. Thus, traditionally, information no matter how stuffy (e.g., the sutras and shastras of India) was transmitted in poetry."

His own more "traditional" music may be represented by the do-it-yourself manipulation of radio dials, or the now more-than-notorious 4' 31" as executed by a pianist who sits at a closed piano for four minutes and thirty-one seconds: the "music" is the undetermined public reaction (discomfited coughs, bridled approbation) as restricted to this predetermined period. Not for nothing has Cage's name, second only to Stravinsky's, become a word to international households less than erudite. His extramusical charm is contagious; the question-and-answer sessions following his concerts are more eagerly awaited than the concerts. But if for households he satisfies a need for the all-but-vanished crazy artist, to the more specialized public he satisfies a solider need.

That need, as I see it, is best explained by the mechanized West being caught with its pants down. So rapidly has industrialization developed since the war that we've not had time for a compensating indigenous growth of introspection. Instead we have reached out for the organized whimsy and wisdom of an Oriental past and superimposed it, come what may, onto our Occidental present. It remains to be guessed whether the adoption was from superficial desperation or whether, in fact, now is the time when finally the twain of East and West shall meet—at least culturally. Surely Japan since 1945 has advanced philosophically toward us as fast as we toward her. And as flocks of her dutiful three-year-olds learn the Suzuki fiddling method while her masterful novelists write of miniskirted murders, a not-insignificant segment of our composers compose according to the reinterpretation of a religion that itself was transplanted into Japan from India where it had evolved centuries before. Much of this indeterminate music becomes, in effect, not all that distinguishable from predetermined serial or even electronic works with which, as we shall see, it has begun to overlap. All the same, its "pure" state had by 1960 outlasted the purity of these other expressions, doubtless because the *act* of chance music, as opposed to the music itself, fulfilled more urgent impulses.

Conservative composers are those who persevered (shall we say logically?) according to European musical traditions set up in the 1600s. By the late 1930s those traditions had progressed through us into a readily identifiable American style. That style, cursorily one of sophisticated diatonic French economy soldered to local hymn tunes, commenced with the practical restrictions of the WPA and reached peak delineation during the war when isolation forced invention. With the armistice the complex chromaticism of Vienna, long latent beneath Hitler and presumably fossilized, was reinvented by the young who deemed it "new." America, seldom secure in matters artistic, again acquiesced to continental domination. From the ensuing recomplication of chromaticism there crystallized an international academy exemplified in the experimental schools just described.

Yet certain Americans abstained. Roy Harris and William Schuman, say, or younger men like David Diamond and Vincent Persichetti, kept their distance from global vogues, a distance maintained, it would seem, less from spite than from oblivion to the radicalism of the preceding two decades. Through pride and through habit they continued a national tradition.

How to label that tradition? Well, it is far from far-out. Yet conservative is as inapplicable as conformist or conventional. For it is conventional to be "in." And since the "ins" are far-out, to be far-out is to conform. Call them the post–avant-garde, since in their concern with sound over device they sailed beyond current modes toward a revival of that dubious preoccupation with self-expression.

Self-expression. Ontogenetically as well as phylogenetically, music drags behind the other arts. Writing and painting had mostly withdrawn from obscurantist fashions by 1960. Who knows if musical self-expression indeed might not also soon triumph as a cultural last laugh?

WHAT IT'S BECOME AND
WHERE IT MIGHT GO

Avant-garde is a term so overused as to have grown meaningless. The French vanguard from which the term derives refers, of course, to those military scouts who go on before. It is not arbitrarily that I date 1960 as the close of our musical world's split; by then the designation avant-garde as applied to "a group that is extremist or bizarre" was de-energized utterly. Perhaps it will regain healthy usage through shifts of sense—like the convolutions of the word *black*, once a patronizing colonial reference that changed to darky, then to colored, to Negro, and finally back to black. By 1960 there no longer existed such disparate groups as *Webster's* names "new, original, or experimental." The "ideas, designs, and techniques" had begun to merge inexorably, willfully and wistfully.

Other kinds of music, too, were reorienting themselves—sometimes subconsciously—toward a simplicity antidotal to our mixed-up times, a simplicity nonetheless expensive and thus ideal for records.

Jazz, for instance, in becoming a thoroughly random expression, had reached the end of the line. Most of the devotees changed cars for another trip propelled by the vocal statement of rock. That statement, in an increasingly wild world, seemed sanely simple, like a troubadour tune. Physical reaction was the byword, and we were allowed again to dance and sing. The singing was to verse which, like that of the 1930s, dealt with "the times," though the commitment now contained a fantasy of surrealist humor. Back too was Big Band backing, but only as a device made feasible through records. If the Beatles, at least, can afford accompaniment by the London Philharmonic, it is a one-shot deal caught and mass-produced in wax. Many of their sound effects are borrowed from the experimentalists; yet sound effects they remain, not integral but arbitrary, like the Zen dice-throwing of "chance" composers. Rock's real starting point is with the community-sing revival dolled up for modern consumption.

Meanwhile, experimental music itself forsook its avant-gardism-at-any-price and became as scholarly an instruction as eighteenth-century counterpoint. To electronic equipment was added a system of composition by computers, cheaper and (they say) potentially unlimited. Not only at Manhattan gatherings were artists of conflicting persuasions united, but in schools as well. At Juilliard alone, four utterly diverse but world-famous composers now teach side by side, uniting their pupils once a week for exchange concerts. These pupils fuse the trends of their teachers. Their other living idols, if they have any, would be personified more in general practitioners like Foss or Henze than in specialists like Babbitt or Cage (who themselves are no longer all that specialized). Lukas Foss, Berlin-bred, reached puberty over here where by 1940 he was already famous for his American style. From that date the length of stylish musical generations (like schools of painting and poetry) telescoped with such acceleration that by the 1960s a trend's survival rate was about two weeks. Fair-haired Lukas kept on the bandwagons, leaping from Coplandian open prairies to Stravinskyan neoclassicism to post-Gregorian romanticism, to serial, to indeterminate, to jazz, to what he called pop-art music, and finally to "unsafe." "Composing once meant writing the music I like," he states. "Now it means to me: writing out of a deep concern for new music and for the cause of new music." Which is to say, for publicity.

Youth today is collective, no longer out for glory à la Beethoven, for "making it" à la Podhoretz; it acts through anonymous or through celebrated groups like the hippies or the Rolling Stones. If chic Andy Warhol still loves his fame, be it said he's pushing forty. But his clan of very young followers is just that, a clan, like Sinatra's. They don't care about masterpieces anymore. Communal offerings such as the Chartres cathedral or *The Chelsea Girls* are not, by definition, masterpieces.

If dance has replaced opera and so-called legitimate plays as the staple of living theater, the "dead" staple of the young art is found at the movies. But curiously, film lacks adventure in mixed-media sound tracks. Very contemporary thinkers in the very contemporary medium of movie making, like Fellini, Antonioni, Godard, with their "in" tone of alienation and violent "lack of communication," use, when it comes to original scores, either straight jazz, as in *Breathless*, Italianized jazz, as in *Juliet of the Spirits*, or no jazz at all, as in *Red Desert*, which dispensed with any music. The occasional American cinema use of experimental sound is predictably restricted to the dream sequence or to drug hallucination.

Thus the conservatives remain the suitable composers for movie scores because they have taken time to perfect their craft. Like rock musicians they borrow, if gingerly, from the experimentalists whose inventions they employ as decoration, not as formal points of departure. Conversely, die-hard experimentalists now revert to traditional instrumentation, especially in the more ambitious Iron Curtain lands. Take Poland, which since the war has given us a Gorecki or a Penderecki who use normal strings to imitate electronic sounds, just as women nowadays tease their real hair to resemble mod wigs.

If mod wigs began in England as a style of living, musically they are covered by an old hat. That nation's inherent conservatism is partly accountable to the overwhelming personal dynamics of Benjamin Britten's eclecticism. (Third stream jazz and neoromantic chromaticism are just starting to take hold there.) And all the young British stem from Britten—even by virtue of denying him—just as Britten stems from Stravinsky, Stravinsky whose retainment of individuality is of itself individual, a last stand.

And France? She has never been musical, despite appearances. Which is to say that, although producing more than her share of great composers plus a number of great performers, she has never produced a viable public for these musicians. If the seven lively arts in the countries of our earth can be distinguished as either aural or visual (and they *can*: no fine art except cooking and sex is dedicated to the sense of taste, touch, or smell), the French have always been leaders in the visual. Always, that is, until Rauschenberg acquired the laurel crown in 1961. Which left Paris with little international prestige, her composers having long since emigrated to Germany.

Soon after the war Germany ironically became a recipient for French "refugees" whose new esthetic, though grudgingly sanctioned, was hardly fostered at home by the old guard. The old guard composers themselves had enough problems getting heard. Led by the dominating Boulez, young French musicians took over the willing government-sponsored radio stations and summer festivals of Germany, from where they dictated what soon was to become the "international style." Back home today the newest flock, typical of the Gallic tradition of naughtiness, has already officially dethroned the mentor by composing, I'm told, *Le Tombeau de Boulez*. Boulez himself has now turned into a conductor of classics.

The open question of what will come is vain but tantalizing. Tantalizing, because it is the primal question of human nature. Vain, because historic events, even history itself, switch focus every year as we funnel faster toward novel philosophies. Certainly we listen now to Mozart in a manner inconceivable to him: he was ignorant of Mascagni and Mildred Bailey who came between to recondition us. And already we hear with different ears the music of only a decade ago. History is a contemporary decision, not what once took place. So forecasts are useless.

Still, is it not fair from all of this to offer some conclusion? As things stand now, music appears in a state of redemption as "an acceptable art." The wild has turned establishment. That is a fact. And an establishment such as the National Institute of Arts and Letters, after long catering to experimental coteries, has this year proposed grants to David Del Tredici, Francis Thorne, William Flanagan, and myself, the last three being hard-core conservatives if ever there were any! As to the symphony situation, our bigger orchestras—doubtless from survival instinct and from sympathy (or rivalry) with schools taking the bit in their teeth— are now commissioning the more intransigent composers. Of necessity these composers will be coerced into writing more playable (and thus, presumably, more listenable) pieces. They won't think so much about being modern.

Anyway the modern as a concept has probably come to a close. Music's future lies, as always, in discovering and then codifying the present. The future, what's more, automatically takes care of itself. Our problem is Now.

(*1968*)

OUR MUSIC NOW

(1974)

Musically speaking, America is the most vital land in the world, and also the most abject. Vital, because composition—music's so-called creative aspect (the first aspect by which the cultural health of a country must be judged)—has finally matured into model independence. Abject, because the dissemination of this composition, through performance and funding, is slow and painful.

The most representative American—unlike Western European—composition is, for the moment, noncollaborative, specialized, and mostly for chamber groups (some quite large), usually without vocalists.

Sonic scenery, once named incidental music, has not been an assumed appendage of our straight theater for years. I don't mean that compact medium called musical comedy, which thrives today, but "background" or "mood" pieces. Economy, not taste, so raised the price of original incidental stage music that drama now uses, when anything, canned sound effects.

Movies? No treatise is yet published on music's conditioning role in film. Bad music wrecks good movies, good music can redeem a bad movie, and any music can radically alter the intention of any given scene. Its abstract (though not neutral) force makes music more subliminally persuasive than any other periphera of film, something cineasts have known from the start. Those handy pianists for silents grew up into the Steiners of talkies. Such studio employees—providers of auditory decor—gave way in turn to "serious" imports from New York. Then nothing. After the high-class wartime documentaries, movies produced no distinguished scores—no non-pop music with sufficient character to stand alone. Unlike stage music, which was priced into starvation, movie music depreciated with the advent of star directors, in Europe as in America.

Advanced directors employ hack composers, as though to join hands with a vital musician would constitute a threat. Or they too use the past. The famous concert accompanying *2001*, for instance, contains not one original note (of course, by definition a movie about the future cannot use music of the future), while our breakthrough movies, which otherwise receive citations, content themselves with theme songs or straight rock.

There is no real collaboration in movies anymore. There is no stage music anymore.

There never was nor will be television music either. Insofar as TV is not real-life reportage, it is not TV. Any music heard on TV is less good than on a stage or phonograph, even music conceived for TV. The long shot is meaningless on TV. The close-up is TV's triumph. Close-ups are arias. An opera made from only arias is not an opera. Even if it were, to present these arias as a series of close-ups would be redundant. Consider the claustrophobia of *Scenes from a Marriage*—sung!

The appetizing possibility of opera conceived for movies, a format that may prove the salvation of the hybrid monster, has yet to be tried. "Tried and true" is what composers meanwhile persist in setting, when not foisting upon us mixed-media propositions self-titled opera.

Barber's revised *Antony and Cleopatra* (on Shakespeare) will soon be granted a second chance after its sabotage years ago, although the new version remains "old opera." Elsewhere the visual distractions of a Berio seem no more musically professional than in high school, and qualify as "new opera" only because the composer calls them that.

If opera, even at its most outrageous, is distinguished from show-biz tantrums by the formality of its word settings for singing actors (i.e., by its superimposition of one set of symbols upon another set that will be interpreted theatrically), then only Stanley Silverman comes close to exemplifying the definition. His vehicles for real singers dadaistically amalgamate all styles past and present. They are small scale (dramatized song cycles really) and financially feasible for schools. Although they could be blown up for production in Tibet or Penn Station, they do not offer themselves as masterpieces.

Those still awaiting a composer of the Great American Opera find their chief candidate in Leon Kirchner. Kirchner, a maker of "abstract" chamber and orchestral works, is not known for vocal settings (if indeed he's done any), much less for lyric dramas. Yet during a decade his musicalizing of Saul Bellow's *Henderson the Rain King* has been the loudest secret since *Who's Afraid of Virginia Woolf?* before its unveiling.

Can Great American Operas be devised from Great American Novels? Previous chauvinist contenders have all been on original librettos. Not that viable music can't be based on preexisting literature (some think Verdi's *Otello* greater than *Meistersinger*); it's just that American composers haven't yet added convincing dimensions to classical European plays. Or even to native blockbusters. (Britisher Benjamin Britten with his *Turn of the Screw* and *Billy Budd* has, for whatever reason, dealt more movingly than any American opera maker with established American texts.)

Need for the "big statement"—still acute for book critics—has become a thing of the past for most musicians, due largely to inroads of pop where breath is short and inspiration collective.

Only two American composers have come up with memorable ballet scores in thirty years—that is, since the happy postwar collaborations of Martha Graham with Copland, Schuman, Barber, Dello Joio. They are Lucia Dlugoszewski, whose concoctions for Erick Hawkins's choreography are a hypnotic joy to both ear and eye (she herself performs on instruments of her own unique construction, thus replacing the late irreplaceable Harry Partch), and Leonard Bernstein, whose accompaniments for dance remain paragons of theatricality even sans dance. Balanchine's caused nothing in American music.

No other serious composer has come so close to inheriting that part of Stravinsky's specialness which allowed for the staginess of sound—which asked that music be visual while retaining its exclusivity as music—than Bernstein. But as exception to prove any premise, he's not to be pigeonholed.

The most traveled composer in the world, he is the least cosmopolitan, his music, all of it, stemming straight from America's most identifiable heritage, jazz. Yet Bernstein is America's first Jewish composer, if Jewish, before meaning Semitic or Talmudic, means viewpoint. This meaning, consciously conveyed to his art, renders Bernstein's sounds and subjects more Jewish than those of, say, Gershwin and Copland, with their Carolinian Negroes and Appalachian cowboys; or Hugo Weisgall and Marvin Levy, with their Strindberg and O'Neill heroines; or David Diamond and William Schuman, with their fondness for Waspish symphonic forms.

And Bernstein is the only "classical" American who stays, in heart and in practice, a collaborator. Nine-tenths of his work is for theater (ballet, musical comedy, the ritual mass, movies) where he joins with others; when composing opera or a straight concert work he collaborates with himself.

There exists no more beguiling melodist. That this gift can be promoted not only charmingly but scarily is shown with a craft ever more distilled. His best piece to date, the *Dybbuk* dances, succeeds in conveying maximum Bernstein volatility through an almost silent tension. His niche in public fancy makes him—as such things are judged—our second most significant (although curiously not very influential) composer over fifty. The first is Elliott Carter.

From Stravinsky, Bernstein inherited the catholic virtuosity and Carter the grand-style fame. And Carter is the only composer in the world, not excluding Boulez, who could wear such a mantle with gravity—none other seems needed anymore.

How balanced with Bernstein's heat is Carter's ice! The difference between theatrics and dramatics. Bernstein is all civilized contrast, sentiment, narrative; Carter is monochrome madness, perfunctory, nonprogrammatic. Storytelling in Carter's music translates only as metaphor—as events occurring to instruments, not to humans. Such strictly instrumental occurrences sometimes cause this composition to be termed uncompromising. It eschews carnal appeal, nor does it presume to charm. Seduction in sound comes facilely through the admixture of orchestral timbres, through richness of color. Though Elliott Carter is skilled with that palette, he is far more colloquial with intimate (though no less huge formally) conveyances. Except for the crimson human voice. Indeed, he most excels in that grayest, that most undifferentiated, and, they say, that most risky (because most exposed) and "pure" of mediums, the string quartet, for which few composers since Bartók have written with much sense of necessity.

Necessity, however, is what Carter projects. Not, as some would have it, the necessity of intellect but the clean-cut urgency of a child's fit. Like never-resting souls tangled in hell proceed his bowed counterpoints, and always in performance after performance they are *tangled in the same way*, like those viscous strands on a Pollock canvas that, actually still, seem to move through time. Nothing great is ever left to chance, and great Carter surely is in his ability to notate insanity with a precision that, after the fifth or twelfth hearing, renders the notes as logical as the placement of beasts in the Peaceable Kingdom. In the unwhorish communicability of the logic of folly (or the folly of logic) lies Carter's force, a force particularly intense for young citizens to whom personal grandeur seems again (after years of mindless group grooving) to be a need.

Our female composers are in all ways equal to their brothers. If Dlugoszewski is queen of the dance, Miriam Gideon has for long decades been, in the cognoscenti's eye, a weaver of vocal fabrics at once taut and tender. Her contemporary Louise Talma, a more muscular craftswoman, is drawn to large instrumental expressions (although she's the only composer ever to have obtained a libretto from Thornton Wilder, the important *Alcestiad*, an opera yet to be heard in America).

No musician mixes more exciting orchestral hues or draws more personal melodic lines than does youngish Barbara Kolb, and none projects more purposeful know-how in vast formats than does Betsy Jolas.

Here are but five of a growing body of women composers. To single them out as such (deftly avoiding words like *lovely*, which I often use for men) is maybe unfair since they no longer do so themselves. They do not wish your ear to recognize their efforts as feminine—as "ladies' music" rather than as music. Nor really do they endure more discrimination than male composers; composers as a species are so foreign to mass consciousness—even to music lovers—that they go undespised in one amorphous lump. (Talma's opera remains unperformed not because she's a woman, nor yet a bad woman, but because she's a woman who writes operas.) Composers are all freaks, yes, but the public doesn't see them. What doesn't exist can't be scorned.

Conducting is visibly a domain of males. Our country boasts less than twenty first-rate orchestras, and the women's committees who largely run these orchestras are not about to let any of their own claim such plums. Even American males aren't much in the running. With notable exceptions our conductors are foreigners.

In a gracefully talkative documentary on the trials of America's sole female symphonic conductor, Antonia Brico, age seventy-three, shows herself more advanced sociologically than musically. Through all her lauding of sacred monsters like Schweitzer and Schubert we hear no word about any American performer or composer of either sex, nor even a passing reference to what we call modern music. Liberated women can remain reactionary artists.

The Russian cellist Rostropovich a decade ago commissioned a number of large-scale vehicles from composers all over the world. That he was also a great interpreter seems slight when you realize that, emerging from a creatively archaic country, he single-handedly caused to exist most of the important cello literature of this half-century. Imagine an American cellist, emerging from this creatively advanced country, pursuing such a notion! Or any of our virtuosos. No Cliburn, no Stern has yet—not even for his immortality—voluntarily paid for a new work, and those few big names who have, have through foundations.

People in the Midwest imagine the Eastern marketplace to be congenial, homogenized. They ask a visiting composer for anecdotes about famous performers. He doesn't know any. Famous performers don't play his music so he has no occasion to meet them. He rationalizes that they wouldn't "know how" anyway.

Expecting her to reply "They don't know what they're doing," I asked Barbara Kolb how the Marlboro contingent sounds when, exceptionally, they rehearse one of her not-easy pieces. (That contingent is, after all, drenched from birth to death in nineteenth-century middle-European chefs d'oeuvre, whereas Barbara is used to hearing her music at the hands of Fromm Foundation specialists.) "They're terrific," she answers. "They play it like music, not like modern music."

On yet another composers' panel, our exchange becomes amiable prattle. The very twentieth-century phenomenon of the Roundtable on New Music suddenly seems obsolete.

There used to be mutual stimulation. Musicians of conflicting persuasions goaded each other about ideology. With cheers and sneers, flying fur and splitting hair, the identical questions and answers were spouted for the thousandth time. It all grew too loud, lasted too long and settled nothing, but it was therapeutic.

In the past years, simultaneous with revolutions in more urgent arenas, composers of quite different schools and aims have become live-and-let-live. They even play each other's music, because they are united in a sort of ho-hum defiance against standard virtuosos who ignore them. When they do join at roundtables their purpose is not to chastise each other but to present a united front before performing units. They want representation, copyright revision, their just rewards through royalty revisions, money from the government. To make these demands heard in high places leaves composers no time to meet on panels. They're too busy scribbling recommendations for each other to the National Endowment for the Arts.

Endowments. We welcome their encouragement, though it's touch and go. Certainly the trumpeted "cultural explosion," if it exists, is independent of private or public sponsorship, and like most explosions exudes a residue of destruction and waste.

Lots of money is being misspent by self-appointed committees (like Fromm, the once noble) to determine "important American works," the result to be funneled to conductors, here and abroad, too lazily busy to examine the music themselves. Both state and national councils of the arts require that not only unknown petitioners but composers with long-standing credentials prove (in words and before the fact) that the music they need money to compose will be both a masterpiece and a profit maker. Ford asks fewer questions, merely slashes the budget.

Do these discouragements change the shape as well as the bulk of fine art today? Qualifications determine recipe proportions, not flavors. Sure, outside restrictions are bad, but limitations, whether imposed by an artist on himself or by the state, do not deter communication. Art is form, form is elastic. While remaining the same size and weight, form stretches itself grandiloquently to cheat censors. Censors anyway make less difference in art than in "life"—less difference to a novelist than to a journalist. For an artist pure freedom is dangerous, controls are good. But he must stay free to control his own controls.

Art does not grow from the collective tension of the left but from individual leisure. Sadly, our most liberal politicos are often the least culture-minded. Bella Abzug, for example, makes no statements on behalf of the arts, yet her district alone houses the most concentrated covey of first-rate creators this side of Paris in the 1920s. God knows she's for human rights, but only the jaded rich seem to have time for the art of artists as well as for their campaign support.

Political art? Military marches impel men into battle. What marches impel them to turn around and walk away?

The next years may overhaul our awareness of serious national music. Every American composer has been called on for the Bicentennial and the results will be heard, like it or not, for a long time, on programs large and small in even the hickest towns. Already this year we celebrate widely the hundredth birthday of Charles Ives. Like Satie in France, our only musical primitive has become the most overrated of underrated composers, but his imposition on the general consciousness is wholesome. Except for Hemingway, greater America has always been a bit embarrassed by her high-culture figures. Now with an Ives festival, a Whitman bridge, and a Gershwin postage stamp, we are finally making a thing of artists rather than of generals. The thing results from the responsibility of growing up.

(1974)

OUR MUSIC NOW

(1984)

The state of contemporary classical music? Worse than ever. Today's classical—or in ASCAP parlance, "serious"—composer is less a pariah than merely an unknown species, not only to the unwashed but to cultivated amateurs, and his situation is unique among creative artists. A fancier of Leonardo, Byron, or Shakespeare knows their current equivalents—Larry Rivers, John Ashbery, Edward Albee—but if he also fancies, say, Vivaldi or even Machaut, he finds *their* equivalents mainly in pop musicians like Michael Jackson or, at best, Stephen Sondheim. Composers such as myself, whatever our relative worth among ourselves, resemble that genus of tree frog, newly discovered in Guyana, which for millennia went about its business without bothering human beings. The situation is worsening (assuming, as we must, that the situation should need bettering) because of the confusion—the merging—in the public ken of pop and classical, genres that in fact are unrelated, one difference being that pop is mainly entertainment and thus, unlike classical, does not ask for more than passivity from its audience. But since pop has become legitimized (because it makes money) by promoters, and because the public is ever more undifferentiated, that public is exonerated from responsibility toward contemporary classical, which is not even scorned. (What doesn't exist can't be scorned.)

Another reason for the worsening state is that composer and performer, often the same person a century ago, now face opposite directions. The performer's repertory being solely of old chestnuts, the living composer flounders in a vacuum. Now, only in the realm of musical art do we find this anachronism. Most of the plays and all of the movies that we enjoy (or detest) are by modern artists, and so are most of the paintings and ballets and novels and architecture. In an area where the past is anathema, we speak of "revivals" of even so recent a dramatist as, for example, Eugene O'Neill; but where the past is sovereign, we never speak of revivals of, for example, Beethoven. Thus for the public all art today, except music, bleeds with the blood of the times. Meanwhile the concert audience, which absorbs strictly the past, is as passive—as dead finally—as the pop audience.

In the specific domain of Song, performers in America don't even know *how* to perform the music of today. Europeans are general practitioners and Americans are specialists in everything except recital-song repertory. Young German or Italian or French singers master the problem of their native tongue first and foremost, learn thoroughly their country's vocal output, and often spend distinguished careers singing solely in their own language. Young American singers learn every language *except* their own. Graduation recitals feature songs in German, Italian, French, and Spanish, none of which the students "think" in; if they do offer an English encore, it's tossed off with a fake foreign accent. Due partly to the high majority of European teachers who deem English unsingable, partly to the opera-oriented bias of students themselves, the voice recital has atrophied in the United States. The students (those not aiming toward musical comedy) sniff neither glory nor money in English-language repertory. They feel no pride in—have scarcely an awareness of—the long tradition of songs in English. To declare as they do that English is ungrateful is to see clearly the thrilling pitfalls, which in foreign tongues are invisible. The only thing bad about English as a vocal medium is bad English. And the only thing bad about modern vocal settings is bad music.

Conductors? The same phony mystique. The United States—or some of them—are vain about concocting ever-grander doom machines, but with high culture we still feel obscured by Europe. Women's committees (and it's they who really make the decisions), through some demented notion of glamour, will hire an inferior foreigner before a superior home boy. Or girl. And the conductors we end up with are not about to push American produce. Adding insult to injury, a Muti openly contends there *is* no American produce. Interestingly in France, where on a superficial level a crass Yankee chic has taken over nearly everything else, outcries are always raised when non-Frenchpersons aspire to musical organizations. (A cold eye is currently cast upon the Italian Massimo Bogianckino, new director of the Paris Opera.) Of course, our James Levine may be an exception that proves the rule, though what really has he done for American—or indeed any new—music?

here's less and less interchange. Choreographers and composers no longer conspire together. How many original dance scores, even bad ones, can you list from the past twenty years? Movies all use either pop sound tracks or none at all. Meanwhile, professional critics of dance and movies seldom mention such music as is used in ballets and film, much less do they mention *how* the music is used (as buffer, springboard, mood setter, whatever). As for straight music critics, they're scarcely worth the paper they write on. Yes, one or two with a classy integrity have emerged since the withdrawal of Virgil Thomson, but their outlets are scant. There's just no room for them anymore. Nor are there outlets for young composers once they leave school. Which is why, during school, they should mercilessly exploit the available executants, because once those confreres become superstars, or even nobodies in the outside world, the give-and-take is kissed good-bye.

Recording too is increasingly mediocre, as everyone knows. Leontyne Price told me only last month that she, the grandest diva of them all, is no longer in a position to impose a disc of so-called art songs by Americans, although she'd sort of like to. If other big names could swing it, I don't see them doing it. Salability is the sole criterion for value in recording, and the same criterion begins to erode publishing. A publisher close to my heart, and one of the world's most distinguished, has just been ordered by its computer to discontinue printing all choral works by a certain composer (close to my heart and one of the world's most distinguished), because "they don't sell." Even the journal *ASCAP In Action* wherein this, my impotent yelp, will appear is 98 percent dedicated to hyping the commercial at the cost of the presumably longer range of the classical (although, in fairness, the latter is fed from the crumbs of the former).

Yet is there truly a longer range? Not if management, which is the most sinister wrongdoer in this melee, has anything to say about it. Impresarios—every one of them—tell you with straight faces that they adore new music but that the public doesn't buy it, so they're forced to edit what their stars play in the sticks. Stars acquiesce, since Mammon's pull is firmer than Euterpe's. Now, impresarios lie. They hate new music. If they didn't, they'd sell it: you can always sell what you believe in. The public will accept what it's given, if given with love and a little enthusiasm. A tenor, for instance, who explains to a women's club that this or that song is actually in their native tongue and that they of all listeners will appreciate it, has won half the battle.

Can we bring about larger audiences for new music? Well, even allowing that managers are of goodwill, there's no such thing as one audience. Mine is hardly Wuorinen's, though they do overlap each other more than with John Kander's whose audience is nonetheless nearer to ours than to John Denver's, whose has little in common with Alban Berg's. You don't see the same people at *Lulu* as at *Tosca,* though if those people occasionally overlap each other, they don't overlap ballet people, who don't overlap Merce Cunningham. Still, the same people who swallow without wincing the Cageian cacophonies that accompany Cunningham would, if they heard those cacophonies in the concert hall, run out screaming. Such is the power of the visual as an aid to appreciation. (Or is it oblivion?)

However, do we really need larger audiences? Is not that notion itself a touch commercial? Must everyone have everything? There are hierarchies and lowerarchies even among the elite. (I, for one, with all my aristocratic penchants, could live on blissfully without Beethoven or Schubert, without ever seeing another art exhibit, and without musing over poetry—despite my small but solid reputation for setting poetry convincingly to music.) Serious composers, if they're good (but who decides?), should be given barrels of emeralds without having to justify their existence in practical ways.

That would be in an ideal world. Then again, since music always reflects the tensions of the times, in an ideal world perhaps there would be no music. Are you hoping I'll close on the conventional upbeat? There is no upbeat. All is down.

(*1984*)

SIX

OF SONGS
AND WORDS

POETRY OF MUSIC

Since music lacks content beyond itself, can it then be compared with poetry? "What does it *mean?*" people ask of a poem. About music they do not ask *why*—at least not in the sense of its dealing a double standard, of being beauty that instructs. When singers question me on the significance of the words to a song, I answer: They signify whatever the music tells you they signify. What more do I know about poetry?

Poems are not "why." They are "because." Comprised of both question and answer they mirror music more singularly than any other human enterprise. Perhaps because of their common quality, poetry and music often marry. Now the marriages, however seemingly ideal to outsiders, are all based on misunderstanding at best, at worst on total perversion.

Having his verse set to music is not necessarily the ultimate compliment a poet may receive from a composer. Yet many poets today covet the idea, at least before the fact. They ponder Beethoven and Schiller, Schumann and Heine, Ravel and Mallarmé, those sublime collaborative unions wherein the poets' words were illuminated while presumably remaining the same—the same, only more so! Actually those unions were not collaborations at all. They were settings of a *fait accompli*, the *fait* being verse able to stand alone, the *accompli* being a denial of that ability, resulting not in "the poem only more so" but in a transformation: a song. The song often bemused the poet who, though maybe pleased (more likely dismayed), never quite recognized his original impulse. After all, had he not heard his own "music" while composing the poem? Naturally no musician hears that poem the same way, or why would he write a song?

Song is the sole example of one preexisting art medium being juxtaposed intact upon another. The words of the poem are not *adapted*, like film scenarios from plays; they remain unaltered while being tampered with, and unlike other musical forms—fugue, for instance, or sonata—there exist no fixed rules for song.

There are as many "right" ways for tampering with a poem as there are poems and good composers, or different viewpoints of a single composer toward the same poem. A composer's viewpoint is right if it works, regardless of the poet's reaction. For the poet will never feel the song as he felt the poem that inspired the song.

Debussy, Fauré, and Hahn all used the same verse of Verlaine, all convincingly, all more or less differently. More or less. "Clair de lune" did suggest a similar built-in musical formula to French composers at the turn of the century.

On the principle that there is no one way to musicalize a poem I once composed a cycle *(Poems of Love and the Rain)* by selecting eight works by as many Americans and setting each one to music twice, as contrastingly as possible. The performing sequence of the sixteen songs was pyramidal: one through eight, then back from eight to one. Although each poem is repeated, none of the music is; thus the poems supposedly take on new impact at second hearing not only by virtue of being sung at a later time, but also by being reinvested with another shape.

It goes without saying that I speak here of poetry as distinct from lyrics. Poetry is self-contained, while lyrics are made to be sung and don't necessarily lead a life of their own. The best lyricists are collaborative craftsmen. When "real" poets write with song in mind they fail both as poets and as lyricists because, in "helping" the composer, they overindulge in presumably felicitous vocables that emerge as self-conscious banality. To argue that they *hear* what they write is irrelevant to musicians; we have come a long way since Homer, and poems today are mostly made and absorbed in silence. A poet declaiming his own verse is no more definitive, no more *inevitable*, than some composer's setting of that verse. This applies as much to readings of always-the-same verse against never-the-same jazz backgrounds as it does to the embarrassing solo histrionics of a Dylan Thomas or the sabotagingly dry delivery of an Elizabeth Bishop.

Elizabeth Bishop in Brazil and I in France corresponded for years on such matters. Finally in 1957 I made a setting of her masterpiece, "Visits to St Elizabeths," recorded it with a mezzo-soprano, and sent the disc to Rio where it was awaited with high expectations. The tact of Elizabeth's disappointment was touching. "I wonder why you picked a female voice," she wrote in 1964, "and how it would sound with a male voice." Again, in 1968: "Sometime I'd like to write you one small criticism— not the music, of course, but the manner of singing it." Finally in 1969: "My complaint is that it sounds too hysterical. I hadn't imagined it that way, somehow. Yes, I had thought of a male voice, I suppose—but I don't believe that is what bothers me. It is the fast tempo and the increasing note of hysteria. Because the poem is observation, really, rather than participation . . . something like that. Two friends have said rather the same thing to me. It is awfully well sung, nevertheless. I don't know whether it could just be *slowed* down, or not? Probably not." (I'm reminded of Saroyan's poignant remark to Paul Bowles about the latter's music for "My Heart's in the Highlands": "Couldn't it be played more—well—in *minor?*")

Poets' work ends with their poems. During the concert they can only weep impotent from the wings, especially when the song succeeds. *"Visits to St Elizabeths"* in fact succeeds more than many of my pieces, being often sung, loudly applauded, and singers say it "feels good." How answer Miss Bishop when the song imposes its own terms of longevity?

As to the singer's sex she has a point, but a point of taste, not quality. In principle, we cannot distinguish blindfolded between male and female pianists, say, or violinists. A composer hence has a stricter concept of piano and violin attributes than of the human voice. He is more lenient of *varieties* of interpretation given one song by many singers, since a soprano is by her nature more limber than a baritone. Nothing precludes a woman's persuasively singing a man's song at a faster speed if within the speed she maintains a logical attitude. (The reverse is less convincing, at least in opera, not for musical but for esthetic reasons. While we can empathize and even weep with Octavian or Cherubino, a man in a woman's role is only good for a laugh.) As for a man performing the Bishop work, I like the idea, though the reality would sound top-heavy, it being a patter song.

Once I judged a contest for young composers. My duty was to select the best from some two hundred manuscripts. An unconscionable percentage were settings of "The Hollow Men," all for male chorus and all starting with the first-thing-that-comes-to-mind solution: open parallel fifths. Which may explain why T. S. Eliot never granted musical rights to anyone.

———

Not that Howard Moss disapproved of my musicalization of his long *King Midas* suite, though certainly his sonorous concept (a concept after the fact) was not like mine. The songs are lean and western, while he saw (saw, not heard) eastern opulence. Yet for the final publication his only request was sizable billing, he being more concerned with rightful recognition than with sabotage. After all, the poetry hasn't been stolen: it's still right there in his book.

Poets' names are seldom seen on song covers and usually omitted from printed song programs. Yet where would the song be without them? Where, though, would the singer be without the song whose composer is given proportionately short shrift? And returning full circle, where is the poet without the singer? "But I am not without the singer," answers the poet. "The singer is myself, and what you call illuminations are to me evasions."

Good poetry won't always lend itself to music, won't of itself make good music even if the composer is good. Some poems more than others cry out to be sung (their authors' wishes, like Eliot's, notwithstanding), though different cries are heeded by different composers with different viewpoints on dealing with those cries—whether to clarify, dominate, obscure, or ride on them.

Still, better good poetry than bad. Music, being more immediately powerful, does tend to invisibilize all poems except bad ones. Despite popular notions to the contrary, it is a demonstrable fallacy that second-rate poems make the best songs.

Theodore Chanler may well have become America's greatest composer of the genre had not his small catalog adhered to mainly one poetaster (Father Feeney), whose words sound even sillier framed by lovely tunes that through some inverted irony end up being subdued by those words. Duparc gained Parnassus on a lifetime output of only thirteen songs; yet I wonder how they'd come off with other verse than Baudelaire's. Chanler just may make it on his eight delicious *Epitaphs* based on the solid words of Walter de la Mare.

Despite whatever reputation I may hold in this area, I am not *just* a song composer in the sense that Duparc was. My three hundred plus songs written since childhood add up to as many hours labor and as many minutes hearing, nothing compared to the long labors of symphonic orchestrations and other works in the larger forms. Yet inasmuch as all real music is essentially a vocal utterance, be it "Danny Boy" or *Petrouchka*, I *am* just a song composer.

If less is more, one great song is worth ten merely adroit symphonies. To say you can have it for a song is to sell the form cheap.

The form, of course, is whatever the composer feels the verse dictates. (The verse, so to speak, dictates its own execution order.) Until the age of twenty-three my songs were built largely upon the dictates of "singable" poetry from Sappho through Shakespeare to Hopkins. Then for a decade in Europe I composed in whatever language I thought I was thinking in. (Incidentally, my songs in French seldom get done, nor do any French songs by Americans. If a French singer condescends to sing an American song, he—or rather, she: it's invariably a she—will go all out and learn one in English, for better or worse. And when an American singer decides to learn a French song, she finds it more "legitimate" to learn one by a Frenchman. Britten has set, in the author's tongue, poems of Hölderlin, Rimbaud, even Pushkin, but they are sung mostly by Britten's ever-faithful Peter Pears. Nor am I aware that Italians, for instance, are given to performing Britten's marvelous *Michelangelo Sonnets*. Of course, Italians only sing arias anyway.)

During those first twenty years of songwriting, I also used regularly the sounds I most normally inhale: American poetry, especially that of friends, some of whom made words expressly for my setting. Words, not lyrics.

Take, for instance, Paul Goodman, who was once my Manhattan Goethe: the poet to whom I as a balladeer most often returned. From 1946 his verse, prose, and theater beautifully served my short tunes, choruses, and opera. Lives shift, ever faster. We seldom meet anymore, in either speech or song. Paul today seems more drawn toward guiding the political thoughts of the young; this can't be done through poetry. And I grow more withdrawn. Yet lately while rehearsing his songs all written in France during the early 1950s (a period of weep-and-the-world-weeps-with-you), I became rekindled with a need for the words and music of that easier decade. The rekindling has not fired more songs of the sort, but it has cast light again on a bit of conversation between old friends.

Or take Frank O'Hara, whose young and recent death placed both a shroud and halo over that vital group called the New York School of

Poets. The last of several occasions for which we conjointly conceived an idea was a Poulenc memorial concert. Alice Esty invited this collaboration. Frank made a poem I couldn't understand and didn't want to set. So he made another which I couldn't understand but wanted to set, and did. As a musician I "understand" poetry not during but only after the fact of setting.

Nor do poets *understand* music, thank God. So-called radical poets, like O'Hara and Goodman, usually in their musical taste are conservative. How often one finds sprinkled through their pages the names of Beethoven, Saint-Saëns, Rachmaninoff.

Take also the poet John Ashbery who writes his *Glazunoviana* while editing *Art News* which is, by definition, about the new (as over in Paris the up-to-date Françoise Sagan drops the name of Brahms!). Ashbery supplied the words to my vocal trio *Some Trees*. The words were no problem, for the music does not make them a problem: I didn't try to illustrate their sense, but to underline their sound. Poets want their words (if not their meanings) comprehended. The farther out the poet, the nearer in must be his musician.

My songs are love letters. To whom? Like Vladimir Nabokov I write "for myself in multiplicate," meaning for friends, those personal extremities. Are unheard melodies sweeter? Intelligence is silence, truth being invisible. But music does not (should not) appeal only to our intelligence, nor is it especially concerned with truth any more than poetry is.

Yet we're all afraid of being misrepresented, as though we didn't misrepresent ourselves every minute. A song is but a single facet of ourself, which the listener takes as the whole self.

Song is the reincarnation of a poem that was destroyed in order to live again in music. The composer, no matter how respectful, must treat poetry as a skeleton on which to bestow flesh, breaking a few bones in the process. He does not render a poem more *musical* (poetry isn't music, it's poetry); he weds it to sound, creating a third entity of different and sometimes greater magnitude than either parent. It too may ultimately stand alone, as those nineteenth-century songs now do despite being disowned at birth by their poetic fathers. *We* hear them as totalities without considering their growing pains.

Indeed much past poetry is known to us exclusively through song settings, hence our unconscious assumption of such poetry's emanations of musical inevitability. Yet when it comes to his own work, today's poet has his own notion of inevitability. He is torn between a need to hear his words sung, yet for those words to retain their initial beat and echo, their identity proper. His "proper" must obligatorily be sacrificed; his notion of inevitability becomes the fly in the ointment. The only inevitable way to set poetry is the "right" way, and there is no one right way.

(*1969*)

SONG SINGING
IN AMERICA

What the world needs is a Society for the Promotion of Last Performances. In declaring a moratorium on The Hundred Masterpieces, the Society would reserve prizes for those artists who are the first to give the last hearings of Beethoven and Brahms. The prize money would go, of course, to new music. And since all living composers have a vested disinterest in standard programming, they would prove useful in drawing up the rules.

Are composers really that bad off? Yes, some. American song composers are.

Vocal contours depend upon language and eventually give music a discernible national character. Vocal music is the source of non-vocal music, and speech inflection is the direct basis of all music of all cultures. So, since music resembles the speech of a nation, it also resembles the people. People therefore resemble their music.

In theory, the definitive interpreter of a country's songs should be a singer from that country.

America is a land of specialists in everything but song literature, while Europe produces general practitioners in everything but song literature. Voice students in Germany, France, and Italy logically master the songs of their own language first, often to the lifetime exclusion of all songs from other countries; the great foreign singers sing primarily in their native tongue. Americans, illogically, learn songs in foreign languages first (languages that they neither speak nor think in), often to the exclusion of American—or even English—works, whose existence they ignore; the most famous American singers sing primarily in foreign tongues.

Famous Americans in local recitals during the current season have sung mostly in German. (One or two may throw in some token Ives learned under duress last year because of that composer's big birthday.) They defend themselves. "Yes, but *my* Schumann is exemplary." "Would you sing him in Munich?" "I wouldn't dare."

Fischer-Dieskau, as the exceptional European general practitioner, is more prepared than most Americans for giving an all-English-language program tomorrow.

Recitals by opera stars? These are not recitals but bouquets of airs cut down to piano size. "I'd far rather do lieder," declares the American diva, "but my fans demand arias." Fans take what they're given. And divas, despite their protestations, sing what they believe in. Alas, since they also believe in fans, the circle turns vicious.

Evelyn Lear states: "Thank God my coach forced me to give up modern stuff, it almost ruined my voice. Composers should take voice lessons if they want to learn to write grateful vocal music."

But Callas and Tebaldi ruined *their* voices on standard stuff. Meanwhile, that tiny handful of specialists—Beardslee, Curtin, Gramm, Wolff—sound better than ever after decades of doing contemporary music along with their "grateful" programs. That's because they don't treat modern music as modern music, but as music. No music of any period, if a singer believes in it, can harm the voice. (But aren't those broad jumps of Mozart and high dives of Bach riskier than anything Stravinsky ever penned?)

As for composers taking singing lessons, that would only reveal their own limitations rather than another's possibilities. Knowing how to sing has nothing to do with composing musically, hence vocally (for all true music, be it Paganini or Varèse, is in essence song). That composers have never been singers has obviously not kept them from creating the definition of vocality. When they follow a singer's suggestion (professional composers do listen), it's always to make a passage not simpler but harder.

"English is bad to sing in," say American singers. Because they comprehend the words, they can no longer hear them, and are slightly embarrassed. Of course, the only bad thing about musicalized English is bad English. But our singers have been geared to language as medium, not message. Indeed, the only language any of us hears purely is the one we don't understand. When we learn to think in a new language we can no longer just listen to it because we know what it "means." Insofar as songs are literary they are not strictly music, and so (as Gertrude Stein says) they make us feel funny. Yet that funny feeling is exactly what all nonvocal music seeks to provide.

Sutherland is a dumb singer of dumb music. Sills is a smart singer of dumb music. Curtin is a smart singer of smart music. (Dumb singers of smart music? No example comes to mind, though there used to be "voiceless" singers of smart music.)

This is not to denigrate but to identify categories. I use *dumb* in the sense of *bête:* appealing to the body—as opposed to the intellect— through beat and tune, avoiding byways of harmonic density and contrapuntal nuance. Thus all rock and bel canto is dumb, while no serial dodecaphony is. The best of Poulenc—himself the best songwriter of this age—is dumb, and Stravinsky is dumber than he's given credit for (the early vocal ballets *Noces* and *Histoire* being pure carnality, as by extension are *The Rake's Progress* and *Requiem Canticles*). Bach is dumb in most of the well-tempered preludes and in the middle movements of his sonata structures, smart in fugues and choral pieces.

Dumbness that tries for smartness fails, like *The Rake's Progress.* Smartness that tries for dumbness fails, like Salzman's *Nude Paper Sermon.* The mixture of innocence and experience jells only when inadvertent, as sometimes in Satie or Scriabin.

Sills is intelligent about analyzing that which requires no analysis, but at least her diction and stage action are cleaner than Sutherland's. Curtin is more "important": she knows what she's up to in scores that ask that she know what she's up to.

Is Billie Holiday a dumb singer of dumb music? Yes, because what she does, and what she does it to, is uncomplicated and unliterary. Is Gerard Souzay a dumb singer of smart music? No, because although his approach to all art is instinctive rather than scholarly, the contemporary music in which he specializes is of the nonintellectual brand, that is, French.

The French, curiously, who are nothing if not practical, have for three centuries produced a music whose attraction is essentially sensual. Germans, who are nothing if not emotional, are the ones who come up with the systems.

———

Awestruck by Mozart, people ask how he made magic from mere scales, and they cite the slow ebbing strings at the climax of *Don Giovanni*. Then they proffer their own nonanswer: He was Mozart!

A real answer: Assuming the strings *are* magic, they are not "mere" scales. Mere scales are just that, mere, and get boring in lesser Mozart sonatas. However, in his opera the composer does turn a seven-note melodic minor mode into two (ascending, then descending) eight-note harmonic minor passages. He immediately repeats this pattern a half-tone higher, then a whole tone higher, and so on up chromatically, ever tightening the screw with this pseudomodulatory device (or vise) much copied in today's pop songs. Meanwhile a human basso intones a pedal "A" whose color alters according to the flux of color beneath, above, and beside it. These independent occurrences are melded by "abstract" chords of sustained lower brass, by a kettledrum heartbeat, and by the Commendatore's "concrete" language. Now, this concrete language—Italian prose—is missing from Mozart's first and only "plant" of the menacing mood, hours earlier, in the overture. But because the plant hints to connoisseurs what is to come (though the curtain's not yet up and human voices haven't yet been introduced), the scales in the overture may justly be termed psychological, a word inappropriate to any wholly nonvocal music, including Beethoven's quartets.

Mozart's "mere" scale was but one of many simultaneous happenings on his page: we may be aware of just that scale while the rest is subliminal; but that rest, while maybe magic, is analyzable magic.

That paragraph voices but one of many warnings about oversimplifying the gift to be simple. It's hard to be easy. Simplicity results from complex tailorings.

Is it time for black concertizers to desist from spirituals? Already years ago Leontyne Price sang hers unaccented (though her Barber and Harrison and even her Sauguet were edged in croon). Today Shirley Verrett, whose German and French are unaccented, fakes that drawl in her encores as white Helen Jepson used to do. Younger black singers learn the drawl from records.

Creatively considered, an ear for speech and an ear for music are never found together. Great composers don't write great verse, great poets don't compose great music. If a great songwriter—Schubert, say—does join through sound his ear for notes and verse, the verse is always by someone else. Often that someone is no one special. (Wagner, Menotti, Blitzstein, Noël Coward, who composed great music on their own words, are not often considered great poets.)

It is common practice for composers to shape fine music around preexisting words, but no poets have ever shaped fine verses around preexisting music, certainly not their own music. Even in pop, that casual yet profiteering domain, words generally come first.

The singing voice is the most satisfying of all instruments, the spoken voice the least. Melodrama, or unmetered speech imposed upon music, like a gnat on a lens, intrudes on the business at hand. A composer may have conceived his music as coexistent with speech (*Le Martyre de Saint Sébastien, A Lincoln Portrait*), but the words always act as irritant.

Metered speech, with the declamation notated, as in Schoenberg's *Pierrot lunaire* or Walton's *Façade*, is more satisfying, the voice part having been rhythmized and hence controlled by the composer. This is song once removed. Even the 1950s habit of reading poetry to jazz background, although inane, worked theatrically, since the musical improviser was in cahoots with the actor.

A case could be made (but I shall not make it) that vocal music is deep or shallow according to its literal sense. Precise meaning is all-important to the enjoyment of melodrama or pop; indeed, the music often can't exist without the words. But no knowledge of Latin liturgy is needed to enjoy a mass of Palestrina; indeed, who can prove that Palestrina even "felt" the words, or that he did not impose these words upon tunes already in his notebook? (Isn't Handel's *Messiah*, that monument of inevitability, actually confected from preexisting scraps of profane operas?)

If you stop to think about it, there is something silly about singing poems. There is something silly about setting poems to music. There is even something silly about writing poetry. If you stop to think about it, what have you left?

(*1975*)

ANATOMY OF
TWO SONGS

During November 1949 in Morocco I kept a Journal of Songs wherein I dissected, after the fact, recollections about the making of a dozen of my vocal works. The following examples pertain to pieces from student days, three years previous.

"Spring and Fall"

Clearly this song owes its existence to Monteverdi's madrigal "Amor." Why apologize? For centuries good friends have been exchanging ground basses (there's not an original plot in all Shakespeare); I simply took this one without asking.

It was composed for Christmas 1946 to delight my sister Rosemary (unmarried at the time), because Hopkins had subtitled his poem "To a young child." But the dedication on the printed music is for Eva Gauthier, easily seventy, because . . .

That printed music is in the key of one sharp. Conceived by me in the key of four flats, it was transposed by the publisher so that it would sell better. Indeed, only a very pure tenor could start "Margaret" and "Come" on so quiet a high G! In four flats, then, the opening figure was an impulse from something by a colleague about a nun. I changed the order of notes, and so rendered the steal invisible. Where the overall melody came from I don't know: it now looks (and sounds) woven improvisationally from fluid threads around the solid ostinato. Probably I wrote first the music to the final verse—"It is Margaret you mourn for"—and proceeded backward. The poem I had known vaguely for ten years (since the time Norris Embry declaimed it into a hear-your-voice-back machine at Chicago's Museum of Science and Industry), but I decided to musicalize it only in the summer of 1946 when Sarah Cunningham sang me her version, which I needed to improve upon.

Good Guy Ferrand, always astute, has pointed out the note-for-note resemblance between the melodic line "This is our Lordly Hudson" and the piano part of "Spring and Fall" against the words ". . . same. Nor mouth had, no nor mind, expressed. . . ." I'd never noticed. But since I pilfered only myself, there is no call for shame.

None of the rests should be literal. A lot of pedal to avoid jerkiness. The "Ah!" must be slightly gasped. "Ghost-guessed" should be practiced two hundred times. Singing is easy.

"On a Singing Girl"

This is one of my few songs written as a temporary emotional release. Composing as a craft can be a permanent release—but not emotionally, only technically: it keeps you busy.

I was sitting, waiting, exhausted, in the lobby of Juilliard. A girl I know came up to say that our mutual friend Teru Osato had only four months to live. Under my arm was a book of American poems. I whispered to myself: Why not write a song while waiting.

Elinor Wylie had made a rhymed transliteration from the Greek of an epitaph for a musical slave girl who had died young. (Oh, the connection with Teru hadn't struck me, really, until now.) I wrote out the vocal line right there on my lap, overtailoring the prosody as was then my obsession.

So the voice was complete in itself, though I had no idea of how the accompaniment would go until I reached home that evening. I'd learned that if a vocal line is conceived alone it will probably take on the rambling curves of nature rather than the artificial curves—square curves, you might say—of folk song; for coherence, a systematized accompaniment is indicated. (Contrariwise, sometimes in our piano improvisations we hit upon a figuration so pretty that any silly tune can be successfully superimposed.)

I needed square curves. Having just come to know Paul Bowles "David," I decided to disguise some of the piano part of that into a background design. Such conscious plagiarism is safe, remorse leads us to sabotage innovators, we sign our names. Who is the wiser? Certainly not Paul. Artists—by definition innocent—don't steal. But they do borrow without giving back.

This song, like most of mine, was made in a couple of hours. Nobody sings it much because it reacts like sandpaper on flayed fingertips. The closing words "dust be light" were originally an octave higher. Povla

Frijsh lowered them to their now-inevitable position. Always listen to singers, even when you can't see them shrieking back there in the brain.

For the record I've mentioned dear Teru, but the music is dedicated to Danny Pinkham because he and I were the only ones writing songs in those days. Singing is difficult.

(*1949*)

LAST POEMS OF
WALLACE STEVENS

An Album Note

Corporeally we are what we eat, and culturally we are what we call ourselves. Without definitions concepts wither and become less human. When ideas shift and fade and change focus with the years, sometimes dividing into new and quite different genres, their definitions alter accordingly; but the *fact* of definition remains stable.

Long ago, when I began to compose vocal music, I narrowed the notion of art song thus: *a lyric poem of moderate length set to music for single voice with piano.* That applied to the medium as it appeared around 1800 and prevailed for the next century and a half. The atrophy of the public song recital began in 1950 and is at its most decayed today. Such composers as still address the solo voice do so usually with an accompaniment of two or more instruments, since so-called chamber groups are now their only outlet. Thus Song has widened its definition while retaining its identity.

What is a song cycle? There would seem to be as many definitions as there are examples. The German cycles of the early nineteenth century were mostly based on narrative sequences by one poet, while today a cycle can be any cluster of settings of quite unrelated poets—or of prosifiers. Generally, though, a theme threads the texts, as with Britten's *Nocturne*, which uses "nighttime" words ranging from Shakespeare to Wilfred Owen, or with Boulez's *Le Marteau sans maître*, which uses words by only one writer but in disconnected fragments. Both of these cycles, in trend with the times, feature exotic combinations of instruments. If such a feature is not quite new (Ravel, Schoenberg, and others were composing vocal chamber pieces in the early 1900s), it is now the rule and not the exception.

The foregoing paragraphs would not have occurred to me had I not been invited to provide this program note. But in trying to "locate" my piece *Last Poems of Wallace Stevens*, I found myself foundering. How to define it? What is certain is that the piece fulfilled the commissioner's specifications. In 1972 the David Ensemble asked for something of about twenty-five minutes using any combination from their nucleus of performers but with a compulsory singer. The result, whatever else it might be called, is surely in the largest sense a wreath of song, since all the instruments "sing." The premiere was in New York's Town Hall on November 13 of the same year, with Sheila Schonbrum, soprano, Jonathan Abramowitz, cello, and Warren Wilson, piano.

I had often musicalized the works of the New York Poets—John Ashbery, Kenneth Koch, Frank O'Hara—but had never before used the verse of their prime progenitor, Wallace Stevens. The unifying device of my piece is the poet's personality, for the poems I selected were not devised by him as a sequence. Since then, I have not made other vocal use of Stevens's poems, although in 1978 I did write a symphonic suite based on a memory of his great *Sunday Morning*. However, *Last Poems* is but one of many works written, or that I plan to write, with one or more solo voices joined with two or more instruments. Someday I hope to compile an *Art of the Song* for five solo singers in every possible arrangement with each other.

How deeply satisfied I am with the present performers. For years I have known separately and felt at home with all of the three artists, but they met each other in this work for the first time. In 1969 I composed a concerto for Jerome Lowenthal, whose hands blend steel with gold so expertly that they seem a tangible replicate of an intellect both logical and compassionate. Ten years later Sharon Robinson became the "onlie begetter" of my suite *After Reading Shakespeare*, which she renders as she renders everything: as though her cello were the very human voice of an androgynous genius. The voice of Rosalind Rees, by contrast, is almost angelic in texture while vastly broader in connotation: there is nothing in a poet's nature that she seems incapable of re-expressing with a sound that winds like a seamless curve of mauve smoke into heaven. Without the lively union of these three, the music would be far less.

That music, planned by its composer to flow unbroken through seven poems by way of a prelude and an interlude, is in form a suite. As to genre (lest according to my own definition I "wither and become less human"), it is simply a song cycle—a cycle for three voices of which one is verbal and the others are not.

(*1983*)

A POSTSCRIPT
ON WHITMAN

"I pour the stuff to make sons," he exclaimed. Those sons cover the earth, singing for better or worse through the impulse of their father.

More than anyone in history save Shakespeare, Whitman has appealed to song composers whatever their style or nationality, possibly because he spoke as much through his voice as through his pen, contagiously craving immortality. "I spring from the pages into your arms," cries the dead author to his living reader.

The act of reading is no more passive than being a spectator at the theater, despite what sponsors of total-audience participation would today have us think. To read is to act, it takes two to make a poem, an attentive reader participates constantly. But with Whitman the participation becomes more than usually evident, more physical.

The reason may lie in his emphasis on immediate sensation rather than on philosophic introspection. At least that explains his century-old appeal to musicians and his more recent revival within our collective poetic sensibility, specifically with Allen Ginsberg and generally with the flower children of pop culture. That explains also why so many primarily instrumental composers, when they do write an occasional song, set the poems of Whitman to music. (Or set their music to the poems of Whitman!) Finally it explains why so many of us primarily vocal composers started early with Whitman, especially during the 1940s when it seemed urgent to be American at any price, and why so many of these songs sing embarrassingly now like the youthful indiscretions they are. During that same period, but for other reasons (reasons of gratitude), certain riper Europeans used Whitman, and used him more touchingly than many of us—Kurt Weill, for example, or Hindemith, whose *When Lilacs Last in the Dooryard Bloomed* is surely his choral masterwork.

My own choices of words have usually been somehow more practical.

When planning to write a song I seek poems more for sound than meaning, more for shape than sentiment. Sometimes (this is a confession), the music being already within me, I'll take literally any verse at hand and force it into the preconceived melodic mold. When the outcome "works," it's precisely because I have not wallowed in the sense of the words so much as tried to objectify or illustrate them.

But Whitman has proved exceptional to this kind of choice. For if I loved form for its own sake and challenge, I also loved and needed Whitman, whose style, in a sense, is lack of style: an unprecedented freedom that, with its built-in void of formal versified variety, offers unlimited potential for formal musical variety. Whitman is content. A poet's content is a musician's form; any other way a song is merely redundant and becomes, in the words of Valéry, like a painting seen through a stained-glass window. Looking back, I find that the dozen Whitman poems I have musicalized over the years were selected less from intellectual motives than because they spoke to my condition at a certain time. I adopted them through that dangerous impulse called inspiration, not for their music but for their meaning.

The first was "Reconciliation," an appeal to my pacifism in time of war. A few years later "Sometimes with One I Love" so sharply described my frame of mind that the music served as a sort of superfluous necessity. But once, when commissioned to provide accompaniments for recitations of Whitman, I of course failed; for if the human voice in song is the most satisfying of all instruments—indeed the instrument all others would emulate—the spoken voice is the least musical, and a sonic background to it simply interferes.

Another time, however, I was so overcome by the sensuality of "The Dalliance of the Eagles" that song was not enough. In a tone poem called *Eagles* for huge orchestra I composed a purely instrumental tissue on Whitman's strophic format and followed (symbolically, if you will) his development of idea. Listeners, aware of the program, are appropriately titillated by the sound picture of aerial carnality, though of course no nonvocal music really connotes an unvariable picture beyond what the composer tells you, in words, it's supposed to connote.

Contrary in resources, if not in intent, were my 1957 settings of five Whitman poems for baritone and clavichord. And in 1966 I turned to this catholic writer for help in still another domain. I was plotting a large-scale suite for voice and orchestra titled *Sun*, and I proposed to use descriptions of that star by eight poets—from King Akhenaton in

1360 B.C. to the late Theodore Roethke. At a loss for a penultimate selection (I required something tranquil, almost motionless, before the final explosion), I turned to Whitman as naturally as some turn to the Bible and found, not to my surprise, in his *Specimen Days* a prose paragraph to answer my prayer, whose low key proved to be the high point of the cycle.

Much current enthusiasm for Whitman, indeed for any admired artist, centers less in quality per se than in how that quality applies to our times. We hear a good deal about protest and involvement, with implicit hints that a committed artist is a good artist—or vice versa. The premise is false, for talent is conspicuously rarer than integrity. An artist speaking politics succeeds on the strength of his name; he is not speaking art. The prime movers of public thought have never been major artists who, almost by definition, are not in positions of authority; when they are, their art atrophies. Romantic though it sounds, artists need time, time for the introspection of creation. That time cannot be spent in the obligatory extroversion of "committed" oratory. Anyone can be right; nor are artists necessarily invested with rightness. Their function is not to convert so much as to explain pleasurably—albeit with sometimes agonizing pleasure. At least that's how I understand *my* function.

Yet when I consider my musical use of Whitman I can, in a sense, see it as *engaged*. Still, the song "Reconciliation" is not the product of a pacifist but of a composer who happens to be pacifist, just as "Sometimes with One I Love" is not the product of a lover but of a composer who once felt the experience. How easy to misread the intent of these songs because they have words! The misreading may declare them good when, in fact, they could be bad. Actually no nonvocal music can be proved to be political or committed, and by extension neither can vocal music nor any other so-called representational art.

Having heart and head well placed, then, does not inherently produce art, though it's safe to assume that most artists are no fools. Genius bigots like Wagner are really exceptional; artistic natures do tend to the compassionate left.

Thus it was not Whitman's good intentions that made him what he was, but his expression of those intentions. And with mere contradictory words, what more can I say of Whitman's intentions that I hope I've not said better with music?

(*1969*)

SEVEN

ODDS AND ENDINGS

WHY I WRITE
AS I DO

What can be told about music that the music itself can't tell? Only how it came to be written.

It is instructive to hear what one composer says about another because, no matter how biased, he quite knows what he's talking about. It is less instructive to hear what a composer says about himself because, no matter how sincere, he doesn't quite know what he's talking about. A composer can clarify his method to others, but not his esthetic. He can tell how he wrote his piece, but not why. His why *is* the piece. All else is a smoke screen through which he explains what you're supposed to hear rather than what you do hear. Unless the smoke screen itself is his music.

A smoke screen is handy but fragile. Let me show you mine—which may blow away even while I'm talking.

Why do I compose the way I do?

What way is that? As with affairs of the heart, each time is the first time, and the way of a new composition is no more predictable than the way of true love. Rules observed last time must be broken this time; vices become virtues in a different setting.

Years later, when one or another of his "ways" has faded from public awareness, a composer himself finds it hard to revive the old flame, nor can he explain why the spark did or did not flare into fireworks. Of course, experience eventually teaches him how to play with fire. And it teaches him not to push comparisons: love, even love for music, is never logical, while music, even music that inspires love, is always logical.

Why do I compose the way I do?

How answer, unless I know the effect the music has on others? That effect can never really be known, least of all while composing. While composing I can only know the effect I want to project.

No artist hopes, or even seeks, to be understood. In his heart he feels understanding to be a bit insulting: he is too complex, too special, and anyway, understanding is no urgent ingredient of art as it is of more critical expressions. What he hopes for is: not to be misunderstood. For an artist, the height of misunderstanding is to be taken for clothed when in fact he is naked, to be praised for finery he has no intention of wearing.

For example. My early emigration to France was not that of an American in need of a change; I had felt myself born out of context and wanted to go back to a different womb. When I first played my pieces for my new countrymen I experienced relief and elation to be finally spilling forth my oh-so-sensual Gallic wit to comprehending ears. Their reaction was: Why so cold and humorless, Ned, so Nordic and inhibited? Be more French.

Do I then compose because of influences?

We all compose, probably, "through" the first music that attracted us. That music in turn was heard through music we already knew. Because I knew Ravel before Bach, I still hear Bach as I hear Ravel: those baroque sequences become static ninth chords. Because I knew French music before German, I still hear (and judge) German music as French. I still hear twelve-tone music as tonal, and still hear my own jagged airs as mere nursery exercises for blues singers. We all grow by taking from our predecessors. To refuse to take from them is itself a taking—an affirmation. The difference between a true and false artist is the difference between a conscious and an unconscious thief. The professional disguises a theft by stamping it with his trademark. The amateur has no trademark; he doesn't know he's stolen; he peddles black-and-white reproductions.

A trademark can be a speech defect. It makes no sense to disqualify a speech defect, or even a language. Criticize only what is said in the language, and despite the defect (which may be engaging). I speak my native tongue as I can. Do you hear? Will you listen? Do I hold your interest?

Aware of those I've robbed, I smile when others don't recognize them. Yet I make no claims to novelty. My sole originality is that I've never sought originality. Though in the end that claim cannot apply to my music, only to a point of view about my music.

Do I compose because I've been encouraged? Been so often singled out as a unique melodist?

I'm not a unique melodist. I am a setter of literature, which has no special claim to tunes. Any uniqueness springs from an unactive competition—at least in the domain of recital song. Every composer worthy of the name is essentially a vocal composer, be his medium a quintet of horns, a percussion ensemble, an electronic synthesizer. He is a setter of literature, which makes no special claim to words. Inasmuch as I've been—against my will—pigeonholed as a songwriter I have, yes, been encouraged. Without the practicalities of praise and performance day after day, I would have given up long ago. And each day is still touch and go. Admittedly there is a professional paradox here. Although others who *know*, because their ideas are published, say my reputation is that of a song composer, of the ample variety of commissions offered me over the past ten years none have been for songs.

My three mottos for songwriting: Use only good poems—that is, convincing marvels in English of all periods. Write gracefully for the voice—that is, make the voice line as seen on paper have the arched flow that singers like to interpret. Use no trick beyond the biggest trick—that is, since singing is already such artifice, never repeat words arbitrarily, much less ask the voice to groan, shriek, or rasp. I have nothing against special effects; they are just not in my language. I betray the poet by framing his words, not by distorting them.

Why do I compose? Less from self-expression than because I want to be an audience to something that will satisfy me. The act dispels the smoke screen between my ego and reality. However my gifts may seem a luxury to others, I compose for my own necessity, because no one else makes quite the sound I wish to hear.

(*1974*)

NOTES ON
SACRED MUSIC

I do not believe in God. I do believe in poetry, which isn't the same thing although people compare them. God explains the unexplainable and, however cruelly, he soothes. Poets reflect; they do not explain nor do they soothe. At least they don't soothe me. But the fact of them is more intelligent and thus rarer than the fact of God, and sometimes for moments they take me out of myself.

If poetry were synonymous with religion, poets in middle age would not so frequently turn toward God. Yet neither they nor God can finally stop wars, nor even change our life in smaller ways. During periods of strife when we need them most, both God and the poets disappear.

Alec Wyton, choir director of Saint John the Divine, writes (*Choral Music*, January 1972):

> Ned Rorem is a typical example of a splendid musician who devotes some of his time to the church. . . . [He] is also the author of one of the more pornographic books in our bookstores today. . . . God is not fussy about the channels of His grace, and the truth may come from the most unexpected source, and I would rather have the music of Ned Rorem with all the integrity and greatness of it than the pious, awful platitudes of [an] Ithamar Conkey, who I am sure never broke one of the ten commandments.

God did not give me a talent for church music, he gave me a talent for music. Nor does his voice necessarily speak through any text I've chosen to musicalize. When I write music on so-called sacred texts it is for the same reason I write music on profane texts: not to make people believe in God but to make them believe in music. Music is not a shortcut to heaven, it is an end in itself. For some that end is hell. What I seek in the Bible is poetry, not sanctity; my best songs are on the verse of sinners.

Integrity? Ulterior motives propel me around every corner. Fortunately, fruits born of bad motives aren't always rotten. Still, some can be unpalatable.

"The Lord's Prayer" is my shame. Years ago I fell in with a publisher's proposal that if Malotte could hit the jackpot I could hit it harder. So I set the prayer to music, it was widely distributed and publicized by the publisher, and then we awaited glory. But not only did my version not displace Malotte's, it never even made money. And that was divine retribution.

My taste in poetry surely has much to do with whatever reputation I may enjoy as a "vocal" composer. Yet commissioners of songs usually have their own favorite poets. These commissioners might concur with my taste (the handful of recitalists interested in American songs are not, as a rule, illiterate), in which case I fulfill the commission without compromise. For example, when Alice Esty and Caroline Reyer, respectively, asked me to set the poetry of Theodore Roethke and Kenneth Koch, I was delighted; the poets had both been on my own list anyway, just waiting for the right moment. But when I agreed, as I once did, to set the verse of Mary Baker Eddy, the result was terrible. Not because her verse was bad poetry, but because it was not my kind of bad poetry.

Then why is my "Lord's Prayer" terrible, since it is good poetry? Because it is not necessarily *my* good poetry. (We can concede to the greatness of certain works which nevertheless leave us cold.) And then, I wrote the piece more for gain than from conviction. It was not the setting but the *kind* of setting that is contemptible, for it panders to a sentimental public. I've often composed, without embarrassment, for the needs of a performer, but the needs of a performer and the tastes of an audience are separate considerations. From its contrived height on the word *glory* down to the footnote advertising an alternative version for organ, the piece drips opportunism, and to this day when congratulated on it I turn over in my grave. Not that gain and conviction can't go hand in hand. Beethoven did write the *Hammerklavier* to pay a laundry bill. But no one told him *what* to write.

Heaven forbid that I preach integrity. I am not a particularly honest person, I don't even know how to fake it. But to be a successful whore is not easy either, and to sell oneself for what one doesn't believe in is to despise the buyer, and finally oneself.

Then can composers write as "good" a piece when on commission as when on their own? They will conform to specifics of dimension so long as specifics of language are left to them. They'll all tell you that hard cash and guaranteed performance are their truest inspiration.

"I do not write experimental music," said Varèse. "My experimenting is done before I write the music."

To experiment with music in the church is to fight a losing battle. If the battle could be won, the church would no longer be the church but a sociopolitical ground. The reason for experiment is to bring action. The church was never a scene of action but of reaction, making rules, not following them. Great classical works sprang from the quite reactionary promotion of the Gaetanis, the papal lines, the Medicis and Borgias, the Esterhazys. Even today the capitalist families, the Rockefellers and Fords, are those who make of art an issue that, being a nonessential, is generally absent from more liberal parties.

Insofar as the church becomes action it dispenses with ritual. Catholics react, Quakers act. Quakers never use music and are the most socially progressive of church groups. By underplaying the motionless symbol of the Trinity, Quakers emphasize the need for political movement. When they reinforce that need politically, they do so in silence.

Brought up a Quaker, meaning in silence, I needed noise. So I became a composer. As a composer I am apolitical. As a Quaker I am superpolitical. There is no halfway point. To give a church concert for war orphans is commendable, but no more intrinsically so than any other benefit that is an admixture of oil and water, like a society ball for cancer.

Belief in God once provided nourishing soil for art. To believe in God today is to be removed, to be impotent before more urgent problems. To reanimate belief by experimenting with, say, rock in church is to underestimate both musical rock and the holy rock.

So much pop expresses extramusical concerns, points of view more than points of heart. When it succeeds it succeeds autonomously; luring youth to church via rock concerts is asking them to accept a diluted version of what they can get better at home.

———

Bernstein's *Mass* or *J. C. Superstar* are absolutely swell, so long as they aren't sold as apocalyptic breakthroughs but as spectator sport. Their foolproof scenarios are from the same book that has provided the stuff of good theater since the medieval passion plays, and the stuff of good fiction from Saint John of the Cross through Anatole France to Gladys Schmitt. But theater and fiction the stuff remains, not revelation.

The difference between a church mass and a stage mass is that one is for participants and the other for spectators. To persuade spectators that they are in fact participants is to insult true believers, although the persuasion is itself show biz and, on its terms, legitimate. Less legitimate is the next turn of the screw: the introduction into the church of the rock mass. Now if a rock mass on stage is entertainment masquerading as revelation, introduced into the church it remains entertainment and thus retains its integrity, while the church sells itself cheap. If Bach's *B-minor Mass* in concert is more impacting as art than as revelation, is a rock mass in church more impacting as revelation than as art?

(What about the frenzy of a Baptist revival meeting? That's quite pop! It's also quite real, emerging as it does from the service. Pop is quite unreal, being superimposed onto the service.)

Although Quakers, our parents used to send Rosemary and me to other denominational Sunday schools from time to time. That was squelched when we came home and confectioned crucifixes. Nonetheless, on holidays our family attended Catholic or High Episcopal services "for the pageantry." One Christmas, arriving late at the Church of the Redeemer on 56th and Blackstone, Father asked the usher: "What time did the show start?" "We don't refer to it as a show," was the chilly reply.

Imagine such a reply today. *The* mass may not be a show, but *Mass* sure as hell is.

Must the compulsion for originality equate the invention of new languages? Aren't new accents, new pronunciations, enough? Must we be polyglot or babel? Is rock in church a new accent, or an old accent in a new context? Is the context so new?

A pleasure not to be underestimated is a composer's knowledge that his dalliance with King James involves no infringement of rights. Woe ye who touch the New English Bible! No living or recently dead poet, no Yeats or Plath or Auden is guarded by a tougher dog in the manger.

This Bible is no longer everyman's property, and permissions are hard come by: the publishers, holding out for a killing on cassettes, make even God serve Mammon. Were this the sole source of sacred texts, a composer would stop composing for the church altogether. Technically a preacher quoting from the NEB should pay a copyright fee, too. Let him meanwhile expose the legal eccentricity that keeps this book out of public domain.

Music's meaning, like the language of dolphins, is not translatable into human prose. If music were translatable it would not have to exist. What we call musical messages actually come through words that have been set to music. Those words used to be of a complex poetic order and highly symbolic, being Latin.

Non-vocal music has no meaning literarily, or even physically. It cannot say happiness, or hot and cold, or death—except by association. It says whatever its composer tells you, in words, that it says.

To assume a need for "message" music is to assume a need for vocal over non-vocal music. The need is not recent. Most of our century's best music has been for voice, and so has most of the worst.

Commerce, which dictates our needs now, knows we want more than a message: we want an easy message. Commerce decrees the greatest good for the greatest number, hence Jesus freaks, the bromidic English litanies of *Superstar*. The same message was always there, but in the Latin masses of Stravinsky, Britten, Penderecki, Poulenc. Today, since it is not music but music's message that is popular, that message must be in the vernacular. By definition the vernacular is not symbolic. To understand a language is, in a sense, to hear it no longer. Because we know what it is saying, we do not listen to our native tongue as to a foreign tongue.

Emerging from the cerebral into the simpleminded, from rococo into barbarity, we realize that though neither genre is inherently "bad," both are decadent because they engender nothing first-rate.

Why have I, an atheist, composed so extensively for the church?

I was not composing for the church but for anyone who wanted to listen, using texts I believed in. I did not believe in them for their subject but for their quality.

That the glory of God is its chief sentiment does not qualify verse, or any Sunday-school primer would be on a par with the Psalms of David.

The glory of God is expressed in, not through, the verse.

I can't prove it, but probably no composer creating for the church today really believes in God. If he does, that belief does not of itself make his music persuasive, if it is persuasive.

As for the church as seat of experiment, that is to let the composer—the non-believer—dictate the rules of service.

(*1972*)

THE WELL-DRESSED
COMPOSER

There is no such thing as a well-dressed artist, much less The Well-Dressed Artist: these two implied occupations cancel each other out, since both are full-time jobs.

By definition an artist does not dress, he undresses. His business—sometimes his pleasure—is to expose himself. Even his skin is ripped off, flung to a wind that sweeps it beyond our horizon. We then applaud a throbbing heart laid bare. The heart's blood drips to the ground. Weakened, the artist stumbles, staining his shoes. Next day red shoes are "in."

What he happens to wear for this striptease is inconsequential to him, since he is not a performer (e.g., the dancer, conductor, tragedian who will ultimately interpret his work) but a creator. Creation is a private affair. A painter at work would only soil his Brooks Brothers shirt, if he had one to soil.

It's the nine-to-fivers who change shirts, keep up appearances, are seen. An artist when seen (I speak always of so-called creative artists, never of executants)—an artist when seen is no longer an artist, but a man *representing* the person who painted that picture or composed that piece. Perhaps this man is well dressed; but if, as people say, he is also "great," whatever he wears is right. What he wears is right if he is the one to wear it. He is "the one" if elected. Who elects? A faceless consensus. (Warhol's dark glasses at midnight are "chic.") It's not "he the artist" but "he the flirt" who dresses. Flirtation and the knack for clothes are both called arts, but they are not arts which here concern us.

Women dress to impress in this order: each other, men, themselves; but they dress to please, in this order: men, themselves, each other. Men dress to impress themselves, each other, women; and to please themselves, women, each other.

Artists—and here I distinguish them less as another sex than as another species—dress to console (or to disdain, which is the same) the public. A beard can be high fashion: Allen Ginsberg's is more emulated than Major Schwepps's—or whatever his name is. And yes, even a stance is habiliment: Glenn Gould's slouch, Corelli's chestiness, Bernstein's hip swing. But these are performers. It is Ginsberg the actor, not the poet, who doesn't shave. Nor is it Bernstein the composer who once sported a Koussevitzky-type cape, or who now employs a private tailor. Composers aren't hams: it isn't the composer within Virgil Thomson but the sometime baton-flashing socialite who is garbed by the men's store of Lanvin.

Lanvin's gorgeous daughter Marie-Blanche, the late Comtesse de Polignac, was a soprano of rare quality. Indeed, were I lost on a desert island with a choice of only five LP records, one would be her singing of Monteverdi's madrigals under the direction of her dear friend and mentor, Nadia Boulanger.

Marie-Blanche once told an endearing story about Mademoiselle Boulanger who, as everyone knows, is still at eighty the world's most consecrated and influential pedagogue of music. Clothes have never been among her chief concerns. Around 1930, for conductorial appearances, she ordered chez Lanvin a *passe-partout* unprepossessing gown of severe black, expensive but no-nonsense. As this gown was still serving her active professional purposes some twenty years later, Marie-Blanche gently offered to have a new one made. Boulanger quickly agreed, returned to Lanvin, and asked for a copy of the very same dress—which she used for many years more.

Taste is not necessarily related to intelligence or education, or even to art. Taste is natural implicitly, art is unnatural. Fashion (which au fond means taste) is comfortable essentially, art is painful: the difference between play and work.

Good cooks deal in taste—literally in taste buds—but make no guarantee against upset stomachs. Good art upsets *before* being tasted; ultimately it purges us—makes us feel good. If it is to our taste. Because great art may be great, yet still not to our taste. I admire Beethoven unqualifiedly, but I don't *like* him.

A dish once tasted and swallowed disappears forever. So perhaps does a Delacroix, a Russian play, certainly a symphony's performance. But the cooking, unlike the painting, cannot remain in the memory. (Art concerns only two of the five senses: sight and sound. No art is devoted to touch, taste, or smell.) It must be repeated forever; tongues forget. Even hearts remember falsely from one moment to the next.

Painters and composers (even poets) make good cooks because they're used to mixing colors, judging volumes. Yet their cooking resembles only the palette or score sheet: it is just a preparation.

"Fashion is beauty that grows ugly, art is ugliness that grows beautiful," bravely stated Madame Chanel.

Yet by a third convolution, fashion emerges from art. Because fashion is the shadow of art, expensively out of date, obtrusively in the background.

In France, always less specialized than America, one sees *les grands couturiers* along with statesmen, authors, and high-ranking policemen in private centers of culture. The couturiers impose this generalized culture onto their product; they rifle not from a rival couturier but from a painter. In America the dressmaker does not steal the painter's canvas but the painter's very clothes off his back, absconds with the superficial blue denim, corduroy, psychedelic patterns, and charges unthinkable prices. Like a Cheshire cat the painter himself sits back, smiles at his cheap sexy pants, then opens his own boutique and, to rich ladies, vends these Emperor's New Clothes.

It has not always been so. Look at the formal busts of Bach and Handel, their wigs and lacy cuffs; they dressed like everyone else of the period. Before the Industrial Revolution an artist pertained to his society; he set the "tone" through his work, not through his public-private style. His bohemianism developed when he was put aside as a superfluous commodity, a luxury. When the newly emerging "businessman" shortened his hair, the composer let his grow longer. Socially he contradicts.

Look then at today's formal busts: the apparel of what's called establishment resembles a rainbow (reflecting ever-so-dimly ex-President Truman's summer shirts) and the sexes merge through their coiffures, while Copland or Milhaud or Stravinsky never go out without a tie. The long-hair composer? Now the definition holds only when hairdos are switched: mod locks are longer than Liszt's, but the "serious" composer clips his as befits the university professor he's become.

Poet Bill Berkson is one of the world's best-dressed men, so he doesn't "look like" a poet (only the non-poets of Tompkins Square look like poets). But he *is* a poet, therefore he looks like one. But therefore he isn't . . . et cetera. By being, he dictates involuntarily, like a king. And only the poor can afford to be well dressed. (Poor means conformist; Afford means frightened; Well dressed means unmusical.)

Artists resemble royalty who, like Henry the Fifth soliciting a kiss from the recalcitrant Katharine of France, observe among themselves: "You and I cannot be confined within the weak list of a country's fashion . . . and the liberty that follows our places stops the mouths of all findfaults. We are the makers of manners."

(1968)

LADIES' MUSIC

The male of nearly all species is bigger, brighter, more eloquent than the female. Consider the peacock or nightingale, the whale or minnow, the tiger or grizzly bear. There are exceptions: one breed of parrot produces a ruby-hued female, while the male is merely emerald. And in various strains of arachnid, males are not only tinier than their mates: after mating they are devoured and become quite invisible.

But with virtually all mammals, the male is physically more conspicuous than the female. All mammals, that is, except humans.

This is fact. Interpretations vary. That the male is gaudier in appearance does not mean he is quicker in mind; it defines his role as protector who diverts enemies away from the inconspicuous egg-sitter. Yet with certain groups—lions, for instance—the female is the provider. As to whether the lioness is less lovely than her shimmering husband is a question of taste, and a human taste at that. In mankind's high periods of art, simplicity takes precedence over the ornate.

Yet even in the highest periods the human female, through her accoutrement, has made herself more visible than the male. Is this her assertion—or is it man's permission—that she is not an animal? Very early woman became, superficially, more brilliant than her masculine counterpart, adopting a wardrobe in simulation (or from the actual skins) of the male animal. If at Louis XIV's court men sported spike heels and twelve-inch perukes, their women bettered them with fifty-foot trains and cages containing live birds woven into their spiraling headdresses. (The stately saraband evolved to accommodate these clothes.) And if our 1930s female impersonators outdid each other in extravagant drag, again they were one-upped, as Parker Tyler elucidates, by somnambulist marvels like Mae West or Marlene Dietrich who, with their feathers and scarlet fingernails, became impersonators of female impersonators.

Only today, with her ardent emancipation program, does woman revert to what opponents name her natural dowdiness. Men meanwhile, casting off gray flannels for gorgeous robes, inasmuch as they still differ from the other sex, differ from it as flowers differ.

Despite what current suffragists contend, women from many points in time and space have been strong in politics: think of Cleopatra of Egypt or Queen Balkis of Sheba, Elizabeth Tudor of England or Catherine II of Russia, Golda Meir of Israel or Indira Gandhi of India.

Women have been strong in poetry and letters, from Sappho to Sévigné, from Sand to Stein. Admittedly there's a vast lacuna between 200 B.C. and 1600 A.D.; I can think of only two women writers—both vigorously Christian—during that span: the tenth-century German playwright Hroswitha, who wrote in Latin, and the sixteenth-century Spanish mystic Teresa, who wrote in Castilian. But today, at least in the English-speaking world, there are as many top-notch female fictionists— not to mention critics—as male.

Strong, too, have they been in visual art, though for a shorter time. France seems first to have spawned them in the 1800s. Rosa Bonheur immediately comes to mind, then Mary Cassatt and Marie Laurencin in the early twentieth century. At present in America there may be more good women painters than men, and treated just as seriously, that is, getting the same fees.

Our century has also produced scientists, anthropologists, historians, reporters, and precedent-shattering choreographers, impresarios, and theater specialists as dissimilar as Madame Curie, Margaret Mead, Edith Hamilton, Janet Flanner, Dorothy Day and Dorothy Thompson, Mary Wigman, Jean Rosenthal, and Jean Dalrymple. And our century gave us the philosopher Susanne Langer who has written as knowledgeably about music as anyone ever.

Yet she has not written music.

Why, when we have seen so many women long excelling in what are commonly thought to be masculine categories, have the few women composers been of such recent vintage?

Is it because music, although probably the oldest art, is nevertheless the youngest in that it is the last to have gained individuality (the composer as individual is hardly three centuries old) and thus corresponds to the distaff's tardy emancipation?

Is it then because until modern times music everywhere was predominantly a religious expression, and in the West predominantly Christian, and among Christians predominantly male? If indeed the church is a man's world, before the Renaissance it was musically not even that, but a domain of asexual anonymous contributors.

Is it because, like the theater (though unlike poetry or sculpture), music is an *interpretive* craft, and women make better interpreters than they do creators, interpretation being artificial, and artifice—use of makeup, of costume, of song—being more socially fitting to girls than boys? Then what of playacting, that great artifice whose golden peaks in Greece and England eschewed women completely?

Is it because, again like the theater, there are problems of execution that need never be faced by poets and painters? Music, before it can exist in the ear of an audience, needs a middleman. And any composer, unless he spends his career writing solely for friends who "play piano," will logically be drawn to the orchestra. Now the orchestra is a man's world, autocratic and closed, ruled by an absolute despot. The orchestral players' reaction to all comers, soloist and conductor alike, is one of "you gotta show me." If to them the living composer in general is an object of contempt, the female composer is an object of derision.

On this last point, an esthetic consideration: music, which is sounded and which exists only in performance, is more assertive than pictures which are mute and which exist in themselves, or than poems which are half mute and half sound. Still, the patron saint of music was a woman, the virgin Cecilia who died a Roman martyr eighteen hundred years ago. From that time until the Freudian revolution, music was often termed a feminine art, and thus an art fit only for men to tamper with. If even today your typical male composer (and there *is* a type) is less extrovert, less aggressive, than your average male painter, the reason lies elsewhere than in the giddy assumption that the arts they practice embody sexual identity.

A rule is not conscious of itself. The white man in a white land seldom thinks of his color, while the Negro in a white land seldom thinks of anything else. By the same token there is no white music when all music is white. Most of what most of us have heard in the Western world has been white for three millennia. For three centuries, however, there has been black music (black, when heard against a white background: the black music of Africa is not black to black Africans). We have absorbed this as slave songs, as spirituals, as jazz, and more recently as an art form by specific conservatory-trained individuals aiming for the concert hall while still (like the best Negro prose, for the moment) using race as subject matter.

Similarly, there is no male music because it is all male. So unquestioned is the premise that we can afford to patronize rather than resent those females who do enter the arena.

I don't mean the glittering plethora of performing ladies—90 percent of whom are singers, from Handel's day through Jenny Lind to Bethany Beardslee, with Marguerite Long and Myra Hess at the ivories. Nor do I mean those black women, Ma Rainey, Josephine Baker, Mary Lou Williams, Marian Anderson, Hazel Scott, Mattiwilda Dobbs, who have instituted new traditions with grace and force. Significantly, we don't yet find major black women soloists in the nonvocal "serious" domain— no concert violinists, for example, or pianists—although in orchestras there are some, notably the percussionist Elayne Jones who, ever since I can remember, has been featured in the special recitals of ultramodern music in the New York vicinity.

I mean composers. There are a handful—and none before 1900. (Oh yes, there *are* earlier examples. Pauline Viardot-Garcia, Rossini's soprano virtuoso, did write at least one apparently delightful opera for performance by herself in the 1830s. And a hundred years earlier Bach's second wife, Anna Magdalena, composed a bit, mostly transcriptions. But these, both in intent and effect, are really exercises, albeit distinguished ones.) The early decades showed us Dame Ethel Smyth in Britain and the Boulanger sisters, Nadia and Lili, in France. France in the 1920s brought renown to Germaine Tailleferre, in the 1930s to Marcelle de Manziarley, in the 1940s to Betsy Jolas. America in the 1940s weaned Miriam Gideon, Louise Talma, Vivian Fine, the black Julia Perry, the Australian-born Peggy Glanville-Hicks, the South African-born Elisabeth Lutyens, and the German-born Ursula Mamlok. Today there is an International Society of Women Composers headed by Poland's Grazyna Bacewicz. All are well-schooled first-rate musicians. Mostly they do not use womanhood as subject matter, and they shudder at the phrase Ladies' Music, a sarcastic classification defensively coined by men during the world-famous popularity of Cécile Chaminade's *Scarf Dance*.

And yet, until around 1950 when the civil-rights pot began to boil, we applauded the subtlest gesture of the creative female as we applauded the black—with the condescension accorded to talking dogs.

What happened in 1950? The time-worn ecological scale balancing church and state began toppling, and ten years later splintered irreparably. By church, of course, I mean concert hall, and by state, the clubs and streets and coffeehouses. All merged and blurred. Ladies were no longer treated as talking dogs, since all music, including ladies', went to the dogs. Each art, in lowering standards toward mass orientation, coincidentally became interchangeable with each other art. Ironically, the older Ladies' Music, high on the crest of a liberation gap, fell into the pollution and drowned, while younger talents of all sexes headed away from art.

What is Ladies' Music? It is easier to define this by first defining the more tangible Ladies' Literature.

On the one hand, it pretends to be nothing more than what is generally considered feminine (instinctive, fluffy), deals with the so-called female psychology from the inside out, and addresses itself to women readers. At worst it is overdressed, rambling, sensational, and lax, like the prose of Hollywood columnists, *Cosmopolitan*, or Margaret Mitchell. At best it bursts from an enviably tight and tailored yet excruciatingly sensitive cocoon, and soars beyond category, like Virginia Woolf, Willa Cather, or the wonderful women of France from Madame de Lafayette to the all-knowing Colette. Some men write high-quality Ladies' Literature, "poetic" prose, elaborately plotted, dealing nonintellectually with "feminine psychology": Pierre Louÿs, Oscar Wilde, Tennessee Williams. Interestingly, an author like Mary Renault, while involved exclusively with male—especially "inverted" male—sensibility more tellingly than any man, elusively retains her female identity (possibly because she treats inverted love as simply love) through the sixth sense compassionately implied in Jean Paulhan's letter to the pseudonymous and supposedly unknown perpetrator of The Story of O:

> That you are a woman I have little doubt. Not so much because of the kind of detail you delight in describing—the green satin dresses, wasp-waist corsets, and skirts rolled up a number of turns (like hair rolled up in a curler)—but rather because of something like this: the day when René abandons O to still further torments, she still manages to have enough presence of mind to notice that her lover's slippers are frayed, and notes that she will have to buy him another pair. To me, such a thought seems unimaginable. It is something a man would never have thought of, or at least would never have dared express.

That paragraph might be a red herring. Responsible rumor maintains Paulhan himself authored the story.

On the other hand, Ladies' Literature may appear so lean of style, so businesslike of content, so precise and yet so deep of insight, so political, in short so masculine, that only a woman could be the originator, no man—not even Hemingway, nor surely Kenneth Burke—feeling *that* impelled to assert his maleness. (It used to be popular to say that Norman Mailer's writing suggested that of a repressed homosexual. Trends change quickly. A cursory reading now of, say, *An American Dream* shows the narrator to be a reasonably adjusted heterosexual posing as a repressed homosexual.)

Mary McCarthy has been said to perform in manly style, as have Brigid Brophy, Susan Sontag, Hannah Arendt, Diana Trilling (though not Doris Lessing or Simone de Beauvoir who are too baroque, too long-winded) because the filtering of intelligence and originality through an economical sieve has, until recently, been considered a masculine operation. What is thought to betray these persons as female is a certain willful coldness, though that too is hardly an exclusive terrain: how about the cynicism of G.B.S., Alexander Woollcott, John Simon!

Women no longer hide beneath noms de plume, like the Georges Eliot and Sand. Yet editors, voyeuristic and discriminatory, still consider it appropriate to engage them for mutual criticism. Like Amazons in the Roman arena they overcompensate (Jean Garrigue's review of Anaïs Nin's diary), over-resent (Joyce Carol Oates's report on Janet Frame's novel), or take it upon themselves to defend their less fortunate sisters (Mrs. Trilling's epitaph for Marilyn Monroe). Somehow this all seems unfair, unfair to themselves, since it calls forth their worst writing. They cancel each other out, like poets reviewing each other poetically. They aren't reviewing other people, but other female people. Any meanness involved is interpreted as prejudicial, as though they are *men* writing about women, or whites who aren't yet permitted to dislike certain blacks on purely human terms.

When Virginia Woolf turns her cutting pity on Katherine Mansfield, or Miss McCarthy clarifies, with an understanding surpassing Nathalie Sarraute's, Nathalie Sarraute, they present exceptions proving the rule.

Then what is Ladies' Music?

The "meaning" of musical art is more mercurial than the meaning of any other art, so Ladies' Music is harder to define than Ladies' anything else. Substitute Music for Literature in the preceding paragraphs, and you will have at least one definition.

Ladies' music isn't what girls used to enjoy playing: *Rustle of Spring*, Chopin *Nocturnes*, anything Romantic with hands crossed. It is music composed by women who lack not talent but discipline, who aim at a low target like wisteria or a robin's egg and *miss the mark*. As for compensatory male music by women (tough ideas that aim high, like an Iris Murdoch—not a Jane Austen—novel), even if it once could have been identified, it is now, as I've explained, lost in the international monochrome mire.

There are no musical equivalents of fiction and nonfiction, so one cannot claim that women composers, as opposed to any composers, excel in certain genres of music.

What is black subject matter? In fiction and essays it is the black life viewed, at present, strictly problematically. In contemporary music it is black folk material (African and American) recast into more complex molds.

What is womanhood as subject matter? In sound it must be the same as in letters, and has sense only in the programmatic or operatic: music depicting a story about a woman. The fact that Louise Talma chose to compose a tragedy about Alcestis, as did Martha Graham (who has also choreographed climaxes in the lives of virtually every female monster from Medea to Emily Dickinson), need not imply that these creators are involved in *women*'s creation any more than Euripides or Racine were so involved. Nor is Miriam Gideon, when setting to music the verses of Francis Thompson, invading a man's territory.

Martha Graham, as you gauge such things, is one of the seven geniuses of any sex in any field today. Although genius and innovation do not inevitably go hand in hand, she has influenced change in dance more than any person or group (certainly more than Balanchine) during the past hundred years. Yet her very preoccupation with the female as female, particularly the more-than-criminal female as Royal Elect, would disqualify her from membership in the Women's Liberation Front.

We quickly throw art into the mire (art that lowers its standards, along with art that does not), and still more quickly we change criteria for judging that art. One can and does, I suppose, listen to, perhaps, Joan Baez, with tears in the eyes, if that means anything (and it does), which is more than can be said of, perhaps, Karlheinz Stockhausen. Yet when Baez is judged, as she is most often by judges with tears in their eyes, the judgment disqualifies itself. Young musicians in Stockhausen's milieu write easily but do not listen. In Baez' milieu they listen easily but do not write. It comes to the same thing.

With certain women in music the ridiculous is serious, thus pathetic. Has anyone forgotten the coloratura of Florence Foster Jenkins? Or the cornet of Giullietta Masina in *La Strada*?

During the 1940s one Mabel McAllister, a blue-haired Texas matron, hired the small Carnegie Recital Hall to perform a program of her own piano works. Her brochure announced, almost as an afterthought, this information: "One fascinating aspect of Mrs. McAllister's compositions is that they are all written exclusively for the black keys."

Last year a London woman received wide acclaim for her communion with dead composers. She took dictation directly from Beethoven, Liszt, and others. Who's to say that the dubious quality of the result was caused by the London woman's lack of talent rather than by the composers' senility?

With men the ridiculous is usually conscious satire: Harpo Marx, Victor Borge. And while some women also display method in their madness—Anna Russell, Jo Stafford—it's difficult to find examples of the converse: men whose tackiness is innocent. Surely Liberace is not fooled by his image.

If Wanda Landowska, like the London woman, was on close terms with the dead, she also delivered the goods—this despite elaborate theatrics, which, for all we know, were standard nineteenth-century fare. I first saw her in 1944. Emerging onto the stage of Town Hall, she spent a full four minutes gliding slow-motion toward her lamp-lit harpsichord (during which she leered like a snake charmer at her public whose accompanying applause was undiminishing), sat down upon seven gold pillows, stood up again to remove one pillow which she cast on the floor, reseated herself, poised her right hand to play, froze it in midair, replaced it in her lap, and turned again toward us. Long pause. "Last night Johann Sebastian Bach came to me. For several hours we compared the fruits of our mutual study. He then bequeathed to me registrations and fingerings which I will perform, and which you will hear, for the first time this evening." From the audience an abject sigh of thanks, from the stage a recital which practiced what it promised. Hers was the grand authenticity that anticipated, and thus automatically disqualified, all sister colleagues.

From the Industrial Revolution until 1950 the artist has commonly been accepted (rejected) as an alienated decoration. Art accordingly was the sole ground whereon men and women theoretically met with equality. In fact, as I have tried to show, women suffered discrimination in art as elsewhere. Less perhaps in the silent arts, painting and writing, which can be practiced "in hiding," than in the noisy ones, theater and musical performance, which require a personal and assertive presence. Such a presence will be almost automatically eccentric, bigger than life, a Streisand, a Leontyne Price, or, against three odds, a black woman playwright like Lorraine Hansberry whose untimely end followed a certain logic.

Why then, finally, so few women in the *creative* musical field? The answer is clear. Whereas poems, even great poems, can be completed in haste at a supermarket or in the maternity ward, and whereas pictures, especially terrible ones, can be drawn by literally anyone from age one to one hundred, because writing and drawing are languages integral to everyone's everyday life, musical composition (great or terrible) is not a language for dabblers. A minimum of professionality and a maximum of time are required to produce a communicable score. If, as is generally conceded, the bringing into existence of a two-hour opera, from conception to production, is a matter of around three years comprised of ten-hour days, days absorbed in the highly technical questions of not only composition but of instrumentation, piano-vocal reduction, supervision of orchestral extraction and copy, interminable conferences and sectional rehearsals, it is hard to picture a woman achieving this proficiency in her art while raising a family with the comparatively unneurotic ease of her sisters "in poetry."

If gift knows no gender, neither does lack of gift. When music reaches, as it threatens, the point of gratuitous simplisticism now reached by other arts, then talent will be more indistinguishable than the sexes have become, and nobody will know, or care, who composed what. Still, that may indicate the route toward an ideal society where, according to Freud, art will no longer be necessary.

(*1968*)

CHARLES ROSEN'S
THE CLASSICAL STYLE

It is harder to review a good book than a bad one. Beyond offering a résumé and a definition, what can a reviewer say that the author hasn't said better? This is especially true in the present case when the book itself is a résumé and a definition: in one sense *The Classical Style* provides its own review. Still, it is not the book's high quality but a generic quandary that inhibits me.

Surely editorial policies fluctuate about who writes up what: should women review women's books? should blacks review blacks? Or musicians musicians? Why not, if the critic knows what the author is talking about? The trouble is, there are as many kinds of musicians as there are women or blacks.

We inhabit distant worlds, Charles Rosen and I. Though both musicians, he is a classical scholar, I a contemporary composer. He seems obsessed with analysis, not only his own but that of others, judging by his discussion in the *New York Review of Books* of certain literary and musical specialists, past and present, who expound about the number of angels that can dance on a pinpoint. Painstakingly he would render tangible that which with me is unconscious and assumed: the principle of métier. Essays centering upon the force and form of creation, whether they inspire the special pedantry of a William S. Newman, whose monumental series on the sonata suggests 6,000 footnotes in search of a text, or the unusual pedagogy of a Sir Donald Tovey, whose literary skill rivals a true maestro's baton, are all (once résumé and definition get settled) after one thing: the secret of greatness. Such essays never prove conclusive, but while their subject continues to beguile both pedagogue and layman, it remains indifferent to artists themselves: the meaning of greatness is not an artistic concern. Artists are less interested in how something came to be than in bringing something to be.

Certainly as a composer I am more enlivened by writing music than by reading about writing music. When occasionally I see program notes regarding my own music I am struck with how correct they are in detail, yet as a whole they never hit the unseen nail on the head. If their annotator reveals, even to me, some convoluted nuance in the score, I'm more touched than instructed by his care and wonder why he bothered. Now although this very stance could arm me with a viewpoint toward music's structuring, it would lack insight, for by definition I'm on the inside looking out. Charles Rosen speaks from a reverse position and knows "about" music far more than I.

He would be the first to appreciate the disparity between musicological and creative approaches, as when he writes: "Reading a composer's mind, retracing the steps by which he worked, is not a viable critical method even when the composer is alive and one can ask him how he did it—he generally does not know."

There are as many kinds of people who write about music as there are those who write about the writing. Three key types are the daily reviewer who explains the "when," the analytic critic who explains the "why," and the practicing composer who explains the "how." There are dozens of combinations of these. One thinks immediately of Schumann, Berlioz, Debussy, Schoenberg, Sessions, Thomson, Hindemith, all first-rank composers, all first-rank critics, some of whom earned at least part of their living as reviewers. One thinks of non-practicing musicians who are authorities like Alfred Einstein and Paul Henry Lang, or popularizers like David Ewen and Joseph Machlis. Other professional authorities are not musicians at all: G. B. Shaw, E. M. Forster, Brigid Brophy. Certain amateurs pretend to discuss music professionally, albeit with no authority, like Gide in his booklet on Chopin or Pound in his treatise on harmony, naive statements from authors who learned the hard way (that is, away from class) what the most casual music student takes for granted. Poets like Auden in his souvenirs of *The Rake's Progress* or John Hollander in *The Untuning of the Sky* write on music with technical know-how, while others bring us "poetic" précis on composers—Frank O'Hara on Morton Feldman or Paul Éluard on *les Six*. Naturally there are novelists who use music intrinsically for character portrayal, as Mann in *Doctor Faustus* and Rolland in *Jean Christophe*, or extrinsically like animated wallpaper, as Proust throughout his big book or Huxley in *Point Counter Point.*

Finally there are executant musicians such as Lotte Lehmann or E. Robert Schmitz who publish practical manuals on how to perform. But there is the performer who is also the scholar. In North America have been Glenn Gould, Robert Craft, Ralph Kirkpatrick, and more recently Charles Rosen combining the virtues and none of the vices of the above categories.

First-generation North American pianists are comparatively young, around forty-five or fifty. A notable preceding generation does not, for whatever reason, exist; the mentors of this first generation were at least twenty-five years older and inevitably central European with a repertory built on the eighteenth- and nineteenth-century masterworks. Reaching their twenties, the pupils spread wings and, more often than coincidence allows, flew to France. Their attraction to that country grew in general from a sharing of the postwar syndrome of American youth seeking "roots" in the now-defertilized pastures of Sartre and Jean Gabin, and grew in particular as an antidote to their intensely German-focused training. For varying periods they centered in Paris, some even becoming French scholars: Julius Katchen, Leon Fleisher, Jerome Lowenthal, Eugene Istomin, Gary Graffman, Alexis Weissenberg (though not William Kapell or William Masselos, special cases and slightly older).

Charles Rosen, born in 1927 in New York City, received his doctorate in French literature and has been recognized for twenty years not only as a virtuoso of French piano music of the so-called impressionist era (his recording of Debussy's *Études* being exemplary) but of modern American music. He and the harpsichordist Ralph Kirkpatrick were the creators of the *Double Concerto* by Elliott Carter, to whom *The Classical Style* is dedicated. Now if what we call classical can be applied to a school of French literature, it was virtually nonexistent in French music. Musical classicism originated, developed, and decayed in the Germany of the late eighteenth century. Rosen thus may be said to straddle three continents in both space and time, and to convince us that he is professionally at home in them all, a posture I cannot begin to comprehend and am in awe of.

The rarest qualities of Rosen the researcher are his good writing and his concern with sound.

His opinions about his vast store of information he expresses with professional economy and contagious devotion. That most musicologists (or music historians, as some prefer to be called) are mere compilers without style is no surprise, but that they seem more preoccupied with how music *looks* than with how it *sounds* may come as a contradiction to many laymen. Rosen seldom errs in that direction; he reacts to music through the ear (to how form is derived from sound, not vice versa), and his words evoke not only the arch of a tune which, after all, must change according to the soprano or viola or bassoon emitting it, but those sensual vertical textures planned orchestrally by the composer. Moreover, he comes as close as anyone to entering the composer's heart and head and uttering what the composer doesn't "know." And yet . . .

The foregoing skirts the actual contents of Charles Rosen's book, although the margins of my copy seethe with penciled notes. Their nature is at once so obvious and so specialized as to be useless to any reader of reviews. Obvious, because I learned from *The Classical Style* exactly what any non-musician would learn; but I dare not divulge what I learned without sounding the fool, for I couldn't make comparisons to other books of this kind, never having read any. Specialized, because I take exception to the meaning (i.e., the cause of the persuasive value) proposed by Rosen for every example he cites in his numerous analyses; but my exceptions are esthetic, based on personal method, unprovable, and I'm no more right than he.

All my life I've been on close terms with much of the music discussed here so elegantly. But I played it unconsciously, for it never occurred to me *not* to understand what the notes "meant," nor to wonder at the numerous *trouvailles*, while Rosen, quite consciously and with no end of skill, has placed himself in the composer's seat. When he himself states that a composer "wants his intentions made audible, not his calculations," I realize that I've always linked the two unquestioningly and cannot help but find such vast amounts of diagnosis a bit—well—superfluous.

In short, insofar as this book is involved, Rosen and I face opposite directions, the past and the future, so I'm incapable of having an attitude toward his work. I cannot, so to speak, face it.

(*1971*)

HOMAGE TO
JULIUS KATCHEN
(1926–1969)

Though possibly no less beloved of the gods than Mozart or Schubert who died young, successful executant musicians—at least nowadays—are mostly governed by healthy longevity as though renown itself (plus the adrenergic drive that seems coupled with renown) nourished their survival. When a great virtuoso dies after a long life of outward appreciation and inner fulfillment, our sadness contains a reassuring calm, as when the curtain falls on a perfect play. But when a youthful performer is stricken at his height we again see Orpheus murdered by those who are jealous of his song. The irony of such a fate today is often its artificiality. Young Ginette Neveu, for instance, or William Kapell, were among the first of the sky-traveling generation to gamble (and lose) at crowding as many concerts into as many parts of the globe as possible. Theirs was a twentieth-century death.

For Julius Katchen none of these generalities holds. Throughout his life his dazzling talent inspired enough adulation—and his intensity of concentration enough energy—to endure for centuries. He gambled (and won) at the international game: he was world famous through annual personal appearances. Yet he died young, not violently, nor even like a performer so much as like those composers of the romantic era he most adored. Not since the similar passing of Lipatti in 1950 has the piano world suffered such a loss. Theirs was a nineteenth-century death.

Precisely because of early fame and jet-orientation, today's crop of pianists maintain they have no time to learn new works, nor do many of them feel impelled to at the fees they get for playing old ones. By contrast Julius Katchen commanded at any given time some fifteen recitals and three dozen concertos performable on a few hours' notice.

This command was due in part, of course, to a loving curiosity about all music (no one is too busy for what really interests him). It was due also to a bizarre endowment. His lightning-quick learning and his notoriously faithful memory of what he learned came not from intellectual retention but from what might be termed eidetic fingertips: his hands had total recall. I remember first hearing him play all five Beethoven concertos on one program. I remember him memorizing the *Diabelli Variations* from scratch in three days and my own *Piano Concerto* in less. I remember him going on tour without his music, not because (like the *incroyable* Yvonne Loriod) it was all photographed in the brain: it was recorded in his hands.

What I remember began twenty summers ago when we met, through Gérard Souzay, on the terrace of a Saint-Germain café. Like his pianism, Julius's social style was not cerebral but emotional, that is, direct and very friendly. We immediately grew as close as a composer and pianist can grow, in that I wrote music specifically for him to play. I tailored my tunes not (consciously) around my abstract interior, but around what I knew he could do, which fortunately—in a sense—was anything. Through him, rather than through the average, did I learn.

Paris, which was then my new residence, had been Julius's home since shortly after the war and was to remain so until the end; he even came to be known as a French pianist. The reason for his choice of domicile was more social than musical. For one thing—and this was his personal tragedy as well as America's—he never was a prophet in his homeland once he left, although Europe considered him one of the greatest U.S. exports and elected him the first pianist to make an LP record (Rachmaninoff's *Second Concerto*). For another, his exceedingly American character was attracted by the urbane exoticism, his palate by the high cuisine, and his Judaic-Quaker training by the sensual freedom of France. The language he spoke perfectly, multilinguality being one of his major talents, a talent, incidentally, mistakenly thought to accompany musicality. He ultimately bought a most Parisian house, married a bright French girl, and had a very French son.

Nonetheless, I cannot remember his ever playing Debussy or Ravel or, in fact, any French music. His musical heart lay generally in Germany, particularly in Brahms. The French, never known for catholicity of cultural taste beyond their frontiers, found Brahms, at least in the 1940s, as novel as Americans then found Ives. In his final years Julius played Brahms almost exclusively, everywhere presenting the complete solo piano works of that composer in a series of four recitals. Once he confided that while performing the *F-minor Sonata* his involvement was so total that he felt he was fertilizing the universe.

Exclusivity of taste, however, excluded only French classics. There exist few major American or Russian piano works that did not appear on his programs, and his encouragement of young composers in Greece, Turkey, and Spain was not merely verbal. He played them.

To assume that his freak gift for quick mastery was a casual process is to ignore that our gifts in the long run are paid for, and sometimes the price is terrifying. Julius Katchen worked very hard. His vitality was such that after some twelve hours of practice he could go out and make the rounds of bars with the rest of us, get up early next day and start again. Repose was not his obsession, not if it precluded knowing all sorts of people and cultivating fans. For me this boundless interest and force, this unifying of day with night, indicated that, like Baudelaire, he lived three lives in one. Which means that when he died last May he was not 42 years old, but 126.

(*1969*)

ROBERT JACOBSON
GONE

The deaths for which we are "prepared" often catch us up short. We have waited so long in the desperate shade that the shade itself has come to seem permanent. Thus what was inexorable never resounds in reality with quite the same timbre of horror (or relief) as in our imagination. This truism seems italicized by the death of Robert Jacobson, as by the deaths of so many of his friends—and ours—who have been devoured by the mysterious plague. AIDS, with its ironic highs and lows, gives the illusion that where there's life there's hope. Then suddenly the hope is gone.

Now that the anxious solace of his funeral is removed by several weeks, I can look back calmly on Robert. We were not so much close friends as staunch colleagues. During our decade-long acquaintance I wrote a yearly essay for his magazine *Opera News*. With one exception, *Carmen*, these essays by mutual agreement dealt with works by twentieth-century composers. Their extramusical details—length, deadline, fee—were discussed at an annual noonday meal, either at the Café des Artistes or *chez moi*. (I went to his office only once, and visited the Tribeca loft for the first and last time a few months before Robert died.) Otherwise we met rarely and casually, at parties or in lobbies where he was always quickly visible, looming o'er the crowd with his likable and intelligent features.

But if in ten years I saw Robert Jacobson no more than twenty times, each time was a pleasure, and the pleasure stemmed from the breadth of his musical tolerance. Far from being a mere opera buff—that is, one who likes opera as opposed to music, singer as opposed to song—his scope was all-embracing. Indeed, Robert sometimes evinced loathing for certain interviews he conducted in the line of duty because of the dullness of the self-referential limits in the average prima donna (if any prima donna can be called average), the very diva the average opera buff would kill to chat with. Robert concurred with the famous starting line of Marianne Moore's "Poetry": "I, too, dislike it: there are things that are important beyond all this fiddle." He did know the fiddler from the fiddle; though if, like devout amateurs, he had necessarily a more intimate humming knowledge than most professional composers with the repertory, from Monteverdi to *Montezuma*, he was rare in recognizing the preeminence of composers over the far more conspicuous performers in our lopsided culture.

That is why I recall him with affection and respect: because he kept the cart behind the horse; because his own affection and respect for others was as noticeable in his play as in his work, which was really the same thing; because *Opera News* was no more urgent than his extramural organizations like the AIDS benefit of 1985; and because he was so personally beguiling, witty, cool, strong, warm, opinionated, and generally correct.

(*1987*)

PETER YATES ON TWENTIETH CENTURY MUSIC

The best minds these days seem more geared to commentary than to creation. Certainly our brightest Western prose lately has not been fiction but criticism. Painting usually turns out to be less amusing (not to say competent) than the advertising announcing it. As for musical composition, its defense has come to sound more intriguing than itself, even though composer and defender are usually the same.

Peter Yates, so far as I know, is not a composer. He is, however, a Music Lover, which few composers are anymore. A Canadian by origin, author of *An Amateur at the Keyboard* and for years a contributor to *Arts + Architecture*, he has long lived in Los Angeles where he founded the now-famous "Evenings on the Roof." His close acquaintance with the likes of Schoenberg and Stravinsky no less than with others less glamorous (mostly West Coasters, it would naturally seem) accounts for his special knowledge of what composers are made of. And it accounts for the dedicated, painstaking, and more or less objective enthusiasm of his extraordinarily wise book, *Twentieth Century Music*. I can't imagine a composer as having written it—as having had the *time*, the time to care in just this way. And Yates cares.

With care, then, he explains how today's music got that way and how we can learn to take it. He does this by discussing the evolution of all of music's components, both as themselves and as exemplified through the works of some dozen key figures of the past century. The discussion is no easy-going appreciation course; the author's intent is not to delight but to instruct, and no such instruction on the current market is more concise. (Virgil Thomson's recent self-portrait is as much of the artist's particular economy as of the general "scene," while Wilfrid Mellers portrayed the scene itself—but only in America.)

Yates is not one of those brainwashed reviewers who, dazed by their own brilliance and the ever more quickly changing world, are inclined to confuse the fascination of a work's analysis with the work itself, then to interpret the complexities of that analysis as the work's virtue, and hence to produce false evaluations. "Musical analysts look for what they know, not for what they do not know." Yates knows that the current state of music is not a suddenly random and perverse perpetration of fast thinkers, but the result of a loving and logical growth of selective doers, a growth that (he feels) occurred as an auditory, not a harmonic, phenomenon and has led from the end of the Harmonic Era to the new Era of Sound which will have as its center the computer.

Making it clear at the outset that music and sound can no longer be counter-distinguished, the author proceeds—with his master Schoenberg acting as a sort of invisible Vergil—through the public hells of misunderstanding, touching gently or ponderously most aspects of the subject at hand, through past and present, until he has cleared for us the complex clouds around the hopefully simple paradise of the future. Early we are introduced to the master himself, newly and keenly, "as natural a melodist as Schubert. . . . If one were to choose a single work to represent the pre-eminent achievement of twentieth century music until the present day, that work would be [Schoenberg's] *Moses and Aron*." Only Stravinsky is treated so unqualifiedly, in as acute an appraisal as any existing.

We are also reintroduced to Satie whom, of course, it is no longer correct to dismiss as trivial; but he too is shown freshly—as a master of parody, "an aspect of art [wherein] convention and the use of it play at cross-purposes." It was not genius, finally, but energy that Satie lacked. He "created a small art that is completely joyous, not innocent but guiltless, without soil." Without soil, perhaps, but presented utterly as a product of France. Ravel, too, and Debussy are thus presented (yet not as twins, for a change; as polarities). For the psychology of a nation, and resultantly of all forms of that nation's output, is another concern of Yates who quotes Vaughan Williams: "If you subscribe to that . . . foolish description of music as a universal language, you will . . . have achieved nothing better than a standardized . . . cosmopolitanism . . . whose mannerisms you have been aping."

"The student, if he is to master what is taught him, must at the same time challenge it." There is not one hackneyed challenge among Yates's major theses. He speaks at length of the "fourth dimension of sound" (ritualistic audience participation); of Just Intonation (his special obsession); of The Integrity of Compromise ("a great artist, in the long view, creates his audience"; "an artist is not a renegade but a workman"); of The Emancipation of the Dissonance; and of the beauty of transcriptions as an ancient musical skill ("music is constantly being made new; the notated score is only a guide," although there can be "a regard for the visual score itself as an esthetic object"). "One purpose of hearing music is to enlarge our capacity for listening," states Yates, yet we are warned that "what gives pleasure is our own tentative recomposing of a type of artistic workmanship with which we have learned to agree!"

The author laments the "dictatorship of popularity" in Russia and America where "reputation does the work of contemplation," and concludes that this attitude will not soon change. He nevertheless suggests that the past quarter century has been the most fascinating in all musical history, and this period contains the unalterable fact of what John Cage calls "the emancipation of music from its notes."

"Is there esthetic work in a destructive force?" we are asked. "The art of tragedy affirms it." The new language is a "fight against routine." What these days we wearily term " 'lack of communication' has been in reality a slow but steady increase in communication between the serious composer, his travelling representative the conscientious performer, and the slowly ripening public intelligence for music as an art on the same level as poetry, painting, and drama, which do not exist solely for public entertainment."

Embedded among his theses are brash *pensées*: "Silence plus one note can be musical, but one note is not music." "For Cage as for Stravinsky, the name 'Beethoven' symbolizes all that is lumped together in misuse of the word *genius*." "No [Jewish] composer . . . whether or not he wished such recognition, has seemed to the Jews in any country to be the musical voice of their tradition." He talks of Elliott Carter's "honest but cautious radicalism" and of Chopin as the last classicist who could not be called a neoclassicist. And he disproves the bromide that jazz is the unique contribution to American music.

Other details strike me as dubious: "A strong libretto can sustain inadequate music, but the best music cannot sustain an inadequate libretto." Or: "Poulenc's . . . guillotine offstage distracts from the music"—

when precisely that guillotine *is* the music, each horrendous crunch of which precipitates a modulation. Or when he takes at face value Cage's faulty syllogism—"Composing's one thing, performing's another, listening's a third. What can they have to do with one another?"—some may wonder at his earlier plea for "the need for good humor."

But he does describe so well (and it can't be done!) how music *sounds*, merely by stating the methods, theoretic and practical, from which a composer—Messaien, say, or Ruggles—proceeds.

The volume represents years of realistic examination in depth. But what Yates has gained in depth he has lost in breadth: his book is too long, and by the same token too short. In a rather unfelicitous no-nonsense style (especially in the first half—in the second he sometimes attains unprecedented, if purple, perception) he reiterates aspects of favored trends while almost ignoring others. No essay can, of course, ever have the last word, but one as ambitious (and redundant) as this cannot afford only a cursory glance toward composers under fifty, and no glance at all toward those under the stigma of what he might term "tiresome conservatism." Yet despite his biases—and all valid historians are biased—Yates does not, except by his silence, come off as a judge. "To keep art in growth," says he, "we should keep it in trial—not on trial."

(1967)

ON NEARING SIXTY

When are you no longer a Young Composer?

When you're a success.

When is that?

When your name is known to those you don't know, and when your music is played by those you've not personally coerced. Of course, by this token there exist fair-haired sexagenarians and hoary youngsters. Their success or failure is not gauged by livelihood: a mere handful of the best-known American composers subsist through the just rewards of their labor, while unknown ones turn a pretty penny writing for church or band. Teaching pays bills. Like poets, composers survive by talking about their art more than by practicing it.

But are they ever a success in their own eyes?

When a piece is done (*abandonned*, as Valéry said), it will lead its own life or death while its bereft maker wonders if he has the right to make love or war or even to eat unless he quickly gets back to work. If the world screams *genius!*, he feels more silly than gratified. What has genius to do with him? A moot question, since the world screams genius only for performers.

The so-called creative artist is sometimes thought to be more egocentric than "real" people. Certainly his egocentricity *shows* more than the butcher's or baby-sitter's or bomb maker's. Not being a needed commodity, he flails pitifully and as a social animal becomes conspicuous. Yet a century from today, if he's the real thing, the artist's work will by definition be more representative of our time than the bomb maker's or baby-sitter's or butcher's. Thus it could be argued that the artist, his work being outside himself, is the most generous of creatures.

Will you, O songwriter, teach us to write a perfect song?

Any hack can teach you that, though he cannot guarantee that it will breathe and bleed. Perfection is no more a requisite to art than to heroes. Perfection palls. Beauty limps. Yes, I know how to write an unflawed song. If only I could write the throbbing airs of forty years ago when I didn't "know how"!

But wouldn't you agree that most creative thinkers and doers grow with the years?

Growth is not of itself an improvement (as, for example, the growth of a cancer). Some artists never improve with the decades, as witness Chopin and Ravel; others would seem to change radically. But are the late works of Stravinsky and Beethoven demonstrably better than their early ones? What is evolution in a composer's catalog? As with mastering a foreign tongue, when after a year we're as good as we'll ever be (accent, speed, reflex) and all we'll improve upon is vocabulary, so with a new piece of music: our intellect and instrument get the point fairly soon (or else never). But though our viewpoint may ripen, ripeness is not always all—it turns to rot.

You often perform with singers. Are you a good pianist?

No, I'm a mime. When people say I play sublimely, it's when I'm doing an imitation of Eugene Istomin. Am I a camera? No, I'm a blotter. Creators don't have notions of their own; they only use what is. There exists no "own." Art is not creation; it is imitation. The artist has no control over what the result ultimately says.

As a composer, what are your origins?

It has been forty years—longer than Mozart's whole life—since my first public performance. William Strickland conducted a short Psalm for male chorus and woodwinds with the Army Music School's forces in the echoing pavilion of the National Gallery. I was nineteen, the age Rimbaud threw in the sponge. We teenagers, mushrooming in the wake of the war after a healthy isolation from European dogma, had no immediate forebears. Copland and Thomson—the Rome and Avignon of American music—were older than even Horowitz, though they did brand many of us as Horowitz branded the young pianists then. The 1940s had few composers in their thirties: Barber, Schuman and Persichetti, Diamond, yes; but how many others? Carter, though older than these, was yet to come into his own (but there exists no "own," etc.).

France more than America stamped me, except for jazz. My bending melodies stem as much from Billie Holiday (her way with a tune, not the tune itself) as from the melismatic Duparc or the syllabic Fauré, my harmonies from Gluck via Benny Goodman, colors from Ravel through Red Norvo, rhythms from the Big Bands rather than from Stravinsky—

square and not eccentric patterns being seductive to me. Since I am contrapuntal and since the French are not, there is a drop of German blood somewhere. The reason for my (shall I say profound?) attraction to French as opposed to German culture lies in terseness. Does the peacock's rainbow fan reveal less than his heart and lungs? Surface is as telling as depth, the casual as touching as the Big Statement, and nostalgia is the bread of creativity.

How do you feel, after the lonely years of treading a diatonic tone row, when atonal philanderers now garner publicity by skulking home to weigh themselves on a C-major scale?

Like the Prodigal Son's brother. To make matters worse, we now can hear that their simple tunes really aren't so good. Flaws show up like bunions on already ugly feet. The sovereign gift of melody is not for the asking.

What of your own style?

Style may not be all, but I do feel that style is most. So-called creators have no more than four or five negotiable ideas in their whole life. They spend that life shaping those ideas into commodities, long or short or merry or sad or multicolored or for solo instrument. What they say has always been said before, but how they say it is *them*. I have never concocted an apology for my musical language; have compiled no syllabus for critics to hang their prose on; nor, when writing program notes, have I felt that words speak as clearly as the music they purport to describe.

It is time, though, to advance a motto: I believe in the importance of the unimportant—in the quotidian pathos. Like sex and food, music exists in the Now (as distinct from love, which, like power and philosophy, exists in retrospect or in anticipation), and this Now must always be pleasurable, even when it hurts. The pleasure comes from economy. I do not know what *meaning* means, except that it is instantly recognizable. All of this will not justify my credentials (only the music can do that), but it will explain an esthetic that already sounds more important than I intend.

Why, like Rimbaud, have you not thrown in the sponge?

Because no one else is making what I need. Success is forever transient, frozen dead. What it represents may live on, but the maker collapses even as he is being misrepresented. Without daily reassurance (in the form of performances and recognition, good or bad), I could not persist; I am not my work which, like a child, seeks autonomy. Yet I ride the crest of the wave. Looking about, seeing death everywhere, I realize that my gaudy past is past. Anyone can be drunk, anyone can be in love, anyone can waste time and weep, but only I can pen my songs in the few remaining years or minutes. The sponge is always there, but where would I throw it? Where could I go?

(1983)

MARGINALIA

On Receiving a Commission to Write a Mass

Brought up a Quaker, meaning in silence, I needed noise. So I became a composer. The texts for my first vocal works were chosen from the Old Testament, not because I was a believer but because the poetry was good. (The shepherd David had, after all, conceived those psalms in song.) But from thirteen to thirty-five I gradually forsook the Bible for Sappho and Chaucer, approached Shakespeare and Herrick, advanced through Jonson and Byron toward Hopkins and Hardy, and finally ended up at home. Home was in the American language as written by E. E. Cummings and Paul Goodman, by Theodore Roethke and Howard Moss, or by "today's generation," my friends Frank O'Hara, Kenneth Koch, Kenneth Pitchford, Kenward Elmslie. Occasionally in a pinch or a hurry I'll revert to the Psalms: they're good for a tune, though my heart's seldom there anymore. Not that tune and heart need be mutually inclusive; on the contrary, "inspiration" is the direct cause of our vulgarest church music.

Now it's rumored God is dead. Long live God! The poems of this time, however they're sliced, are for my time, however I'm sliced, though I'm called behind the time; yet who by that can prove I'm not instead ahead? Despite or because of God's death, American churches now commission vociferously, even Catholics, who want vernacular masses. Though I no longer feel the call, I heed the call. Remunerative deadlines have always been (as all composers will tell you) the palpable inspiration par excellence.

(*1967*)

On Movie Music in General

A musically untutored movie audience accepts without flinching a score whose audacity, if heard in concert, would send the elite yelling for mercy. The public is, and should be, mostly unconscious of movie music;

356

a background fails when it distracts from central business. But such is music's strength that it may sugarcoat a tasteless film or poison one of quality. A recent drama on capital punishment, *I Want to Live*, excited extra tension through its sound track of progressive jazz. *On the Beach*, whose subject was more timely still (terrestrial death through radioactivity), was devitalized by a score with old-fashioned associations.

Any music may persuasively accompany any image or story while inevitably dictating the *tone* of the joint effort. Music's power lies in an absence of human significance and this power dominates all mediums it contacts. When Auric composed the score for Jean Cocteau's film, *The Blood of a Poet*, he produced what is commonly known as love music for love scenes, game music for game scenes, funeral music for funeral scenes. Cocteau had the bright idea of replacing the love music with the funeral, game music with the love, funeral with game. And it worked—like prosciutto and melon. Nor did Cocteau commission a composer for his ballet of a modern young painter who hangs himself onstage; he used a passacaglia of Bach whose clash with the present ignited the eternal.

(1959)

On the Music for 2001: A Space Odyssey

Stanley Kubrick in *2001: A Space Odyssey* uses three "kinds" of music: (1) For "The Dawn of Man" we hear the noble opening bars of Richard Strauss's *Zarathustra*, unfamiliar and hence spookily effective—like Cocteau's earlier use of Bach—to ninety-nine out of a hundred. But to the hundredth—or at least to me—the tone poem's previous associations render its present location not noble but ludicrous. (Similarly, twenty years ago, the very young Kenneth Anger, to save money and doubtless banking on the music's unfamiliarity for its effect, garnished his unusual *Fireworks* with an old recording of Ernest Schelling's *Victory Ball*. Again then, my previous acquaintance canceled the score's pseudo-impressionist powers in mixed media.) 2) For the first visions of deep-space travel we hear in toto Johann Strauss's *Blue Danube Waltz*, quite familiar and hence campily effective—like Kubrick's earlier use of pop song in *Doctor Strangelove*—to ninety-nine out of a hundred. For the hundredth—at least for me—I couldn't tell why (though why anything, really, in art!) he chose a familiar rather than unfamiliar camp tune, or even camp at all. 3) For ensuing exposition, and for the final infinity-shattering sequence, we hear snatches of works composed years earlier and for other purposes by the Armenian Khachaturian and the Hungarian Ligeti, works already known to that unhappy few who feel such works to be non-accompanimentory, self-sufficient. Yet the Ligeti especially contains those "current" sonorities (an out-of-focus heavenly choir singing what sounds like *Kyrie*) that, wrongly or rightly, have come to be as identified with science fiction as Debussy's *La Mer* is with travelogues on Tahiti.

None of the above-mentioned pieces were specifically written for the movie; all were torn from context and superimposed on the finished sound track—though not, we suppose, for economic reasons (as in the case of Anger) so much as because Kubrick already knew and just had to have these sounds.

My point is that familiarity does not breed contempt, it just breeds more familiarity. A film about the future cannot, by definition, employ music of the future. Yet the medium's artifice requires music (unless dispensing with music altogether, which amounts to the same thing, since planned silence fulfills the same soldering purpose). The question is, with a movie like this, what *kind* of music? Kubrick, in not running a risk, found no answer. As to what risk he should have run, I have no answer either. I'm only a composer.

(*1968*)

On the Timeliness of Art

Some art dates well, some badly, but all art dates, the worst and the best. Even *within* a work of any scope, because time passed while he created it, an artist may have inadvertently introduced anachronisms; the sole purpose of his technique is to solder these anachronisms convincingly, to make them cohere in the flow of the work. Inspiration, of course, does not concern the artist. Nor will a conscious timeliness in the long run make his work seem inspired. Certainly timeliness doesn't add to worth. *Lysistrata* and *The Trojan Women* may strike us as ironically pertinent to the present, but *The Birds* and *Oedipus Rex* do not obtain to us at all. Paintings and movies from the 1930s are bad or good, embarrassing or thrilling, junky or skillful, but all are old-fashioned in both matter and style. Whatever period a work of art purports to depict, the work itself can be situated only in its own period. Jules Verne's visions of the twenty-first century are strictly from the nineteenth. Shakespeare's Cleopatra is strictly Elizabethan, while De Mille's Cleopatra is less involved with ancient Rome than with ancient Hollywood. Thus

Bartók's *Bluebeard's Castle* is not about medieval mores but about the dawn of Freudianism in Hungary as observed through musical explorations of 1911.

(1975)

On Comparing Architecture with Music

If the arts inherently expressed or even resembled each other, we wouldn't need but one. Still, oftener than they are differentiated they are likened. The most frequent comparison is of music with architecture, though these are the farthest apart. (Architecture is no more "frozen music" than music is "melted architecture.")

Music serves no purpose beyond itself, and the identifying property of that self is motion. Architecture does serve a purpose beyond itself, and its identifying property is static. Architecture would thus seem closer to painting or sculpture, while music—as flow—obviously resembles dance, or even prose. Yet unlike prose, or even dance, music has no innate content, no symbolic sense. If a building has symbolic sense, the primary function is nonetheless practical. An architect cannot improvise, thinking up a plan and the plan's execution as he goes along the way artists can. An architect who omits a beam will see his structure collapse; if he overlooks a bathroom the tenants collapse. When an artist fails, no one but himself really gets hurt; his work is not useful.

Music, then, inhabits an opposite pole from architecture, with prose and painting falling somewhere between.

(1969)

On Listening to Music Chez Marie-Blanche

The musicale never thrived in our practical land. Even in France, after a long red- (I mean blue-) blooded activity, the salon has died of anemia. The final transfusions were offered by a beautiful widow, the Comtesse Jean de Polignac, née Marie-Blanche Lanvin and nominal head of the *maison de couture*. Twelve regulars gathered weekly in her dining room where, beneath a fresco created by Bérard to suit the countess's coloring, they would consume breasts of guinea hen, pure-gold lemon soufflés, and champagne from the Polignac vineyards. They then adjourned to a grand upstairs parlor where more guests would arrive, and there followed three hours of musicalizing: sometimes Auric and Février rambling through Chabrier at the two huge Pleyels, sometimes Poulenc accompanying his own nasal wail in the premiere of a recent cycle, perhaps Marie-Blanche herself informally singing Monteverdi with her friend Nadia Boulanger, or more formal recitals by eminent soloists or composers who happened to be passing through Paris—Menuhin, maybe, or Copland. Thus were all Sundays until Madame de Polignac's death in 1958, Sundays of dedication among friends, of music in the home.

But such a home! My first visit there rendered me tone-deaf. The wall of that upstairs parlor happened to be covered with Vuillards, the floor with velours, the twenty-foot couches with satin, the ashtrays with pearl, the air with Arpège, and the hostess with a never-the-same Lanvin creation of apple-green chiffon or fairy-tale organdy, all this garnished (between "numbers") with that theatrically succinct résumé of which French is made, be it Sartre's or Suzy Solidor's.

Is this any way to hear music? Yes, once the grave young U.S. composer that I was had grown accustomed to luxury as "tone" rather than as vice.

The rich American living room is remarkable for functional spick-and-spanness, for expensive necessities, the owners feeling a bit guilty about beauty for its own sake (their Matisse is for investment more than joy); wealthy European counterparts, though the ceiling may need drastic repairs, will glow with be-rubied objets d'art serving no other purpose than to be looked at. My first evening chez Marie-Blanche I *heard*. Not until my third could I *listen*. One Sunday we repaired for our music to a hall that I had never seen. The hall, permeated by tuberoses, Renoirs, and be-diamonded guests, obliged me, as a listener, to begin from scratch. That evening's mixed media was a preview of our Electric Circus.

Being a subtler mechanism than the eye, the ear is crushed by new environments. From the premiere of a new ballet, albeit one by Stravinsky and Balanchine, it is sights more than sounds we bring home.

(*1969*)

On Originality

Originality as an artistic concept is less than two centuries old. Radiguet: A true artist has his own voice and cannot copy, so he has only to copy to prove his originality. The act of creation has, in a sense, always been an act of plagiarism; even the iconoclast in refuting the past makes use of the past. But plagiarism is a crime. So artists, who are also craftsmen, remodel their stolen clay into something resembling themselves, and when they succeed they look new. A professional is someone sufficiently aware of his influences to wish (and to know how) to disguise them. An amateur proceeds willy-nilly reproducing picture postcards.

(*1970*)

On the Artist Talking about His Art

Half of being an artist today lies in promotional skill, yet to accept this condition is to be half an artist.

What a work of art says, and what its maker says it says, need not jibe. Critics will tack on meanings after the fact; that's their job. An artist who supplies meanings cheats.

To offer a technical analysis of his work is for an artist to repeat himself, but with less eloquence. To dismantle a structure is to divulge uninteresting secrets, secrets that he half forgets once the work is done. Even if he could recall each compositional process, to reveal this would be to kiss and tell, like psychotherapy.

For a composer—at least this composer—just having his piece played in public is an embarrassment (albeit sometimes a rewarding embarrassment). Discussion afterward insults the delicious injury. Although I've a point of view toward music, I've no point of view toward *my* music, since I'm not outside looking in. Nor have I an outlook, since the music is its own outlook. Nor have I a philosophy of songwriting: if I had, I wouldn't write songs but would write philosophy. Furthermore, no composer can even possibly conjecture what distinguishes his music from that of others, other than (hopefully) its quality. Conscious influences he will not readily admit to. Unconscious ones, by definition invisible to the composer, are apparent only (again hopefully) to critics and presumably musicologists. Thus, only as a musicologist can a composer discuss all music except, for the above reasons, his own.

(*1969*)

Envoi

In the foregoing do I contradict myself? Very well then, taking good Walt Whitman's prerogative, I contradict myself. Not that, like him, I am large or contain multitudes; but he taught me not to fear contradictions. The purest demonstration of fearlessness is nudity, whose purest demonstration is song, whose purest demonstration is the poet's eternal Myself.

(*1969*)

INDEX